Classical Social Theory

Investigation and Application

Tim Delaney, Ph.D.
State University of New York at Oswego

PEARSON
Prentice Hall

Upper Saddle River, New Jersey 07458

Library of Congress Cataloging-in-Publication Data

DELANEY, TIM.
    Classical social theory : investigation and application / TIM DELANEY.
      p. cm.
    ISBN 0-13-110900-6
    1. Social sciences—Philosophy. I. Title.

H61.D33768 2003
300'.1–dc21   2002192957

AVP, Publisher: *Nancy Roberts*
Editorial Assistant: *Lee Peterson*
Editorial/Production Supervision: *Arny Spielberg, Victory Productions, Inc.*
Prepress and Manufacturing Buyer: *Mary Ann Gloriande*
Director of Marketing: *Beth Mejia*
Marketing Assistant: *Adam Laitman*
Cover Art Director: *Jayne Conte*
Cover Design: *Bruce Kenselaar*
Composition/Full-Service Project Management: This book was set in 10/12 Palatino by
   Victory Productions, Inc.
Printer/Binder: Hamilton Printing Company.
Cover Printer: The Lehigh Press, Inc.

Portions of chapter 2 (Herbert Spencer) and chapter 4 (Karl Marx) appear in *Values, Society & Evolution*
   published by Legend books and are printed with permission from the publisher.

Pearson Education LTD.
Pearson Education Singapore, Pte. Ltd
Pearson Education, Canada, Ltd
Pearson Education–Japan
Pearson Education Australia PTY, Limited
Pearson Education North Asia Ltd
Pearson Educación de Mexico, S.A. de C.V.
Pearson Education Malaysia, Pte. Ltd
Pearson Education, Upper Saddle River, NJ

10 9 8 7 6 5 4 3 2 1
ISBN   0-13-110900-6

The one who tells the story . . . is the survivor.

Contents

Preface

Humans often attempt to find a meaning for life and aspire to understand the world around them. Understanding is derived from a number of sources that include: faith, tradition, common sense, and science. All of these approaches, except science, have major flaws. Sociology is a science. It is a science as much as any of the so-called "natural" sciences. Sociology teaches us to look beyond the limits of common sense—that not everything one was led to believe is necessarily true. This contradiction often leads to culture shock. Culture shock is evidence contrary to previously held beliefs regarding a social group, place, or phenomena. Social thinkers, including sociologists, have long fought the validity of a reliance on a religious belief system or a social order maintained by tradition (e.g., "royalty"). Sociology has its roots strongly entrenched in empirical science and moral reform. It analyzes human social behavior from a socio-historic perspective.

C. Wright Mills recognized that an individual's meaning of inner life is linked to external social events. A series of previous events all shape the formation of current events. In other words, human behavior and social reality is a product of historically linked events of behavior and phenomena. Mills (1959) used the term *sociological imagi-*nation. The sociological imagination allows its possessor to understand individual events from the historical perspective. It allows us to comprehend individual biography and history and the relationship between the two within society. From this perspective, individuals come to realize that their problems are a result of the greater societal strain. For example, an individual may feel bad about him/herself after being laid off from work. But these feelings of self-remorse subside with the realization that the socio-economic structure in society has changed and consequently, a large number of people are losing their jobs through no fault of their own.

When teaching theory, it is important to analyze the biography of social thinkers and provide a glimpse of the historic events occurring in conjunction with the theorist. In addition, it should be obvious that students need to be exposed to key concepts and contributions of each theorist. However, the most important goal to teaching social theory is, perhaps, demonstrating the relevance of such material to the students' daily lives. Teaching the relevance of sociology should be the *focus* of the discipline. This goal can be attained by incorporating everyday events into the classroom (and textbooks). Some of the sources of relevance to students' everyday lives include newspaper and magazine articles; recently released movies; the news; sports; arts and entertainment (especially television); campus activities; professors' first-hand accounts of behavior in different cultures; and pop culture.

Classical Social Theory: Investigation and Application provides an excellent overview of classical social theory with a concentration on sociological thought. This book reflects the convergence of social science, natural science, philosophy, and history into a collective body of classical discourse.

Chapter One provides a brief overview of the many social, political, and philosophical antecedents that preceded the founding of sociology. The story of social theory is generally acknowledged as beginning with Machiavelli's *The Prince*, a book published in 1513, at the height of the Italian Renaissance. *The Prince* was a controversial book for its time, as it provided a realistic view of human actions and challenged the long-held belief in the Divine Rights of Kings. In 1517, Martin Luther challenged the Catholic Church by nailing his 95 Theses to the door of the cathedral in Wittenberg, Germany, lighting the fires of the Reformation and Protestantism.

A review of the impact of the works of Thomas Hobbes, John Locke, and Jean-Jacques Rousseau follows, as these early thinkers had a tremendous impression on early sociological thinkers. The chapter concludes with a review of the importance of the Enlightenment, the large number of revolutions (industrial and political), and the contributions of Claude-Henri Saint-Simon. This chapter is important because it establishes that all social thinkers were influenced by the works and thoughts that preceded them.

Chapters Two through Thirteen provide a review of specific social thinkers critically important to the development and expansion of the field of sociology. All of these specific theorists provided major contributions in their own unique ways. In each chapter, a biographical sketch of each theorist is provided (family background, education, personal life, publications, and so on); a review of those significant intellectual influences on each theorist that helped to shape his own thoughts; a concise and clear review of the concepts and contributions of each theorist; and an application of the relevancy of their concepts and contributions to contemporary and future society.

The biographical sketch of each theorist has proven to be of special value to students in my social theory classes. It is an interesting way of making these "names" more "real" and human to the student as they learn about the challenges, pitfalls, and accomplishments of each theorist. It also reveals that people are most definitely a product of their time and place in history. The section concerning the influences on each theorist demonstrates the fact that ideas are not created in a vacuum. Instead, they are the result of the knowledge and wisdom of those enlightened thinkers who came before each of them. From a purely academic standpoint, the section on concepts and contributions attributed to each theorist is perhaps the most critical and therefore represents the bulk of each chapter. These concepts and terms are explained in a clear manner that the reader should be able to comprehend.

What should stimulate students the most is the section on the relevancy of these social concepts to today's world. The ability to link social thought with everyday real events becomes the critical challenge of any social theory text. The relevancy section provides glimpses of the application of specific concepts. The examples do not represent an exhaustive list, but rather an attempt to show its practicality to present-day reality.

Critical thought and pragmatic discussion in the application of this material will help to develop the student's rational thought processes and analytical skills, as well as to instill an appreciation for synthetic thought. It is this section, Chapters Two through Thirteen, that separates and distinguishes this book from all other social theory texts.

Chapter Fourteen, "Contributions from Women to Classical Social Theory," is dedicated to the progressive, and reformist, contributions from a select number of significant women in the areas of classical social theory and the advancement of sociology. This is a meaningful chapter as it provides a solid foundation to the role of women in the development of sociological thought, and symbolizes the discrimination felt by women throughout the classical era. To place this chapter anywhere else in the book seemed to *force* it upon the reader. As a final chapter, it serves as a statement that the role of women in sociological theory is just beginning. Thus, Chapter Fourteen partially serves as the transition chapter into the contemporary social theory era.

The women discussed in Chapter Fourteen include Harriet Martineau, Beatrice Potter Webb, Anna Julia Cooper, Ida Wells-Barnett, Charlotte Perkins Gilman, Jane Addams, Marianne Weber, and the Ladies of Seneca Falls—Elizabeth Cady Stanton and Lucretia Coffin Mott. Far too often, women are ignored in classical social theory books; and indeed, other women such as Alexandra Kollontai could have been included in this chapter.

In fact, making a decision as to which theorists to include and exclude is often difficult. Certain theorists such as Auguste Comte, Karl Marx, Emile Durkheim, Georg Simmel, Max Weber, and George Herbert Mead are "givens" for any classical social theory book. Other theorists such as Herbert Spencer, Charles Cooley, Karl Mannheim, Talcott Parsons, and George Homans have a high probability of appearing in such a textbook. Other theorists (e.g., W. E. B. Dubois, E. F. Frazier, and Vilfredo Pareto) received a great deal of consideration for inclusion, but ultimately the decision was made to use the theorists found in this current edition, as they seemed the most representative of a comprehensive approach to social theory. Additionally, there is always a concern of whether or not a book gets too lengthy.

A couple of reviewers suggested a companion reader filled with quotes from theorists so that students might better interpret the works of these great thinkers. What a wonderful suggestion for a future book, thanks!

Acknowledgments

As all social thinkers are influenced by those who preceded them, I owe a great deal of gratitude to a number of brilliant people. As a student I greatly benefited from Lewis Coser's *Masters of Sociological Thought*. Coser provides a wealth of information on a social thinker's biography, influences, and contributions. In *Classical Social Theory: Investigation and Application*, I attempt to articulate sociological concepts so that they are more student-friendly, and emphasize the importance of demonstrating their relevancy. In the classroom I was inspired by such talented theorists as Jonathan Turner, Herman Loether, Dmitri Shalin, and Andrea Fontana—thank you to all.

I especially want to thank Tim Madigan, who not only proofread the first draft of this book, but also offered valued and insightful comments from both sociological and philosophical points of view.

My thanks also go to the following people who reviewed the text and provided additional insight and guidance:

Karen A. Callaghan, Barry University; Jeffrey A. Halley, University of Texas–San Antonio; Arthur J. Jipson, University of Dayton; Marguerite Marin, Gonzaga University; James P. Marshall, University of Northern Colorado; George McCarthy, Kenyon College; and John D. Murray, Manhattanville College.

I am deeply grateful to the support given to me by Nancy E. Roberts and Lee W. Peterson of Prentice Hall. They are perfect examples of why Prentice Hall is such a prestigious publisher. It is a pleasure to work with such professional and wonderful people. Special thanks to Lee Shenkman and Victory Productions for their assistance in the final editing process.

As always, a special thanks to my inspiration, Christina.

Tim Delaney, Ph.D.

About the Author

Dr. Tim Delaney, Assistant Professor of Sociology at the State University of New York at Oswego, holds a B.S. degree in sociology from the State University of New York at Brockport, an M.A. degree in sociology from California State University, Dominguez Hills, and a Ph.D. in sociology from the University of Nevada, Las Vegas.

Delaney is the author of *Community, Sport and Leisure, Second Edition* (2001); co-editor of *Values, Society and Evolution* (2002); and co-editor of *Philosophical and Sociological Implications of Deviant Behavior* (2003). He has published nearly forty book reviews, numerous book chapters, journal and encyclopedia articles, and served as Guest Editor for *Philosophy Now*. Delaney is an international author.

Dr. Delaney has presented thirty papers at regional, national, and international conferences, including papers that were presented for the Russian Academy of Sciences during international conferences at both St. Petersburg (1999) and Moscow (2001). He is the Associate Founder of The Anthropology Society (Western New York) and is in the process of creating the Social Theory Society, an academic society that promotes "learning through thinking and experience." Delaney maintains membership in ten professional associations, including the American Sociological Association, Pacific Sociological Association, and the North American Society for the Sociology of Sport. In 2002, he was selected as a charter member to the "Wall of Tolerance" sponsored by the National Campaign for Tolerance, co-chaired by Rosa Parks and Morris Dees, in recognition of his community activism and scholarship efforts in the fight against social injustice. Delaney has also been selected for inclusion in the 2003 Marquis *Who's Who in America* for his outstanding achievements.

Antecedents
Social, Political, and Philosophical

There has been philosophical speculation on the nature of society and social life at least as far back as the ancient Greeks. However, for the most part, the Greek philosophers were more concerned with the way things should be than with the way they actually were. They did not engage in scientific-empirical research. These philosophers assumed that intelligent observers could learn about the nature of reality simply by thinking and talking with other intelligent individuals about it. They created an ideal type of society and called upon it to conform to that ideal. Consequently, it is safe to say that the roots of sociological social theory do not lie with the ancient Greek philosophers.

According to Garner (2000) the story of sociology begins with Niccolo Machiavelli and *The Prince,* a book he published in 1513, at the height of the Italian Renaissance. During the period of 1450 to 1525, Europe was experiencing dramatic social change. For example, in 1453 the Turks captured Constantinople (now Istanbul) from the Greeks and demonstrated the proficient use of cannons and gunpowder. The eastern Mediterranean became part of the Islamic world and European rulers, merchants, and adventurers felt pressure to expand westward and southward beyond the Straits of Gibraltar. In 1458, Johann Gutenberg printed the Bible on his movable type printing press and spearheaded the movement of mass dissemination of the printed word. In 1492, Columbus "discovered" the "New" World, triggering the burst of expansion by European nations onto the rest of the world. In that same year, the sovereigns of Christian Spain completed their reconquest of the peninsula from Islamic rule and expelled the remaining Moors and Jews (Garner, 2000).

Martin Luther (1497–1546), one of the first advocates of mass education, challenged the Catholic Church and its assertion that the only true interpretation of the Bible should come from religious leaders. Luther, in contrast, believed that it was the right, even the duty, of all Christians to interpret the Bible for themselves. For this to happen, everyone had to learn to read, which required mass education (Farley, 1998). In 1517, Luther challenged the Catholic Church by nailing his 95 theses to the door of the cathedral in Wittenberg, Germany, lighting the fires of the Reformation and Protestantism. Germany declared 1996 as "Luther Year" in honor of the 450th anniversary of his death (*Los Angeles Times,* 1996).

It was Machiavelli's work that sparked sociological theory. *The Prince* was a controversial book for its time, as it provided a realistic view of human actions and challenged the long-held belief of the Divine Right of Kings and others (e.g. slave owners) who held "legitimate" power. Until the Renaissance, most books upheld general notions of normative behavior, were non-empirical, and did not observe, describe or analyze actual human behavior. Machiavelli included into his book all the violent, fierce, savage, coercive, and sometimes even compassionate acts that the ruler must implement in order to stay in power. *The Prince* was based on reality—the observations of real people, not just moral ideals. It is for this very reason that *The Prince* shocked its readers and was widely censored and banned. This is the very type of publication that illustrates modern social science—to write about society as it really is, not only as the power elite says that it is, or should be.

Hobbes, Locke, and Rousseau

After Machiavelli, many social thinkers would make contributions to the study of society and human behavior. Three of the more influential theorists are Thomas Hobbes, John Locke, and Jean-Jacques Rousseau. In the following pages a brief review of their significant contributions are discussed.

Thomas Hobbes (1588–1679)

Hobbes was born in Wiltshire, England, on April 5, 1588. His father, the vicar of the parish, could only read the prayers of the church and the homilies, and did not value learning. One of the surviving stories about the senior Hobbes was that he was an irresponsible and unpleasant fellow. Consequently, after a fight with a fellow clergyman, he was threatened with excommunication. As a result, he soon "disappeared from history" (Martinich, 1999). The young

Hobbes lived a sheltered and leisured life. His education was provided for by an uncle, a solid tradesman and alderman of Malmesbury. By the time he reached fifteen, Hobbes had mastered Latin and Greek and was sent to Oxford to continue his education. Hobbes would travel throughout Europe and did not begin academic writing until he was forty years of age.

Hobbes's primary contribution to social thought is his belief that social order was made by human beings and therefore humans could change it (Adams and Sydie, 2001). Even under authoritarian rule, Hobbes believes that authority is given by the subjects themselves; that, by their consent, the rulers maintain sovereign power.

As a political and social theorist, Hobbes wondered what life and human relations would be like in the absence of government. In 1651, Hobbes published his greatest work, *Leviathan*. In this book he provides a disturbing account of society without government. From his viewpoint, society would be filled with fear and danger of violent death; and the life of man would be solitary, poor, nasty, brutish, and short.

In his brief introduction to the *Leviathan*, Hobbes describes the state as an organism analogous to a large person. He shows how each part of the state parallels the function of the parts of the human body. He notes that the first part of his project is to describe human nature, insofar as humans are the creators of the state. To this end, he advises that we look introspectively to see the nature of humanity in general. Hobbes argues that, in the absence of social condition, every action we perform, no matter how charitable or benevolent, is done for selfish reasons. Even giving to charity is a way of showing one's power to do so. Today, this concept is often referred to as psychological egoism. Hobbes believes that any description of human action, including morality, must reflect the reality that man is self-serving by nature. Hobbes also noted that there are three natural causes of conflict among people: competition for limited supplies of material possessions, distrust of one another, and glory insofar as people remain hostile to preserve their powerful reputation. Given the natural causes of conflict, Hobbes concludes that the natural condition of humans is a state of perpetual war of all against all, where no morality exists and everyone lives in constant fear.

It is interesting to note that Hobbes certainly had his own fears. In November 1640, when the Long Parliament began to show signs of activity threatening civil war, Hobbes was one of the first to flee to France, and he even described himself as a "man of feminine courage." Additionally, when *Leviathan* was one of two books mentioned as blasphemous literature, Hobbes was seriously frightened and it is said that he went to church more regularly.

Hobbes offers evidence that the state of nature is as brutal as he describes. We see signs of this in the mistrust we show of others in our daily lives. In countries that have yet to be civilized, people treat others in barbaric forms. In the absence of international law, strong countries will prey upon the vulnerability of weak countries. Further, humans have three motivations for ending this state of war: the fear of death, the desire to have an adequate living, and the hope to attain this through one's labor. Yet, during war, each person has a right to everything, including another person's life.

For Hobbes, the state of nature is not a specific period in history, but rather a way of rationalizing how people would act in their most basic state. Advancing on the individualism put forth by René Descartes ("I think, therefore I am"), Hobbes uses the individual as the building block from which all of his theories spring. He formulated his theories by way of empirical observation. Hobbes believed that everything in the universe was simply made of atoms in motion, and that geometry and mathematics could be used to explain human behavior.

According to his theories, there are two types of motion in the universe: Vital (involuntary motion such as heart rate, etc.) and Voluntary (things that we choose to do). Voluntary motion is further broken down into two subcategories that Hobbes believed were reducible to mathematical equations—Desires and Aversions. Desires are things one is moved toward or that are valued by the individual, while aversions are fears or things to be avoided by the individual. Further, individuals' appetites constantly keep them in motion, and in order to remain in motion, everyone needs a certain degree of power. Thus, the pursuit of power is the natural state of humans; humans are in a constant struggle for power and above all else, they want to avoid a violent death.

Consequently, humans must find a way to maintain peace. Hobbes draws on the language of the natural law tradition of morality, which emphasized the principles of reason. Hobbes reasoned that people would be willing to give up "individual rights" for the security offered by a peaceful cooperative society. He believed that a "social contract"—an agreement among individuals—would accomplish this. But, because human nature would never allow this to happen (because of greed, jealousy, etc.), and with no way to enforce the contract, people would eventually break it in an attempt to control a greater share of power over others.

Realizing this, Hobbes proposed that an authoritarian government would come to power in order to enforce the social contract by whatever means necessary. He gave this government the name Leviathan (from the Bible), meaning monster. Individuals would give up all of their rights to the Leviathan except for the right to self-preservation. People might give up their rights to the Leviathan, but by their very nature, they would not be able to abandon their passion and quest for power. This drive would be channeled into what Hobbes called "commodious living," things such as trade, industry, and other business ventures. The government would insure that all individuals were free to maximize their self-interests while protecting them for each other.

Hobbes was certainly considered a "liberal" in his day. He emphasized the importance of the individual and made them the center of politics. Government should derive from human beings, and not some divine sense of purpose or birthright. Since Hobbes is often referred to as the first liberal thinker, then it is only fitting that attention is now turned to John Locke, considered by some as the father of liberal democratic thought.

John Locke (1632–1704)

John Locke was born in a village in Somerset, on August 29, 1632. Locke was the son of a country attorney and small landowner (John Locke Sr.) who served as a captain in the parliamentary army when civil war broke out, and Agnes Keene Locke (Cope, 1999). Not much is known about Locke's mother except the fact that she was nearly ten years older than Locke's father (Cope, 1999). Both sides of the family came from the Puritan social class, but Locke Sr. rose a step up on the social ladder by becoming an attorney. Locke had two siblings, but only his brother Thomas survived past infancy (Cope, 1999). His father had hoped that John would follow in his footsteps and become a lawyer, but Locke decided on medicine instead.

John Locke grew up amid the civil disturbances that were plaguing seventeenth-century England. He was educated at home until the age of 14, when he went to

John Locke (1632–1704) seventeenth-century English philosopher.
Source: Courtesy of the Library of Congress

Westminster School (Thomson, 1993). In 1652 Locke attended Christ Church, Oxford, where he studied Aristotelianism and remained a student for many years. He would come to revolt against the medieval scholasticism of the Oxford curriculum and became more interested in the "new science" or "natural philosophy" introduced by Sir Robert Boyle, who ultimately founded the Royal Society (Thomson, 1993).

Locke became friends with many of the leading scientists of his era, among them Boyle (known as the "Father" of chemistry), the pre-eminent physician Thomas Sydenham, and perhaps the most recognizable, Isaac Newton (Ayers, 1999). For many years Locke pursued his medical studies and finally obtained a Bachelor of Medicine degree in 1674. Although he did practice medicine intermittently, it never became his regular profession (Thomson, 1993).

Locke was interested in the great philosophical and scientific questions of his time. He was a secretary and confidante of Lord Ashley and held a number of government posts while Ashley was in office. He gave economic advice to the government, and held the important position of Secretary to the Board of Trade and Colonies from 1696 to 1700 (Ayers, 1999).

Locke embraced many of the ideas presented by Hobbes in his theories on the state of nature and the rise of government and society. They differed, however, in that Locke believed that God was the prime factor in politics. He believed that individuals were born with certain natural rights given not by government or society but by God. This divine right is what gives all people equality. Locke and Hobbes shared a common view of the importance and autonomy of the individual in society. The extent to which they agreed varies, but one important belief was constant between the two—people existed as individuals before societies and governments came into being. They each possessed certain rights and all had the freedom to do as they pleased, unrestricted according to Hobbes, and with some restrictions placed on them by God, according to Locke. This individual freedom was important, for it was the foundation for modern liberal democracy.

Besides a general right to self-preservation, Locke believed that all individuals had a natural right to appropriate private property. This natural right carried with it two preconditions of natural law. First, since the earth was given by God to all individuals, people must be sure to leave enough property for all to have, and secondly, nothing may be allowed to spoil. These conditions met, an individual was granted exclusive rights to any object that they mixed with their labor.

Locke agrees with Hobbes that, human nature being the way it was, people eventually would find a way around the natural law restrictions on property accumulation through the creation of money. People were granted the ability to accumulate unlimited money based upon their industriousness. This meant that some people acted more rationally than others, and thus were more deserving of property. Locke so despised the use of money that he argued it led to the disproportionate and unequal possession of the Earth.

However, Locke recognized that money "turns the wheels of trade." He argues that riches consist of gold and silver, and countries filled with mines have an interest in maintaining the gold standard. Such countries grow richer either through conquest or commerce. In his *Some Considerations of the Consequences of the Lowering of Interest and Raising the Value of Money* (1691), he states the importance of a uniform code and a steady measure of values. A few years later in *Further Considerations* (1695), he argues against devaluing the standard that he had proposed earlier. He reestablishes his commitment to maintaining standards in money *An Essay for the Amendment of the Silver Coins* (1695).

For Locke the state of nature was still a horrible place, but God's law created moral imperatives preventing humans from partaking in the total free-for-all that Hobbes described. According to Locke, people left the state of nature not out of fear of violent death, but as a matter of convenience and proprietary protection. They would not have to give up all their rights to an absolute authoritarian government; instead, they formed two distinctively separate agreements: the contract of society, and the contract of the majority of society and government or "trustee relationship" as it is often referred to. The contract with society takes place when people give up the total freedom that they enjoyed in the state of nature. This society was made up of two types of people: property and non-property owners. Property owners being rational individuals were given the right to suffrage, while non-property owners, viewed as not being industrious, were not. In order to fulfill the contract of the majority of society and government, the society as a whole contracts an impartial third party to act as the government. This agreement is often referred to as a trustee relationship because the government has no rights, only responsibilities to the people, and therefore acts only in the best interest of the members of the society. The government is given its power to act by the property-owning portion of the population, not by society as a whole.

Locke's *Two Treatises of Government* (1690) has been viewed as the classic expression of liberal political ideas. It is read as a defense of individualism and of the natural right of individuals to appropriate private property. It served as an intellectual justification for the British Whig Revolution of 1689 and stated the fundamental principles of the Whigs (Ashcraft, 1987). It would also serve as a primary source to the American Declaration of Independence. The key elements in Locke's political theory are natural rights, social contract, government by consent, and the issue of private property. Labor becomes the source and justification of property. Contract or consent is the ground of government and repairs its boundaries. Locke also believed that society had the right to overthrow the government. Since a majority created it, they have the power to remove it. This introduces the idea that government should be accountable to the people. Clearly, Locke was in favor of a limited government, not an authoritarian one, as Hobbes described.

The constitutional and cultural life of the United States was deeply influenced by Locke's *A Letter Concerning Toleration* (1689), which argued for the rights of man and the necessity of separating Church and State. Locke wrote that the commonwealth seems to be a society of men constituted only for procuring, preserving, and advancing their own civil interests. Locke referred to civil interests as liberty, health, and indolency of body; and the possession of outward things, such as money, lands, houses, furniture, and the like. It is the duty of the civil magistrate, by the impartial execution of equal laws, to secure unto all the people in general and to every one of his subjects in particular the just possession of these civil interests.

In *A Letter Concerning Toleration*, Locke detailed in great length the need for the separation of Church and State. Locke states that whatsoever is lawful in the Commonwealth cannot be prohibited by the magistrate in the Church. Any law created for the public good overrides the Church and any conflict with interpretations of God's will shall be judged by God alone, not religious zealots. Further, the magistrate ought not to forbid the preaching or professing of any speculative opinions in any Church because they have no manner of relation to the civil rights of the subjects. Locke argued that the Roman Catholic Church was dangerous to public peace because it professed allegiance to a foreign prince. Locke generally goes out of his way in many of his theological writings not to take issue with the Christian faith and adherence to the Bible. He treated religion like any other subject, he uses an intellectual approach, something quite admirable and ahead of its time.

Together with Newton's *Principia*, Locke's *Essay Concerning Human Understanding* (1690) effectively decided the issue in the battle between "gods" and "giants." Locke details in *Essay* the need for analysis and study in regard to issues of morality and religion. The *Essay* represents Locke's greatest philosophical contribution and centers on traditional philosophical topics: the nature of the self, the social world, God, and the ways in which we attain our knowledge of them. His initial purpose of thought was to halt the traditional analyses of the Cartesians (or the medievalists) and to derive a method of dealing with the important difficulties in normative conduct and theological discussion. In book four of the *Essay*, Locke reveals that he is at one with the rationalist theologians of his century in their antagonism toward those who would ignore reason. Locke (1690) states, "Reason must be our last judge and guide in everything" (Book 4:19:14).

Whether or not Locke can be labeled a "rationalist" is debatable. Some social thinkers come to view a person as a rationalist if they ground their thoughts with reason as a means to interrupt the social world. Philosophers insist on labeling Locke an empiricist. Thomson (1993), for one, argues that Locke was an empiricist, and describes empiricism as beginning "with sense experience and claims that all knowledge must be derived from it . . . Empiricist principles reject the possibility of a priori knowledge of the world" (p. 210). A long-standing interpretation of an approach that is labeled "empirical" is based on information obtained through our senses; the information must be something that can be seen, heard, felt, tasted, or smelled, and that can likewise be verified independently by others' senses (Goode, 1988). Modern sociologists are empirical because they collect evidence that involves real things that happen in the real world, a world that is visible. Consequently, modern science demands that claims of empiricism must refer to information carefully gathered in an unbiased manner (Kornblum, 1991). Systematic data collection and statistical interpretation are requirements of modern empiricism, and therefore in order to be labeled an empiricist, one must collect data

and employ statistical analysis of such data. Thomson provides no evidence that Locke conducted empirical research; in fact, Locke's pursuit of a medical degree was hampered by this critical limitation. The philosophers may label Locke as an empiricist during his era, but as the criteria of empiricism has evolved, there are few modern social scientists that would label him an empiricist based on a contemporary perspective.

During the first few decades of the eighteenth century the *Essay* and *Principia* gradually overshadowed their Cartesian rivals, as their great philosophical movement of idealism gradually acquired its strength (Yulton, 1956). His contemporaries, especially among those in England, felt the impact of Locke's theories on morality, government, and religion. His lasting impact of society rests with the fact that he laid the foundation for much of the groundwork of the U.S. Constitution and the U.S. Federal Government.

Jean-Jacques Rousseau (1712–1778)

Rousseau was a fascinating individual whose unorthodox ideas and passionate prose caused a flurry of interest in eighteenth-century France, and his republican sentiments for liberty, equality, and brotherhood led eventually to the French Revolution. He was born to artisan Isaac Rousseau and his wife, an academic elite, Suzanne Bernard, on June 28, 1712, in Geneva, Switzerland. He was baptized into the Calvinist faith. Suzanne Bernard was forty years old when she gave birth to Jean-Jacques and died of puerperal fever (an infection of the female reproductive system caused by improper disinfecting during labor) within ten days of his birth. Although puerperal fever was fairly common during the eighteenth century, Jean-Jacques' father blamed him for his mother's death. This was not his only suffering; "like many other children of aging parents, Rousseau was born with physiological defects; he had a deformity of the urinary tract which caused him much pain in later life and affected his sexual activities in a way which added to his humiliations" (Cranston, 1983:23).

In his autobiography, *Confessions*, Rousseau offers details of his childhood, describing it as such, "the children of kings could not have been more zealously cared for than I was . . ." (Cranston, 1983:28). He speaks with the greatest respect and admiration for his father, and yet he is unable to hide the fact that he was given a very unstable upbringing. His father did not really deserve the praise Rousseau lavished upon him. Rousseau's fa-

Jean-Jacques Rousseau (1712–1778) proponent of the French republican sentiments of liberty, equality, and brotherhood.
Source: CORBIS

ther home schooled him. In *Confessions*, Rousseau recalls having the ability to read by the age of three. His father had him reading romances and classical histories such as Plutarch's before apprenticing him to an engraver. Reading such French novels may account for his "highly romanticized and sentimental vision of the world" (Cranston, 1983:24). Rousseau claimed himself a Roman by the age of twelve, allowing him the ability to possess a free and republican spirit. Meanwhile, Isaac Rousseau was revealing his emotionally unstable personality by constantly beating his two sons; François, the eldest, was neglected after his brother's birth and received the brunt of the beatings. Cranston (1983) reports that Jean-Jacques was left in the care of his uncle, Gabriel Bernard, when his father fled Geneva to avoid imprisonment and fines resulting from a dispute (leading to a physical attack) with Captain Gautier, a patrician living just outside Geneva. Isaac's abandoning of Jean-Jacques would prove detrimental in the future treatment of his own children, as he would abandon all his own children, sending them at birth to an orphanage (Cranston, 1983).

Rousseau left home at age sixteen. He studied music and devised a new system of musical notation which was rejected by the Academy of Sciences. Throughout his life, Rousseau often earned his living by copying music. In Paris in the 1740s (he arrived for the first time in 1742) he entered literary society and wrote both words and music for an opera *Les Muses galantes*. Rousseau lived for thirty years with an uneducated servant girl who bore him five children, according to his *Confessions*; all of them were given to an orphanage in infancy. His life was consumed with sexually deviant behaviors, including the desire for erotic sensuality from the pain of spankings by way of dominatrix Mademoiselle Lambercier. He had numerous affairs —particularly with older women.

Rousseau has a number of significant published works. As Broome (1963) states, Rousseau's first discourse was published in 1750, entitled *Discourse on the Arts and Sciences*. This publication was a prize-winning essay written for the Academy of Dijon. He argued that the more science, industry, technology, and culture became developed and sophisticated, the more they carried human societies from decent simplicity toward moral corruption (Cranston, 1986). In his second publication, *Discourse on the Origin of Inequality*, Rousseau elaborated on the process of how social institutions had developed extreme inequalities of aristocratic France, where the nobility and the church lived in luxury, while the poor peasants had to pay most of the taxes. The theme of *Inequality* is that society alienates man from his natural self, thus creating a situation of inner dissension and of conflict with other men (Crocker, 1968) In his *Discourse on Political Economy*, he suggested remedies for these injustices. He suggests that the individual should choose to regard himself as part of the whole society. He argues that civil freedom must be accompanied by moral freedom. Through the practice of moral freedom, the citizen reaffirms his original integration in the civil unity. Rousseau states, "men are trained early enough never to consider their persons except as related to the body of the State, and not to perceive their existence, so to speak, except as part of the State's, they will eventually come to identify themselves with this larger whole; to feel themselves to be members of the homeland; to love it with that delicate sentiment that any isolated man feels only for himself . . ." (Cullen, 1993:87).

In 1756 he retreated to a simple country life and wrote a romantic novel, *La Nouvelle Heloise*, which won the hearts of many. Some historians consider Rousseau the initiator of the romantic rebellion in art and literature.

In 1762 Rousseau published his famous *The Social Contract*. According to Rousseau, society could only be accounted for, and justified, as a means for enabling men to advance to a higher level of achievement than could be arrived at in its absence. Society had to be regarded as a necessary means to the development of the moral potentialities of man's original nature. Man's development from primitive to organized societies would provide the foundation for his conception of the necessary elements of social obligations—Man is born free and everywhere he is in chains.

Rousseau believed that nature ordained all men equal and that the State's conformity to natural law involved the maintenance of public order and the provision of opportunities for the happiness of individuals. Rousseau's idea of a "perfect" society would include:

- A society that grew only to the extent that it could be well governed.

- A society in which every person would be equal to his occupation; no one would be committed to another's function.

- That society and individuals have the same goals.

- That all members of society have an equal voice.

- That no single member is above the law, and further, that no such individual would be able to dictate to the State to be obliged to recognize individual superiority of power.

- That society should be aware of a dramatic increase of new members, and take measures to make sure that these new members do not restructure the state so that they enjoy unequal power.

- That the society should be free from threat of conquest by other societies and should not attempt to gain control of others.

- That as society grows, it becomes necessary for magistrates to "run" it, but their power must be limited.

It is clear that Rousseau wanted a democratic society, but he was also aware of the potential of individuals acting in self-interest. He believed that the only primitive instinct of man is the desire for self-preservation. He will love what tends to conserve it and abhor what tends to harm it. Man's attempt of societal order would be the source of all evil. For man in his earliest or natural condition was an isolated being; there were no institutions, political or social; no government, no family, no property, none of the usages of society. Man survived in nature by self-sufficiency. The first moment that man becomes aware of self-consciousness signals the beginning of the decline of man. For now, reflection led him to the fatal knowledge of his superiority to other animals. Thus, with human pride comes the divorce from nature. Man, now apart from nature, sets out to subdue the world, to advance himself in knowledge and power, and to perfect his place in the environment by this awakening reason. Man now must agree to created laws, equally binding all, and assuring the peace and well-being of everyone. However, the very vices that had rendered government necessary rendered the abuse of power inevitable. Rousseau, therefore, believed that the State is to have a limited role in societal matters with its primary function to protect the members from outside threat as well as internal self-concerning individuals.

The work of social thinkers like Hobbes, Locke, and Rousseau emphasized the grand, general, and very abstract systems of ideas that made rational sense. Their work, along with many other thinkers, such as Voltaire, Charles Montesquieu, and René Descartes, would spearhead a new movement of social reasoning known collectively as the "Age of Enlightenment."

Age of Enlightenment

The "Age of Enlightenment," the collective term used to describe the trends and writings in Europe and the American colonies during the eighteenth century, appeared prior to the French Revolution. The phrase was frequently employed by writers of the period itself, convinced that they were emerging from centuries of darkness and ignorance into a new age enlightened by reason, science, and a respect for humanity. The Enlightenment was a period of dramatic intellectual development and change in philosophical thought. A number of long-standing ideas and beliefs were being abandoned and replaced during the Enlightenment (Ritzer, 2000).

The Enlightenment thinkers kept a watchful eye on the social arrangements of society. "Their central interest was the attainment of human and social perfectibility in the here and now rather than in some heavenly future. They considered rational education and scientific understanding of self and society the routes to all human and social progress" (Adams and Sydie, 2001). Progress could be attained because humans hold the capacity for reason. Further, reason should not be constrained by tradition, religion, or sovereign power.

The roots of modern sociology can be found in the work of the philosophers and scientists of the "Great Enlightenment," which had its origins in the scientific discoveries of the seventeenth century. That pivotal century began with Galileo's "heretical" proof that the Earth was not the center of the universe (as the Church had taught), and ended with the publication of Sir Isaac Newton's *Principia mathematica* (Kornblum, 1994).

The work of Enlightenment thinkers was not dispassionate inquiry, for they were deeply disturbed by the power of the Church and its secular allies in the monarchy. Freedom of inquiry and diversity of thought were not tolerated, and free-thinkers were often tortured and executed (Garner, 2000).

The Enlightenment is most readily characterized as "liberal individualism." It was a movement that emphasized the individual's possession of critical reason, and it was opposed to traditional authority in society and the primacy of religion in questions of knowledge (Hadden, 1997). According to Seidman (1983), liberalism arose as a reaction against a static hierarchical and absolutist order, which suppressed individual freedom.

Of the basic assumptions and beliefs of philosophers and intellectuals of this period, perhaps the most important was an abiding faith in the power of human reason. The insistence on the ability of people to act rationally was anathema to Church and State (Hadden, 1997). Social thinkers were impressed by Newton's discovery of universal gravitation. If humanity could so unlock the laws of the universe, God's own laws, why could it not also discover the laws underlying all of nature and society? Scientists came to assume that through a rigorous use of reason, an unending progress would be possible—progress in knowledge, in technical achievement, and even in moral values. Following the philosophy of Locke, the eighteenth-century social thinkers believed that knowledge is not innate, but comes only from experience and observation guided by reason.

Through education, humanity itself could be altered, its nature changed for the better. A great premium was placed on the discovery of truth through the observation of nature, rather than through the study of authoritative sources, such as Aristotle and the Bible. Although they saw the Church, especially the Catholic Church, as the principal force that had enslaved the human mind in the past, most Enlightenment thinkers did not renounce religion completely. They saw God as a Prime Mover, a motivator of sorts (Garner, 2000). Yet they still believed that human aspirations should be centered on improving life on earth and not on the promises of an afterlife. Worldly happiness was placed before religious promises of "salvation." No social institution was attacked with more intensity and ferocity than the Church, with all its wealth, political power, and suppression of the free exercise of reason.

The Enlightenment was more than a set of ideas, it implied an attitude, a method of thought. There was a clear desire to explore new ideas and allow for changing values. It is important to note that not all of the social writers that comprised the collectivity of enlightened reason were intellectuals. There were many popularizers engaged in a self-conscious effort to win converts. They were journalists and propagandists as much as true philosophers, and historians often refer to them by the French word *philosophes*.

For the most part, the homeland of the philosophes was France. Political philosopher Charles de Montesquieu, one of the earliest representatives of the movement, had begun publishing various satirical works against existing social institutions. Voltaire was another famous French writer of political satire, poems, and essays, and aided tremendously in popularizing the works of the philosophes. Voltaire and other philosophes relished the concept of a philosopher–king enlightening the people.

The philosophes valued both education and practical knowledge. They believed that educated persons would exercise their critical reason for their own happiness and consequently, their acts and deeds would benefit society overall. The philosophes also placed a great deal of importance on practical knowledge—how to farm, how to construct bridges and dams, how to relate to follow citizens (Adams and Sydie, 2001).

Hard work and education were believed to be the foundation to human and social progress. As quoted in Gay (1969:170), Denis Diderot (co-author of the *Encyclopedie*, volumes from 1751 to 1765) believes that "nature has not made us evil; it is bad education, bad models, bad legislation that corrupt us." Thus, reason is learned, it is not innate.

The Enlightenment was also a profoundly cosmopolitan and antinationalistic movement with representatives in many other countries: Immanuel Kant in Prussia; David Hume in England; Cesare Beccaria in Italy; and Benjamin Franklin and Thomas Jefferson in the American colonies. All maintained close contacts with the French philosophes but were important contributors to the movement in their own right.

The Conservative Reaction

History will show that whenever a new and radical movement begins to challenge and change the very core beliefs and values of society, a corresponding, usually negative, conservative backlash will result. The Enlightenment and the French Revolution created a powerful backlash. The Enlightenment thinkers are generally considered to be the intellectual forbearers of the French Revolution (1789–1794). Intellectuals who represented the interests of the absolute monarchy and the aristocracy wrote against the new ideas of freedom of thought, reason, civil liberties, religious tolerance, and human rights (Garner, 2000). They argued for a return to rigid hierarchies, with fixed status groups, established religion and misery for the masses. Many of the conservatives questioned the legitimacy of individual freedom and rights, including the right to happiness. They argued that society is not a collection of individuals, but is instead a social unit in its own right, and must be protected from free thought.

The extreme irrationality of the conservatives included suggestions from some that society should go back to the medieval-era style of rule. Louis de Bonald (1754–1840), for example, was so disturbed by the revolutionary changes in France that he yearned for a return to the peace and harmony of the Middle Ages. In his view, God was the source of society and therefore, reason, which was so important for the Enlightenment thinkers, was seen as inferior to traditional religious beliefs. Furthermore, de Bonald opposed anything that undermined such traditional institutions as patriarchy, the monogamous family, the monarchy, and the Catholic Church (Ritzer, 2000).

The conservatives had idealized the medieval order, conveniently forgetting, or not caring about, the misery that the vast majority of people were subjected to throughout their short, labor-filled lives. As a challenge to the principles of the philosophes and a critique of the post-Revolutionary "disorder," the conservatives advanced a number of propositions about society. Zeitlin (1981) outlines ten major propositions of this conservative reaction about society, which are shown in abbreviated form as follows:

1. Society is an organic unity with internal laws and development and deep roots in the past. Society is greater than the individuals who comprise it.

2. Society is superior to individual man, for man has no existence outside of a social group or context, and he becomes human only by participating in society.

3. The individual is an abstraction and not the basic element of a society. Society is composed of relationships and institutions.

4. The parts of a society are interdependent and interrelated. Therefore, changing one part undermines the stability of the whole society.

5. Institutions are positive entities because they provide for the needs of individuals.

6. All the various customs and institutions of a society are positively functional, nothing is dysfunctional, not even prejudice (which can serve the function of unifying groups).

7. The existence and maintenance of small groups is essential to society. The family, neighborhood, religious groups, and so forth, are the basic units of society (not individuals).

8. The conservatives wanted to preserve the older religious forms—Catholicism, not Protestantism—and sought to restore the religious unity of medieval Europe.

9. The conservatives insisted on the essential importance and positive value of nonrational aspects of human existence. Man needs ritual, ceremony, and worship. The philosophes were merciless in their criticism of those activities, labeling them irrational vestiges of the past.

10. Status and hierarchy were also deemed as essential to society. A hierarchy was necessary to assure that the Church remained on top of the social order.

The propositions brought forth by the conservatives would greatly influence such thinkers as Saint-Simon, Comte, and Durkheim. But what is most important is that both the conservatives and the Enlightenment thinkers contributed substantially to the foundation of sociological thought. The Enlightenment thinkers stressed liberal individualism with its emphasis on reason, individual freedom, contractual relations, and a reverence for science as the way to examine and explain all spheres of experience, including the social. The conservatives stressed collectivism, which emphasized the importance of maintaining social order for the good of society itself. Tradition and church authority are sacred and must be maintained.

Revolutions

Reactionary beliefs and hopes of the Conservatives that society should turn back to a way of life that existed in the Middle Ages were, of course, never to be realized. Progress can never be stopped and the rise of reason and science had already transformed the social order. The vehicle of social change was not science itself, since relatively few individuals of any society were practicing scientists. Instead, social change was a product of the many new social ideas that captured people's imagination during the Enlightenment. A series of revolutions took place in Europe and America that were, at least in some part, a result of the social movements unleashed by the triumphs of science and reason. The ideas of human rights for all, not just the elites, of democracy versus rule by an absolute monarch, of self-government for colonial peoples, and of applying reason and science to human issues in general, are all streams of thought that arose during the Enlightenment (Kornblum, 1994).

Political Revolutions

The Age of Reason allowed for the questioning of the traditional order of society. Faith and tradition was slowly challenged by secular thinking. Knowledge was replacing sacred tradition and ritual. The concept of individual, natural rights for all people influenced the study of law and law-making, and debates about justice in society began to replace the idea that kings had a "divine right" to rule. From the Renaissance on, especially in Western societies, social thinkers and political revolutionists would extol the virtues of reason and scientific discovery.

From the standpoint of Europeans, the American Revolution and the Declaration of

Independence indicated that, for the first time, some individuals were going beyond the mere discussion of enlightened ideas and were actually putting them into practice. The American Revolution would encourage further attacks and criticisms against existing European regimes. "Thomas Jefferson's preamble to the Declaration of Independence, a prime example of Enlightenment thinking, assumed that all 'rational' individuals would agree with the 'self-evident truths' that 'all men are created equal' and endowed with 'inalienable rights' of 'life, liberty, and the pursuit of happiness'" (Adams and Sydie, 2001:12). By praising the value of democracy and citizen's rights, Jefferson was striking a blow against tyrannical authority.

The British empire directly felt the impact of the American Revolution, as they learned that the convictions and desires of the oppressed would not be tolerated by free-thinking citizens armed with the tools to fight back. Indirectly, it was the French who were perhaps influenced the most by the revolution in America. The citizens of France were no longer willing to be subjected to traditional forms of authority. The ideas of democracy had a great impact on the French people and provided a spark to ignite the French Revolution of 1789.

The Age of Enlightenment is usually said to have ended with the French Revolution of 1789. As mentioned earlier, some see the social and political ferment of this period as being responsible for the Revolution. The French Revolution brought the French people the opportunity to build a new social order based on the principles of reason and justice. The changes were indeed revolutionary, as many nobles were killed and their dominant role in French society was ended forever (Cockerham, 1995). A series of laws enacted between 1789 and 1795 produced a number of other fundamental social changes. Churches were now subordi-

nated to the state and forbidden to interfere in politics and the conduct of civil government. Each social class was given equal rights under the law, and each son in a family was entitled to equal amounts of inherited property (opposed to just the eldest son). The total impact of the French Revolution was far more intense than the American Revolution. The Americans were fighting for freedom from the imperial British government, while the French were fighting for the near-complete restructuring of society.

While embodying many of the ideals of the philosophes, the French Revolution in its more violent stages (1792–1794) served to temporarily discredit these ideals in the eyes of many European contemporaries. France was forced to fight several wars against Britain, Russia, and virtually all its neighbors in order to preserve its new social and political order. The French society was at total war and would reach its zenith of power under one of its generals, Napoleon Bonaparte, who became a dictator in 1799. For the next fifteen years Napoleon was the dominant figure in European politics. In a series of brilliant battles, Napoleon would conquer most of Europe. He met his political demise at Waterloo in 1815.

As France returned to a period of stability under an imposed peace settlement, intense debate erupted among French intellectuals about the many social changes that had occurred. As Giddens (1987) states, the French Revolution marked the first time in history that an entire social order was dissolved by a movement guided by purely secular ideas of universal liberty and equality.

The long series of political revolutions ushered in by the French Revolution and continuing into the nineteenth century was a dramatic factor in the rise of sociological theorizing. The impact of these revolutions on many societies was enormous, and resulted in many positive changes. It also attracted the attention of many early theorists who concentrated on the negative effects of such changes. These writers were particularly disturbed by the resulting chaos and disorder that revolution and war brought with them, especially in France. An interest in the issue of social order was one of the major concerns of classical sociological theorists, especially Comte and Durkheim.

The Industrial Revolution

The Industrial Revolution was at least as important as the political revolutions were in shaping sociological theory. It began in the late eighteenth century in England and quickly spread through many Western societies, including the United States. The Industrial Revolution was not a single event but, instead, a number of interrelated developments that culminated in the transformation of the Western world from a largely agricultural to an overwhelmingly industrial system.

The Industrial Revolution involved the substitution of machines for the muscles of animals and humans, which resulted in a dramatic increase in productivity. This increase in productivity led to an increased demand for more machines, more raw materials, improved means of transportation, better communication, better-educated workers, and a more specialized division of labor.

Large numbers of people left their farms and rural ways of life in hopes of finding employment in the rapidly developing urban cities. Industrialized factories created a high demand for labor. More and more people left their agrarian lifestyle behind them, not sure of what to expect in the city. Large sections of many medieval cities were transformed into sprawling, chaotic slums characterized by poor sanitation. Laborers worked long hours for little pay.

The Industrial Revolution changed the face of Western society. No longer did the majority of people live in small, rural villages with an extended kinship system and produce for themselves most of what they needed in order to survive. The rise of trade had dissolved the subsistence economy of medieval society and created a system of political power based on financial wealth rather than ownership of land. A wide range of social problems that had never existed before industrialization became the new topic of concern among intellectuals and social thinkers. Issues of social change and social order were joined by questions of why modernization was not occurring elsewhere in the world. Why weren't Africa, China, India, and other nations experiencing the same social changes as the West? These concerns would soon come under the domain of sociological thinking.

Claude-Henri Saint-Simon (1760–1825)

Born in 1760 into a noble family, Saint-Simon lived in comfort as a member of the aristocracy. He was the eldest of nine children and was educated by private tutors. Saint-Simon met Rousseau and was taught the leading ideas of the Enlightenment philosophers of France. Every morning his servant would greet him with "Remember you have great things to do." In 1776 Saint-Simon joined the military. Three years later he became a captain, as the common practice of the aristocracy was enjoying rapid promotion. Saint-Simon served in the American Revolution as a volunteer on the side of the colonists. He fought under the command of George Washington at Yorktown. Fighting with the French in a colonial war in the West Indies, he was captured (1782) by the English and served a prison term of several months. In 1783 Saint-Simon went to Mexico and designed the concept of building a canal across Panama. The following year Saint-Simon returned to France. He took no part in the

French Revolution, believing that the old regime was weak enough so why bother with war? He did, however, use the opportunity to make a fortune through land speculation.

Saint-Simon spent the first forty years of his life as a soldier and speculator. It is said that Charlemagne, the first and greatest Holy Roman Emperor, appeared in a dream and told him to become a "great philosopher." This vision persuaded him to pursue a career in "saving humanity." Saint-Simon's desire for social improvement led him into the purchase of an aristocratic and church property from the government, and a financial partnership he formed to this end met with great success. He lavished his wealth on a salon for scientists but spent his later years in poverty, sustained by the faith that he had a message for humanity. With the support of a former servant, Saint-Simon found time for full-time study and would soon begin his scientific studies.

Saint-Simon maintained that Newton had uncovered the structure of the universe (structure is viewed here as recurrent patterns that could be observed and studied in astronomy). He thought it was possible to study the structure of society and uncover its laws. In his work, Saint-Simon wrote about the necessity of creating a science of social organization. The very term organization meant "organic structure" to him. He maintained that society, like an organism, was born and grew. The major challenge was to understand such growth (social change) and the forces behind social stability (social order). He believed that laws exist to explain these issues of organization and social stability.

In his *Introduction to the Scientific Studies of the 19th Century* (1807), Saint-Simon stated that the observation of patterns over a long period of time was essential. Those observations must then be brought together in a general theory of history capable of explaining the fundamental causes of historical change, not only in the past and at the present time,

but also in the future; for the causes of future events must already be in existence. The implication was, if one could forecast the future, then one might be able to shape the future as well. This line of thought was influenced by Nicolas de Condorcet's belief that he could document the operation of progress in the past and project the course of history for the future. For Condorcet, the idea of infinite perfectibility was a foregone conclusion (Coser, 1977). Ironically, Condorcet was a victim of the terror of the French Revolution.

In his 1813 *Essays on the Science of Man*, Saint-Simon suggests that the methodology of a social science should be the following:

1. Study the "course of civilization" and look for regularities, patterns, and processes of change.
2. Observations will disclose patterns or "laws of social organization." The broad historical trends will outline the history of social evolution.
3. Once the laws are discovered they can be used to reconstruct society on the basis of a plan.

Consequently, the study of society should be based on science, including the use of history and observation, in the search of regularities.

Foreseeing the triumph of the industrial order, Saint-Simon called for the reorganization of society by scientists and industrialists on the basis of a scientific division of labor. He had an essentially authoritarian and hierarchical view of society, believing that it was inherently divided into rigid social strata. Social classes would be determined by the new social order being ushered in by positivism. Positivism (the reliance on scientific study, laws, regulations, and reason) was to be directed by the most "competent" members of society. Saint-Simon referred to the competent class as people like bankers, lawyers, industrialists, and intellectuals.

Saint-Simonian thought dictated that action taken by this class was to be evaluated and analyzed from a positivistic perspective.

The control over the social order created by this science would come in the form of a religious force. Saint-Simon was associated with a religious revival outlined in his most significant publication, the *New Christianity* (1825). He called for a newer, more humanistic, approach to Western religion. Saint-Simon believed that science and religious ideas would eventually combine to form a positivistic religion, or a *terrestrial morality* as he called it. Saint-Simonian groups sprung up all across Europe preaching the message of Saint-Simon's philosophy. They were bourgeois intellectuals and officeholders (both public and private) who were, not surprisingly, mainly bankers, industrialists, and intellectuals considering themselves to be the "competent" class. They emphasized the need for order, discipline, efficiency, public control of the means of production, and the gradual emancipation of women. Being in their predominant social position, Saint-Simonians were mainly interested in material productivity and control of society by qualified experts (the competents, like themselves). Partly because of their eccentricities the Saint-Simonians achieved brief fame. And, although the movement developed into a moral-religious cult and had split and was disintegrated by 1833, it exerted much influence, especially on later socialist thought.

Ideologically, Saint-Simon envisioned a planned society, an international community, and as such, he was in favor of technological growth and industrialization. He believed that all societies would unite, forming a worldwide community. Because "common" people could not grasp such a concept of a worldwide community based on science, the elites would be needed to oversee and lead society. Worldwide protests in 2000 against globalization and organizations such as the World Trade Organization and the World Bank, would seem to support Saint-Simon's contention that the masses still cannot, or will not, grasp the concept of a world-community. Saint-Simon felt that the ideas of science should be introduced to the masses through artists and their art, therefore reducing it to a level that common people could understand.

Saint-Simon employed an adaptation of the survival-of-the-fittest attitude believing that everyone must work and be productive members of society, and if you do not, you do not eat. He was against welfare (care for the elderly, homeless, etc.) because he believed that it leads to a dependency on the state, which would eventually drain productive societies.

The most lasting and important influence of Saint-Simon lies with one of his former pupils and one-time personal secretary—Auguste Comte. For it was Comte who would more successfully transform many of Saint-Simon's ideas and formulate them into a new and highly challenging discipline called sociology.

Auguste Comte

(1798–1857)

Isadore Auguste Marie François Xavier Comte was born January 19, 1798, in the southern French city of Montpellier during the height of chaos and instability in France. To add to the instability in his own immediate setting, his parents were devout Catholics and ardent royalists, affiliations not conducive to one's personal safety (Hadden, 1998). His father, Louis-Auguste Comte, was a petty government official who was employed at a tax office, and a serious man who was opposed to the French revolution (Standley, 1981). The senior Comte was an earnest, methodical, and straight-laced man, devoted to his work, his religion, and his family, whose only pastime was to cultivate his garden (Coser, 1977). Like his father, Auguste Comte (he had shortened his name early on in life) disliked Napoleon and the Restoration. He and his father disagreed about most of their beliefs except for the idea that social order was of the utmost importance (Thompson, 1975).

Louis-Auguste married Felicite-Rosalie Boyer in 1797. They had to conceal the wedding ceremony because the revolutionary government had closed the churches of Montpellier. Both Louis and Felicite were conservative Catholics. Felicite was a gentle person who devoted her life to the love and care of her husband and children. Auguste was coddled by his mother. He was small and fragile, and prone to many illnesses. His father, a humble employee of the tax office in the Department of Herault, and sister would also suffer from poor health. At the age of fourteen, Comte announced that he had "naturally" ceased believing in God. At the same time, he abandoned the royalist sympathies of his family and became a republican. As a result, Comte's relationship with his family was strained throughout the remainder of his life. He never appeared to be close to his parents or his three siblings (two sisters and one brother). Later in life, Comte would call his family covetous and hypocritical. He complained, rather vocally at times, that because of the ill-health of his father and sister, the family rarely had enough money to support his literary career.

Despite the limited finances of the Comte family, they were able to send Auguste and his brother to the Lycée at Montpellier. It is believed that they may have received some sort of scholarship aid because their father was a civil servant. Auguste entered the school when he was nine years old. Under the Napoleonic regime, the Lycées were boarding schools, which served as training grounds for future soldiers and civil servants of the Empire. The students wore plain uniforms and had to march under the orders of a de-

Auguste Comte (1798–1857) French philosopher who coined the term sociology for his positive philosophy.
Source: Courtesy of the Library of Congress

manding drill sergeant. The better students were honored with the distinctions of sergeant or corporal. Despite the mundane routine of the school, Auguste began to show astonishing prowess. It should be noted that these schools were not popular with the bourgeoisie.

There are two outstanding events in Comte's early life, which help to explain and shaped his more mature thought. The first was his attendance at the Ecole Polytechnique in Paris. Founded in 1794 at the height of the radical phase of the French Revolution, the Ecole Polytechnique trained military engineers and was quickly transformed into a school for the advanced sciences. Under Napoleon, it grew to become the foremost

French scientific institution. For Comte, however, the Ecole Polytechnique became a model for a future society ordered and sustained by a new elite of scientists and engineers. Ecole was organized and modeled under the guise of military efficiency.

Comte arrived in August 1814 and enjoyed the privilege of meeting many of the eminent scientists of France. Auguste was admitted as a corporal on the basis of his good examination grades. He soon felt that this was *his* school, a school from which he not only wished to graduate with honors, but where he hoped to teach after the end of his studies. His classmates saw early on Comte as the leader of his class, but he continued the disorderly and unruly behavior of childhood days. In 1816, Comte led a protest of students against the teaching methods of geometry instructor M. Lefebvre. When the school tried to punish the six ringleaders, the whole student body was in an uproar. The school's general, trying to keep in line with the new conservative government, ordered the removal of Comte and his whole class. They were dismissed for their rebelliousness and their political ideas of anti-Enlightenment thought. The government sent troops to the school and sent the offending students home without further incident. Comte and some of his friends tried to organize an Association of the Students of the Ecole Polytechnique, but this amounted to little more than further signaling to the government that these students could no longer be trusted (Standley, 1981). The government responded by ordering police surveillance over Comte's activities. No evidence was found against Comte.

This expulsion would have an adverse effect on Comte's academic career (Ritzer, 2000). He spent a few months with his parents and then returned to Paris. Comte supported himself by tutoring, and lived in hopes of the imminent overthrow of the

Bourbon oppressors. He met a general who had a number of connections in the United States and who promised to find him a teaching position in an American version of the Ecole Polytechnique, which was about to be organized. Comte was ecstatic over the possibility of obtaining a teaching position in the United States. He dreamed of emigrating forever to the land of the free, but the U.S. Congress postponed the opening of the school and Comte, brokenhearted, would never make it to America. When Ecole began to permit other student leaders of the rebellion to reenter the school, Comte also applied for admittance. Unfortunately, he failed to send in his application before the deadline. Consequently, although it was true that Comte received a formal education he never earned a college level degree. This reality would cost him dearly.

Growing up, Comte's math teacher, a former Protestant pastor named Daniel Encontre, was the only one who impressed him. It was perhaps Encontre who awoke the young Comte and inspired a wide-ranging intellectual course of action (Coser, 1977). Comte's knowledge of mathematics would help him in his later years when he attempted to establish the validity of "laws" existing in society. Comte was an extraordinary student, excelling primarily in math and physics, and was able to demonstrate unusual feats of memory such as reading pages of text and immediately reciting it backwards by heart (Hadden, 1998).

The second great event in Comte's life took place in the summer of 1817 when he was introduced to the French utopian socialist Claude-Henri Saint-Simon, then the director of the periodical *Industri*. Comte became Saint-Simon's secretary, or more accurately his protégé and the two were very close despite the vast differences in their ages. Saint-Simon was nearly sixty years old when the two met, but he was attracted to Comte's brilliant mind and came to view him as his "adopted son." As Saint-Simon's apprentice, Comte was paid quite handsomely, but when Saint-Simon experienced financial troubles, Comte continued to work without pay.

It is difficult to determine who benefited the most from this collaboration and scholars have debated this for some time. In acknowledging his debt to Saint-Simon, Comte states, "I certainly owe a great deal intellectually to Saint-Simon . . . he contributed powerfully to launching me in the philosophic direction that I clearly created for myself today and which I will follow without hesitation all my life" (Durkheim, 1928: 144). Eventually, Comte came to dislike Saint-Simon's method of developing theories, and he "became critical of Saint-Simon's lack of scientific knowledge and his unsystematic approach" (Standley, 1975:20). Comte and Saint-Simon split over publishing rights for the *Plan des Travaux Scientifiques*, which Saint-Simon later published in 1824, failing to acknowledge his secretary. This falling out caused Comte to reassess his opinion of Saint-Simon, and in his later years, he described his relationship with Saint-Simon as "catastrophic," adding, "I owe nothing to this personage" (Pickering, 1993:240). Suffice it to say that his mentor influenced Comte in a major way, but the ideas of Comte were most likely already in formation.

After the break with Saint-Simon in 1824, Comte supported himself by tutoring in mathematics. One year later, Comte believed that he had found personal security and happiness when he married Caroline Massin, a young woman whom he had known for several years, more recently as the owner of a small bookstore and earlier as an alleged streetwalker in the neighborhood of the Palais Royal. Comte's bourgeois parents objected to the marriage based on the fact that she came from a lower social class and provided their son with no dowry. Massin was the illegitimate child of two actors, and was raised by her grandmother (Pickering, 1996). The union proved unhappy and ended in separation years later. Refusing a position as a chemical engineer, Comte earned a meager living by tutoring the sons of wealthy and prominent families. This allowed him to maintain close ties with prominent members of society.

During these years Comte's major preoccupation was centered in the elaboration of his positive philosophy (Coser, 1977). When the work appeared to be suitable for a proper audience, Comte concocted a scheme by which he would present a series of seventy-two public lectures (held in his apartment) on his philosophy (Ritzer, 2000).

Beginning in April 1826, his lectures on his new philosophy began, attracting many outstanding French thinkers. It was from these lectures that Comte developed his six volume *Course of Positive Philosophy*, which was published between 1830 and 1842.

Unfortunately, after just three lectures, Comte fell ill, having suffered a nervous breakdown. He was treated for "mania" in the hospital of the famous Dr. Esquirol, where this author of a *Treatise on Mania* attempted to cure him by a cold-water treatment and bloodletting. Esquirol objected when Madame Comte finally decided to bring him back to their home. The register of discharge of the patient had a note in Esquirol's handwriting stating that Comte was "not recovered" (Coser, 1977). He continued to suffer from mental problems and he attempted suicide in 1827 by throwing himself into the Seine River. After an extended trip home to Montpellier, Comte slowly began his recovery. The lectures were resumed in 1829, and Comte was pleased with an audience of several prestigious attendees. But, as we will see, as time went on, he gradually became an object of ridicule in the scientific community.

In 1832, Comte began teaching part-time at Ecole Polytechnique. Five years later he was given the additional post of admissions examiner, which now allowed him economic freedom from his family for the first time. It should be pointed out that he was barely living above the margin of poverty. As the years passed by Comte became more isolated from society. Around this time, he began the practice of "cerebral hygiene," where he no longer read or followed the current literature in his field, eventually leaving him hopelessly out-of-touch with the scientific community. Despite these tribulations, Comte slowly began to acquire disciples. In England, John Stuart Mill became a close admirer and spoke of Comte in his *System of Logic* (1843). Mill even arranged for a number of British admirers to send Comte a considerable sum of money to help him with his financial difficulties.

Comte was publicly humiliated in 1844 when the Ecole refused to reappoint him. Just when things appeared to be at their worst, Comte met Clotilde de Vaux, an upper-class woman not yet thirty years old, and fell deeply in love. Madame de Vaux had been married previously. Her first husband was a minor official who had embezzled government funds and disappeared, leaving Clotilde in financial difficulties (Adams and Sydie, 2001). Auguste and Clotilde shared a romantic, yet platonic relationship, that never led to physical culmination. Tragically, she was stricken by tuberculosis, and died within a few short months after they had exchanged their first love letters (Coser, 1977). Comte now vowed to devote the rest of his life to the memory of his "angel" and credited Clotilde with providing the inspiration for his last major work, "A Religion of Humanity" (Adams and Sydie, 2001). In its pages (found in *System of Positive Polity*, 1851–1854) Comte now proclaimed the validity of emotion over intellect, of feeling over mind, and suggested that it was time for the warm powers of femininity for a humanity too long dominated by the cruelty of masculine intellect. With this deviation from scientific thought Comte lost most of his rationalist followers that he had worked so hard to acquire.

He managed to publish two more works, *The System of Positive Polity* (1851–1854) and *The Catechism of Positive Religion* (1852), but neither work captured his audience as had *Positive Philosophy*. Comte was undeterred by the loss of disciples. He believed that he would attract an infinite number of followers with his positivist religion. Comte began referring to himself as "The Founder of Universal Religion, Great Priest of Humanity." He wrote to all the powerful leaders of the world in an attempt to convert them to the new social order that would be known as Positive Society. He promised them that he had all the answers to the world's problems and was willing to be the world ruler. It was clear that this once brilliant mind was consumed with mania. His body, meanwhile, was consumed with cancer and the illness spread quickly, killing him on September 5, 1857. A small number of disciples, friends, and neighbors witnessed his burial at Père Lachaise. His tomb became the center of a small positivist cemetery where, buried close to the master, his most faithful disciples are.

Intellectual Influences

In response to the scientific, political, and industrial revolutions of his day, Comte was fundamentally concerned with an intellectual, moral, and political reorganization of the social order. Adoption of the scientific attitude was the key, he thought, to such a reconstruction. Comte was an ardent positivist. He insisted that the goal of sociology involved the discovery of knowledge that would aid in the progressive improvement of society. Comte was intellectually influenced by a number of theorists and schools of thought, including: English philosopher

Francis Bacon, who emphasized inductive experimentation; astronomer Galileo; English philosopher Thomas Hobbes; French philosopher Baron de Montesquieu; German philosophers Kant (whom Comte considered the metaphysician closest to the positive philosophy), Wilhelm, and the French philosopher Bossuet; and, above all, Saint-Simon (Ashley and Orenstein, 1985). During the early period of his life, Auguste Comte was deeply influenced by liberal political economists Adam Smith and J. B. Say. Comte was also impressed by historians William Robertson, David Hume, and G. W. Hegel. In short, he was in debt to many traditions but did not fully belong to any one of them; instead he assimilated various doctrines in order to present a synthesis of his thinking. The following is a quick review of the major influences on Auguste Comte.

The Effects of the Enlightenment

Comte believed that the purpose of science (especially sociology) was to study objective relationships of both structure and change in order to predict future events. For Comte, the Enlightenment notions of natural rights and individual freedom of thought and action were metaphysical ideas ungrounded in scientific analysis. Comte was greatly disturbed by the anarchy that pervaded French society and was critical of those thinkers who had supported both the Enlightenment and the revolution. He developed his scientific view of positivism to combat what he considered to be the negative and destructive philosophy of the Enlightenment (Ritzer, 2000).

Comte was a thinker in line with the French counterrevolutionary Catholics, especially de Bonald and de Maistre, and a resolute antagonist of the individualistic approach to human society that had predominated throughout the eighteenth century. However, Comte's work can be set apart from theirs on at least two points. First, he did not think it possible to return to the Middle Ages, because advances of science and industry made that impossible. Second, he developed a much more sophisticated theoretical system than his predecessors, one adequate enough to shape early sociology.

The Tradition of Progress

From the intellectual school of thought emphasizing the tradition of progress, Comte was deeply influenced by Nicholas de Condorcet. Condorcet's *Esquisse d'un tableau historique des progrès de l'esprit humain*, written while he was hiding from Robespierre's police, continued Turgot's focus on the long, historical chain of progress culminating in modern rational man. Condorcet believed that he could document the operation of progress in the past and project trends that would continue. He saw science and technology as the means by which mankind would propel society into the future. Taking his viewpoint from Bacon's *New Atlantis,* he elaborated a plan for a new scientific society in which an elite group of scientists would collaboratively share their knowledge and enhance scientific productivity. These men of science would act as the vanguard of society, ushering the dawn of a more perfect society. Although certain inequalities would continue to exist, the high level of achievement established by the human race as a whole would lead to the end of suffering and deprivation. Comte was very much impressed with Condorcet and yet he never followed his two major tenets: the belief in individualism and in relative equality. Instead, Comte's doctrine has a strongly hierarchic, anti-individualist, and inegalitarian composition.

The Tradition of Order

The traditionalists taught that a society not bound together by the ties of a moral community would collapse as a number of unre-

lated individuals. (This line of reasoning is similar to the adage "United we stand, divided we fall.") Society must have a legitimate authority with a hierarchal structure and the full support of its citizens. From this standpoint, society is viewed as an organic whole. The idea of social contracts between individuals, and the concept of society based on natural individual rights, was considered hubris or madness by the traditionalists of order. They believed men had duties rather than rights (Coser, 1977). Rousseau, in particular, was a target of their contempt, with his assertion that man, unspoiled by society, had been naturally good. Contrastly, de Bonald (1864) asserted that man becomes good through society. Disagreeing with Condorcet's belief in the perfectibility of man, de Bonald (1882) said that it was society which perfects man.

The traditionalists believed that society is healthy only when the different parts are functioning in harmonious order. Comte embraced many of the ideas of the traditionalists: order, hierarchy, moral community, spiritual power, and the primacy of groups over individuals. In fact, Comte's concept of social statics can be directly traced to their influence. Still, he could not give up on the idea of progress and the illogic of attempting to go back to medieval society.

The Tradition of Liberalism

Comte (1896) had the highest regard for Adam Smith, calling him "the illustrious philosopher." But he was also critical of Smith and his successors for their belief in the self-regulating character of the market. Comte viewed laissez faire as a system conducive to anarchy. Comte's belief in the beneficial effects of the division of labor comes directly from Smith. He agreed with Smith that the industrial form of the division of labor had awoken a potent form of social cooperation, which would allow mankind to drastically increase their production capacity. Comte would later recognize the potential for negative aspects of the specialization that takes place with the division of labor. Namely, the worker could reach the point where he would not have to exert creative understanding of his task and may develop a lack of desire to exercise invention.

There is one additional area in which Comte is directly indebted to the liberal economists: his recognition of the creative functions of "industrialists" or the modern term "entrepreneurs." Comte followed Smith's French disciple, Jean Batiste Say, in making distinctions between the capitalist and the entrepreneur. Comte believed that the entrepreneur would guide and direct activities in the new industrial system, whereas the capitalist controls the production and distribution.

Saint-Simon

As mentioned earlier, Comte met Saint-Simon in the summer of 1817. Comte would collaborate with Saint-Simon on a number of works. In 1824, Comte finally broke from the master over a quarrel involving intellectual as well as material issues. Saint-Simon, ever the activist, wished to emphasize the need for immediate reform. What he wanted above all was to inspire the liberal industrialists and bankers who were his backers to take prompt steps for the reorganization of French society. Comte, in contrast, emphasized that theoretical work had to take precedence over reform activities, and that establishing the foundations of the scientific doctrine was more important for the time being than effecting any practical influence. Despite this departure, Comte was clearly influenced by Saint-Simon.

Saint-Simon stated that changes in social organization take place (and are necessary) because of the development of human intelligence. According to him there was a direct relation between ideas and social organiza-

tion—the former influenced the latter. He suggested that any scientific study has to look at the moral ideas of a period because at any particular time in history the form of organization of a society is a direct reflection of the prevailing social code. He claimed that there were three different moral ideas in western Europe and each was separated from the others by a transition—during that period one moral system declines and another replaces it. The process of replacement–transition results from accumulated scientific knowledge that changes the philosophical outlook of the society. For Saint-Simon the three moral systems are:

1. Supernatural–Polytheistic Morals: Greece and Rome

2. Christian Theism: Socratic science, feudalism, and Middle Ages

3. Positivism: Industrial society

Saint-Simon's three moral systems would have a direct influence on Comte's "Law of Three Stages." Many other ideas of Comte are derived from Saint-Simon's writings: the emphasis on the key role of industrialists in ordering the temporal affairs of society; stressing the need to reconstitute spiritual power in the hands of elite scientists; the realization that society must be rebuilt after the chaos of the Enlightenment and the Revolution; and the emphasis on the need for a hierarchy and on the creative powers of the elites. These are but a few of the influences of Saint-Simon on Comtean notions (Coser, 1977).

Concepts and Contributions

In the fourth volume of the *Course of Positive Philosophy*, Comte proposed the word *sociology* for his new positivist science. The word "sociology" is a hybrid term compounded of Latin and Greek parts. Comte preferred "social physics" to describe his new social science but later found out that Belgian social statistician Adolphe Quetelet had "stolen" the term from him (Coser, 1977). As Ritzer (2000) notes, the use of the term *social physics* made it clear that Comte wanted to model sociology after the "hard sciences." Comte acknowledged that physics was the first field of knowledge to free itself from the grip of theology and metaphysics; the decisive moment was Galileo's struggle with the Catholic Church, which tried to suppress his findings and teachings in astronomy, especially the Copernican model of the solar system and the discovery of the moons of Jupiter (Garner, 2000). Though Galileo was silenced and confined to virtual house arrest for the last ten years of his life, his findings soon were accepted by all educated people in Europe. Chemistry was the next discipline to liberate itself from theology and metaphysics. The struggle was still underway in biology and sociology, the fields closest to human affairs and therefore most likely to challenge religious doctrine.

Since the French Revolution had failed to establish a stable order based on Enlightenment principles, Comte attempted to organize those principles that, he thought, could do the job. Above all, the reorganization of society required intellectual reform. It would also involve replacing Catholicism with his positive philosophy (Hadden, 1998). Comte's idea of positive philosophy, or positivism, is one of many major contributions to sociology.

Positive Philosophy

Although many individual sciences, such as physics, chemistry, and biology, had been developing at a steady pace, none had yet synthesized the basic principles of these sciences into a coherent system of ideas (Hadden, 1998). Comte envisioned a system that was led by an intellectual and moral basis, and that allowed for science to intervene on behalf of the betterment of society.

There are social thinkers who believe that the social world can be studied in the same manner as the natural sciences and their belief in the existence of natural laws. This approach is generally referred to as *positivism*. Social positivists seek to discover social laws that will enable them to predict social behavior. Through observation of behavior certain social relationships and arrangements should become identifiable; these observations could be explained as "facts" and in causal terms without interference of the researcher's value judgments. Therefore, positivism claims to be the most scientific, objective research tradition in sociology (Adams and Sydie, 2001).

Comte is remembered to this day in sociology for his championing of *positivism* (Scharff, 1995, and Turner, 1990). Comte's idea of positivism is based on the idea that everything in society is observable and subject to patterns or laws. These laws could help explain human behavior (Simpson, 1969). Comte did not mean that human behavior would always be subjected to these "laws," rather, he saw positivism as a way of explaining phenomena apart from supernatural or speculative causes (Simpson, 1969). Laws of human behavior could only be based on empirical data. Thus, positivism was based on research guided by theory, a premise that remains the cornerstone of sociology today. The very purpose of sociology as a discipline is to define and create social patterns of development in society (Thompson, 1975). Comte believed positivism would create sound theories based on sufficient factual evidence and historical comparisons to predict future events. The discovery of the basic laws of human behavior will allow for deliberate courses of action on the part of both individuals and society.

Decision-making guided by science would, indeed, be positive.

The Law of Three Stages

Comte's first major publication was *A Prospectus of the Scientific Operations Required for the Reorganization of Society*, which he referred to as the "great discovery of the year 1822" (Hadden, 1998). It is here that he describes the plan for an empirical science of society by introducing his evolutionary theory of "The Law of Three Stages." It involves the notion that the history of societies can be divided rather neatly into three distinct periods and that each kind of society is produced and supported by a different form of thought or philosophy (Hadden, 1998). Since society of his day was experiencing a period of crisis and great disorganization, he set out to discover the causes or reasons for this phenomenon. He concluded that European societies were in the midst of a difficult transition from one stage to the next.

For Comte, evolution or progress was a matter of the growth of the human mind. The human mind evolved through a series of stages, and so too must society, he proposed. The transition is always difficult, filled with periods of great disorganization and reorganization based on the newly emerging form of thought. Comte argued that an empirical study of historical processes, particularly of the progress of the various interrelated sciences, reveals a law of three stages that govern human development. He analyzed these stages in his major work, the six-volume *Course of Positive Philosophy* (1830–42). The three different stages are:

1. **Theological.** Relies on supernatural or religious explanations to explain what man otherwise could not. Intellectual efforts were hampered by the assumption that all phenomena are produced by "supernatural beings." The highest point of

this stage is the idea of a single God replacing the former proliferation of gods.

2. **Metaphysical.** This stage is a mere modification of the first stage and centers on the belief that abstract, even mysterious forces control behavior.

3. **Positive.** In this final stage of societal development, there comes the realization that laws exist. Through the use of reason and observation to study the social world, human behavior can be explained rationally. This stage is highlighted by a reliance on science, rational thought, empirical laws, and observation.

The theological stage occurred prior to 1300 A.D. This was a time when religion dominated society and unexplainable phenomena were attributed to supernatural beings or divinities. In this stage, the human mind is searching for the essential nature of things, especially one's origin and purpose of life. Comte felt that this was a period of inferior and primitive knowledge. During the theological stage, priests and military men maintained social order, and the gods did man's thinking for him (Simpson, 1969).

There are three transitional stages that make up the theological stage: fetishism, polytheism, and monotheism. Fetishism is described as a point in time where man and his surroundings lived "harmoniously." By this he means that man accepted the things that occurred around him without speculation. Polytheism marks the time where humans desired explanations and they began speculating and attributing phenomena to various supernatural beings. During this time, man was haunted by feelings of "awe" and "fear" (Scharff, 1995). The movement into the monotheistic stage occurred when people became overwhelmed with the many gods, who appeared to always be at conflict with one another. The worship of one single divinity is the final step of the theological stage.

The metaphysical is the second stage, which occurred between the 1300s and the 1800s, and is only a slight progressive step beyond the thinking of the theological stage. This was a time of philosophical thought and there was a heavy reliance on nature and abstract forces. Comte deemed this stage as the least important of the three stages. It was merely a transitional stage necessitated by Comte's belief that an immediate jump from the theological to the positivist stage would be too much for humans to handle. Comte believed that the use of philosophy was useless, for it was far to unsystematic (Simpson, 1969). Comte summarized the metaphysical stage as the sunset of theologism and the sunrise of positivism (Simpson, 1969).

The final stage is known as the positivist stage, which began in the 1800s. This stage relies on science and knowledge based on empirical laws and observations. The insistent search for absolutes, origins, and purpose is refocused into the study of laws. In this stage the individual became the "object of science" as well as the "subject making science possible" (Simpson, 1969:43). Industrialization and scientific moral guidelines of reasoning and facts dominate the scientific positivistic stage (Thompson, 1975).

Acceptance of Comte's positivistic views entails acknowledging that there is an existing order of the universe that occurs in a progressive stage. Comte believed that the cause of every phenomenon was not supernatural but natural (Mill, 1873).

Although Comte recognized an inevitable succession through these three stages, he acknowledged that at any given point in time all three might exist. Comte envisioned a future world where positivism dominated and theological and metaphysical thinking would be eliminated (Ritzer, 2000).

Each of the stages, Comte believed, is correlated with certain political developments. The theological stage is reflected in such notions as the divine right of kings. The metaphysical stage involves such concepts as the social contract, the equality of persons, and popular sovereignty. The positivist stage entails a scientific or "sociological" approach to political organization. Quite critical of democratic procedures (primarily because they would allow the uneducated masses too much say in how future society would operate), Comte envisioned a stable society governed by a scientific elite who would use the methods of science to solve human problems and improve social conditions.

Research Methods

Comte stressed four research methods of investigation as a means of obtaining knowledge:

1. Observation

2. Experimentation

3. Comparison

4. Historical

When using observation, the scientist looks for specific social facts in order to validate laws or theories involving the phenomena of social behavior. It is based on social facts and not simply an unguided quest for miscellaneous facts. Comte claimed that no social fact can have any scientific meaning until it is connected with some other social fact (Simpson, 1969). In using observation, one must develop ways and means of assuring that different sociologists will be able to see, hear, and experience the same phenomena. This observation cannot be assured unless it takes place on the basis of established sociological laws, no matter how simple they are at the beginning. Without laws, and the testing of hypotheses based upon them, there would be a scattering of random observations. Comte also felt that astute observers would be rare because most people cannot systematize their observations through laws and hypotheses. He was optimistic that this situation would improve as science continued to develop. Comte thought an individual trained in the scientific method will be able to convert almost all impressions from the events of life into sociological data when experience is combined with a talent to interrelate them.

The second research method of investigation is experimentation, which is rarely done in sociology, and is best suited for the "natural sciences." Conducting an experiment is extremely difficult in the social world because there is a near infinite number of variables to control. For both moral and practical reasons, sociologists do not have many opportunities to perform experiments. There is, however, ample research in contemporary sociology, and especially social psychology that warrants the continued use of experiments. Field experiments provide situations in which the researcher observes and studies subjects in their natural setting.

The third research method of investigation is comparison, which Comte divided into three subtypes. First, we can compare humans to lower forms of animals. Second, we can compare a variety of societies from different parts of the world. Third, we can compare societies to others in the same stage of development (Ritzer, 2000). In the first type of comparison, Comte felt that there was great value in comparing whatever rudiments of social life are found among the lower animals with those found among humans. Comte thought that the first germs of social relations could be discovered among the lower animals, and according to Simpson (1969), this method has since proven of some advantage in such subsidiary fields of sociological study as the family, the division of labor, and socialization. By Comte comparing humans to lower animals, he undermined ruling classes that considered mankind a special species above all other species.

According to Comte, the primary use of the method of comparison is the discovery of social structures, social classes, social functions, and patterns of social behavior, which are universal. This discovery is made through the study of coexisting states of society in different parts of the world. Comparing coexisting societies is an important tool for positive sociology, but Comte believed that the comparison of consecutive stages through which society passes over time was also needed.

This is where the fourth, and "chief scientific device" of sociology, comes into play. The fourth method is the historical investigation of human evolutionary growth. Comte states, "Our existing state cannot be understood simply through study of it as it is, but only by seeing it as part of the series of social states from which it has emerged and which have left their imprint upon our minds" (Simpson, 1969:21). By attributing human reason to history, history provides more than "counsel" and "instruction," it provides a "general direction" for humans to proceed.

It should be noted that Comte wrote about conducting research but he most often engaged in speculation or theorizing in order to get at the invariant laws of the social world. He did not derive these laws inductively from observations of the social world; instead, he deduced them from his general theory of human nature (Ritzer, 2000).

Social Statics and Social Dynamics

Through his notions of social statics and social dynamics, Comte established a direction for social research. He believed that just as biology found it useful to separate anatomy from physiology, it was just as desirable to make a distinction in sociology between statics and dynamics (Coser, 1977). *Social statics* is a term used to describe the social processes that hold society together, while *social dynamics* refers to mechanisms of change. Thus, Comte not only gave sociology its name, but its initial orientation, which distinguished it from other disciplines (Cockerham, 1995).

In his description of social statics (sociologists today would refer to this as *social structure*), Comte was anticipating many of the ideas of later functionalists. Through the use of social statics, Comte maintained that the units or levels of investigation were the individual, the family, the society, and the species. The individual, by nature, according to Comte, had a tendency to let the affective (emotional) faculties predominate over the intellectual. The development of society depended on some type of stimulation, and an extension of intellectual faculties. As civilization grew, individuals would become more stimulated, and hence, develop further (Hadden, 1998). Social statics depends on the interaction and cooperation of individuals in a society and assumes that the state of nature for humans is social. The family represents the simplest aspect of society, but it is not an accurate representation of society as a whole. The government functions as the whole of society helping families, thus government is not a necessary evil but a positive force for achieving a continually shifting consensus (Simpson, 1969). Subordination to government authority is necessary to establish and maintain an orderly existence. Individualism is not hindered by social statics, but it is an attribute that is needed in order for social structures to function properly (Lewes, 1853).

Comte devoted more attention to social dynamics (today's term would be *social change*) because he found it more interesting than social statics and of far greater importance. It was more important because the evolution of society would make the conditions of society better. Social dynamics deals with the laws of social movement, or progress. Comte believed that human social development was firmly rooted in the development of human intelligence. Social development, based on the growth of intellect, leads to the primacy of the "preponderant powers of human existence," namely to the development of the positive philosophy (Comte, 1975). As civilization begins to develop, population will become more concentrated. This provides a stimulus to further intellectual and moral development. Reason, in turn, becomes more developed and influential in the general conduct of man and society (Comte, 1975).

Society is always changing, and Comte believed that "man looks for stability in change" (Simpson, 1969:87). Change is ordered and subject to social laws; it is an evolutionary process. Comte believed that there was a parallel change in society's material development and intellectual development. The changes in humankind occurred between the growing intellect and conduct of man and the gradual advances that took place as a result. Comte thought that periodical reforms were needed to help move this evolutionary process along. Because invariant laws control this process, there is relatively little, beyond intellectual and moral development, that individuals can do to affect the overall direction of this process.

Comte believed that the development of the intellect and society makes itself felt differently in different sciences. In general, the theological stage sparks the understanding, the metaphysical maintains speculative activity on all subjects, and the positive, or final stage allows for the extraction of laws and general principles which can be applied to alter nature and society (Comte, 1975). It was Comte's ultimate goal to make sociology a positive science. He developed a hierarchy of sciences beginning with the simplest and rising in order to the most complex. For Comte, a positivistic classification of the sciences would demonstrate how the human mind works at its rational best, and would show the necessary interconnection of all the sciences.

Hierarchy of the Sciences

Comte's theory of the hierarchy of the sciences is connected with the Law of Three Stages. Just as mankind progresses through determinant stages, each successive stage building on the accomplishments of its predecessors, scientific knowledge also passes through similar stages of development. Comte believed that the simplest forms of science evolved the quickest. He arranged the sciences in the order of their ability to make laws (Simpson, 1969). He claimed that the natural sciences are the simplest. Consequently, the sciences on the top of the hierarchy are the most complex. At the base was mathematics, strictly speaking not a field of empirical research, but an area of knowledge that was foundational to scientific work (Garner, 2000). The sciences placed above mathematics in this hierarchical structure were astronomy, physics, biology (physiology), chemistry, and sociology at the very top, which Comte crowned "the queen of the sciences" (Garner, 2000). Each stage of scientific development represents a more complex organization of matter, from atoms (physics) to molecules (chemistry) to cells and tissues formed into organisms (biology)

to the grouping and interrelationship of human organisms into society (sociology). Comte ignored psychology because he thought that individual behavior could be explained either at the sociological level of society and culture or at the biological level (Garner, 2000).

Sociology is located at the highest level of the hierarchy because of its obvious complexity of subject matter. Clearly the "natural" sciences are far less complex because they do not study dynamic human behavior. Sociology offers attributes of a completion of the positive method, with all the other sciences preparatory to it. Thus, the sciences are not independent, but dependent on one another for validity. The classification of the sciences is necessary because, "the relation which really subsists between different kinds of phenomena, enables the sciences to arrange in such an order, that traveling through them we do not pass out of the sphere of any laws but merely take up additional ones at each step" (Mill, 1866:37). In short, as a new science emerges, it has the advantage of utilizing the methods created by the preceding sciences, and it can further develop the scientific method.

An interesting note: Comte, in his later work, added a seventh science that ranked above sociology—morals (Ritzer, 2000).

Division of Labor

Comte believed that the development of individual gifts and specialties helps to contribute to human solidarity because it creates within each individual a sense of union with others. This attachment of individuals to a society helps the community function as a whole. Thus, Comte's division of labor is a functionalist approach, where all the parts (individuals) function for the greater good of the whole (society). The division of labor within a societal setting is productive for the individual because man cannot function as effectively in solitude. The division of labor is a natural phenomenon and begins in the family. Each individual within a family carries out tasks to achieve survival for their domestic unit. At the macro level, the division of labor assists humanity as a whole through dependency on one another based on specialties. Comte wrote, when a regular division of employment has spread through any society, the social state begins to acquire a consistency and stability which places it out of danger from particular divergences (Thompson, 1975). The distribution of labor enables everyone to do a job that is suitable for their talents. This creates interdependency between every individual and a natural place for everyone in society. Comte believed that social order could be maintained through the division of labor. As social beings, humans are inclined to interact with others. The division of labor acts as a natural adhesive amongst individuals in their pursuit of survival (Thompson, 1975).

The Religion of Humanity

Although he rejected belief in a transcendent being, Comte recognized the value of religion in contributing to social stability. In his four-volume *System of Positive Polity* (1851–54), he proposed his religion of humanity, aimed at encouraging socially beneficial behavior. Comte's sociology was overly intertwined with his own ideas of the correct polity. In his view, society had broken down as a result of the French Revolution. In one regard, the Revolution was a good thing because it allowed French society to move out of the obsolete theological stage of knowledge and toward the scientific/positivistic stage of development. It was the progress of science that was triumphant. But, the Revolution offered no plans for the reorganization of society—that is, the

Revolution destroyed the old regime without creating a new one.

The task then, was to provide a new religion, a new faith, and of course, a new clergy. To replace the Catholic clergy, Comte proposed a scientific-industrial elite that would announce the invariable laws of a new social order. The *ancien régime* and its destruction by the French Revolution had to be synthesized and made meaningful by a new clergy of elites: the technocrats. This was absolutely necessary to meet the problems brought about by the collapse of the ancient regime as well as those problems created by industrial society. This insight, religious in nature and intuitive in form, was then reformulated by Comte and his disciples as "positive science."

Positive science led to the construct of a "positive religion." Comte set about establishing the "positivistic church" and "the religion of humanity" (Ashley and Orensteim, 1985). Comte declared that the center of his church was in Paris, that he was its first high priest, and that his religion involved the worship of the "great being of humanity." The optimistic Comte expected to amass a large following quickly, especially among women and working men. He expected support from women and members of the working class because of the way he romanticized their lives. His new religion had its holy days to reaffirm positivism; its positivistic calendar which was to be composed of thirteen months, each divided into twenty-eight days; its secular hero of saints—Adam Smith, Frederick the Great, Dante, Shakespeare, and others; a specified number of priests and vicars required in each of the temples; priests that were supported financially, very handsomely, by bankers; and its positive catechism (Comte, 1854).

It was a nontheistic religion, a religion of man and society, and illustrates Comte's shift away from philosophical and scientific interests to what most generously could be described as a form of mysticism. The primary goal of this religion was to achieve what Comte had spent a lifetime working on, moral social order. The positive religion urged everyone "to live for others." He wished to see an end to class conflict, not by the destruction of one class by another as Marx had suggested, but instead, to moralize one and all. Positive religion was to inspire all the servants of the Great Being with a sacred zeal to represent that Being as fully as possible (Comte, 1852).

Views on Race, Class, and Women

On the issue of race, Comte had little to say. He did believe that Europeans, and especially the French, were superior, although others might, over a period of prolonged time, advance to the same level of development (Adams and Sydie, 2001).

Comte had far more to say about social class. As stated earlier, Comte expected to replace his scientific followers with disciples from his church of humanity, of whom many were expected to be from the working class and women. Comte believed that he was a champion of the working class. He romanticized their lifestyles by attributing a number of traits that were supposed to be honorable: The working class members have more affectionate ties at home (compared to the elites); they have genuine types of friendship; sincere and simple respect for superiors; experience with life's miseries, which stimulates them to nobler sympathies; and a greater likelihood of engaging in prompt self-sacrifice at the call of a great public necessity (Comte, 1851).

Comte believed that the people of the higher classes had to concentrate on matters of business and finance during the working hours because their level of occupation and importance to society demanded such diligence. The working people on the other hand, because their work was not so demanding, were able to think best during working hours on matters beyond their immediate need. Assumingly, Comte felt that the working class had more time to reflect on the benefits of positivism than do the upper classes. Comte believed that the working people would turn to his positivism instead of Marx's communism. In fact, Comte understated the spread and importance of communism during this period by referring to it as a moral, rather than an economic, movement so that it would fit into his general scheme (Ritzer, 2000).

Comte believed that there were a number of reasons that the working class would benefit more from positivism than communism. First, positivism focuses on moral responses rather than on political and economic issues. Second, positivism encourages individuality, at least to the point of encouraging entrepreneurship, whereas communism seeks to suppress it. Third, positivism deems leaders of society as essential, communism seeks to eliminate the leaders of industry. Fourth, communism seeks to eliminate inheritance, while positivism sees inheritance as a means for providing historical continuity from generation to generation (Ritzer, 2000).

Comte's interest in the working class was not so unique among social thinkers of his time. However, the importance he placed on the role of women, in his later life, was quite unmatched. Feeling the pain of a love lost, Comte's writings became centered around the role of women. He believed that their affectional component was the critical missing piece of the positivistic puzzle. He wrote that women are the "best representatives of the fundamental principle on which Positivism rests, the victory of social over selfish affections" (Comte, 1851). He flattered women as the purest and simplest impersonations of Humanity who are always deserving of loving veneration.

Comte was not a feminist. He contends, "Women's minds no doubt are less capable than ours of generalizing very widely, or of carrying on long processes of deduction . . . less capable than men of abstract intellectual exertion" (Comte, 1851:250). Further, Comte did not believe in equality, saying that equality between the sexes is contrary to nature (Comte, 1851). Women were also excluded from being priests in his "Religion of Humanity."

Language

Comte had made reference to the analogy of society as a biological organism, but realized that there were many problems with this. One critical issue was the fact that a biological organism has physical boundaries and limitations, while individuals in society are free to move about. Comte believed that what kept members of society bound to one another was language. He believed that language was a critical social institution because it allows people to interact with one another. From this standpoint, language helps to promote unity among people. It not only connects people with their contemporaries, but serves as a vessel in which the thought of preceding generations, the culture of our ancestors, is stored and therefore can be retrieved. Language binds fellows to the long chain that links a living community to its remote ancestors. Without a common language; solidarity, consensus, and social order would be impossible. Comte viewed a common language as indispensable to a human community, but it was only a medium, not a guide to behavior. Religion would serve as the guide and language was the tool.

Relevancy

Comte's place in sociology is secure. He not only came up with the name *sociology*, he provided it with its initial direction and course of action. For that reason, he can be seen as the "founder" of sociology. Comte made it very clear that sociology was a positivistic science. He believed that there are invariant laws of the social world and it was the task of sociologists to discover those laws. The contemporary and future relevance of Comte begins with his systematic and theoretical presentation of society as a scientific discipline, emphasizing empirical analysis. Critics of Comte will point out that he never conducted empirical analysis himself, but the point remains, he started sociology in this critical direction.

As contemporary sociology accepts the overwhelming necessity of maintaining an empirical discipline, it is nearly impossible to fully appreciate the influence of positivism as it existed more than a century and a half ago. Comte enjoyed various levels of esteem during his lifetime. His reputation as a scholar and social thinker reached high levels in and outside of France.

In the same way as Saint-Simon's legacy depended on his religious devotees, the Saint-Simonians, Comte's fame rests securely on the unflagging effort of his most ardent disciple, Emile Littre (1801–1881). It was Littre, a French lexicographer and philosopher, who refused to follow Comte into the nebulous gray area of his positivist religion. He considered this part of positivism to be the product of Comte's tired and troublesome mind. In 1867, Littre founded *The Positivist Review*, a journal that maintained that the real value of positivism was its ability to demonstrate that philosophy could profit, as had the natural sciences, by using scientific methods. He accepted Comte's notion that social improvement depended on the advancement of the sciences. Positivism offered the only hope for the future development of society along rational lines. Positivism directed human efforts toward work, social equality, and international peace by means of four things: industry, the diffusion of science, the cultivation of the fine arts, and the moral improvement of man.

In line with his doctrine of positivism, Comte insisted that sociology utilize the methods of the natural sciences (observation, experimentation, comparison) and the historic analysis of social events. These methods are still used by sociologists today, and will surely be used throughout the third millennium.

Central to Comte's sociology was the distinction between the study of social statics and social dynamics. This continues to be an important differentiation in sociology, but the concepts are now referred to as *social structure* and *social change* (Ritzer, 2000). Sociologists continue to study society as it is in the present, they examine its changing nature, as well examining trends to predict future events.

Comte defined sociology in macroscopic terms as the study of collective phenomena and viewing society as the "whole" consisting of many individuals, families, and communities as the "parts." Although he never used the term "organic analogy," as many theorists shortly after him did, Comte's ideas played a key role in the development of a major contemporary sociological theory—structural functionalism. Comte's macro-perspective is employed by many sociologists today, although many others find validity in the study of small groups.

However, the focus on macro-structures as being the product of past structures and as possessing the seeds of future structures, gives Comte's work a strong sense of historic continuity. It also allowed for Comte to create an evolutionary theory of the social world. His Law of Three Stages, admittedly with empirical validity as "suspect" at best, allows for evolutionary analysis and critical thought. If he had not limited his "law" to *three* stages we might be able to apply his

analysis to the changing social structure of society in the early years of the third millennium. Societies of the West have been experiencing a major transition from an industrial-based economy to a service-based one. The transition is indeed difficult, filled with great disorganization and reorganization, just as Comte would predict. Perhaps, we are experiencing a *fourth* stage in the evolutionary process of human society.

Comte had correctly predicted that intelligence in man would continue, and creations from such elite innovators would transform all of society. The validity of this perspective is evident all around us, as technology has completely changed social behavior. The internet, cell phones, air travel, and so on, have allowed for "less-intelligent" persons to benefit from the advancements created by others. Unfortunately, it also makes us vulnerable to nuclear warfare and terrorist attacks, and a questionable "quality-of-life."

Comte's ideas on language would foreshadow many other social thinkers who would come to recognize the value of a one-language policy as a means to unite a society. In regions of a society that have multiple-language debates there is almost always an ethnic and/or racial difference as well, thus illustrating a lack of solidarity and consensus, elements which Comte believed could make social order impossible. The province of Quebec, Canada, has reached a "secession" debate level amongst its citizens, with language as the primary focal point. There are many other examples throughout the world that are experiencing this same type of problem.

Another dichotomy in contemporary sociology that parallels Comtean thought is the positivistic distinction between pure and applied sociology. The dominant motive of Comte's positivism was not speculative but practical. His purpose was, for him, most clear—the reformation of the social order. Comte was not happy with simply developing abstract theory but was interested in integrating theory and practice (Ritzer, 2000). Although some of his later bizarre ideas have scarred his reputation as a great social thinker, his ambition remains the same as many contemporary sociologists—the integration of theory and practice. Today, sociologists simply use the term *applied sociology*.

Comte's legacy is a mixed one. On the one hand, he has made a number of lasting contributions to the field of sociology. Many of his ideas are still used in contemporary sociology, and will continue to find validity in the future. Unfortunately, Comte is as well-known for his outrageous beliefs, such as his practice of "cerebral hygiene" and self-proclaimed label of the "Great Priest of Humanity."

3

Herbert Spencer
(1820–1903)

Herbert Spencer was born in Derby, England, on April 27, 1820. Derby was a bleak and dismal British industrial town. He was the oldest of nine children and the only one to survive infancy. One can only speculate how this would affect his personality and subsequent development. Spencer was a weak and sickly child. Even so, he lived a long life. His father, George Spencer, wrote to his brother Thomas regarding the young Spencer's name. The letter stated, "the name we call him at present is Fredric, but we are undecided between that and Herbert" (Spencer, 1904:72). Herbert was finally chosen because the letter, which was written back from his uncle, contained a copy of verses by a recently deceased young poet named Herbert Knowles.

The senior Spencer, a staunch Wesleyan with rigid political views, imbued these philosophies into Herbert at a young age. George Spencer taught his son from his extremist nonconformist perspective in light of the burning political, social, and philosophical issues of the day. All members of the Spencer family were staunch nonconformist Dissenters and highly individualistic in their outlook. George Spencer was a well-built man, who, along with his brothers, was known for acts of endurance, including walking sixty miles in one day (Spencer, 1904).

George was a school teacher and was very punctual. Herbert said that his father had one drawback, he was unkind to his wife. His father did not show love to his wife, Harriet. Spencer's mother is described as a patient and gentle woman whose marriage was most likely not very happy. After being wed, Harriet showed little interest in their marriage, and this disappointed her husband. It would appear that Herbert did not think too highly of his mother, having described her as simple-minded, and nothing special intellectually speaking (Spencer, 1904).

Spencer received no formal education but was trained by his schoolmaster father and his clergyman uncle at home. His lessons were heavily scientific and he was strong in mathematics and the natural sciences. At age ten, Spencer's father decided that Herbert's primary education of biology, botany, entomology, life drawing, and mechanics left him lacking in ordinary curriculum. Herbert was then sent to Mr. Mather's day-school; however, this would not last long. Bored by this type of teaching, Herbert left and pursued his education with his uncle William. At age thirteen, he moved near Bath, where his uncle Thomas furthered his education. Thomas Spencer was a clergyman, who was also an advanced social reformer, a Chartist sympathizer, and an advocate of temperance.

Herbert Spencer (1820–1903) English philosopher and social evolutionist coined the term "survival-of-the-fittest."

Source: Courtesy of the Library of Congress

Thomas taught Herbert the principles of Philosophical Radicalism as well as the rigid code of dissenting Protestantism (Coser, 1977). Thomas Spencer was a highly driven, hard-working man, who would die in January 1853, leaving Herbert a large sum of money, which would later allow him the comfort to live the life of an independent scholar. By age sixteen, Herbert was strong in mathematics and science but weak in his grounding in Latin and Greek. He received no formal education in English, and his knowledge of history was superficial. He was not, nor was he ever to become, a generally cultivated man (Coser, 1977).

Spencer's lack of formal education made him feel unfit for a university career.

Consequently, Herbert decided to follow his scientific interests, and in 1837 he began work as a civil engineer for the London and Birmingham Railway. A year later he took a better position as a draftsman with the Birmingham and Gloucester Railway staying there until the construction of the railroad was finished in 1841. At first, this gave him the opportunity to travel and stretch his intellectual ambition, while paying him a very good salary. He enjoyed his job very much and became very successful. Spencer was rather withdrawn, introspective, and quite individualistic, at peace with his personality. Subsequently, his co-workers did not think too highly of him. He also had a tendency to antagonize senior personnel and generally got into arguments where he was routinely found to be in the right (Wiltshire, 1978). Thus, he was not a well-liked man, but well-respected none the less. However, he soon grew tired of the railway business and felt that it stifled his intellectual development. The call from the radical politics of his youth was about to be answered.

During the construction work necessary for the building of railways, numerous fossil remains were found. This sparked Spencer's interest in geology and paleontology and, in turn, led him to an interest in evolution. Yearning for more knowledge about fossils, Spencer read Charles Lyell's *Principles of Geology*, which contained a rebuttal to the ideas of Jean-Baptiste Lamarck on the origins of species (Adams and Sydie, 2001). Lamarck had suggested that acquired traits could be genetically transmitted and that humans developed from a lower species. Spencer did not completely agree with Lyell's argument and leaned toward Lamarck's assertion of evolutionary process.

Spencer would continue to study on his own throughout his years as a railway engineer and he began to publish scientific and political articles in the radical press (e.g., *The*

Leader, The Fortnightly, and *The Westminster Review*). A series of his dissenting papers, including, "The Proper Sphere of Government," appeared in *The Nonconformist*. The young Spencer provided early glimpses toward his future course of action by arguing for extreme restrictions on government. He felt that the whole field of human activity, except for policing, should be left to private enterprise. He was against welfare (he advocated the abolishment of "Poor Laws"); national education programs; an established church; restrictions of commerce; and factory legislation (Coser, 1977). He also showed signs of his "laissez-faire" beliefs.

Spencer struggled on the fringes of radical journalism and radical politics for a number of years. In many ways this period led to the cementing of his political beliefs and in other ways, it meant adjusting certain views. Whereas Spencer was raised in a strong liberal background—the restricting of governmental action—he was now being influenced by other points of view. George Eliot (pen name for Mary Ann Evans), for one, had an effect on him whereby he now came to view democracy as a natural right. Though still committed to reform, he began to shift to conservatism (Wiltshire, 1978).

In 1848, Spencer moved to London and was employed as a subeditor with the London *Economist*. "The *Economist* not only widely propagated laissez-faire, it helped to formulate and elucidate it" (Wiltshire, 1978:48). Social commentators such as Jeremy Bentham and Adam Smith were postulating free trade and advocating a more limited role of the government. While in London Spencer became a social friend to many of the brilliant thinkers of his time. This circle included Charles Kingsley, Frances Newman, Francis Galton, Robert Browning, James Froude, Frederick Harrison, and John Tyndall. At this time Spencer showed his disdain for authority and con-

vention, which he viewed as limits of man's freedom.

During this time Spencer also met important life-long friends who would greatly influence him, among them George Lewes and Thomas Huxley. Huxley became a confidant and advisor, campaigning endlessly for the evolutionary cause and to whom Spencer gave all his biological proofs for factual accuracy. Spencer wrote, "there is no one whose judgment on all subjects I so much respect, or whose friendship I so highly value" (Wiltshire, 1978:55). Thus began the long road for Herbert Spencer and his writing career. He was a freelance journalist with a tight circle of friends who would have great influence over his life.

In 1851, he finished his first book, *Social Statics*. It was well received by the radical public, which welcomed him as a new recruit to the position of laissez-faire. In *Social Statics*, Spencer groups the upper class with the working class, stating that they share a sense of moral depravity and ignorance. He believed that the working-class predicament was natural, and not alterable in the foreseeable future. Here, Spencer also disparaged reform measures and government intervention; he felt that power should be given to the whole society, so that the few would not abuse it. His radical views had changed somewhat, out of fear of revolution and political violence. He believed that government intervention was a great waste of energy that could otherwise be put to better use. Spencer's railway engineering and draftsman experience in many ways opened his eyes to the world of capitalism and politics. As he began to realize from the age of seventeen, the world was far from perfect, but more importantly, that he had a place in the world, which he now tried to help. His laissez-faire attitude of government developed into an overall conservative attitude about reform, and politics in general. Spencer's experience with the railroad had shown him the ugly side of the capitalist system, and corporate greed in shareholding and stocks alienated Herbert from the profession of business altogether.

During the writing of *Social Statics*, Spencer began to experience insomnia and the suffering was so intense that he often attempted to overcome it by smoking heavy doses of opium. Over the years his mental and physical health problems mounted and he was never able to work more than a few hours a day. He was to suffer a series of nervous breakdowns throughout the rest of his life.

When his uncle died in 1853, Herbert received a large sum of money from him. Spencer quit his job with the London *Economist* and pursued a life as a private scholar without regular employment or university ties. Spencer never married and stated, "I was never in love" (Raison, 1969:77). As a lifelong bachelor, and having been raised in the strict abstemious discipline of Derby Dissent, he lived frugally in successive lodgings and rooming houses about London. He was close to marriage once. It seems that she (George Eliot) was willing, but he eventually changed his mind. Spencer not only died a bachelor, but there is every likelihood that he also died a virgin (Coser, 1977).

As a result of his burgeoning friendship with George Henry Lewes (Lewes and Eliot lived together; after Lewes's death, Eliot married John Cross), Spencer began to read Lewes' *A Biographical History of Philosophy* (1845/1846). Within a short time he found himself so absorbed in the topic that he decided to make a contribution of his own to philosophy in the form of an introduction to psychology. In 1855, Spencer published his second book, *The Principles of Psychology*. It is a complex and difficult book, hardly an introduction to the topic; and, like Bain's *The Senses and the Intellect*, it too marked a turning point in the history of psychology. While

Bain had linked movement to the sensations of associationism and arrived at the first fully balanced sensory-motor associational view, Spencer went even further and grounded psychology in evolutionary biology. In particular, Spencer stressed three basic evolutionary principles that transformed his view of mind and brain into one to which the cortical localization of function was a simple logical corollary. In so doing, he laid the groundwork for Hughlings Jackson's evolutionary conception of the nervous system and extension of the sensory-motor organizational hypothesis to the cerebrum. Spencer's key principles were: adaptation, continuity, and development. Spencer wrote in *Principles*, "that different parts of the cerebrum subserve different kinds of mental action. Localization of function is the law of all organization whatever . . . every bundle of nerve-fiber and every ganglion, has a special duty" (607–608). Due primarily to its complexity, *Principles* was not as well received by the public as *Social Statics*.

Soon after the publication of *Principles of Psychology*, Spencer suffered from a nervous illness of some sort, although it was never diagnosed. (Today, psychiatrists would most likely diagnose the illness as a severe neurotic disorder.) There were times when he would wander about aimlessly, and other times when he simply was unable to read or write. He would often retreat from public life, and in his later years even the idea of a public lecture became intolerable (Coser, 1977).

Despite the many physical and emotional problems that confronted Spencer, he was a very successful author. *The Social Organism*, published in 1860, provided a functional analysis of society. In 1862, he published *First Principles* (of his overall *Synthetic Philosophy*), which was followed by the several volumes of the *Principles of Biology* (1864–67), *The Study of Sociology* (1873), the many volumes of the *Principles of Ethics* (1870s), volumes of the *Principles of*

Sociology (1890s), *The Man Versus the State* (1884), and the *Autobiography* in 1904.

Although Spencer complained that he was remembered the most for his book *Social Statics*, he did enjoy much recognition. *Principles of Biology* was used as a textbook at Oxford, *Principles of Psychology* as a textbook at Harvard, and William Graham Sumner taught Spencerian ideas at Yale. Sumner, a Social Darwinist, is credited with being the first person to teach a course in the United States that could be called sociology. Sumner claims that he began teaching sociology years before any such attempt was made at any other university (Curtis, 1981). By the turn of the century, most of Spencer's work had appeared in French, German, Spanish, Italian, and Russian translations. His theories were as agreeable to some business people as Marx's were to some labor groups. For example, James J. Hill, railroad magnate, argued that the fortunes of railroad companies are determined by the law of the survival of the fittest (Hofstadter, 1955). John D. Rockefeller described the growth of large business as merely a result of the survival of the fittest (Hofstadter, 1955). American industrial giant Andrew Carnegie reveals that his reading of Darwin and Spencer was a source of great peace of mind. "I remember that light came as in a flood and all was clear. Not only had I got rid of theology and the supernatural, but I had found the truth of evolution" (Carnegie, 1920). Carnegie wrote to Spencer just prior to his death in 1903. In this letter Carnegie wrote, "Dear Master Teacher . . . you come to me everyday in thought, and the everlasting 'why' intrudes—Why lies he? Why must he go? . . . The world jogs on unconscious of its greatest mind . . . But it will wake some day to its teachings and decree Spencer's place is with the greatest" (Peel, 1971:2). Spencer's ashes are buried in a grave directly opposite that of Karl Marx's in Highgate Cemetery, London.

One of Spencer's most interesting characteristics was his unwillingness to read the work of other people. He resembled Comte and his practice of "cerebral hygiene." Spencer did not believe in the need to read others, having said, "All my life I have been a thinker and not a reader, being able to say with Hobbes that 'if I had read as much as other men I would have known as little" (Wiltshire, 1978:67).

A friend once asked Spencer's opinion of a book, and "His reply was that on looking into the book he saw that its fundamental assumption was erroneous, and therefore did not care to read it" (Wiltshire, 1978:66). Charles Darwin said of Spencer, "If he had trained himself to observe more, even at the expense of . . . some loss of thinking power, he would have been a wonderful man" (Wiltshire, 1978:70).

So where did Spencer's ideas come from? According to Spencer, they emerged involuntarily and intuitively from his mind. He said that his ideas emerged little by little in unobtrusive ways, without conscious intention or appreciable effort. This, of course, is not completely true, for there are many documented influences on Spencer's life.

Intellectual Influences

There are a number of sources that contributed to Spencer's works. A quick review of some of these influences will demonstrate the relationship between them and his own concepts and ideas.

Thomas Malthus

Malthus was a conservative thinker who believed that social problems were inevitable, and that the role of government in society should be limited. Malthus' famous book, *An Essay on the Principles of Population*, centered on a premise that humans tend to reproduce in numbers greater than could be easily supported by available resources—in short, the time was rapidly nearing when the number of people were going to outnumber the available food supply. The lack of resources would then lead to crime, poverty, and greed.

Malthus used the laws of mathematics to apply to this societal problem of overpopulation. In his theorem, Malthus stated that the world's population grew geometrically (1, 3, 9, 27 . . .); while the world's food production grew arithmetically (1, 2, 3, 4 . . .). The ratio of people to food would eventually deplete the natural resources available to humankind. Malthus claimed that nature would provide forces of relief from the strain created by these increased demands in the form of "The Four Horsemen." The four horsemen were: war, pestilence, famine, and disease. The purpose of the four horsemen was, of course, to provide population control; they are the destroyers of life. Thus, the geometric growth of population would create the very conditions favorable to conflict, starvation, pestilence, disease, and death.

Spencer had read Malthus' *Essay on Population*, and although his outlook on the problem of overpopulation was not quite as pessimistic as Malthus, he believed that overpopulation would lead to the "survival of the fittest." (It must be noted that this term was coined ten years before Darwin's "natural selection.") The "survival of the fittest" doctrine had two basic outcomes. First, the excess of fertility could stimulate greater activity, because the more people there are, the more ingenuity or intelligence is required to stay alive. This need for greater production causes the need for a more intelligent force to develop that is capable of producing more. Those who cannot adapt or evolve become extinct, ultimately supplanted by those able to meet the challenge.

Second, the conflict for scarcity of goods would accelerate into political and territorial conflicts. In fact, Spencer was one of the first sociologists to understand fully the significance of war and conflict on the internal patterns of social organization in a society. It is with Spencer's model of the macrostructure that we see how the problem of overpopulation leads to an increased level of competition among social units for resources. It is at this point where the concept of the survival of the fittest comes to the forefront. Increased competition results in a differentiation among the social units. This differentiation and increased pressures for coordination and control put society in the position of dissolution. Dissolution will occur with increased opposition to regulatory authority.

George Lewes and Karl Von Baer

Until he began his friendship with Lewes, Spencer had paid little attention to philosophy. Spencer admits in his *Autobiography* that in 1844 he had begun to read Kant's *Critique of Pure Reason*, and after reading just the first few pages he rejected the basic premises. He further admitted to a disdain toward and non-interest in psychology, as well as philosophy. Reading Lewes' work provided Spencer with the general background of philosophical thought. Lewes asserted that functional adaptation is the sole cause of development, but Spencer believed in a more systematic, cyclical development.

Karl Von Baer's principle of universal transformation from homogeneity to heterogeneity had a more profound effect, compared to Lewes, on Spencer's subsequent theory of evolution and dissolution. Von Baer was of Prussian decent. He attended the University of Dorpat to study medicine. He received his degree in 1814, and trained in comparative anatomy. In addition, he contributed a great deal of time to embryology. In 1827, he made discoveries in the mammalian ovum and concluded that humans developed from eggs. The fact that human development originates from an egg, where the cells must multiply until it forms the human, supported the process of evolution.

Von Baer's principles allowed Spencer to organize his ideas on biological, psychological, and social evolution. It was during his writing of *Psychology* that Spencer discussed the trend of homogeneity to heterogeneity, where he hit upon the idea of "multiplication of effects," the concept that every cause produces more than one effect (Wiltshire, 1978:65). For as Spencer came to emphasize, evolution is a process of development from an incoherent, undifferentiated, and homogeneous mass to a differentiated and coherent pattern in which the functions of structures are well-coordinated. Conversely, dissolution involved movement from a coherent and differentiated state to a more homogeneous and incoherent mass. Thus, Spencer came to view the major focus of sociology as the study of the conditions under which social differentiation and de-differentiation occur.

Biology

In 1864, Spencer wrote the first volume of the *Principles of Biology* and wrote the second volume in 1867. Spencer took three main elements from biology: through competition, individuals and societies emerge; social evolution occurs through interrelated functions; and differences between individuals and society occur due to varying environmental conditions. Spencer agreed with post-Newtonian views of science. That is, universal laws exist that could explain the phenomena in the world. Spencer proposed three propositions:

1. The law of persistence *force*

2. The indestructibility of *matter*

3. The continuity of *motion*

These three laws would occur throughout Spencer's theories.

Spencer reluctantly gave credit to Comte for reintroducing the organic analogy back into contemporary thought. However, Spencer stressed that Plato and Hobbes had made similar analogies and that much of his organismic thinking had been influenced by Von Baer. The organic analogy involves the comparison of society to an organism. Spencer acknowledged the role of environmental variables on social organization and agreed that the Super Organic (society) and the Organism (body) had six similarities:

1. Society and individuals grow.

2. As size increases so does complexity.

3. Progression in structure is accompanied by a differentiation in function.

4. Parts of the whole are interdependent of one another.

5. Every organism is a society.

6. Some parts die, and some parts go on. (In a society all humans do not die simultaneously.)

Spencer did however, feel that there were some distinct differences between an organism and society:

1. The degree of connectedness—In the organism there is a concrete hold, close contact. Society has a discrete hold. (Members can come and go as they please.)

2. Communication—The organism communicates in molecular waves. Society has language.

3. Differences in Consciousness—In an organism the units exist for the benefit of the whole. In society, the whole exists for the good of the people.

Thomas Huxley and Charles Darwin

Among contemporaries who influenced Spencer, his lifelong friend Thomas Huxley stands out. The two met in the early 1850s and Huxley convinced Spencer to focus his arguments and sharpen his logic. Huxley introduced Spencer to many scientific findings. In fact, many of Spencer's friends and associates would help him with details and supply new facts. Yet, they never succeeded in diverting him in any significant way from the theoretical path he had chosen. This was cleverly expressed in Huxley's laughing remark that, for Spencer, the definition of a tragedy was the spectacle of a deduction killed by a stubborn fact (Coser, 1977).

Huxley was much more than just a friend to Spencer, he was also known as Darwin's "bulldog," his most vocal supporter and defender. When Darwin's *Origin of Species* appeared in 1859, Spencer welcomed it warmly. He accepted the idea that natural selection was a key ingredient of evolution. Darwin, in turn, expressed his esteem for Spencer's "development theory" even before the *Origin of Species* was published. Darwin was even moved to call Spencer "about a dozen times 'my superior'" (Coser, 1977).

Lamarck's beliefs about acquired traits ran counter to Darwin's idea of *natural selection*, which suggested that individuals born with advantageous genetic traits were the ones that survived to reproduce and contribute to the evolution of the species. "Spencer believed, however, that Lamarckian adaptation and Darwinian natural selection proceeded together and, with the elimination of traits no longer useful to society, human beings and society progressively improved" (Adams and Sydie, 2001:63).

Darwin's theory of evolution offered Spencer a respected intellectual tool for justifying his laissez-faire beliefs. Darwin's theory of evolution and Spencer's survival of the fittest concepts have become mistakenly interchangeable. It is surely incorrect to call Spencer a "social Darwinist," for his main doctrine was developed before Darwin had published anything on evolution.

Auguste Comte

Spencer met Comte only once, toward the end of the latter's life, and was not overly impressed by him (Coser, 1977). Although, he noted in his *Autobiography* that upon hearing of Spencer's nervous disorder, Comte advised him to marry, saying that the sympathetic companionship of a wife would have a curative influence. As to Comte's overall influence on his thought, Spencer denied it with vehemence, in a number of impassioned statements. The French were labeling Spencer as a disciple of Comte's Positive Philosophy, a claim that Spencer said was totally inaccurate. While it is true that the lives of Comte and Spencer overlapped, the two men were separated by the English Channel and a substantial difference in their ages (Comte was twenty-two years old when Spencer was born, and Spencer lived for forty-six years after Comte's death). Consequently, Comte had finished much of his work before Spencer had published *Social Statics*. However, comparisons between the two began to be made immediately following *Social Statics*. Spencer was so upset with these comparisons that he wrote an essay entitled "Reasons for Dissenting from the Philosophy of M. Comte" (1864). It is perhaps advisable at this point to list the similarities and differences between Comte and Spencer.

Areas of agreement between Comte and Spencer:

1. Knowledge comes from positive methods (e.g., experiences and/or observed

facts) and metaphysical speculation is pointless.

2. There are invariable laws in the universe that can be discovered and utilized.

3. The different branches of knowledge form a rational whole.

4. Social phenomena form an interdependent whole.

5. Both developed theories of evolution and progress.

6. Spencer accepted Comte's term of sociology for the science of superorganic bodies.

7. Spencer reluctantly gave credit to Comte for reintroducing the organismic analogy back into thought. (However, Spencer stressed that Plato and Hobbes had made similar analogies and that much of his organismic thinking had been influenced by Von Baer.)

Spencer disagreed with Comte over the following issues:

1. Societies passed through three distinct stages.

2. Causality is less important than the building of social theory.

3. Government can use the laws of sociology to reconstruct society.

4. Sciences have developed in a particular order.

5. Psychology is merely a subdiscipline of biology.

6. Spencer especially disagreed with Comte's sense of a positivist religion and sociologist–priests.

7. Concerning the emphasis of evolutionary thought; where Comte was focused on the evolution of ideas, Spencer was interested in structural (and functional) evolution.

8. Comte believed that individuals could be taught morality, largely through the positivist religion, but Spencer ridiculed the idea that morality could be taught by any means, let alone religion or the government.

In short, Spencer emerges as an individualist, whereas Comte presents a combination of liberal–individualist and conservative–collectivist approaches.

Concepts and Contributions

Throughout most of Spencer's life, he enjoyed critical acclaim for his works and theories, and during the early years of American sociology, his ideas were much more influential than those of Comte, Marx, Durkheim, and Weber. His most significant contributions, including his ideas on social evolution, differentiation, evolution and dissolution, survival of the fittest, and social types are discussed in the following pages.

Social Evolution

Darwin's theory of evolution was based on his empirical observations of the natural world, especially those he had made during an extensive exploration voyage abroad the *HMS Beagle* in the early 1830s. It is in Darwin's *The Voyage of the Beagle* (2000 [1859]) volume where he provides his evolutionary framework. Darwin observed that various species of birds, tortoises, and other animals had modified their physical form in ways that seemed to "fit" or "adapt" to their environment. Darwin concluded that God had not created all the species on earth at once—instead, they had been evolving over many millions of years. Further, this theory could be applied to the human species as well.

The essence of Darwin's theory of evolution is that mutations (unexpected physical changes) in organisms occur more or less randomly from one generation to the next. When these "mutations" are beneficial in improving individuals' ability to survive their environment, then they are "selected for" survival. These new traits would be passed on to the next generation, forming a natural selection process of survival.

Human beings are distributed widely throughout the planet and face an array of climates and environments. Why is it, then, that humans did not evolve into separate species, as occurred among other animals? According to Spencer, the fact that humans, unlike other species, have remained similar even on different continents must be explained by the fact that we adapt to changes in our environment through the use of culture rather than biological adaptation. Geertz (1973) terms this process "cultural evolution," in that the most successful adaptations are handed down to the next generation. Spencer simply called this process the *survival of the fittest*, meaning that those who are most successful at adapting to the changing environment are most likely to survive, and to have children that will also be successful. "These successful individuals pass on their adaptive advantage to their offspring, the cumulative effect of this process over many generations is the adaptation of the entire population to its environment" (Andreski, 1971:221).

Spencer believed that this process of cultural evolution could not be stopped, and therefore, the government should not intervene with social policies other than to police and protect the public (both from internal and external threat). Spencer used the industrial revolution to explain the idea of cultural evolution and why some people prospered

while others barely scraped by. The people who were leaving their farms behind and moving to the slums of the city to work in factories were less well-equipped culturally to succeed in an urban environment than those who could innovate and invent. Ideas such as these made Spencer very popular in the Western world during the mid-1800s, for it justified the prevailing economic sentiment of competition and capitalism by those who controlled industry and growth.

Growth, Structure, and Differentiation

Spencer believed that increases in the size of both organic and social aggregates were invariably accompanied by an increase in the complexity of their structure. According to Spencer, the process of growth, by definition, is a process of integration. Furthermore, integration in its turn must be accompanied by a progressive differentiation of structures and functions if the organism or the societal unit is to remain capable of survival. Social aggregates, like organic ones, grow from relatively undifferentiated states in which the parts resemble one another into differentiated states in which these parts have become dissimilar. As the level of complexity increases, so too will the level of interdependence among the parts of the organism and the social unit.

Spencer (1898) argued that societies change from "a state of relatively indefinite, incoherent, homogeneity to a state of relatively definite, coherent, heterogeneity" (371). By this, Spencer meant that what distinguishes premodern societies from modern societies was differentiation—the development of increasing societal complexity through the creation of specialized social roles and institutions. Premodern societies were seen as characterized by relatively few roles and institutional distinctions, requiring *upwards and onwards?*

people to have a wide range of skills that allowed them to act independently of one another. In modern societies, however, people master a limited number of skills within a large number of highly specialized institutional roles, thus leading to a great deal of interdependence.

Societies differ in development and their level of differentiation. Structural differentiation occurs through regulatory function, operative functions, and distributive functions. The internal needs of a complex society will lead to specialization. Because of specialization, no one body can survive without the whole. Thus, society becomes interdependent on itself. Spencer believed that specialization also allowed for a quicker response in times of environmental changes. Regulatory systems develop in response to either internal needs or external threat. However, as these regulatory functions develop, they continue to grow in order to maintain their need. A highly developed regulatory system would be especially important in time of war. Spencer argued that war could be good in that a more "organized" race could help organize "inferior" races.

In short, the fundamental processes of growth, differentiation, integration, and adaptive upgrading are, to some extent, conditioned by:

1. **External Factors.** Such as the availability of natural resources.

2. **Internal Factors.** Such as the nature of interior units.

3. **Derived Factors.** Such as the existence of other societies or internal values and beliefs.

Evolution and Dissolution

In Spencer's early writings, one might come to the conclusion that he believed that the evolutionary process was inevitable and that human societies were destined toward continued progress. The mature Spencer recognized that, although the evolution of mankind as a whole was certain, particular societies may retrogress as well as progress. He did not believe that societies develop irreversibly through predetermined stages, as Comte had stated, but rather, they developed in response to their social and natural environment.

Many people fail to recognize that Spencer viewed the universe as in a constant and cyclical process of "structuring" and "destructuring" or in his terms "evolution" and "dissolution." Too often Spencer is viewed by his detractors as a strict evolutionist, when in fact he was interested in the transformations of structures, whether these transformations involved development or dissolution of phenomena. He felt that evolution is the change of the matter from homogeneous and incoherent form to heterogeneous and coherent form, by means of the dissipation of movement and the integration of matter. In *First Principles*, Spencer uses the example of gas to explain evolution. He elaborates that the evolution of gas is an absorption of motion and disintegration of matter.

Spencer recognized that evolution and dissolution are related processes. Dissolution occurs when a society ceases to proceed. If there is no advancement of society, Spencer believed it would fall. Further, if surrounding societies are evolving, while one society remains stagnant, it will be unable to compete, and risks being conquered or overwhelmed by more dominant and advanced societies. He believed that the history of mankind had generally been one of evolution, but some populations and societies have evolved and then completely dissolved.

Earlier in this chapter it was mentioned that Spencer created "laws" to explain social phenomena. Utilizing his laws might make Spencer's definition of evolution a little more understandable. Some *force* (e.g., economic capital, a new technology, a deed to gather resources, new values and beliefs) sets into *motion* system growth. This *motion* as it acts differently on various units, sends them in different directions and "segregates" them such that their differences are "multiplied." Conversely, to the extent that integration is incomplete and/or the *force* that drives the system is spent and cannot be replaced, then dissolution of the system is likely. Thus, social systems grow, differentiate, integrate, and achieve some level of adaptation to the environment, but at some point the system may fall into a phase of dissolution. *Social institutions arise from structural requirements;*

Functionalism

Most functionalist theories share the assumption that as societies develop they become ever more complex and interdependent. Within sociology, this assumption can be traced to Spencer (1860), who argued that societies change from "incoherent homogeneity to coherent heterogeneity." Much of Spencer's discussion of social institutions and their changes are expressed in functional terms. He analyzed social institutions in relation to the general matrix in which they were variously embedded. Spencer makes great efforts to show that social institutions are not the result of deliberate intentions and motivations of actors, but arise from structural requirements.

In his *First Principles*, Spencer links the role of industry with that of an evolving government. The growth of regulative structure is important in both government and industry. An industry evolves within itself a structure, regulated by the parts, which also have to be directed. Now comes the operative part of each industry. The division of labor is grouped into producers and distributors, each with various grades and kinds. Thus, each industry affects other industries and

these effects advance each other. This is similar to governments (societies) effecting other governments in various ways (the multiplication of effects).

Survival of the Fittest *1864*

In 1864, in his *Principles of Biology*, Spencer first uses the phrase *survival of the fittest*. This would be Spencer's greatest contribution to social thought, and ironically, it is often credited to Darwin. Spencer, of course, coined the term some ten years before Darwin published his ideas on *natural selection*. Darwin later suggested that he actually preferred Spencer's phrase (Hadden, 1997). Carneiro (1967) further explains Darwin's potential preference for the term survival of the fittest over his own concept because his term, natural selection, suggests an intelligent agent—Nature—doing the selecting for humanity's benefit. In contrast, Spencer's term reveals the fact that nature does not select so much as it eliminates the "unfavorable" variations of species. Spencer's survival of the fittest has an even greater implication than Darwin's natural selection, in that Darwin focused on the process of transformation for each species, while Spencer focused on both the biological and the social processes, and on the end result—the survival of the fittest (Peel, 1972).

The evolution of species or societies, for Spencer, is ultimately a matter of the survival of the fittest. According to this notion, evolutionary processes filter out the unfit species, with the eventual outcome of a more perfect society. Since he viewed this outcome as a result of a natural process, he was adamant about his laissez-faire or non-intervention policy. Adaptation is the key to this process; if individuals are to survive in society, they must change with the changing society (and environment).

This radical idea, suggesting that the natural process of adaptation should not be

survival of the fittest = adaptation

For the Good of the whole

interfered with, indicated that the "unfit" (the poor, weak, ignorant, or unhealthy) would be "weeded out." Spencer came to view the conception of a natural process of conflict and survival as a kind of biological purifying process (Martindale, 1981). In *Social Statics*, Spencer (1908:150) states,

> It seems hard that widows and orphans should be left to struggle for life or death. Nevertheless, when regarded not separately but in connection with the interests of universal humanity, these harsh fatalities are seen to be full of beneficence—the same beneficence which brings to early graves the children of diseased parents, and singles out the intemperate and the debilitated as the victims of an epidemic.

Spencer was just as cold-hearted toward the poor. He was against government legislation designed to help the poor.

> By suspending the process of adaptation, a poor-law increases the distress to the borne at some future day; and here we shall find that it also increases the distress to be borne now. For be it remembered that of the sum taken in any year to support paupers, a large portion would otherwise have gone to support labourers employed in the new reproductive works—land-drainage, machine-building, etc. An additional stock of commodities would by-and-by have been produced, and the number of those who go short would consequently have been diminished. (Spencer, 1908:154–55)

Spencer was opposed to practically every form of state interference with private activity. Competition would see to it that the biologically and socially unfit persons would die out. This same principle could be applied to the world of business. Spencer's laissez-faire individualism had special appeal to American capitalists, for if one were at "the top" one might find this a comforting justification of one's own superior qualities.

Spencer argued that humans' progress resulted from being advanced over inferior competitors. Kennedy (1978) notes that Spencer claimed that the fittest thrive under conditions that the unfit cannot. Spencer's own survival was aided by his uncle's money, but even this reflects the fact that he was "fit" due to family finances.

In Spencer's model of the macrostructure, he describes how the problem of overpopulation leads to an increased level of competition among social units for resources. It is at this point where the concept of the survival of the fittest comes to the forefront. Increased competition results in a differentiation among the social units. This differentiation and increased pressures for coordination and control puts society in the position of dissolution. Dissolution will occur with increased opposition to regulatory authority. The concern over the problem of overpopulation has continued as one of the leading factors of conflict. Karl Marx, a contemporary of Spencer, wrote in his *Economic and Philosophic Manuscripts of 1844* that, "Man's very existence is a pure luxury. If the worker is ethical he will be sparing in procreation" (Tucker, 1978:97).

As Spencer's concept of the survival of the fittest is perhaps his most important contribution, it will be discussed in greater detail in the Relevancy section of this chapter.

Social Types: Militant and Industrial Societies

Spencer attempts to classify societies in terms of their stage of evolutionary development. They are arranged in a series and consist of:

1. *Simple societies* which are characterized as "headless" because they form a "single working whole unsubjected to any other." They cooperate without regulation because they know all members of the society will benefit (Spencer, 1898).

2. *Compound societies* result when simpler societies merge together, either through peaceful cooperation or because of war. There is some sort of central regulatory power (Spencer, 1898).

3. *Doubly compound societies* are far more complex with political structures that are rigid and complex, possess a formal legal system and have progressed by demonstrating value placed on education and the arts. As with compound societies, there is a single authority and the societies emerged either through peaceful means or by conquest (Spencer, 1898).

4. *Trebly compound societies* are the "great civilized nations" of the past and present in which the complexity of structures and the increased mutual dependence is very apparent (Spencer, 1898).

Spencer (1898) notes that in all cases, the stages must be passed through in succession. He proceeded to state that societies were ranked by their modes of settlement, which were: nomadic, semi-settled, and settled.

Spencer's primary analysis of social types rests with his classifications of militant and industrial societies. These are differentiated by the structures of social regulation. This theory relies on comparing the social structure of one society to that of another. Whether it is peaceful or militant affects the internal structures of a society's system of regulations. Peaceful nations have weak internal regulations, while militant nations have coercive and centralized control. Internal structure is no longer dependent on the level of evolution, but the presence or absence of conflict with other societies.

According to Spencer (1898), a militant society is geared primarily toward warring and preservation. Militant societies are highly centralized with a strong authoritarian government; characterized by little division of labor; have incorporated a defensive and offensive strategy; and have little trade. Citizens are controlled through compulsion and are subject to internal control. Individuals who do not bear arms spend their lives in furthering the maintenance of those who do. Warriors will often outnumber the body of workers. Personal characteristics of loyalty, courage, obedience, faith in authority, and discipline are generally valued among the people in this type of society.

Spencer perceives the industrial type as the "perfect" state, every society that falls short is only semi-evolved. Much of this discussion is explained in Spencer's *The Man Versus the State*. The dominant activity is a peaceful, mutual rendering of individual services. Industrial societies are decentralized, with the state existing for the benefit of individuals; private enterprise is encouraged; movement between the levels of the social class system is possible; and free trade exists. Valued social and personal characteristics include independence; respect for others; resistance to coercion; individual initiative; and privacy.

The social types of militant and industrial societies offer some valuable insights in Spencer's evolutionary theories. Unfortunately, the classification of just two categories of societies is far too limited, and seems trivial and lacking. However, he does clearly illustrate the role of regulatory systems in determining responses to external threat, and internal control through social regulation.

War and Militarism

Spencer felt that societies could be classified in two ways. The first category of militant and industrial types of societies were described in the previous pages. He also distinguished types of societies by their level of integration or according to the prevalence of "organs" which favor conflict or welfare (Battistelli, 1993). Spencer believed that society was similar to an organism; that is, different parts of society have different roles and jobs to perform, and each part must function properly for society to survive. Although Spencer repeatedly denied any pure and simple comparison between the biological and social organism, he nevertheless identified, in *Principles of Sociology*, a "general law of organization" that was common to both: "distinct duties entail distinct structures." (p.254). Consequently, the structures (organs) used to deal with "outside" variables belong to one category, while the "internal" structures and organs, used in maintenance and support, belong to another type.

He applied this principle to war and conflict. "Each society has structures for carrying on conflict with other societies and structures for carrying on sustention" (Battistelli, 1993:195). Spencer believed that the defense structure and the sustention structure were extremes of each other. They exist on opposite levels of society and should interact as little as possible. However, they must also co-exist as both carry out essential functions of society (Battistelli, 1993). Spencer argued that in order for a military to work, there must be an indispensable centralized authority. A military must be kept in a state of readiness during peace so that it can defend society in the event of war. He believed that all societies must have some means of defense. If they do not, they risk dissolution when threatened by hostile outside forces.

Spencer was disgusted by the barbaric acts that the British military were committing in the latter parts of his life. While he knew that a military was essential for a society to survive, he disagreed with how England was trying to colonize many different parts of the world in the late-nineteenth century. Spencer believed that the purpose of a military was not to conquer other nations, but to keep one's own nation safe from outside predators that might attempt to take advantage of a "weaker" nation. Thus, England was one of these "outside" predators because it was colonizing parts of Africa and Asia. (He was particularly upset over the Anglo–Boer war in 1899.) He defined England in terms of *barbarianism*, and this reality saddened Spencer (Battistelli, 1993). Spencer often commented, "I am ashamed of my country" (Duncan, 1908:449).

Individualism and the Organic Analogy

As outlined earlier in this chapter, Spencer was influenced by the field of biology. A comparison of an organism to a society led Spencer (1898) to conclude that society is a collective name for a number of units. Society is merely a name for the units within the society. A society is a coherent mass, and entity, formed by units that are molded and arranged for centuries. Social evolution establishes connected differences. Thus, single units maintain a level of individualism, but are connected by their similar attachment to the given society. The combined actions of these mutually dependent parts make up the life of the whole; therefore, establishing a parallelism between the national and individual life.

The integrity of the whole and of each large division is always maintained notwithstanding the deaths of its component citizens. Even if some of the parts (e.g., citizens) die off, the fabric of the whole is not changed. Private unions (e.g., families), local bodies (e.g., towns), secondary institutions (e.g., clubs) may decay, while the nation, maintaining its integrity, evolves in mass and structure (Spencer, 1898).

Spencer takes the individual, representing the society, to a whole new level of cohesion. The body of the whole is coherent, while its essential units form a whole only relative to the layers within the society.

Individuals equal the mind of the whole, a comprehensive consciousness. Thus, coherence is maintained through communication, which can only be accomplished through a shared language. Though the social organism (society) does not prevent subdivision or mutual dependence of parts, it does prevent parts from becoming out of balance with each other. The want of physical cohesion brings fixity of function (Spencer, 1898). The want to be a part of the group is mutually beneficial, thus creating a strong social cohesion. The society exists for the benefit of its members, not for the benefit of the society (Spencer, 1898).

Spencer's series of ever-increasing complexities portray society as an entity with increasing social function and structure. As parts of the social whole become more unlike, and the roles of individuals become more differentiated, their mutual dependence increases. Whereas, simple societies can substitute one part for another, more complex societies cannot. Thus, a regulating system is needed to ensure their coordination. These later regulating systems take the roles of internal regulation and social control when the complexity of functions cannot allow spontaneous adjustment of parts to one another. Therefore, the social function of a society is to protect its parts and continue the whole. As outside threat increases, internal control also increases, and vice versa. As the structure becomes more differentiated and complex there is an increased need for internal integration. As society evolves and increases in differentiation and complexity, there becomes a stronger, firmer need for internal control and development, or the whole risks disintegration into its many parts, thus leading to dissolution.

The Role of Language

As Spencer explains, societal comprehensive consciousness is attained through language.

The value of language for a society, both written and spoken, is its integrating function. The smooth functioning of the whole necessitates that the individual members all speak the same language. In fact, Spencer states that the value of language is paramount as growth is accompanied by increasing complexity. Multiple languages spoken in the same society represents an internal threat to the state's security.

The development of language, knowledge, morals, and aesthetics, is aided by social evolution. As social complexity increases, so does the complexity of language, ultimately leading to the permanence of a dominant language. Therefore, a progress in intelligence, which is associated with a progress in language, is a result of social progress. Spencer (1898) elaborates:

> Not only do all the above enumerated organization, domestic, political, ecclesiastical, ceremonial, industrial, influence one another through their respective activities; and not only are they all daily influenced by the state of language, knowledge, morals, arts; but the last are severally influenced by one another. Among these many groups of phenomena there is a *consensus*; and the highest achievement in Sociology is to grasp the vast heterogeneous aggregate, as to see how each group is at each stage determined partly by its own antecedents and partly by the past and present actions of the rest upon it (Spencer, 1898:568).

By comparing different societies at different stages one can understand the functions and structures of each and, therefore, understand all societies. Language becomes one of the critical variables as society increases in complexity (Spencer, 1898).

Utilitarianism

Spencer developed an indirect approach to utilitarianism. Spencer is a curiosity because he holds some liberal views but is not un-equivocally a liberal. Spencer is at his most utilitarian in *Social Statics*, but here he is as much a critic as an apostle of the theory. He rejects the conventional Benthamite view of the public interest, as the greatest happiness for the greatest number of people, on the grounds that it is incoherent and indeterminate; and he replaces it with an equal liberty principle (Weinstein, 1998). The equal liberty principle is itself based on a broadly utilitarian view of the goal of human action (to evolve) which is consistent with his evolutionary theories. Spencer believed in the absolute rights of individuals governed by the equal liberty principle that applied to all citizens.

Relevancy

Spencer's last years were characterized by a collapse of his initial optimism, and were instead replaced by a pessimism regarding the future of mankind. Nonetheless, Spencer devoted much of his efforts to reinforcing his arguments and preventing the misinterpretation of his monumental theory of non-interference. He was admired and respected by many intellectuals, including American philosopher William James and American sociologist William Graham Sumner. Although criticized by many contemporaries, Spencer has his proponents today. Libertarian thinkers, such as Robert Nozich, have invoked Spencer's views on natural rights. Jonathan Turner has actively campaigned to revitalize Spencer's substantial theory. Still, others fear or resent his evolutionary thinking.

Some people fear evolutionary theories because of ethical implications. Spencer's evolutionary theory argues that societies, like living organisms, evolve from simple states into highly complex forms. He incorporates Darwin's concept of natural selection with his own concept of survival of the

fittest to study how social systems evolve and/or dissolve. He argues that stronger societies survive and grow, while weaker ones disappear. This viewpoint had great appeal in Britain and the United States during the mid-1800s because it made their high level of advancement look like a great success story. More importantly, it helped to justify colonialism, since it implied that developed societies had a duty to control lesser ones and improve their level of civilization. Spencer goes so far as to suggest that war could be beneficial because it allowed a more organized and "advanced" society to help organize "inferior" societies.

Spencer believes that the evolution of societies not only followed a pattern but also produced a best-case scenario. Any tampering with this natural process of evolution on the part of the government would only have negative consequences for society.

Therefore, Spencer was against governmental welfare programs, and the like, because they would allow the physically and mentally unfit to reproduce and populate the next generation. This would in turn cause a gradual degeneration of society. Today, in "civilized" societies, most people would have a hard time justifying this philosophy. There are, however, some who view individuals dependent on the state as a weakness that must be discontinued. Ethical implications abound with this subject matter.

Civil law is often designed to combat the force of the survival of the fittest concept. A civilized society cannot allow the physically stronger to dominate the weak. A mundane example involves *Popov* v. *Hayashi*. When San Fransisco Giant Barry Bonds hit his historic 73rd homerun in 2001, a crush of fans on a walkway above right field fought for the baseball, a ball worth an estimated $1 million. Alex Popov caught the ball, but after a scramble, he lost it to Patrick Hayashi. The law of the bleachers is clear, it is every person for themselves. The law of the land states that, if one can show ownership (catching the ball) than one is granted ownership. Specifically, California law entitles one to own something if no one else owns it and it's in your physical control, even if for just a second. Civil law is often in direct contrast to the survival of the fittest concept.

Equating evolution with progress allowed "advanced" societies to view themselves as morally superior. Spencer (1851) writes that, "Progress is not an accident but a necessity. Surely must evil and immorality disappear; surely must man become perfect" (p.32). Spencer believes that more-evolved forms of behavior were superior to earlier forms not only in affording a better adjustment of man to his environment, but also in being more pleasurable for the individual and less-detrimental for the community at large. This smug attitude reflected the Victorian age and contributed to the appeal of Spencer.

Industrialization led to the disappearance of many relatively simple crafts and the emergence of a much more complex division of labor, along with the accompanying "alienation" that industrial forms of production bring. Spencer's explanation of change in terms of progressive differentiation of functions may have proved attractive to those who were not satisfied with the usual utilitarian schemes. Evolutionary necessity made intellectually palatable what might have appeared ethically unsettling. His theory helped to reduce cognitive dissonance of those whose previous lifestyles were radically changed.

Spencer had no problem equating evolution with progress. Progress made society better, and for those who adapt to the changing environment, their lives will become more beneficial. Progress has been made in many spheres of life since the time of Spencer, but we can still see irrational reactions among those who fear change and/or technological advancements. If we examine briefly the ethical ramifications of cloning and genetic engineering we can see the effects of the survival of fittest philosophy.

Genetic engineering involves the manipulation of deoxyribonucleic acid, or DNA. Important tools in this process are restriction enzymes, which are produced by various species of bacteria. Restriction enzymes can recognize a particular sequence of the chain of chemical units, called nucleotide bases, that make up the DNA molecule and cut the DNA at the location. Fragments of DNA generated in this way can be joined using other enzymes called ligases. Restriction enzymes and ligases therefore allow the specific cutting and reassembling of portions of DNA (Singer, 1995).

The possible benefits of genetic engineering are immense. For example, the gene for insulin, normally found only in higher animals, can be introduced into bacterial cells by way of a plasmid vector. The bacteria can then be grown in large quantities, giving an abundant source of recombinant insulin at a relatively low cost. Another important use of genetic engineering is in the manufacture of recombinant factor VIII, the blood-clotting agent missing in patients with hemophilia. There are many other possible benefits, as well as risks, involved in genetic engineering. As science continues to evolve in this area, many lives will be saved, and the quality of life for others will increase dramatically.

Two very different procedures have been referred to as "cloning"—embryo cloning and adult DNA cloning. Embryo cloning has been successfully carried out for years on many species of animals. Some limited experimentation has been done on human embryos. Adult DNA cloning has been used to clone a sheep, but research involving humans has been limited. Nature itself is the greatest cloning agent. In about one of every 75 human conceptions, the fertilized ovum splits for some unknown reason and produces monozygotic (identical) twins. Each has a genetic makeup identical to the other. With the exception of the sperm and egg, every cell in the body contains all the genetic material in its DNA to theoretically create an exact clone of the original body. But cells have been "biochemically programmed to perform limited functions" (Bohlin, 1997).

Recently, adult DNA cloning has been attempted on humans, especially in terms of creating "replacement" organs (e.g., livers and bladders), a feat that could herald the beginning of a biotech revolution in solving the perennial problem of insufficient organ donors (Maugh, 1999). Replacement tissues are being developed to treat degenerative diseases as well. This process is referred to as "therapeutic cloning." Through the therapeutic cloning process replacement tissues, which are genetically identical to the patient, are far less likely to be rejected by the patient's immune system. By the end of 2001, U.S. researchers had announced that they had cloned human embryos for the first time. Their aim is to create genetically matched stem cells to treat a wide range of diseases. There are many other possible benefits of cloning, along with possible risks. Those who fear or cannot understand advancements in science want to halt the increase study of cloning and genetic engineering. They equate the progress in this field as interfering with "God's work."

These fears can be put in their proper place when one realizes that some 35 years ago people responded the same way in regards to heart transplants. It is doubtful that many people would refuse a heart transplant today if it meant extending their life, and few people see this form of medicine as interfering with "God's work." In short, advancements in society are constantly being made. One can refuse to change with the environment if they choose, but they most assuredly risk being left behind.

Throughout most of Spencer's life he enjoyed critical acclaim for his works and theories. But when the intellectual tide turned in the late 1800s, Spencer's fortunes in England turned with them. Although still a highly respected man of science, he lost much of his loyal audience. But as Englishmen turned away from him, a new American public eagerly embraced his ideology. Additionally, admirers of his doctrine were to be found throughout western Europe.

In the early years of American sociology, Spencer's ideas were much more influential than those of Comte, Durkheim, Marx, and Weber. There are several explanations for this. First, Spencer wrote in English, while the others did not. Additionally, Spencer did not write very technically, thereby making his work broadly accessible. Indeed, some argue that this lack of technicality is a result of Spencer's not being a very sophisticated scholar. Spencer offered a scientific orientation that was attractive to an audience becoming consumed with science. He offered a comprehensive theory that seemed to deal with the entire sweep of human history. The large volume of work produced by Spencer offered many things to many people. Finally, and perhaps most importantly, his theory was soothing and reassuring to a society undergoing the wrenching process of industrialization. Society, according to Spencer, was steadily moving in the direction of greater and greater progress. Spencer's most famous American disciple was William Sumner, who accepted and expanded many of Spencer's evolutionary ideas. Sumner argued that a failure to accept the *survival of the fittest* concept left just one alternative, accepting a *survival of the unfittest* doctrine

(Curtis, 1981). Spencer also influenced other early American sociologists, among them, Lester Ward, Charles Cooley, and Robert Park.

However, by the 1930s, Spencer was ignored in the intellectual world in general as well as in sociology. His Social Darwinist, laissez-faire ideas seemed out of place in light of massive social problems, a world war, and a major economic depression.

Spencer's place as a mastermind of sociology had been well secured by this point in time. He had book sales in America alone, from the 1860s to his death, totaling 368,755 volumes, an unparalleled figure in such difficult spheres as philosophy and sociology (Coser, 1977). And now, in the twenty-first century, a renewed interest in Spencer continues in American sociology. This renewed interest was sparked by (among others) Jonathan Turner, one of the greatest contemporary American thinkers. Turner (1981) states, "We could venture that [Spencer's principles] have been used in empirical research far more often than principles developed by Marx, Weber, and Durkheim. We can further speculate that had sociological theorists and researchers begun the 20th century with Spencer's models and principles in hand, it is likely that sociology would be a more mature science" (p.95). Turner (1985) further states that he hopes to rekindle interest in this forgotten giant.

There are many specific examples of the relevancy of Spencer's ideas and concepts to contemporary and future society. For one, many people (e.g., academic scholars, social policy–makers, and environmentalists) are concerned about the issue of global overpopulation, an idea first articulated by Malthus, and then Spencer. Consider that it took the Earth's population until the year 1800 to reach one billion. Only 130 years later—in 1930—the population reached two billion. Less than 70 years later—in 1999—the

world's population reached an alarming figure of six billion. The effects of the scarcity of critical goods and raw materials, such as timber, minerals, water, and oil, are just now beginning to be fully realized. The damage caused to the ecosystem in an attempt to meet the needs of six billion people may be unchangeable. The *Four Horsemen* are clearly running rampant throughout the planet.

The *Four Horsemen* concept has been applied in a completely different manner through the marriage and counseling studies conducted by John Gottman and his team of researchers at the University of Washington. Gottman describes the four signs of trouble in marriage as "The Four Horsemen of the Apocalypse." These four horsemen include:

1. Criticism

2. Defensiveness

3. Contempt

4. (Emotional) Withdrawal

In tests conducted over a twenty-five year period on thousands of couples, Gottman has a 90% accuracy rate in predicting which couples will end up in divorce (*ABC News Special*, 1997). Even marriage is governed by the rules of survival.

Spencer's analysis of militant and industrial societies still holds validity today. Spencer had correctly identified a number of critical elements that characterizes each social type. Industrial society during times of relative peace can enjoy great prosperity. This was true in the United States during the post-Cold War period as the Clinton administration was able to cut costs in its military budget. Ever since the United States was brutally attacked without provocation, or warning, on September 11, 2001, the American government has become far more militaristic in its social policy. The Federal government has taken a far more authoritarian approach in the supervision of everyday life in America (e.g., a military presence at airports with extreme forms of security). This increased role of regulatory systems often comes at the cost of decreased civil liberties and individual rights. As Spencer acknowledged, citizens of the military society respond with such characteristics as loyalty, courage, obedience, and faith in authority. America's patriotism and President Bush's approval rating were both soaring in the months immediately following 9-11. Spencer was certainly correct when he stated that, as external threat increases, internal control also increases.

Naylor (2002) has identified a large number of guerrilla movements over the past twenty-five years that directly lead to increased military policy on behalf of the central government. Among the examples are National Union for the Total Independence of Angola (UNITA); Peru's Sendero Luminoso; rebel groups in North Acheth, Indonesia; the Bougainville Revolutionary Army in Papua-New Guinea; and the Afghan Taliban. These rebel groups, in an attempt to overthrow the existing governmental structure and cultural values, cause such chaos that the government has no choice but to respond in a military fashion. "Military expenditures escalate as the size and firepower of military units increase along with the frequency and scale of operations" (Naylor, 2002:47). Often, these rebel groups attempt to destroy the industrial society and replace it with a reactionary agricultural system (e.g., Pol Pot in Cambodia). Sometimes, as Spencer clearly articulated, societies simply cannot adapt to the changing environment and they fall victim to dissolution. This has been especially true in Africa as new nations have replaced numerous old nations for the past few decades.

There is strong evidence for supporting the validity of Spencer's evolutionary ideas in contemporary and future society, especially his *survival of the fittest* concept. One must first recognize the difficulty in predicting social change with any degree of accuracy. The one thing that seems certain is that the process of globalization will continue for some time. The increasing societal complexity anticipated by Spencer in the mid-nineteenth century is today being realized at the global level. Different societies are progressing at different rates while the process of globalization itself initiates an increasing level of integration of the world into a single economic unit. And while international borders still exist and remain partial barriers to the free flow of goods, they are less likely to hinder the global exchange of information via the Internet.

Technological advancements of computers and especially the Internet mandates the necessity of persons to master computer-related skills. The *survival of the fittest* doctrine is clearly exemplified in the possession of computer skills. The employment sector demands knowledge and skills in this area. Private entrepreneurs recognize that it is imperative to be computer savvy. Many people have made large sums of money in the stock market simultaneously while others lose their life savings. The economic sector of the western world has long abandoned its dependence on industrialization and the service economy now dominates. Those who fail to adapt to the changing environment run the greatest risk of economic failure.

There are countless other examples of the need to adapt to the changing environment. This principle applies to nearly all social encounters, as norms and values change, so too must the behaviors of persons. In the professional world these changes are often even more dramatic: medical doctors must be aware of the latest advancements and techniques; lawyers must keep informed with new court rulings; police officers must enforce new laws; and so on. Students must maintain high grades for they are in competition with thousands of others applying for the same graduate schools and/or career opportunities. Athletes and fans of sport have long realized the *survival of the fittest* principle. Only the "fittest" remain on the team, for there is always someone else ready to take their place. On the playing field, for every winner there is at least one loser.

Spencer teaches us that one should never be satisfied with simply surviving, one must learn to succeed. In society, only those who adapt to changes in the social system will succeed. This has always been, and remains to be, the truth.

Karl Marx

(1818–1883)

Carl Heinrich Marx was born on May 5, 1818, in Trier, Prussia, a city in the far western province of the Rhineland. Its proximity to France, and its temporary rule under Napoleon, allowed . the rationalism of French culture to function as an alternative to the conservatism of Prussian-dominated Germany (Seidman, 1983). Trier benefited from the progressive philosophy of the Enlightenment in ways such as its public works projects. As such, the young Marx could directly observe the positive impact of enlightened reason.

Carl was one of nine children, and the only male among four who lived to be over 40. In the mid-1820s Carl—later called Karl—and his sisters, and eventually his mother, were baptized as Christians (Adams and Sydie, 2001). Karl's parents, Heinrich and Henrietta Marx, were both descended from a long line of rabbis, Heinrich's in the Rhineland and Henrietta's in Holland (Carr, 1934). Heinrich Marx was a successful lawyer, who would rise to become head of the bar, and was able to provide for his family a fairly typical bourgeois existence. Heinrich broke away from his religious heritage by becoming the first to obtain a secular education. This was a very significant event, for it not only signaled a departure from Jewish teaching, it highlighted the fact that the doors of trades and professions were now open to Jews. It was the Napoleonic regime that created equality for the Jews, and since they owed their emancipation to Napoleon, they supported his regime with great zeal. The doors of trades and professions, which had hitherto remained rigidly barred, were open to Jews under Napoleon. With the fall of Napoleon and the assignment of the Rhineland by the Congress of Vienna to Prussia, the Jews were once again deprived of their civil rights. Threatened by the potential loss of his law practice, Heinrich Marx decided in 1817 to convert to the mildly liberal Lutheran Church of Prussia. Having no real contacts with the synagogue, Heinrich did not regard the conversion as an act of moral significance; rather it was simply the practical thing to do.

As a youth, Karl Marx was influenced less by religion than by the critical, sometimes radical, social policies of the Enlightenment. His Jewish background exposed him to prejudice and discrimination that may have led him to question the role of religion in society and contributed to his desire for social change. His father's conversion to Lutheranism most likely influenced Marx's deep concern that all people should have the opportunity to reach their full

Karl Marx (1818–1883) German philosopher, historian, political activist, economic determinist, and humanist.
Source: Courtesy of the Library of Congress

human potential and certainly lead to his questioning of the validity of religion.

Karl's father had an excellent education, unlike his mother who was so poorly educated that she had difficulty writing correct sentences. Needless to say, his mother had little significance upon his life. His father, on the other hand, taught him the importance of a proper education. Early on in his life, Karl formed and developed an intellectual bond with his father, who introduced him to the value of knowledge while exposing him to the works of the great Enlightenment thinkers and both the German and Greek classics. His father had become aware early on that while his other children were in no way remarkable, in Karl he had an unusual

and difficult son, with a sharp and lucid intelligence combined with an obdurate and domineering temper (Berlin, 1971).

Another significant figure in the young Marx's life was Baron Ludwig von Westphalen, a next-door neighbor. Westphalen was a very intelligent man who would encourage Karl by lending him books, and conversing with him on frequent walks about classical works by Shakespeare and Cervantes. Often on these walks they would discuss political as well as social doctrines. The bond between the two was close, with Westphalen, a distinguished upper-class Prussian government official, becoming the spiritual mentor of the greatest general thinker in the history of socialism.

Karl Marx attended high school in Trier and participated in customary student activities. The school was under police surveillance because it was suspected of harboring liberal teachers and pupils. In fact, the principal was a disciple of Kantian liberalism (Seidman, 1983). During this time Marx wrote about Christian idealism and a longing for self-sacrifice on behalf of humanity. Marx's high school papers revealed his absorption of the Enlightenment legacy of liberal humanism.

Marx went off to college at the age of seventeen, based upon his father's advice, to the University of Bonn where he enrolled in the faculty of law. Marx spent a great deal of time reading and writing romantic poetry. His poems reflect the primary themes and ideas of the romantics: idealism, expressionism, and the search for spiritual renewal and unity (Seidman, 1983). Marx would eventually abandon writing poetry, but his romantic concern for individual and collective fulfillment would continue throughout his life's work. While at Bonn, Marx also reveled in his rebellious nature as he fought duels and spent a day in jail for being drunk and disorderly. Marx presided at the Tavern Club, which was at odds with the more aristocratic student associations, and joined a poets' club that included some political activists.

In 1836, Marx abandoned Bonn and the study of law for the University of Berlin and the study of philosophy. The move to this more exciting and lively capital city would prove to be the decisive turning point in the young man's life (Coser, 1977). Hegel was already dead when Marx enrolled at Berlin, but his spirit still dominated. It was here that Karl was first introduced to the radical band of heretic philosophers known as the Young Hegelians, and he was soon initiated into their spirit. The informal *Doktorklub* (Doctor's Club), was comprised of young marginal academics. They were a radical, somewhat antireligious and bohemian group of thinkers. Most outstanding among them were the brothers Bruno and Edgar Bauer, both radical and freethinking Hegelians of the Left, and Max Stirner, the later proponent of ultra-individualistic anarchism (Coser, 1977). Under the influence of these men Marx resolved to devote himself to philosophy. He also became a "social" drinker who frequently was found in saloons around Berlin, where the Young Hegelians debated for hours on the fine points of the Hegelian doctrine.

This group had many interests concerning the German society. They debated everything along the lines of religion to politics. Specifically, the Young Hegelians criticized traditional Christianity, the Prussian monarchy, and the lack of democratic freedom (Pampel, 2000). The Young Hegelians are even considered to be Germany's first known political party. "They began in other fields, and only slowly concentrated on politics as the process of secularization advanced" (McLellan, 1969:28). Marx was important to the Young Hegelians because he and his young associates, who included Friedrich Engels, Moses Hess, Lorenz von Stein, and Michael Bakunin, represented the second generation of Hegelians (Brazill,

1970). Marx did not stay with the Young Hegelians for long, due primarily to an opposition to the teleological spiritual idealism of Hegelian philosophy. The heart of the Hegelian philosophy Marx declared to be nothing but, "the speculative expression of the Christian-Germanic dogma of the opposition between spirit and matter, God and the world" (Hook, 1962:268).

During the University of Berlin days, Marx had envisioned himself as a future professor of philosophy. Bruno Bauer had found a teaching appointment at Bonn and promised Marx that he would find him a position there as well. Unfortunately, Bauer's position was short-lived as he was fired for his antireligious, liberal views. Marx abandoned forever his hope of an academic position (Coser, 1977). Marx's student life would end in 1841 with the submission of his dissertation *On the Differences Between the Natural Philosophy of Democritus and Epicurus.* Marx's doctorate was a dry philosophical treatise, except for a burning antireligious preface which, upon advice of his friends, was not submitted to the academic authorities.

In 1841, after spending five years in the "metropolis of intellectuals" Marx returned to Bonn. At that time the first "New Era" was in vogue in Prussia. Frederick William IV had declared his love of a loyal opposition, and attempts were being made in various quarters to organize one (Engels, 1869). Moses Hess, an admirer and socialist friend of Marx, asked him to become a regular writer for the new liberal–radical and bourgeois paper *Rheinische Zeitung* in Cologne. Hess, Germany's first communist, viewed private property as a source of evil and had recently converted a young Friedrich Engels to his philosophy (Pampel, 2000).

At this time, Marx knew little about communism but he impressed Hess with his own opinions about philosophy. Marx jumped at the opportunity to write for this paper, and exhibited an unprecedented daring to criticize the deliberations of the Rhine Province Assembly in articles which attracted great attention. Marx wrote a series of articles on social conditions, among them the misery of the Moselle vine-growing peasantry and the horrible treatment the poor received for the theft of timber in forests to which they thought they had a communal right (Coser, 1977). The government had passed laws forbidding the wine-growers from using firewood available in the nearby forests during the winter (Pampel, 2000). Ten months later he took over the editorship himself and was such a thorn in the side of the censors that they did him the "honor" of sending a censor from Berlin. Battles with the censors would continue until Marx wrote an article condemning the Russian government. Russian emperor Nicholas I, who had read the article, complained to the Prussian ambassador, and shortly after, the *Rheinische Zeitung* ceased publication. As editor, Marx had increased circulation from 400 to 3,400 (Pampel, 2000).

At seventeen, Marx had become secretly engaged to Jenny von Westphalen, a charming, beautiful, auburn-haired daughter of one of Trier's leading citizens (Baron von Westphalen). Because of social differences, most of her family did not approve of the relationship (Yuille, 1991). They revealed religious and class bigotry in their concerns over Marx's Jewish origins and lower social position. Jenny's family was wealthy and informed her that she would be cut off financially if she married Karl. Only her father, a follower of the French socialist Saint-Simon, was fond of Karl. Karl and Jenny's daughter, Eleanor (Tussy) Marx recounts the love relationship between her father and mother in her 1897 paper "Biographical Comments on Karl Marx." Karl was a young man of seventeen when be became engaged to Jenny, but for them the path of true love was not a smooth one. Karl's parents did not want him to get married at such an early age, so he waited seven years, which seemed so much longer "because he loved her so much." Having played together as children, the couple went hand in hand through the battle of life. And it was a battle, as Eleanor would explain, years of bitter pressing need and, still worse, years of brutal suspicion, infamous calumny, and icy indifference. But through it all, in happiness and unhappiness, the two lifelong friends and lovers never faltered, never doubted, and they were faithful unto death. (It should be noted that Karl fathered an illegitimate child with a maid and Engels claimed paternity to protect Marx). Karl kept with him in his breast pocket a poem he had written to Jenny and pictures of his wife, daughter, and father. Engels laid them to rest in Marx's coffin (Marx, 1897).

Four months after their marriage, the young couple moved to Paris, which was then the center of socialist thought and of the more extreme sects that fell under the name of "communism." This is where Marx first became a revolutionary and a communist, and began to associate with communist groups of French and German working men. Influenced by communist thought, Marx published his *Critique of Hegel's Philosophy of Right* and *On the Jewish Question* in 1843. One year later, Marx wrote a series of articles that were posthumously published as the *Economic and Philosophical Manuscripts of 1844*. It was in a Paris café in 1844 that Marx had his first conversation with a German traveler, Friedrich Engels, who was on his way home from England. The two had met briefly earlier but they now realized the commitment and strength of their common beliefs and agreement on philosophical and political matters (Yuille, 1991). In 1845 he published his *Theses on Feuerbach*.

By the beginning of 1845 Marx was expelled from France by the Guizot government, acting under Prussian instigation. The Prussian government viewed his writings as acts of treason (Marx and Engels, 1978). Marx, now with family and unemployed once again (as he would be most of his life), moved to Brussels where he pursued established contacts with German refugees. In particular, he sought out the remaining members of the dissolved radical League of the Just, an international revolutionary organization formed in 1836 by German radical workers. In 1847 it would change its name to the "Communist League" and commissioned Marx and Engels to draw up a manifesto on its behalf (Marx and Engels, 1978).

Meanwhile, in Manchester 1845, Friedrich Engels had made the acquaintance of Mary Burns, a factory worker who was involved in organizing the English workers' movement (Adams and Sydie, 2001). The two became and remained friends until her death in 1863. From Burns, Engels learned of worker solidarity and social movements. When Engels returned to Germany later in the year, he learned of the German working-class movement and continued to explore communist ideas. By the end of 1845, Engels had joined Marx in Brussels where they enjoyed trips to the country and late evenings in cafés. Ever focused, Marx devoted most of his time to developing his materialistic theory of history. Together, Marx and Engels collaborated on *The German Ideology*, in which they sought to disparage the views of other contemporary philosophers (Yuille, 1991).

Marx and Engels formed the Communist Corespondence Committee, which served as the model for the future International Association. The primary purpose of the Committee was to establish links between the Communists in France, Germany, and England. Close ties were made with the London Communist League, at the time the largest and most organized group, composed mainly of German refugees. At the end of 1847 Marx and Engles attended the Second Congress of the Communist League, where they presented a detailed program of how the League should be organized. This became *The Communist Manifesto*. Viewing himself as an international revolutionist, Marx attempted to organize German and Belgian dissidents. He critiqued the current version of socialism in a 1847 paper titled *The Poverty of Philosophy*. In that work can be found the many essential points of theory that would be presented at the Second Congress conference. Additionally, in December 1847, Marx gave a series of lectures in Brussels, later published as *Wage, Labour and Capital* (1849).

The year *The Communist Manifesto* was published was a year of general unrest in Europe, involving uprisings in eight European countries or city states (Yuille, 1991). In March of 1848, Marx was suspected of taking part in preparations for a revolt in Brussels and was expelled from Belgium, together with his wife and three children. Marx returned to Paris at the invitation of the French provisional government that had just exiled King Louis Philippe. The tidal wave of the revolution throughout European cities had pushed all scientific pursuits into the background; what mattered now was to become involved in the movement.

Shortly after his arrival in Paris, news came of an uprising in Berlin. Marx and his communist followers traveled immediately to Germany. Marx and Engels took active parts in the revolution of 1848–1849 in Germany, co-editing *Neue Rheinische Zeitung* in Cologne. Marx and Engels took freedom of the press to the extreme in their attacks on the Prussian government. Twice Marx was put before authorities for inciting people to refuse to pay their taxes, and was acquitted on both occasions. Marx called for German unity, a German constitution, and a revolutionary war against Russia.

Frederick William IV, King of Prussia, rejected the proposed constitution and a violent uprising occured in Dresden. Eventually, martial law was declared and the rebellion was silenced. Marx wrote an article expressing his sympathy with revolutionaries and his condemnation of the King. Because he was no longer viewed as a Prussian subject, the government expelled Marx from Germany and he returned to Paris. Shortly after, Marx was expelled from Paris again, triggering his move to London, a city that he would reside in until his death.

In London at that time were refugees from all the nations of the continent. Revolutionary committees of every kind were formed. For a while Marx continued to produce his *Neue Rheinische Zeitung* in the form of a monthly review, but later he withdrew into the British Museum and worked through the immense, and as yet for the most part unexamined, library for all that it contained on political economy (Engels, 1869). Marx had now become known as a social historian of distinction. He was a regular contributor to the *New York Tribune*, for an eleven-year period until the outbreak of the American Civil War, as the editor on European politics. Some of Marx's most brilliant historical pamphlets were published during this time: *The Class Struggles in France* (1850) and *The Eighteenth Brumaire of Louis Bonaparte* (1852).

As the London years passed by, Marx and Engels continued to wait in anticipation of the communist revolt. Along the way Karl and his wife Jenny had been arrested for selling arms to revolutionaries and were constantly involved with planning revolutions in hopes of spearheading the new ideology. Such a revolution never occurred in his lifetime. His brilliant works would continue to be published, chief among them *Capital*, Volume One in 1867 and Volumes Two and Three by 1880. *Capital* was published in Russia in 1872.

Economic deprivation and family tragedy played a significant role in the Marx family life, and Engels would often have to assist Karl financially. Toward the end, Engels had become quite prosperous and gave Marx an annuity, enabling him to spend his last few years in relative comfort. Earlier in their lives, Karl and Jenny lost two children in infancy, and their son Edgar in 1855, at age eight, died of tuberculosis. Karl would have to borrow money from Engels for his son's burial. For the most part, Marx was devoted to his wife and daughters. He read his children stories, encouraged educational pursuits, and would often go on day-long picnics with them. Marx was fully conscious of the burden to his family his devotion to the communist cause had cost. Jenny accepted her husband's priorities and willingly spent hours copying Karl's illegible manuscripts. In 1881, Jenny passed away and on March 14, 1883, Karl Marx died. Only Engels and eleven others attended his funeral. Mourners throughout the world sent letters expressing their sympathies. The following year a demonstration was held on March 16 to commemorate both Marx and the Paris Commune. Between five and six thousand people marched with bands and banners along Tottenham Court Road to Highgate Cemetery. They were greeted by five hundred policemen who had locked the gates to the cemetery and refused them entry. Even Eleanor and a few close family friends with flowers were refused admittance.

Today, people pay money at the Highgate Cemetery entrance to visit the grave of Karl Marx.

Intellectual Influences

There were many influences on Karl Marx. Noting that Marx was born in Trier, a city in the far western province of the Rhineland with its proximity to France and temporary rule under Napoleon, the French culture, dominated by thoughts of rationalism, influenced the young Marx. Then later, it was the conservatism of German idealism that would affect Marxist thought. The decisive turning point in Marx's intellectual development occurred when he met Friedrich Engels in Cologne, in November of 1842, with the two developing a lifelong friendship. The primary influences of Marx are discussed in the following pages.

The Enlightenment and Romanticism

During the formative years of Marx's intellectual development, he was consumed with the liberal spirit of the Enlightenment. Karl's father and Ludwig von Westphalen had a deep love for the Enlightenment and for the philosophy of Spinoza. Marx's early college years were dominated by the composition of poetry with chief concerns including idealism, expressionism, and the search for spiritual renewal and unity. By 1839, Marx no longer composed poetry, but the romantic concern for individuals, collective struggles, and personal and societal integration remained central components of Marxian thought.

There were many divergent doctrines of Enlightenment thought. The French *philosophes* were rationalists; the British, including Locke, sensationalists; others like La Mettrie were materialists. But they all shared the common belief in the possibility of altering the human environment in such a way as to allow a fuller and more wholesome development of human capacities. Most believed that man does not have a divine soul, that he is an object in nature, but that he has the capacity for self-improvement through education and environmental changes (Coser, 1977). Man must learn to release himself from superstitions and the irrational beliefs of religion in order to come into his own true sense of being. People are creatures of circumstances and socialization; consequently, changes in such social conditions can lead to self-fulfillment. Marx sought revolutionary change as a precondition for the realization of liberal ideals of secularism, universalism, and rationalization. Marx's ideas of self-realization, human potential, guidelines for society, and the search for "laws" and regularities of the evolutionary form were all influenced by the Enlightenment and romanticism.

German Idealism

The doctrines of the Enlightenment, which stressed the gradual and amicable progress of mankind, were countered toward the end of the century by the harsher philosophy of Kant. Kant took a more pessimistic view of human progress, believing that the antagonism between men was the ultimate driving force in history. He believed that men were given to an "unsociable sociability" (Coser, 1977). Progress came about through antagonistic cooperation. Thus, as Marx would come to believe, conflict is inevitable.

In his *Second Discourse*, Rousseau provides a vivid description of the natural goodness of man being corrupted by society. He believed that individuals were deprived of their natural desires and needs by oppressive and unjust societal laws. In his *Social Contract*, he would demonstrate how people could form a new community, by associating together voluntarily, by forging new bonds. Many German thinkers were influenced by Rousseau's insights. Others, like Friedrich Schiller, were unimpressed by his idyllic description of the "nobility of savages."

Schiller (1967) called it "the tranquil nausea of his paradise." Despite the debate among German thinkers as to the validity of his theories, Kant's *Second Discourse* was an early source for Marx's notion of alienation.

Marx's philosophical studies took place in an intellectual climate dominated by the thought of Hegel and his followers. In many ways Hegelian thought follows the ideas found in the Enlightenment, in the conservative reaction, and in Comte. The Enlightenment's emphasis on reason, the conservatives' on tradition and culture, and even Comte's focus on the primacy of forms of thought can be seen in the development of German Idealism from Kant to Hegel (Hadden, 1998). Kant believed that Newton's science had provided adequate evidence that permanent "laws" existed in nature. He questioned how such insights of nature were possible since nature does not provide any privileged access to its operation. Kant believed that man was capable of sorting data into categories of knowledge. The foremost of these categories were "space," "time," and "causality" (Hadden, 1998).

As German Idealism developed from Kant through to Hegel, the focus of attention shifted outside the human subject. Hegel (1770–1831) viewed human development as a historical process. Whereas Comte had seen historic progress in terms of the development of mind, Hegel did not. Hegel did not believe that any amount of hard, positivist thinking or analysis could make any ultimate claims of "truths." The world and its contents simply do not form a rational whole, Hegel believed, because reason (mind, spirit) had not, as of yet, developed adequately. In Hegel's German the word "spirit" (Geist) does not have the supernatural meaning it does in English; rather it refers to culture or "spirit of the times" (Hadden, 1998). Hegel thought that every process of change—and above all, the unfolding of human history—moves forward through simultaneous negation and transformation of what existed before (Garner, 2000).

Hegel taught that objectivity is a product of the mind's activity, and that we fall into "bondage" of the laws and events that we create. Hegel emphasized that we must be aware of the fact that we are the producers of such categories of thinking, and through participation in society we help maintain (reaffirm) it. Marx's concept of reification came from these ideas of Hegel.

As Ritzer (2000) explains, there are two concepts that represent the essence of Hegel's philosophy—the dialectic and idealism. The *dialectic* is both a way of thinking and an image of the world. It is a way of thinking that stresses the importance of processes, relations, dynamics, conflicts, and contradictions. It is also an image of the world that assumes structures are not static. The philosophy of *idealism* emphasizes the importance of the mind and mental products rather than the material world. It is the social definition of the physical and material worlds that matters the most according to Hegel. We can see why Hegel would have difficulty accepting positivism with his belief in idealism.

Hegelian philosophy was the most dominant during Marx's early years. What attracted Marx to Hegel, after the romanticism of his year at Bonn and his brief enthusiasm for the idealism of Kant and Fichte, was the bridge he conceived Hegel to have built between what is and what ought to be. In a letter written to his father in 1837, Marx wrote:

> A curtain had fallen, my holy of holies had been shattered, new gods had to be found. Setting out from idealism—which, let me say in passing, I had compared to and nourished with that of Kant and Fichte—I hit upon seeking the Idea in the real itself. If formerly the gods had dwelt above the world, they now become its center. (Marx and Engels, 1980:8)

Marx's general aim was to evaluate Hegel's political philosophy, which gave him scope to criticize existing political institutions and, more broadly, to discuss the question of the relationship of politics to economics. He treated Hegel's philosophy dialectically; he negated or discarded Hegel's spiritual mystification and Hegel's enthusiasm for the state as an institution. Marx retained the concept of the logic of historical change, but eliminated spiritual notions and emphasized instead the material and political dimensions of human history. He believed that during the course of history, human beings grow in their understanding of nature and society, and in the sophistication of their modes of production; as this understanding expands, they develop a consciousness of, and an ability to create, society as a collective undertaking. Society, then, is no longer viewed as a taken-for-granted god-given "natural" force, but as a social construct that can be shaped and reshaped. Therefore, it is possible to construct a society in which all human beings can realize their unique and full potential, be creative, develop both their individual talents and their sense of community, and experience freedom as well as solidarity.

During the Berlin days Marx was exposed to the thoughts of Hegel through a group of his disciples collectively referred to as the "Young Hegelians." The Young (or left) Hegelians debated the current issues of the day, and religion was one institution that they believed must be eliminated. For the Old (or right) Hegelians, religion was seen as the true moral bond of human beings in society. Authority and tradition guided by religion were seen in a positive light by the Old Hegelians. German culture was still dominated by an unenlightened and oppressive religiosity during this period. Hence, for the Young Hegelians, the critique of religion was the major philosophical task of importance. In 1835, David Strauss, a Young

Hegelian, published the critical *Life of Jesus*, in which he used the Hegelian historical method to show that certain portions of the Gospels were pure creative inventions, whereas others were only reflections of semi-mythological beliefs common in primitive Christian cultures. Bruno Bauer, a more radical Young Hegelian, went even further in his critique by denying the very existence of Jesus, and treating the Gospels as works of pure imagination—as simple reflections of the ideology of the time. According to the Young Hegelians, if you rid the world of religious illusions, you remove the misery from peoples' real condition. On the other hand, the Old Hegelians believed that if you maintain religious authority and tradition, you provide the final ingredient that binds people together in a proper and reasonable human society (Hadden, 1998).

During the early 1840s, Marx was infatuated with the Young Hegelian position, especially in their battle against religion. But Marx would soon become quite critical of the Hegelian perspective, whether it was the Young or Old Hegelians. From his point of view, they both granted religion more influence than was justified. In a series of articles published as the *Critique of Hegel's Philosophy of Right* (1843), Marx describes his philosophical differences with Hegelian thought. There are four primary areas of criticism (McLellan, 1990, and Marx and Engels, 1978):

1. A general criticism of Hegel for starting with abstract ideas instead of with concrete reality.

2. A criticism of Hegel's defense of the monarchy.

3. Disagreement with Hegel on the role of bureaucracy. Hegel believed that bureaucracy represents the "spirit" of society; whereas Marx's analysis of bureaucracy revealed its tendency to form a state within a state.

4. Disagreement on the issue of the sovereignty of the state. Hegel treats the state as an independent entity that is objectified. Marx saw the state and people as one and the same.

Despite these criticisms, the influences of Hegel and the Young Hegelians would have an impact on Marxian thought. Marx learned of the *holistic* approach through Hegel's ideas of totality. The totality approach states that everything should be considered, that the truth is a whole, not just a part. To find the truth, then, one must look at the totality of incidents that leads to a particular point in time or behavior. The German Ideology would influence Marx's idea of the division of labor, which was a product of a historic process that begins with the family and is maintained by the ownership of private property. Marx's version of communism was to free mankind from the division of labor. In fact, as Marx learned through the ideas of Kant, the entire history of mankind was marked by class struggle.

Ludwig Feuerbach

Although Feuerbach can be categorized as a Young Hegelian, special attention is given to him here. Ludwig Feuerbach (1804–1872) was an important link between Hegel and Marx. Feuerbach was critical of Hegel for, among other things, his excessive emphasis on consciousness and the spirit of society (Ritzer, 2000). Because of Feuerbach's adoption of a materialistic philosophy, he stressed the importance of the material reality of real human beings, rather than the subjective idealism of Hegel. Feuerbach is said to have commented on the importance of materialism over spiritualism, "To think, you must eat." Feuerbach was also highly critical of Hegel's emphasis on the value of religion. To Feuerbach, God is merely a projection created by humans. People set God above themselves, believing that He is perfect, almighty, all loving, and holy, while believing themselves as flawed humans. Feuerbach argued that, through reification, religion serves as an alienating force that must be eliminated. Real people, not abstract ideas like religion, were the cornerstone of Feuerbach's materialist philosophy.

Karl Marx had read and was influenced by Feuerbach's *Essence of Christianity* (1841), where he described religion as the self-alienation of man. Marx believed that Feuerbach had successfully criticized Hegel's concept of the spirit of man, and agreed that the "Absolute Spirit" was a mere projection. Marx was also struck by the *humanistic* aspects of Feuerbach's work. Marx read *Essence* just before submitting his dissertation. Most people attribute Feuerbach's writings as of permanent importance and a major influence on Marx (McLellan, 1969). Breckman (1999) suggests that Feuerbach had an influence upon Marx far earlier than has been recognized. Marx's philosophical efforts can be seen as a combination of Hegel's dialectic and Feuerbach's materialism.

However, Marx certainly did not agree with Feuerbach on everything. In the spring of 1845, as he and Engels were starting their collaborative work on *The German Ideology*, Marx wrote the *Theses on Feuerbach*. More than forty years later, Engels found them in one of the notebooks that had come into his possession after his friend had died. He published them as an appendix to his essay of 1888 on *Ludwig Feuerbach and the End of Classical German Philosophy*, and described them in the foreword to this publication as "the brilliant germ of the new world outlook" (Marx and Engels, 1978). The following eleven points summarize Marx's disagreements with Feuerbach:

1. Feuerbach does not conceive human activity itself as objective reality, hence he does not grasp the significance of "revolutionary," practical activity.

2. The question whether objective truth can be attributed to human thinking is not a question of theory, but is a practical one. The dispute over the reality or non-reality of such thinking is purely a scholastic question.

3. The coincidence of the changing of circumstances and of human activity, or self-changing, can be conceived and rationally understood only as a revolutionary practice.

4. Feuerbach starts from the fact of religious self-alienation and believes the world should be secular. Marx believes that this is just the starting point. The secular world must detach itself from itself and establish itself as an independent realm.

5. Feuerbach, not satisfied with abstract thinking, wants contemplation; but he does not conceive sensuousness as practical, human-sensuous activity.

6. Feuerbach resolves the religious essence into the human essence. But the human essence is no abstraction inherent in each individual. In its reality it is the ensemble of the social relations.

7. Feuerbach, consequently, does not see that the "religious sentiment" is itself a social product, and that the abstract individual whom he analyzes belongs to a particular form of society.

8. All social life is essentially practical. All mysteries that mislead theory into mysticism find their rational solution in human practice and in the comprehension of this practice.

9. The highest point reached by contemplative materialism, that is, materialism that does not comprehend sensuousness as practical activity, is the contemplation of single persons in civil society.

10. The standpoint of the old materialism is *civil* society; the standpoint of the new is *human* society, or social humanity.

11. In one of Marx's most famous quotes, he criticizes philosophers by stating, "The philosophers have only *interpreted* the world, in various ways; the point, however, is to *change* it" (p.145).

Marx did not agree with Feuerbach on all aspects of human social life, but he was most definitely influenced significantly by him. From Feuerbach's ideas, Marx was able to use religion as a good example of reification; he agreed that God and Heaven are mere projections based upon human activities; he viewed human history as man-made, not a creation by God; and, therefore, held that we should realize our happiness in this world, for there is no guarantee of an afterlife. Utilizing Feuerbach's materialistic approach, Marx conceived of the world as an often distorted view. He believed that religion was the root cause of this distortion. From this line of thinking Marx would develop the concept of *false consciousness*.

Friedrich Engels

The most important and influential person in Karl Marx's life was, by far, Friedrich Engels (1820–1895). Engels was born on November 28, 1820, in Barmen, in the Rhine Province of the kingdom of Prussia. His father was a successful manufacturer. In 1838 Engels, without having completed his high school studies, was sent to Bremen for business training. Engels worked as an unsalaried clerk in an export business. Commercial affairs did not prevent him from pursuing his scientific and political education. He had come to hate autocracy and the tyranny of bureaucrats while still at high school. The study of philosophy, especially that of Hegel, led him to further despise the autocracy. Although Hegel himself was an admirer of the autocratic Prussian state, his teachings were revolutionary, and Engels, like Marx, would initially find himself an admirer of Hegelian philosophy.

During 1841–1842, Engels served in the Household Artillery of the Prussian Army, attended lectures at the University of Berlin, and joined the circle of Young Hegelian radicals, "The Free." He wrote articles for *Rheinische Zeitung*. In November of 1842, Engels and Marx meet for the first time in the office of *Rheinische Zeitung* in Cologne (Marx and Engels, 1978). Engels had stopped there while on his way to join his father's business in Manchester, England. Engels would stay in Manchester, to complete his business training in the firm of Ermen and Engels, until 1844. While in Manchester, Engels studied English life and literature, read political economists, joined the Chartist movement, published in the Owenite paper *The New Moral World*, and wrote *Outlines of a Critique of Political Economy*. Engels was gathering materials for a social history of England and on the condition of the English working class. Residing in the center of English industry, Engels made himself familiar with the proletariat by wandering about the slums in which the workers were cooped up, and saw their poverty and misery with his own eyes.

Even though Engels was not the first to describe the sufferings of the proletariat and of the necessity of helping it, he *was* the first to say that the proletariat would rise in revolution to help save itself. He believed that the working class would inevitably realize that its only salvation lies in socialism. Additionally, socialism would only become a force when it becomes the aim of the political struggle of the working class. These are some of the main ideas of Engels' book *Condition of the Working Class in England* (1845). This book was written in an absorbing style and filled with the most authentic and shocking pictures of the misery of the English proletariat. The book was a terrible indictment of capitalism and the bourgeoisie and created a profound impression; never before or since had there appeared so striking and truthful a picture of the misery of the working class (Lenin, 1896).

During this same time, Engels was sending Marx articles for publication in *Deutsch-Französische Jahrbücher*. A double issue of *Jahrbücher* was published (1844) in Paris under the editorship of Marx and Arnold Ruge. Ruge was a radical left-Hegelian writer. Returning from Manchester to Germany, in August of 1844, Engels visited Paris for a second meeting with Marx. This would mark the commencement of their many future collaborations. Their first collaborated work, *The Holy Family*, was published in 1845. The "Holy Family" is a facetious nickname for the Bauer brothers, the philosophers, and their followers. The Bauers looked down on the proletariat as an uncritical mass. Marx and Engels vigorously opposed this absurd and harmful tendency. In the name of the worker, who was trampled down by the ruling classes and the state, Marx and Engels demanded a better order of society. They, of course, regarded the proletariat as the force that is capable of waging this struggle. Even before *The Holy Family*, Engels had published in Marx's and Ruge's *Deutsch-Französische Jahrbücher* his "Critical Essays on Political Economy," in which he examined the principal phenomena of the contemporary economic order from a socialist standpoint, regarding them as necessary consequences of the rule of private property. Contact with Engels was undoubtedly a factor in Marx's decision to study political economy (Lenin, 1896).

In April 1845, Engels joined Marx in Brussels. During the summer of that year, Marx visited Manchester with Engels, returning to Brussels in late August. Here Marx and Engels established contact with the secret German Communist League, which commissioned them to expound the main principles of the socialism they had worked out. Thus arose the famous *Manifesto of the Communist Party*, published in 1848.

The revolution of 1848, which broke out first in France and then spread to other West-European countries, brought Marx and Engels back to their native country. The two friends were the heart and soul of revolutionary-democratic aspiration in Rhenish Prussia. They fought for the freedom and in the interests of the people. Marx was exiled and lost his Prussian citizenship. Engels took part in the uprising in South Germany as an aide-de-camp in Willich's volunteer corps in the unsuccessful Baden rising (Marx and Engels, 1978). After three battles, the rebels were defeated, and Engels fled, via Switzerland, to England. Marx had settled in London.

Engels soon became a clerk again, and then a shareholder, in the Manchester commercial firm in which he had worked in the 1840s. He lived in Manchester until 1870, while Marx lived in London, but this did not prevent their maintaining a most lively interchange of ideas, as they corresponded almost daily. In 1870, Engels moved to London, and their strenuous intellectual life continued until 1883, when Marx died. On August 5, 1895, Engels died in London.

Through Engels, Marx was introduced to the concrete conditions and the misery of the working class. Marx and Engels were the first to show that the working class and their struggles were a result of the ruling class's attempts to oppress the proletariat. They believed that all recorded history hitherto had been a history of class struggle, of the succession of the rule and victory of certain social classes over others. This would continue until the foundations of class struggle and of class domination—private property and anarchic social production—disappear. The interests of the proletariat demand the destruction of these foundations, and therefore the conscious class struggle of the organized workers must be directed against them. Further, every class struggle is a political struggle. Marx and Engels attempted to organize the working class in revolution, for their own good, so that they could attain economic and political freedom, thus allowing for each individual an opportunity to reach his or her full human potential.

Concepts and Contributions

As one of the most influential social thinkers of all time, Marx's contributions are immense. Entire books written on Marx's contributions often fall short of grasping the true impact of Marxist thought. Consequently, a modest effort to touch upon some of the major concepts and thoughts of Marx are presented here.

Human Potential

Marx was a humanist who was deeply hurt by the suffering and exploitation that he witnessed among the working class under capitalism. Marx believed that capitalism was a necessary evil stage toward communism. Capitalism was necessary because it increased the capacity for surplus food and shelter; and the technological advancements helped to free many humans from hard labor. The nature of societies prior to capitalism had been too repressive to allow the masses to realize their potential. Still, Marx saw capitalism as too oppressive an environment to allow most people to develop their human potential. It was Marx's belief that communism would provide the type of environment wherein people could begin to express that potential fully. Marx believed that the communists would lead the proletariat to victory over the bourgeoisie and to the formation of a society free from class antagonisms, in which the free development of each is the condition for the free development of all (Acton, 1967).

The basis of much of Marx's thinking rests with his ideas on the potential of human beings, or what he called species-being (Ritzer, 2000a). Marx was concerned with the powers and needs of people. Powers refer to the faculties, abilities, and capacities of humans, not just as they are now, or as they were in the past, but what they could be in the future under different circumstances (Ollman, 1976). Needs are the desires people have for things that are not immediately available to them in their social setting (Heller, 1976). The use of the concept "species-being" allowed Marx to distinguish between animals and humans. Marx believed that *natural* needs and powers are those that people share with other animals, whereas *species* needs and powers are those that are uniquely human. The primary distinction between animals and humans is the fact that people possess a sense of consciousness. For example, while animals just "do" things, people can set themselves off mentally from whatever they are doing. Humans can choose to act or not to act, they control their own course of action. Though Marx thought that human beings take meaningful action, he also recognized that external, societal forces shape the way in which we act. Thus, as Marx indicated in *The Eighteenth Brumaire of Louis Bonaparte* (1852), human beings make their own history, but not in circumstances of their own choosing.

The German Ideology

Marx and Engels declared *The German Ideology* (1845–1846) to have been written to settle accounts with their former philosophical views (McLellan, 1990; Marx and Engels, 1978). Most of this very bulky work consisted of satirically written, rather arid polemics. It is no coincidence that the largest sections are devoted to Feuerbach and Max Stirner, The Holy Family, and the Young Hegelians. There was also a section that critiqued the followers of Feuerbach who wanted to start a socialism based on the ethical ideal. Marx and Engels were upset over the Young Hegelians' claim that they had repaired, merely by their writings, several centuries of historical troubles. Because of the nature of these exaggerated claims for intellectual work, Marx was to call them "heroes of the mind," for all their activities had taken place in the realm of pure thought (Hadden, 1997). As far as Marx was concerned, the Young Hegelians were simply fighting mere phrases with more phrases. The relationship between consciousness or thought and the reality which the thought or consciousness is about had not been addressed. What, for example, was the relation between German reality and Young Hegelian thought (Hadden, 1997)? In *The German Ideology*, Marx and Engels were wrestling with the relationship between class structure and ideas. They were writing at a time when many historians and philosophers—especially German ones, hence the book title—were convinced that ideas are the major force for social change (Garner, 2000).

The German Ideology represents one of Marx's (and Engels') major achievements. Cutting through the cloudy metaphysics of the Young Hegelians, it sets out the materialistic conception of history with a force and detail that Marx never afterward surpassed. In spite of strenuous efforts, Marx and Engels did not succeed in finding a publisher for their manuscript and left it "to the gnawing of the mice," until it was first published in 1932 (McLellan, 1990).

Historical Materialism

The general conception of historical materialism is established in *The German Ideology*. Marx wanted to achieve a reconciliation of materialism and idealism; to combine the critical and scientific aspects of materialism with the dynamic and historical components of idealism. In opposition to monistic and dualistic theories, Marx sought a dialectical theory which he first called "Naturalism" or "Humanism" and later specified as "Historical Materialism" (Giddens, 1971). In Marx's dialectical approach, mind and matter, spirit and nature, constitute the unified structure of reality. Thus, Marx was attempting to combine material and ideal factors or structural and cultural factors, and to illustrate a reciprocal relationship. Marx's dialectical position regarding the unity between thought and being, structural and cultural factors was connected to a normative model of the individual and society, and the developing harmony between members of society.

Marx was rejecting both the notion of simple nonbelief and Hegel's view of reality, while accepting the materialist view of Fererbach and combining it with Hegel's dynamic and dialectical process (Adams and Sydie, 2001). The result of this process is *historical materialism*: the procss of change in the real world of material, physical reality. Marx explained that freedom and slavery are not just ideas, they exist in the real world; in contrast, religions that hamper the human condition are useless, even "opiates" used to dull the senses of society's citizens.

Marx maintained that bourgeois society was but one phase of historical development, but it was a critical stage, for it creates the universal conditions for the realization of the harmonious development with the individual among other individuals, nature, and the community. It was in the *1844 Manuscripts* that Marx wrote about his desire for the unity of material and ideal factors.

The Historic Process

The importance that Marx places on using an historic perspective reflects his evolutionary ideas of human society. Whereas Comte

and Hegel based their evolutionary theories on *ideas*, Marx's evolutionary theory was based on man's need for *material* satisfaction. Marx's focus on social change lies with his insistence that men make their own history. Human history is the process through which mankind changes itself, even to the point where they pit themselves against nature and attempt to dominate it. During the course of history mankind has increasingly transformed nature to make it better serve its own purposes. By changing nature, men change themselves. Whereas animals can only passively adjust to nature, man has created, among other things, tools that allow him to become actively involved with nature. Mankind distinguishes itself from animals as soon as it consciously realizes that it can *produce* its own means of subsistence, rather than being dependent on what nature provides.

Marx explained that ancient society resulted from the union of several tribes into small towns and cities. They were able to produce little more than what they needed to survive; consequently there was little class distinction. Through the period leading to the Middle Ages, the process of feudalism allowed an elite few to enjoy the benefits of the labor of peasants. By the early period of the sixteenth century, there existed in England the beginnings of a new economic order highlighted by the rapid and vast expansion of overseas commerce. This allowed a slightly larger number of people to enjoy a high level of economic success, while most people struggled to get by. Marx believed that this led to two broad stages of productive organization that would signal the beginning of the capitalist period. The first stage was dominated by manufacture and the second stage was the ushering in of the Industrial Revolution.

The cornerstone of the historic process, then, is the production of material life. This is especially true in the quest for sufficiently securing the basic needs of food, clothing, and shelter. Once the primary needs have been satisfied, humans seek new *needs*, or secondary needs. This is also the first sign of a division of labor, because some people reach the secondary level before others. Class struggle becomes the next inevitable stage in the historic process. Class distinctions are influenced heavily by the possession of personal property, which is determined simply by family lineage. These property relations give rise to different social classes. Different locations in the class system lead to different class interests. The poor pursue primary needs satisfaction, while the wealthier classes pursue secondary needs (e.g., self-esteem, self-actualization, the arts, leisure). People are aware of their position within the class structure and this, according to Marx, leads to class consciousness.

Class Consciousness and False Consciousness

Marx believed that people differ from animals in their possession of consciousness as well as their ability to link this consciousness to their activities. Marx recognized that all of human history is one of class struggles. Antagonism exists between the exploiter and the exploited, the buyers and sellers, and so on. Class consciousness is illustrated by one's relative position to the means of production and access to scarce resources. Class consciousness is the sense of a common identification among members of a given class. False consciousness refers to the inability to clearly see where one's own best interests lie. Marx believed that once the exploited (workers/proletariat) become conscious of their plight and misery, they would unite in revolution. Communism was to be the economic and philosophical force that would eliminate class struggle.

When discussing the related terms of class consciousness and false consciousness, Marx was not talking about individual levels

of consciousness, but rather the consciousness of the class as a whole. Additionally, the concepts of class and false consciousness are not static; instead, they are dynamic idea systems that make sense only in terms of social change and development.

Religion

Marx viewed religion as an example of false consciousness. Agreeing with Feuerbach, who had claimed "Man makes religion; religion does not make man," Marx viewed religion as another abstract creation that had become reified throughout time. Aside from economic issues, Marx believed that religion was one of the biggest factors hindering man's attempt to reach his full human potential. Marx believed that earthly misery was not lessened through prayer or hopes of a possible "eternal salvation" after death. He challenged people to consider a possible reality that there is no life after death, and therefore one should strive for one's full potential while alive on Earth. Marx believed that the power elites encouraged the weak-minded masses to embrace afterlife consideration because the support of the status quo kept them in power. In fact, Marx went so far as to suggest that "Religion is the opiate of the masses" (McLellan, 1987; Hadden, 1997). An opiate is a drug used to dull the senses; if one is not thinking clearly, one is likely to believe most anything. Religion exists only because individuals will its existence (Carlebach, 1978).

Marx was against religion for three reasons. First, he believed that religion was a distraction for man from his essence. Second, he felt that while man was in this distracted state he allowed himself to become shamefully exploited and controlled. Third, because man is being distracted, exploited, and controlled, he loses sight of his human essence. In other words, a religious person is no longer in control of his own destiny (Carlebach, 1978). Marx referred to religion as a form of slavery; it was not healthy, it was explicitly evil, or at least, harmful to society. Further, Marx felt religion was responsible for secular deficiencies, and that religions contain forms of prejudice (McLellan, 1987). Marx believed that religion is based upon the imagination of man. Over time, man's imagination has elaborated to form stories which have become historic events passed on from one generation to the next. He believed that there is no higher form than man.

Marx's family, it will be remembered, had converted to Christianity for practical reasons. The Jews, and even those who had converted, were victimized by discrimination and prejudice. Many of Marx's Jewish contemporaries, including those who had attained intellectual eminence, were still considered socially inferior. Marx was among those who employed an expression of Jewish self-hatred. Marx's lifelong attempt to dissociate himself from his Jewish heritage led him to be highly critical of Jews. In his *On the Jewish Question* (1843), Marx wrote of the Jew as the usurer and the moneychanger; the Children of Israel forever danced before the Golden Calf. In his later career, Marx was subjected to anti-Semitic abuse and it is evident that even before that time he suffered tremendously from his marginal status as a Jew and never came to terms with it (Coser, 1977). Marx was close to his father, but he was always embarrassed by the way his father constantly exhibited attributes that he associated with a specifically Jewish defect: weakness and submissiveness (Coser, 1977).

In 1843, Bruno Bauer wrote *The Jewish Question*. He criticized the Jews for requesting civic and political emancipation, saying that no German was emancipated, so why should the Jew be? Bauer would continue his tirade throughout the essay. He also addressed the issue of why Jews and Christians could not get along with each other. Bauer concluded that religious opposition is im-

possible to overcome. Therefore, the only solution was to abolish religion. When religion was no longer a barrier between people, human harmony and cooperation would occur. In Marx's response *On the Jewish Question*, he agreed with Bauer, that peace was impossible between major religious groups. Marx believed that Christians, Jews, and all others, must abandon religion in order to become free.

Class Theory

Uniting members of different religions would prove to be as difficult a challenge as uniting the working class. Marx frequently uses the term *class* in his writings, but he does not have a systematic treatment on its usage (So, 1990). Various meanings of the term appear in his works, but it does seem clear, at the minimum, that he viewed social classes as structures that are external to, and coercive of, people (Ritzer, 2000a). Ollman (1976) interprets Marx's usage of social classes as reified social relations or relations between men that have taken on an independent existence. Dahrendorf (1959) describes Marx's social classes as interest groupings, emerging from certain structural conditions, which affect structural changes. Marx regarded the theory of class as so important that he postponed its systematic exposition time and time again in favor of refinements by empirical analysis.

The relations to production are the result of the distribution of property. The possession of property becomes the critical issue of industrial production, which in turn, constitutes the ultimate determination of the formation of classes and the inevitable development of class conflicts. Marx's thesis that political conditions are determined by industrial conditions seems to stem from the generalized assertion of an absolute and universal primacy of production over all other structures of economy and society. Inherent in capitalistic society, there is a tendency for the classes to polarize. As the classes polarize, their class situations become increasingly extreme. At the same time, the two classes become more and more homogeneous internally. Once history has carried these tendencies of development to their extremes, the point is reached at which the fabric of the existing social structure breaks and a revolution terminates it (in this case, capitalist society). Marx's image of capitalist society, then, is the image of a society undergoing a process of radical change.

The existence of classes is bound only to the particular, historical phase of development of that society. Social classes, understood as conflicting groups arising out of the authority structure of imperatively coordinated associations, are in conflict with one another. The class struggle necessitates the dictatorship or control of the proletariat. Because conflict is variable, the intensity of authority and control over the workers, by the ruling class, is also variable. Marx believed that this dictatorship, or control, itself only constitutes the transition and eventual abolition of all classes through communism.

Grundrisse

The *Grundrisse* is a very long manuscript, comprising seven notebooks, written by Marx in 1857–1858, which remained unpublished until 1941, and even then it was virtually inaccessible until 1955. It was first published by the Institute of Marx–Engels–Lenin in Moscow as *Foundations* (Grundrisse*) of the Critique of Political Economy*. It was a hastily written, preparatory effort by Marx to put together the results of his economic studies. What grew from this work was his *Capital*, and because of the very rawness of much of the text, it enhances its value as a revelation of Marx's creative mental process (Nicolaus, 1973). The *Grundrisse* is of wider scope than

any later writings and takes up themes from the earlier works, in particular the *1844 Manuscripts*. The ideas of alienation, man as a social being, the dialectical categories of Hegel, and the communist man as the aim of history, reappear here, though mediated through a much more profound study of history and economics than was available to Marx in 1844.

The Critique of Political Economy, intended as a write-up of the first section of the *Grundrisse*, is of little intrinsic interest, as its ideas are largely taken up again in the first two chapters of *Capital*. However, the preface is interesting on two counts. First, it begins with a short intellectual autobiography and second, it contains a summary statement of the materialistic conception of history which has become—often too exclusively—the classical limited focus when reviewing *Capital*. Indeed, the scope of *Capital* was so broad, it concluded with a discussion of the timeless character of great art (Marx and Engels, 1978).

Marx had said that every child knows that a social-economic structure that does not reproduce the conditions of production at the same time it is in production, is doomed to fail (Althusser, 1971). The process of production sets to work the existing productive forces in and under definite relations of production. It follows that, in order to exist, every social formation must reproduce the conditions of its production at the same time it produces. In order to produce it must, therefore, reproduce the productive forces and the existing relations of production. The reproduction of labor power thus reveals as its "sine qua non" not only the reproduction of its skills, but also the reproduction of its subjection to the ruling ideology or of the practice of that ideology.

In brief, the ruling class must keep the workers subjected to their authority, but they are also dependent upon the labor of the workers. Reproduction of labor occurs through wages paid to the workers. As far as Marx was concerned, the social structure is the result of the mode of production (the economic base). The prevailing ideology of a society is directly tied to its form, or structure, of economic production. The state represses the plurality of ideologies in order to maintain its own economic structure. This is why Marx is often referred to as an economic determinist.

Alienation

As noted earlier, Marx demonstrated how the history of man included an increasing positive ability to control the forces of nature. Simultaneously, history revealed that man was becoming increasingly alienated. *Alienation*, according to Marx, was a condition in which humans become dominated by the forces of their own creation, which confront them as alien powers (Coser, 1977; Cooper 1991). They are distortions of human nature that cause one to feel alien and mechanical in the process of labor. The capitalist society, by the very nature of its structure, was responsible for four general types of alienation on the worker, all of which can be found in the domain of work.

First, workers are alienated from the object(s) they produce. The product of their labor does not belong to them, it belongs to the capitalists to do with as they please. This implies that they sell it for a profit. Furthermore, the workers often lack detailed knowledge of aspects of the production process in which they are personally involved. The object produced by labor becomes alien to the worker. The worker does not receive the product, but instead a wage.

Second, workers in the capitalist system are alienated from the process of production. They are not actively involved in the productive activity, that is, they are not working for themselves in order to satisfy their own needs; instead, they are working for the capitalist. This becomes an alienating force because it is not satisfying for the worker, and he often becomes bored from the monotonous, tedious activity.

Because the worker feels alienated from the productive activity and the object being produced, it is no surprise that he also becomes alienated from himself. Through the process of specialization, the worker is not allowed to fully develop his skills. This underscores one of Marx's primary concerns; namely, that the worker cannot reach his full human potential if he is alienated from self. The result is a mass of alienated workers, because individuals are not allowed to express themselves fully. Consequently, the worker feels more like himself only during times of leisure, when he is allowed the opportunity to express himself as he pleases.

Finally, the worker is alienated from his fellow workers, the human community, i.e., from his species-being. Marx's assumption was that man basically wants and needs to work with others cooperatively in order to appropriate from nature what they require to survive. In capitalism this cooperation is disrupted, and in fact, the worker may find himself isolated, or worse, in a position where he must compete with fellow workers. This isolation and competition tend to make workers in capitalism feel alienated from their fellow workers.

In short, Marx believed that capitalism alienated man from reaching his full human potential and the community of his fellows. Communism would be a system that reestablishes the inter-connectedness that had been destroyed by capitalism. One of Marx's most brilliant examples of the perversion of humanity by capitalism is found in his discussion of money. From his *Early Writings*, Marx describes money as the alienated essence of man's work and existence; the essence dominates him and he worships it. In the *Economic and Philosophic Manuscripts of 1844*, Marx states that money is the pimp for man's needs. Money becomes the object of desire and alienates man from his true essence. Marx, in his *Essay on Money*, states that money leads to the distortion of society and that money equals power.

Commodities and the Production of Surplus Value

Marx's conception of *commodity* is rooted in his materialist orientation, with its focus on the productive activities of actors. People produce objects they need to survive. A commodity is an object that satisfies some want or need. If we have a particular need, we attempt to acquire an object that is capable of satisfying that need. For example, if one is hungry, one must find food. Objects that are produced for use by oneself have *use* value. Objects are products of human labor and cannot achieve independent existence, because they are controlled by the actors. However, under capitalism, actors produce objects for someone else (the capitalist). These products take on an *exchange* value.

Marx distinguishes between *use value* and *exchange value* when describing the role of production found under capitalism. Products produced by the capitalist, such as yarn or boots, have a use value in that they are useful commodities for people. In *Capital, Volume One*, Marx acknowledges that the capitalist is a "progressit," and yet he does not manufacture boots for their own sake (the need for boots) but rather, because books possess an exchange value. Marx states, "Our capitalist has two objects in view: in the first place, he wants to produce a use-value that has a value in exchange, that is to say, an article destined to be sold, a commodity; and secondly, he desires to produce a commodity whose value shall be greater than the sum of the values of the commodities used in its production, that is, of the means of production and the labour-power, that he purchased with his good

money in the open market" (Tucker, 1978:351). In short, Marx is against someone making a profit based on the labor of others. He begrudges the cunning mind of the capitalist the opportunity to profit because of his organizational skills.

Fetishism of Commodities

The *fetishism of commodities* involves the process by which actors fail to recognize that it is their labor that gives commodities their value (Dant, 1996). Actors tend to believe that value arises from natural properties of things; the exchange value of one commodity is expressed in terms of its use value. Thus, the "market" takes on a function in the eyes of actors that only actors should perform. It appears natural, and this is due to the historic development of capitalism. Marx borrowed the term *fetishism* from the early French anthropologist Charles de Brosses. De Brosses used "fetishism" to describe certain features of animistic religions, where some cultures created attributions of demons or spirits and then found themselves controlled by their very own mental products.

Capital

The most general economic structural element in Marx's work is *capital*. Capital involves the social relationship between buyers and sellers of labor power. Marx believed that the workers were exploited by a system that they had forgotten they produced through their labor, and therefore, have the capacity to change. Actors tend to reify capital by treating it as a natural phenomenon. In *The Economic and Philosophic Manuscripts of 1844*, Marx states, "Capital itself does not merely amount to theft or fraud, it requires still the cooperation of legislation to sanctify inheritance" (Marx, 1844:136). Capital becomes a governing power over labor and its products. The capitalist possesses this power, not on account of his personal or human qualities, but inasmuch as he is an owner of capital (Marx, 1964).

Capital, Volume One published in 1867, is the book generally referred to simply as *Capital* and consists of two distinct parts. The first nine chapters contain very abstract discussions of such central concepts as value, labor, and surplus value. It is not only this abstraction that makes them difficult to understand; it is also the Hegelian mode of expression and the fact that, while the concepts used by Marx were familiar to mid-eighteenth–century economists, they were abandoned by later scholars. Modern economists have tended to discuss the functioning of the capitalist system as given and concentrate particularly on prices, whereas Marx wished to examine the mode of production that gave rise to the capitalist system and that would, he believed, bring about its own destruction.

Following the first nine chapters, there is a masterly account of the genesis of capitalism which makes pioneering use of the statistical material just then becoming increasingly available. It is one of the best illustrations of applied historical materialism (McLellan, 1990). *Capital, Volume Two* is rather technical, and discusses the circulation of capital and the genesis of economic crises. *Volume Three* begins with a discussion of value and prices and the tendency of profits to fall, but trails off toward the end with the dramatically incomplete section on classes.

In short, Marx believed that the sum total of the relations of production (raw materials, labor, and the technology used for production) and those who control the means of production (the capitalist) constitute the whole cultural *superstructure* of society. Consequently, those who control the means of production and private property are in the position to impose their will onto those do not.

Private Property

Private property is derived from the labor of workers and is reified under capitalism. Marx generally meant by private property the private ownership of the means of production by the capitalist. Thus, it is a product and is external to the worker. It is the product of alienated labor. In order for people to realize their human potential they must overthrow the validity of private property. The overcoming of alienation, Marx declared, hinges upon the suppression of private property, and what is demanded is a reorganization of society, based upon the eradication of the contemporary relationship between private property and wage labor (Giddens, 1971). Marx believed that the means of production should be shared equally through public ownership.

Division of Labor

In *The German Ideology*, Marx and Engels traced the origins of the modern division of labor to the early family, describing the wife and children as the slaves of the husband. The capitalistic system forced the worker to specialize, which was not only dehumanizing, but also alienating. This alienating process, which stunts individuals from reaching their full human potential, was accelerated by the division of labor.

Through capitalism, the existence of a surplus was created. Those who controlled the means of production also controlled the surplus. The existence of a surplus made it possible for classes to develop. Heilbroner (1970) explains that with the appearance of surplus comes as well the appearance of a class division within society. The material surplus is accompanied by an unequal appropriation of this surplus among the members of the community, which, in turn, creates a struggle between the bourgeois and the proletariat. Social classes were directly linked to the division of labor. Through communism, Marx believed that structural barriers such as the division of labor would be eliminated. Not that Marx ever believed that under communism all people could become, for example, doctors, artists, or lawyers, but rather the artificial barriers preventing people from developing to their fullest would be eliminated.

Communism

Marx is perhaps best known for his ideas on *communism*. Throughout the discussion on Marx's concepts and contributions, reference to communism has been commonplace. It has provided a glimpse into the applied aspect of Marx's use of communism. Marx wanted all humans to reach their full human potential. He hoped to eliminate alienation, the division of labor, private property, and other obstacles that he believed hindered this goal. Marx believed that capitalism was a major barrier, and therefore, he hoped to overthrow it. Marx devoted a great deal of his life to understanding capitalism through scientific study, and to ending capitalism through revolution (Pampel, 2000).

Philosophically, Marx's primary ideas of communism were described in *The Communist Manifesto*, a book co-written with Engels. *The Communist Manifesto* has four sections. The first section provides a history of society indicating that throughout time all societies suffered from class conflict; which in the long run had always ended either with the destruction of the society, or with the emergence of the subordinate class as victors. With a new dominant class comes a new mode of production and a new social order. The bourgeoisie emerged from feudal society in western Europe and with it came a growth in colonization, manufacturing, new technologies of production and transportation, and the growth of global markets. The second section describes the position of communists within the proletariat class; rejects bourgeois objections to communism; characterizes the communist revolution and the measures to be taken by the victorious proletariat; and the nature of the future communist society. The third section contains an extended criticism of other types of socialism—reactionary, bourgeois, and utopian. The final section provides a short description of communist tactics toward other opposition parties and finishes with an appeal for proletarian unity.

Marx and Engels believed that the capitalist class would be overthrown and that it would be eliminated by a worldwide working-class revolution and replaced by a classless society. The *Manifesto* influenced all subsequent communist literature and revolutionary thought in general. Marx and Engels truly believed that the world would be a better place with communism. They believed that class inequality would end with the collective control of property and with the size and growth in power of the working class. Under Marxist communism, government was deemed unnecessary. Consequently, the governmental abuse of workers would end with the dismantling of government (Pampel, 2000).

Relevancy

Karl Marx was many things: he was a poet; philosopher; socialist theoretician; economist; historian; and a major contributor to sociological thought. He was a brilliant thinker, whose ideas have been subjected to many diverse interpretations, and in some cases, outright misinterpretations. Add to this, his thought is opposed by many who have not read much, if any, of his works. Marxist thought is without question the most fraught with controversy and opposing interpretations (Hadden, 1997).

On March 17, 1883, Marx was buried at Highgate Cemetery in London. Perhaps the best summary of Marx's immense and profound works and contributions can be found in Engels' speech at his friend's funeral:

> An immeasurable loss has been sustained both by the militant proletariat of Europe and America, and by historical science, in the death of this man. The gap that has been left by the departure of this mighty spirit will soon make itself felt. Just as Darwin discovered the law of development of organic nature, so Marx discovered the law of development of human history: the simple fact, hitherto concealed by an overgrowth of ideology, that mankind must first of all eat, drink, have shelter and clothing, before it can pursue politics, science, art, religion, etc.; that therefore the production of the immediate material means of subsistence and consequently the degree of economic development attained by a given people or during a given epoch from the foundation upon which the state institutions, the legal conceptions, art, and even its ideas on religion, of the people concerned have evolved, and in the light of which they must, therefore, instead of *vice versa*, as had hitherto been the case (Engels, 1883).

Engels described Marx as a revolutionist who wanted to overthrow capitalist society and the state institutions which it had brought into being, and to contribute to the liberation of the modern proletariat. Marx fought with a passion and a tenacity for the rights of workers. Although it is true that only a few people attended Marx's funeral, telegrams from throughout the world, including such groups as the French Workers' Party, the Russian Socialists, and the Spanish Workers' Party, were received expressing their condolences.

There is no question that Marx was a highly influential person during his lifetime, but what relevance does Marx have today? After all, it has become commonplace to refute his ideas of communism, especially as an inevitable outcome following the proletariat's awareness of inequality, and therefore, attaining class consciousness. Furthermore, the concept of communism serving as a guiding force toward some sort of perfect society is naive and utopian.

Marx failed to envision the many changes that would occur in the capitalist system. As he and Engels observed the misery of the working poor throughout western Europe, they failed to realize that they were merely seeing the initial stages of capitalism; where it is common that societies first introduced to industrialization witness many forms of exploitation against the workers. As the capitalist process continues in any given society, changes introduced to the system bring about many potential benefits. For example, governments can create laws to protect the workers from exploitation. Political pressure targeting the government will be far more effective than aiming it toward the capitalist. Workers can form unions and make demands for higher wages, more sick days and so on. The creation of joint-stock ownership helps to eliminate feelings of alienation. Along with the decomposition of both capital and labor a new stratum emerged within, as well as outside, the industry of modern capitalist societies. This development was of course, the middle class. All of these changes led to another unforeseen phenomenon, that of social mobility.

Although it is true that Marx failed in some of his analyses of capitalism, he can hardly be blamed for not properly predicting the future. After all, few are capable of such vision. Despite his lack of complete understanding of the role of capitalism in the future, many contemporary authors continue to use Marxist economic analysis in their own attempts to understand modern capitalism. Evidence of this exists in publications such as *Marxism and the Metropolis* (1984), where contributing authors discuss such topics as capitalist development, urbanization, the tenants' movement, and political conflict.

Marx's analysis of the differences between use value and exchange value are relevant in the criticism of globalization. The capitalist, in his/her continuous attempts to maximize profits, has entered the labor markets of the economically poor nations. Cheap labor and the necessary raw materials are constantly sought out and exploited by the capitalist. This pattern was established by explorers centuries ago.

The new world order of global capitalism is under attack from many protest groups. They appear to be suffering from the same near-sightedness of Marx and Engels. Namely, they are merely witnessing the initial stages of globalization. Through proper cultural assimilation, all societies of the world should be capable of finding a way to benefit from this economic reality. The beginning of the third millennium has included worldwide demonstrations against capitalist entities. The targets include the World Bank and the International Monetary Fund (IMF). Demonstrators accuse global corporations of perpetuating the economic division between the economically poor countries and the rich, powerful ones.

Through much of its history, the World Bank has functioned as the finance division of a global construction company, paying for roads, dams, and power plants. The goal was a better life for the locals. Its level of effectiveness is in dispute between the World Bank and its critics (Burgess, 2000). The IMF has operated as an international auditing firm that oversees lending programs for poor countries. The IMF recently created the Poverty Reduction and Growth Facility (Burgess, 2000). The institution's defenders claim that real changes have been made in an effort to aid poorer countries.

The third millennium began with protests. On May Day 2000, for example, worldwide protests targeted global corpora-

tions. In Portland, Oregon, police officers used clubs to shove protestors whose demonstration was organized by a loose coalition of workers' rights groups (*Buffalo News*, 5/2/2000). Among the damage was a Nike store, which had attracted much attention for its labor policies in its Vietnam factory. In London, protestors clashed with police, tearing down the golden arches of a McDonald's restaurant and spray-painting a hammer and sickle on a statue of Winston Churchill in a May Day protest. Marx would surely be proud of such proletarian demonstrations. However, placing the blame solely on a global corporation is problematic. Why is it that the local governments allow such alleged harmful working conditions to exist? Is Nike the only group that must examine its conscience? Economically poorer countries must examine their own culture and values and determine for themselves whether they really want to be excluded from, and fight against, the capitalist system, instead of simply embracing it, and benefiting from it.

Relevance can be found in almost every other concept discussed by Marx. Reaching one's full human potential has never been a more important goal, especially in American society. There is an entire industry related to assisting individuals reach self-fulfillment goals. There are a number of service and self-help organizations designed to help people feel good about themselves, and thus strive for maximizing their full potential. Parents are told of the importance of enhancing their children's self-esteem. Psychologists have created a number of labels designed to lessen the burden and responsibilities of individuals so that they can feel good about themselves—a kind of "don't blame me, it was someone else's fault" mentality.

On the other hand, there are more positive efforts being made to help one reach their full human potential by feeling good about themselves through voluntarism. At many colleges and universities professors (including this author) implement service learning in their classes. Service learning techniques generally include a number of options for students to volunteer as little as one hour a week at various community centers and agencies (e.g., Habitat for Humanity, the Boys and Girls Clubs, etc.). Service learning is designed to help eliminate social problems and social injustice through activism. Marx would support the efforts of people helping others, especially if it involves the "haves" assisting the "have-nots." Community involvement should benefit the volunteer, those receiving the help, and the community. It could potentially decrease the level of violence and tension found in many communities.

Marx was not optimistic about future society as he believed that conflict was inevitable. It exists at multiple levels. At the class level, because of the growth and complexity of modern societies, conflict has become institutionalized. Conflict exists between social classes, races, ethnicities, and competing religions. Marx has been proven correct that religion continues to serve as a barrier against peace and accord. The world continues to be ravaged by religious conflicts and war. For example, there most certainly will never be peace in the Middle East unless Jews and Muslims abandon religion. Marx would argue that this idea needs to be extended to other religions if mankind has any hope for a lasting cooperation.

George Will (2000) reviews Marx's idea that classes inevitably conflict, and are defined by their means of production. Will then states that, "the bohemian and the bourgeois classes have melded, producing Bobos—the bohemian bourgeoisie, defined by consumption. In an America swimming in discretionary income, consumption is an assertion of Bobo cultural values." According to Will, Bobos are households whose incomes exceed $100,000, and there are 9 million of them in America.

Humans often fail to reach a level of class consciousness. In any society, oppressed and dominated groups will form. The oppressed group, wanting equality, envisions a better life, but rarely knows how to go about attaining it rationally. In *The Utopian Mentality*, Mannheim (1968) describes such oppressed groups as possessing a "collective unconscious," that is, behavior guided by wishful representation and the will to action. The collective want change, but they are disorganized, and therefore go about trying to change things irrationally—they rely too much on unconscious action. Not that the action itself is unconscious, but the collectiveness of rational action toward specific goals is missing. The Los Angeles riots of 1992 are a perfect example of such behavior. African American citizens of Los Angeles had complained for years about poor treatment from the police and a lack of justice in the courts. The acquittal of four LAPD officers of the beating of Rodney King was the spark that flamed the Los Angeles riot. Unfortunately, there were no clear goals spelled out, and behavior was chaotic and damaging to all, producing few results that would benefit the Black community (Delaney, 1993).

Marx's term of false consciousness applies today as well. For example, in an attempt to reach economic freedom and the material goods that accompany it, some people purchase lottery tickets, a type of gambling. The odds of winning a big payoff are very slim, and yet African Americans and Hispanics are the most likely to participate in it (Stashenko, 2000). These are two groups that are disproportionately found in the lower economic classes, and therefore have less disposable income. Pursuing the lottery is not the best course of action for economic riches.

Many people still suffer from forms of alienation, and have indeed pursued leisure pursuits as a means to attain a level of identification and form a sense of community (Delaney, 2001). Humans have a need for community and they seek it from many diverse sources. Marx would most likely be happy with the Internet, for it is the consumer—the proletariat—that is using the Net to gain control (Maney, 1999). The Internet has become a powerful force in providing information to the oppressed of the world. For some, it lessens feelings of alienation.

It is safe to say that Karl Marx will continue to command a great deal of attention from social thinkers whenever they attempt to chronicle the giants of social thought. "Karl Marx was and remains the greatest general thinker in the history of socialism and its most powerful ideologist" (Eddy, 1979:1). In a poll conducted by the British Broadcasting Corporation, Karl Marx was voted as the greatest thinker of the second millennium, ranking above, in order of finish, Albert Einstein, Isaac Newton, and Charles Darwin (*Syracuse Post-Standard*, 11/24/99).

5

Emile Durkheim
(1858–1917)

Emile David Durkheim is one of the most influential figures in French sociology and is acknowledged as the founder of modern sociology (Garner, 2000). Durkheim did more than anyone else to establish sociology as an academic discipline (Hadden, 1997). Compared to Karl Marx, he had little influence on world politics and social movements. But Durkheim, more than any other theorist, defined sociology as a separate discipline with its own goals, methods, and objects of study (Pampel, 2000). "No one, not even Weber, has so eloquently set forth for us the essentials of the scientific method as it bears upon social phenomena. No one else has seen so clearly the legitimate boundaries of sociology among the sciences" (Nisbet, 1974:vii). Durkheim would become the first full professor of sociology. He is described as "a master to whom all students of human nature and of the nature of society owe a great debt; he set an example of the great humanist or, rather, of the genuine sociologist, and left behind him a promise and vision of great achievements to be undertaken by future generations of social scientists" (Roche de Coppens, 1976:46).

Emile Durkheim was born on the evening of April 15, 1858, at Epinal, the capital town of Vosges in the eastern French province of Lorraine, France. His mother, Melanie, came from a family that was involved in "trade-beer and horses" (merchants) (Mazlish, 1993:196). His father, Moise, was the Rabbi of Epinal since the 1830s and was also Chief Rabbi of the Vosges and Haute-Marne. Raised in a very strict Jewish home, Emile spent part of his early school years in a rabbinical school, studied Hebrew and the Talmud, and seemed destined to follow in the footsteps of his patriarchal lineage of Jewish rabbis (Mazlish, 1993). Emile's grandfather, Israel David Durkheim, had been a Rabbi in Mutzig (Alsace), as had his great-grandfather Simon, appointed in 1784 (Lukes, 1972). His desire to become a rabbi was short-lived, and by the time he reached his teens, he had largely disavowed his heritage (Strenski, 1997). At the age of thirteen, he was influenced by a Catholic school teacher, which eventually led Durkheim to become agnostic. From that point on, Durkheim's lifelong interest in religion was more academic than theological (Mestrovic, 1988).

Durkheim was the youngest of four children. His siblings were Felix, Rosine, and Celine. All the children were raised in the Ashkenazi Jewish faith and tradition characterized by such traits as: scorn for the inclination to conceal effort; disdain for success unachieved by effort; and, horror for everything that is not positively grounded

Emile Durkheim (1858–1917) French sociologist generally acknowledged as the "Founder of Modern Sociology."
Source: CORBIS

(Lukes, 1972). The Jews of eastern France had been emancipated for more than two generations at the time of Durkheim's youth, but they still maintained a cultural identity. Matters that concerned the Jewish community were generally overseen by appointed elders (parnassim) or rabbis. Rabbis and their families were, consequently, assured a certain level of prestige within the community. Economically speaking, the Durkheim household would be considered a middle class family by today's standards. Durkheim's eventual break from his father and the Jewish tradition must have been quite a traumatic event in his life.

When Durkheim was twelve years old, France was defeated in the Franco-Prussian

War. During the time that the Germans occupied France, Durkheim was exposed to a great deal of anti-Semitism. He wrote later in life about those experiences: "Anti-Semitism had already been in the regions of the East at the time of the war of 1870; being myself of Jewish origin, I was then able to observe it at close hand. The Jews were blamed for the defeats" (Lukes, 1972:41).

The level of anti-Semitism experienced by Durkheim led him to abandon his Jewish faith and drove him to higher levels of patriotism toward France and a desire to help reshape its society. The intervening century had been politically uncertain, but after the defeat those who favored a rational, industrial society (in order to compete with Germany) began to carry the day (Hadden, 1997). In his *Professional Ethics and Civil Morals*, Durkheim wrote, "As long as there are states, so there will be national pride, and nothing can be more warranted. But societies can have their pride, not in being the greatest or the wealthiest, but in being the most just, the best organized and in possessing the best moral constitution" (p. 154–155).

Durkheim was a brilliant student who possessed a razor-sharp intellect and excelled at the College d'Epinal, earning a variety of awards and honors. With his driving ambition to continue his education, Durkheim transferred to one of the great French high schools, the Lycée Louis-le-Grand in Paris. Here he prepared himself for the rigors of the prestigious Ecole Normale Superieure, home to many of the intellectual elite of France. The Ecole accepted only the brightest and most intelligent students, and those young men who were accepted into this elite institution were expected to go on and become great influential people. Candidates went through a rigorous selection process. The governing board did not accept Durkheim in his first two attempts. Unfortunately, his father had become very ill and the emotional distress experienced by Durkheim had negatively affected his studies.

Finally, in 1879, he passed the entrance examinations. Academic life at the Ecole was nothing like the college experience that students enjoy today. The school monitored the students' comings and goings; they were under strict curfews that allowed off-campus activities, of any kind, only on Sundays and Thursday afternoons (and only once a month) (Lukes, 1972). The strict instruction generally encouraged bonding and a sense of camaraderie among students. The intense training that existed at the Ecole was something the students remembered for a lifetime. Students rose at 6:30 A.M. (6:00 in the summer), ate a quick breakfast, and proceeded to attend classes and study for the next 11 hours (Pampel, 2000). It was almost like an educational "boot camp."

Durkheim had two close friends while at the Ecole: Henri Bergson and Jean Jaures. It is thought that these two friends influenced Durkheim in his final break from Judaism (Lukes, 1972). Bergson, who was to become the philosopher of vitalism, and Jaures, the future socialist leader, had entered the Ecole the year before Durkheim. Maurice Blondel (a Catholic philosopher who generally demoted/deemphasized, at least in his earlier thinking, the role of rational demonstration as a basis for action) was admitted two years after Durkheim. Pierre Janet, the psychologist, and Goblot, the philosopher, were classmates of Durkheim. The Ecole, which had been created by the First Republic, was now enjoying a renaissance with leading intellectual and political figures of the Third Republic (Coser, 1977).

Once admitted to the prestigious Ecole Normale, a major achievement for anyone, Durkheim became uneasy with the course curriculum. He longed for training in scientific methods and moral principles opposed to the more general academic approach at the Ecole. Durkheim would earn the nickname "the metaphysician" by his peers (Coser, 1977). He rebelled against a course of studies in which the reading of Greek verse and Latin prose were deemed more important than actually learning philosophical doctrines or recent scientific findings. Durkheim viewed his professors as showy and shallow, knowing a little about a lot of subjects, but not knowing a lot about a few specialized subjects. When he pressed them for further details they demonstrated a lack of true in-depth knowledge (Pampel, 2000). His professors were not happy being challenged by a student and generally punished him with low grades. Durkheim did, however, admire a few professors. He became friends with Charles Renouvier and Emile Boutoux, both philosophers. He also became a friend with Numas-Denis Fustel de Coulanges, who was an historian who taught him the use of critical and rigorous method in historical research. Durkheim dedicated his Latin thesis to the memory of Coulanges, and his French thesis, *The Division of Labor*, to Boutroux.

After graduating from the Ecole in 1882, Durkheim decided that he would concentrate on the scientific study of sociology. However, because there was no field of sociology at that time, Durkheim taught philosophy in a number of provincial schools in the Paris area between 1882 and 1887 (Nisbet, 1974). His thirst for science was satisfied during a visit to German universities (1885–86) where he was exposed to the scientific psychology being pioneered by Wilhelm Wundt (Durkheim, 1887). In the years immediately following his visit to Germany, Durkheim began to publish extensively. At age 29, he had been recognized in Germany as a promising figure in the social sciences and in social philosophy. This recognition, along with his recent publications, helped him to gain a position in the department of philosophy at the University of Bordeaux in 1887. Not everyone was pleased by his appointment because he was a social scientist and the Faculty of Letters at Bordeaux was predominately humanist.

At Bordeaux, Durkheim offered the first course in social science in a French university. This was an astounding point in French sociology, for only a decade earlier, a furor had erupted in a French university by the mere mention of Auguste Comte in a student dissertation (Ritzer, 2000a). That student, Alfred Espinas, would become a colleague of Durkheim at Bordeaux. Espinas refused to delete the name of Comte from the introduction of his thesis. Throughout the Bordeaux period, Durkheim emphasized the value of sociology and moral education. Durkheim enjoyed teaching courses in education to schoolteachers. He was trying to encourage educators to emphasize morality in an effort to help reverse the moral degeneration he saw around him in French society (Ritzer, 2000a). He felt education was important because it was an area where sociology could make the greatest impact on society (Gidden, 1978).

Around the time of his academic appointment to Bordeaux, Durkheim married Louise Dreyfus. They had two children, Marie and André, but little is known of his family life. Louise seems to have followed the traditional Jewish family pattern of taking care of the family as well as devoting herself to Emile's work by performing secretarial duties including proofreading. Durkheim's marriage and family life are described as a "happy family existence" (Mazlish, 1993).

In 1893, Durkheim published his French doctoral thesis, *The Division of Labor in Society*, as well as his Latin thesis on Montesquieu. In *The Division of Labor*, Durkheim demonstrates his abiding concern with unity and solidarity, and he defends

modern society as capable, in principle, of rational integration while fostering individual autonomy (Hadden, 1997). Two years later, his major methodical statement, *The Rules of Sociological Method*, was published, and within another two years *Le Suicide* appeared. *Rules* represents the formal presentation of frameworks and procedures already initiated in *The Division of Labor*.

In *Suicide*, Durkheim becomes the first social scientist to actually apply the scientific method to the study of social phenomena. He demonstrates that suicide, an individual, antisocial act, can be understood sociologically. For whatever the "reasons" individuals may have for this act, sociology alone is capable of understanding factors contributing to varying *rates* of such behaviors, factors having to do with faulty regulation of individual tendencies (Hadden, 1997). In addition, Durkheim notes in the preface of *Suicide* that sociology was now "in fashion." These works were major accomplishments that pushed Durkheim to the forefront of the academic world. In 1898, Durkheim became a full professor at Bordeaux. In the same year, Durkheim put aside his work on the history of socialism and put all of his efforts into establishing a single scholarly journal devoted entirely to sociology.

Within two years, he had established *L'Année Sociologique*, the first social science journal in France. *Année* was successful from the beginning, and the continued collaboration between Durkheim and its key contributors helped to form a cohesive "school" of thought eager to defend the Durkheimian approach to sociology. Also in 1898, Durkheim published his famous paper *Individual and Collective Representations*, which served as a kind of manifesto for the Durkheimian School. Durkheim would add a number of other publications to his résumé including the famous *The Elementary Forms of Religious Life* in 1912. In this book, despite his agnostic and scientific mentality, Durkheim held that society could not exist independently of religious forms of sentiment and action (Cuzzort, 1969). He argues that the basis of religiously conceived moral authority and suasion lie, in fact, in an impersonal, anonymous, collective, social, and moral authority. Whereas the religious believer sees this force as divine in origin, Durkheim argues that it represents the complex assertion of collective group forces (Hadden, 1997). These group forces are developed through the socialization process inherent in human society, and modified throughout history.

Emile Durkheim returned to Paris, summoned to the famous French university the Sorbonne in 1902, with a reputation as a powerful force in Sociology and Education. Durkheim was the first to be promoted to full professorship in the social sciences in France. He occupied the chair for six years, and in 1906 was named Professor of the Science of Education. In 1913, the title was changed to Science of Education and Sociology. After more than seventy-five years, Comte's brainchild had finally gained entry at the University of Paris (Coser, 1977).

André Durkheim, Emile's son, who himself was a brilliant linguist, was killed in April 1916, at the Bulgarian front in the war between Germany and Belgium. This was a terrible blow to Durkheim from which he never fully recovered. He suffered a stroke and died a year later on November 15, 1917. He is considered to be one of the most influential men in the development of sociology, and was a celebrated figure in French intellectual circles. It was twenty years later, with the publication of Talcott Parson's *The Structure of Social Action* (1937), that Durkheim's work became a significant influence on American sociology.

By today's standards Durkheim's works are considered relatively conservative. But in his time, he was considered a liberal. He was a "Dreyfusard," meaning a member of the group of generally liberal, anticlerical, humanitarian thinkers of the left (Nisbet, 1974:8). This is best exemplified by the active public role he played in the defense of Alfred Dreyfus, a Jewish captain in the French army, whose court-martial for treason (he was convicted of spying for Germany in 1894) was considered by many to be anti-Semitic. Despite proclaiming his innocence, Dreyfus was sentenced to Devil's Island for life. Devil's Island was the collective name given to three small islands in the Atlantic Ocean, 20 miles off the coast of French Guiana, which once contained leper colonies (Farrington, 2000). Devil's Island served as part of France's penal colonies and for months Dreyfus was the only prisoner held at this facility. Meanwhile, evidence pointed to a conspiracy against Dreyfus by army officials and the right-wing government. Luminaries and a few newspapers were proclaiming his innocence, and Durkheim was among the first to sign a public appeal on Dreyfus' behalf. In 1899, the French government issued a pardon, permitting Dreyfus' return from Devil's Island. He was exonerated following a further inquiry in 1906.

The Dreyfus case divided the entire educated elite of France. Durkheim did not attribute this anti-Semitism to racism among the French people; instead, he saw it as a symptom of moral sickness confronting French society as a whole (Birnbaum and Todd, 1995). Durkheim's interest in the Dreyfus affair stemmed from his deep and lifelong interest in morality.

Intellectual Influences

Durkheim was an ardent reader and a highly cultivated man open to a variety of intellectual ideas. Consequently, it is difficult to establish all the major influences on his thoughts. It is well-established that

Durkheim has roots in the French tradition; especially with the works of Montesquieu, Saint-Simon, Comte, and Rousseau; and both German and British social thought. The significant influence over Durkheim's mature intellectual position came from distinctly French intellectual traditions. The overlapping interpretations, which Saint-Simon and Comte offered of the decline of feudalism and the emergence of the modern form of society, constitute the principal foundation for the whole of Durkheim's writings (Giddens, 1971).

The French Tradition

Many French thinkers influenced Durkheim. Rousseau and his concept of a *volente generale* (general will) influenced Durkheim's idea of "solidarity" (let the people unify). French democracy is characterized by its defense of the intrinsic connection between liberty and equality (Seidman, 1983). Rousseau had insisted that genuine freedom and social progress presuppose social equality and participatory democracy. Of Rousseau's idea of freedom Durkheim (1965) wrote, "Man is only free when a superior force compels his recognition, provided, however, that he accepts this superiority and that his submission is not won by lies and artifice. He is free if he is held in check" (p. 88). Freedom, then, presupposes a social and moral framework of rules and regulations that must be self-imposed or based on consensus. Rousseau saw this moral framework as the general will.

Durkheim (1965) acknowledged that he learned of the distinction between social and psychological phenomena from Rousseau when he wrote that, "Rousseau was keenly aware of the specificity of the social order. He conceived it clearly as an order of facts generically different from purely individual facts. It is a new world superimposed on the purely psychological world" (p. 83). For

Durkheim, a society of solidarity has *body* (an organic effect), but also an *attitude/sentiment* (feeling of belonging). Thus, Durkheim reveals thoughts of functionalism, but also, a social psychological effect.

Durkheim believes that, "Man is himself only in and through society. If man were not a part of society, he would be an animal like the rest" (Aron, 1979:105). Thus, Durkheim believes that man's investment into the creation and maintenance of society is what separates him from the other animals; society is what makes a human human. Durkheim states, "Rousseau demonstrated a long time ago, if we take away from man everything he derives from society, all that remains is a creature reduced to sensation and more or less indistinguishable from the animal" (Aron, 1970:106). Clearly, Rousseau influenced Durkheim in this regard.

Rousseau and Durkheim differed on at least one issue—politics. For Rousseau, politics were "the essence" while Durkheim, "although keenly interested in the political state, saw it as but one of the associative influences on man" (Nisbet, 1974:25).

In his Latin doctoral thesis, Durkheim expressed an indebtedness to Montesquieu for pointing to the interrelatedness of social phenomena and the idea of the connectedness of all social and cultural phenomena. Montesquieu held that all the elements of society form a whole and that if taken separately, without reference to the others, they cannot be understood. All elements of society are related to one another: law and morality, trade, social structure and culture, religion, and so on. Durkheim's holistic, or functional, view of society owes much to Montesquieu.

Studying with his teacher Boutroux, Durkheim came to view sociology as having a distinct method and field. Durkheim found philosophy a very important subject, but only within certain criteria. He believed that in order for philosophy to be valid, it must be applied to either politics or society. Perhaps of greater influence was the philosopher Charles Renouvier, whose brand of rationalism recommended a scientific approach to social cohesion and morality while upholding the notion of the autonomy of the individual (Hadden, 1997). Renouvier's long life, from 1815 to 1903, enabled him to live during the same time as Saint-Simon, Comte, and Durkheim. Renouvier was once a student of Comte, and was greatly influenced by Saint-Simon. During the Revolution of 1848, he was involved in distributing socialist propaganda to the people of France. Later, Renouvier served as editor of *La Critique philosophique*, which enabled him to have tremendous influence over the people of France. Although Durkheim disagreed with Renouvier's rejection of historical laws and their relationship with society, he did agree with Renouvier's beliefs that ethical and moral considerations occupy a central role in philosophical thought; that there is a need for a science of ethics; that philosophy should serve as a guide to social action; that the reconstruction of the Third Republic must include a moral unity; and that the fundamental moral concept of modern society is the dignity of the human process.

French sociologist and social philosopher Gabriel Tarde, considered to be Durkheim's major rival, was another person to influence Durkheim. They had many debates and confrontations that most likely helped to sharpen both their intellect and earn the respect of each other. Tarde was a provincial magistrate, not an academian, but his successful legal career provided adequate financial income and free time to allow him to devote much of his energy to developing a system of social theory (Coser, 1977). Tarde was primarily concerned with crimi-

nology and social theory. Tarde published a number of works with *The Laws of Imitation* (1890) as the most noteworthy. He was interested in how ideas and new innovations spread throughout a society. He believed that new ideas became diffused when members communicated with another. Tarde referred to this process as "imitation." He believed that society was an aggregate of individuals in interaction, and human behavior was imitated by the masses from the actions of social elites/leaders. Durkheim's contrary notion was that society is a reality, and therefore explanations of human behavior must be grounded in structural, rather than in social–psychological, terms.

The French theorist Saint-Simon was another influence on Durkheim, especially Saint-Simon's ideas on socialism. "Unquestionably it was from reading Saint-Simon that Durkheim got his full measure of the effects on French thought generally of the politically conservatives who flourished immediately after the French Revolution" (Nisbet, 1974:25). Durkheim states, "for all of us, all that is essential in socialist doctrine is found in the philosophy of Saint-Simon" (LaCapra, 1972:189). Moreover, Saint-Simon's theories on class conflict in the post-Revolutionary society of France was of the utmost importance in influencing Durkheim's theories on the same subject. Saint-Simon believed that "the new conditions could lead to a hierarchical but *nonetheless organic* order of social peace and stability. Intergration was to be achieved primarily by instituting the appropriate moral ideas" (Zeitlin, 1968:236). This theory helped Durkheim formulate his system with regard to the division of labor. It appears evident that it was Saint-Simon and not Comte whom Durkheim regarded as his intellectual master (Zeitlin, 1968:236).

Durkheim accepted Comte and Saint-Simon's concept of positivism. Durkheim credits Saint-Simon with being a more consistent formulator of positivism than Comte. Saint-Simon had not only emphasized the growth of mind as the percursor of science, but also the growth of forms of social organization (Hadden, 1997). Comte's position on sociology lies with his insistence on empirical research. Science, unlike theology and Hegelian philosophy, does not recognize *a priori* that a pattern or an inner logic of things defined by ideal concepts exists. Scientists have to find patterns by studying phenomena (Garner, 2000). Durkheim was the sociological pioneer in the use of positivism, or the scientific method: collecting data, use of statistics, and quantitative data analysis. Statistics based on large numbers of individuals provide the proper insights into human behavior and social patterns. It is the ability to hypothesize, collect data, and test the hypothesis against the data collected that made sociology a legitimate science. Durkheim utilized the scientific method extensively when writing his dissertation and his work on suicide. Commenting on the use of the scientific method when analyzing society, Durkheim states, "No further progress could be made until it was established that the laws of societies are no different from those governing the rest of nature and that the method by which they are discovered are identical with that of the other sciences. This was Auguste Comte's contribution" (Lukes, 1972:68).

It is clear that Comte did have a major impact on Durkheim and his work. In some regards, Durkheim can be viewed as a successor to Comte (though others say he is a successor to Saint-Simon). *The Division of Labor* contains seventeen references, most of them favorable, to Comte. Durkheim points out that Comte recognized the division of labor as a source of solidarity, Durkheim viewed the division of labor as a way of binding one to another within a society because each member is dependent on the others. Further, Durkheim believed that the members of society are consciously aware of this important interdependent relationship. Comte's idea of *consensus* directly influenced Durkheim's notion of a *collective conscience* (common morality).

Durkheim did not agree with all of Comte's ideas. He was not at all impressed by Comte's later "theological" writings or by his metaphysics, and he disagreed with many other Comtean approaches. Durkheim was especially critical of Comte's view of social order, with its obvious ties to conservative values. By professing a cosmological worldview as a necessary basis of social order, Comte failed to grasp the differing modes of solidarity characterized by modern society (Seidman, 1983). Durkheim argued that modern society was characterized by a decline of a worldview cosmic order and was replaced by an increase in secular order and appearance. Durkheim believed that the most recent religions were not cosmologies, but are disciplined morals. In distinguishing secular from cosmic worldviews, Durkheim was able to incorporate the idea of a moral order founded upon collective beliefs (Seidman, 1983).

The English Liberal Tradition

Historians have pointed out that the philosophes drew their inspiration and ideology from the English liberal tradition (Lichtheim, 1970; Sabine, 1965; and Smith, 1962). The primary figures for the French Enlightenment were Newton and Locke. The French philosophes looked to the English constitution and its pluralistic social order as a model of a sound society. English liberal themes included: the doctrine of the constitutional balance of powers; parliamentary government; economic individualism; the ideal of a market economy; and miminal role of the government (Seidman, 1983). In the English tradition, freedom implied the separation of the individual from the artificially created social constraints of society. A polarized relationship was inherent between the individual and society.

Durkheim's sociology was a response to the underlying problem of the Third French Republic: the crisis of liberalism. Durkheim attempted to account for the recurring failure of French liberalism by pointing to such factors as class polarization, the tradition of agrarian France, and moral disorder (Seidman, 1983). He believed that the social and political failure of liberalism was due to the conceptual shortcomings of its doctrine.

Among the non-French influences on Durkheim, Spencer had perhaps the most profound effect on his thoughts. In fact, there are forty references to Spencer in the *Division of Labor*, far more than to any other social thinker. Spencer never abandoned or substantially modified the chief tenets of English liberalism. Spencer compared society to an organism, believing that all the parts make up the whole. Durkheim viewed Spencer's social theory to be of immense historical significance. Durkheim consistently praised Spencer for his analytical accomplishments: grounding society more rigorously as a "natural" entity; specifying social types and the diversity of social development; and orienting sociology to particular problems of an empirical nature. Durkheim appreciated how Spencer was able to examine institutions and classify societies into categories. Most of Durkheim's evolutionary views are derived from Spencer, as evident by Durkheim's conception of evolution as moving from systems of mechanical to systems of organic solidarity. This concept is very similar to Spencer's observation regarding evolution that societies evolve from incoherent homogeneity to coherent heterogeneity. In *Division of Labor*, Durkheim used

a "reliance on Spencer's ideas of evolution as a movement from homogeneity to differentiation" (LaCapra, 1972:119–120).

Despite his admiration of Spencer, Durkheim did not view him as a sociologist. Instead, he viewed Spencer as he did Comte— as a philosopher. Durkheim remained unimpressed both by Spencer's overall hypothesis and by his particular social theories (Lukes, 1972). Specifically, Durkheim disagreed with Spencer's individualistic premises (because self-interest cannot account for or help maintain social order); the aspects of Spencer's organicism; and, to his simplistic extension of the biological paradigm to sociology. Durkheim especially criticized Spencer's sustained attachment to the ideology of English liberalism. Durkheim criticized the English liberal idea of private property attained through inheritance. Durkheim believed that inheritance creates inequalities among persons at birth, that are unrelated to merit or service. Durkheim recommended a recasting of the morals of property so that property ownership by individuals should be equivalent to the services they have rendered in the society. In opposition to English liberalism, Durkheim formulated a doctrine that was responsive to the needs and critical disposition of the working classes, yet in accord with the tradition of moral idealism among the democratic middle class (Seidman, 1983).

German Idealism

In regard to German social thinkers, the philosopher closest to Durkheim was Immanuel Kant (the one-time bearer and destroyer of Western rationalism). In his positive view of the role of *a priori* reason and his methodical pursuit of knowledge, Kant expanded the Western rationalist tradition. However, once Kant rejected the concept of a complete system of knowledge because he believed the world to be unknowable in itself, he turned away from the dogmatic claims of rationalism (Seidman, 1983). Regardless, by stressing the active role of mind in the origins of knowledge and moral law, Kant created a uniquely German form of rationalism.

What attracted Durkheim to Kant was not his epistemology nor his general philosophy, but rather his commitment to the examination of moral duty. Durkheim acknowledged that his version of sociology, which emphasized the desirability of moral acts, was just an extension of Kant's notion of duty and moral obligation. In regards to morality, Durkheim (1938) wrote, "Everything which is the source of solidarity is moral, everything which forces man to take account of other men is moral, everything which forces him to regulate his conduct through something other than the surviving of his ego is moral, and morality is as solid as these ties are numerous and strong" (p. 398).

Durkheim had published a number of lengthy critical reviews of the works of many German thinkers, including Simmel, Schäffle, Gumplowicz, and Toennies. The influence of Ferdinand Toennies, author of *Gemeinschaft und Gesellschaft*, can easily be traced to Durkheim's similar distinction between organic and mechanical societies.

Another German thinker to influence Durkheim was his personal friend, Wilhelm Wundt. Wundt has been called the father of experimental psychology, but worked in other academic areas as well. Durkheim was very impressed by the amount of work that Wundt produced—he wrote or revised 53,735 pages (Coser, 1977). Durkheim appreciated Wundt's commitment to scientific methodology and the scientific research conducted at his famous psychological laboratory at Leipzig. Specifically, Durkheim agreed with Wundt's notion of the *Volksseele*

(the group soul), which he substituted for the more common Hegelian term *Volksgeist*. This notion is again similar to Durkheim's concept of the collective conscience.

In addition, Durkheim enjoyed Wundt's contention that moral phenomena had to be treated as "facts of social existence, *sui generis*"—meaning, as facts irreducible in "origin and operation to individual acts (Thompson, 1982:36). Durkheim would come to see social facts as "things"—objective and measurable things.

Concepts and Contributions

With such credits as the "Father of Functionalism," the "Father of French Sociology," "Founder of Modern Sociology," and the first full Professor of Sociology, it is clear that Durkheim contributed greatly to social thought. He offered a more coherent theory than any other classical sociological thinker. He articulated a clear theoretical orientation and utilized a variety of specific concepts in his works. A brief review of his key contributions to social thought begins with his doctoral dissertation *The Division of Labor*.

The Division of Labor

Durkheim is considered one of the founders of "empirical" sociology, but as he states in the *Division of Labor*, "having begun from philosophy, I tend to return to it; or rather I have been quite naturally brought back to it by the nature of the questions which I met with on my route." *Division* was an attempt to treat the facts of moral life according to the method of the positive sciences. Durkheim believed that the simpler societies were founded on moral consensus or a collective conscience. Organic solidarity is the essential basis of the modern social order.

Durkheim believed that the object of sociology as a whole is to determine the conditions for the conservation of societies. He argued that social solidarity, which is the bond that unites persons, is the key to maintaining society. In his conception there are two ideal types of society. The more primitive type, characterized by *mechanical solidarity*, has a relatively undifferentiated social structure, with little or no division of labor. "Mechanical solidarity is a solidarity of resemblance" (Aron, 1976:11). The modern society is characterized by *organic solidarity*, which develops out of differences in the economic and social structure, and has a much greater and refined division of labor highlighted by specialization. "Organic solidarity is one in which consensus, or the coherent unity of collectivity, results from, or is expressed by, differentiation" (Aron, 1967:11).

Durkheim was bothered by the question: If pre-industrial societies were held together by common ideas and sentiments, by shared norms and values, what holds an industrial/modern society together? Durkheim believed that changes in the division of labor have enormous implications for the structure of society. Whereas primitive societies are held together by their similarities and generalism, modern societies are held together by the specialization of people and their need for the services of many others. Further, Durkheim indicated that large-scale societies can only exist when there is specialization within it (Lukes, 1985).

The role of the division of labor is critical in Durkheim's analysis of society. "Social harmony comes essentially from the division of labor. It is characterized by a cooperation that is automatically produced through the pursuit by each individual of his own interests. It suffices that each individual consecrate himself to a special function in order, by the force of events, to make himself solidary with others" (Durkheim, 1993:200). The division of labor is simply the separa-

tion and specialization of work among people. As industry and technology advances, and population increases, society must become more specialized if it is to survive. In modern society, this is especially evident, as labor has never before been so concentrated, and the current trend is toward an even further increased specialization.

However, as Comte had pointed out, it is the same specialization that holds a society together that pulls it apart. Durkheim too was concerned with the social implication of increased specialization. As specialization increases, people are increasingly separated, values and interests become different, norms are varied, and subcultures are formed. Because people perform different tasks, they come to value different things than others. "A society made up an extremely large mass of unorganized individuals, which an overgrown state attempts to limit and restrain, constitutes a veritable sociological monstrosity" (Durkheim, 1984:liv). Since the era of industrialization many social thinkers have expressed concerned over the changing social structure. "The man of today is no longer able to understand his neighbor because his profession is his whole life, and the technical specialization of this fate has forced him to live in a closed universe" (Ellul, 1964:133).

Durkheim did not see the division of labor as the downfall of the social order, but he did recognize that it gave rise to a new social order, or solidarity: *organic solidarity*. He believed that even as mankind and society continue to evolve, the whole common conscience does not cease to exist. There will always remain a cult of personality, of individual dignity, and of individual consciences. The primary characteristic of modern society—specialization—forces individuals to remain in contact with one another, which in turn, strengthens the bonds between persons. These bonds help to create a group morality within the division of labor. The individual becomes cognizant of his dependence upon society and the forces that keep him in check and restrain him. As Durkheim (1933) summarizes, "Since the division of labor becomes the chief source of social solidarity, it becomes, at the same time, the foundation of the moral order" (p. 401).

Solidarity

Durkheim's *Division of Labor in Society* is, in part, an attempt to discover the grounds of solidarity and unity in modern, industrialized society (Hadden, 1997). He wanted to carry out a systematic, scientific study of solidarity so that the field of sociology could aid in the restoration of France. Durkheim wanted to quiet the detractors of modern society and its increased division of labor. As previously described, Durkheim believed that the division of labor actually provides a firm basis for solidarity.

For Durkheim, solidarity was defined as the bond between all individuals within a society. He was particularly interested in social cohesion. In *Division of Labor,* Durkheim traces examples of social cohesion throughout human history; he uses demographic and economic factors—namely, increasing social density and an increasingly complex division of labor—for an explanation of the changes he observes. He found that in societies characterized by *mechanical solidarity* social cohesion was based upon the likeness and similarities among individuals in a society, and largely dependent on common rituals and routines.

> The major characteristic of a society in which mechanical solidarity prevails is that the individuals differ from one another as little as possible. The individuals, the members of the same collectivity, resemble each other because they feel the same emotions, cherish the same values, and hold the same things sacred (Aron, 1970:11).

It follows that in a society of mechanical solidarity, a consensus should not be difficult to attain, as the bond is strengthened by similar beliefs, opinions and values. Furthermore, it follows that there would not be as much of a division of labor, as people would be performing similar duties. "The society is coherent because the individuals are not yet differentiated" (Aron, 1970:11). Durkheim believes that primitive societies are characterized by mechanical solidarity because of the lack of technological advancements. Technology mandates specialization, which results in the formation of a division of labor.

In modern societies, highlighted by *organic solidarity,* social cohesion is based upon the dependence that individuals have to one another. A society characterized by *organic solidarity* is "one in which the consensus, or the coherent unity of the collectivity, results from, or is expressed by differentiation" (Aron, 1970:11). Even though differences in values and priorities exist among the people, the very survival of society depends on their reliance on each other to perform their specific task. "The individuals are no longer similar, but different; and in a sense . . . it is precisely because the individuals are different that consensus is achieved" (Aron, 1970:12). As a result of the fact that there is a distinct division of labor in a society with organic solidarity, consensus occurs as a result of the fact that members must rely (social bond) upon each other for services.

Collective Conscience

A central concept in Durkheim's work is the *collective conscience,* which he defines as, "The totality of beliefs and sentiments common to average citizens of the same society forms a determinate system which has its own life; one may call the *collective* or *common conscience* . . . . It is, thus, an entirely different thing from particular consciences, although it can be realized only through them" (Durkheim, 1933:79–80).

The *collective conscience* is an example of Durkheim's nonmaterial *social fact*. It occurs at the societal level as a sum of all individual conceptions of conscience, and is a determinate of cultural expectations on individual behavior. The *collective conscience* can be differentiated on four dimensions:

1. **Volume.** The number of people involved.

2. **Intensity.** How deeply individuals feel about it.

3. **Rigidity.** How clearly defined it is.

4. **Content.** How it is formed.

In *The Division of Labor in Society,* Durkheim shows that societies have moved from harsh, punitive, and universally shared collective conscience to a more attenuated and individualized form. In "primitive" societies, the collective conscience is harsh, intense, rigid, and universally shared. Law associated with this level of conscience is usually repressive; the deviant is severely punished for violating rules. In "modern" societies, the collective conscience is less harsh, less punitive, less intensely felt, and less shared than in primitive societies. For example, white collar criminals (embezzlers, tax cheats, insider traders) almost never experience the level of public loathing they deserve. Law shifts from largely repressive normative regulation to restitution, such as payment for fines.

Durkheim also spoke of *collective representatives,* which may be seen as specific states or substrata of the collective conscience. These are similar to today's usage of the term *agents of socialization,* family, religion, occupation, and so forth. According to Durkheim, collective representations comprise a realm of moral facts. These representations not only have authoritative power in the form of obligations, but they are also desirable. Moral phenomena, in Durkheim's view, have this dual character of obligation and desirability.

It was Durkheim's belief that the essential problems of modern society were moral in nature and that the only real solution to modern societies' problems rests with reinforcing the strength of the collective morality. He labeled the modern form of the collective conscience as the *cult of the individual* (Chriss, 1993; Tole, 1993). This was an interesting concept for Durkheim, because it seems to fuse the seemingly antagonistic forces of morality and individualism (Ritzer, 2000a). The basic idea conveyed by Durkheim here is that individualism is becoming the moral system of modern society.

Methodology

The notions developed in *Division of Labor* constitute the foundation of Durkheim's sociology. In his classic *The Rules of Sociological Method* (1895), Durkheim explicates the methodological suppositions already applied in the *Division of Labor.* In *Rules,* Durkheim states that it is not enough to look abstractly at a phenomenon; rather, it should be studied empirically. Since sociology grew from philosophy, it must separate itself (empirically) to become a science. Researchers cannot study by a priori reasoning or by introspective examination, they must study social facts, which are external, and therefore, physically observable. He argues for the existence of a collective realm of facts, which are accessible by the scientific method.

Durkheim's analytical commitment to methodological holism and social idealism and his concern with social solidarity fall squarely with the theorizing of the French tradition. He believed that the sociological, empirical approach to research allowed for generalization; which was critical in order to discuss such concepts as solidarity, collective conscience, and social facts. His methodological critique was aimed at the liberal tradition, and rooted in a basically a priori, deductive, and subjective methodology (Seidman, 1983).

In the preface to the second edition of the *Rules,* Durkheim addresses the objections made to his most basic premises: treating things as social facts. According to Durkheim, being able to treat things as social facts allows the researcher to be objective and detached, which is critical to empirical science. In *Rules,* Durkheim states, "to treat phenomena as things is to treat them as data, and these constitute the point of departure of science" (p. 101). He defines *social facts* as, "ways of acting, thinking and feeling, external to the individual, and endowed with a power of coercion, by reason of which they control him" (1938:3). Individuals act, think, and feel, but the *ways* in which they do this are not of their creation. Social forces, or *social facts*, are imposed on individuals; hence they are external to them; they are powerful and regulate their behavior.

Social Facts

In order to distinguish itself from philosophy, Durkheim argued in the *Rules* that the distinctive subject matter of sociology should be the study of *social facts*. Since *social facts* are treated as things, they can only be studied empirically, not philosophically. Durkheim (1895) believed that ideas can be known introspectively (philosophically), but *things* "cannot be conceived by purely mental activity," they require for their conception "data from outside the mind" (p. xliii).

Social facts are the social structures and cultural norms and values that are external to, and coercive of, actors. They are independent of individuals and they cannot be ignored or wished away. They are rooted in group sentiments and values. They are coercive in the sense that if you ignore them, you

may be subject to punishments, public ridicule, and/or sanctions. *Social facts* are manifested in external indicators of sentiments such as religious doctrines, laws, moral codes, and aphorisms. Social facts comprise a distinct subject matter for sociologists because, as collective representations, they are independent of psychological and biological phenomena. Even though persons have individual actions, thoughts, and feelings, they tend to live their lives through social institutions: family, work, school, sporting events.

Durkheim (1895) made distinctions between two types of *social facts: material social facts* and *nonmaterial social facts. Material social facts* are the clearer of the two types, because they are real, material entities that are external to the individual. Examples of *material social facts* include: any given society; structural components of society (social institutions); and morphological components of society (housing arrangements, income distribution, access to technology). *Nonmaterial social facts* are more complex because they deal with mental phenomena: morality; collective conscience; collective representations; and social currents (trends, great movements, which do not arise in any one individual consciousness).

Durkheim's major explanatory variable—suicide—became the model for the development of American empirical research. In *Suicide* (1897) he demonstrated that social facts, and particularly social currents, are external to, and coercive of, the individual.

Suicide

In *Suicide*, Durkheim firmly established the method and discipline outlined in *Rules* (Hadden, 1997). *Suicide* provides an example of a sociological study that emphasizes social facts rather than individual experiences (Phillips, 1993). Durkheim chose to study suicide because it is a relatively concrete and specific phenomenon. He applies empirical methods to a behavior that seems to be exclusively an individual act. Individuals can be seen as having many "reasons" for committing the act of suicide, but Durkheim wanted to establish sociological "causes" that influence suicide. He also hoped to explain differences in *rates* of suicide. Durkheim noticed that rates of suicide appeared to vary from country to country (note: Durkheim examined data on suicide in Austria, France, England, Switzerland, Denmark, Prussia, Greece, and Italy, among others), and there appeared to be a different "predisposition to suicide" in different societies. Durkheim attempted to find out what caused this predisposition (Hadden, 1997).

Le Suicide is among the very first modern examples of consistent and organized use of the statistical method in social investigation. *Suicide* is an outstanding work in the study of causation, and the application of his concepts of *collective representations* and the *collective conscience*. Durkheim believed that there were a number of social factors that explained why some people are more likely to commit suicide than others. He also felt that groups differ in the degree of their integration, and that suicide varies inversely with the degree of integration. When society is strongly integrated it holds individuals under its influence and control. Integration refers to the degree to which collective sentiments are shared.

Durkheim outlined four types of suicide: *Egoistic, altruistic, anomic*, and *fatalistic*. He linked each of the categories of suicide to the degree of integration into, or regulation by, society. *Egoistic suicide* is associated with a low degree of integration, whereas *altruistic suicide* occurs when there is a high degree of integration. *Fatalistic suicide* is associated with high regulation, and *anomic suicide* with low regulation. Durkheim defined regulation as the degree of external constraints on the members of society. The following is a brief description of Durkheim's four types of suicide.

High rates of *egoistic suicide* are more likely to be found in those societies, collectivities, or groups in which the individual is not well integrated into the larger social unit. These societies are characterized by excessive individualism. Durkheim defined integration as a product of social interaction and the strength of shared beliefs among group members (Pampel, 2000). In the case where society has a stranglehold on a person with egoistic tendencies and a person considers himself at society's service, that person considers killing himself (Durkheim, 1951). *Egoistic suicide* is usually committed by people of the higher social class because they have more things to have an ego over. These persons are generally highly depressed. This type of suicide occurs because society allows for the separation of society and the individual; being insufficiently amassed in some parts or even the whole. *Egoistic suicide* is deeply rooted in the refined ethics which places personality on an extremely high pedestal.

The second type of suicide described by Durkheim is *altruistic suicide*, which occurs when social integration is too strong, and the individual is literally forced into committing suicide. Durkheim believed that if extreme individuation can lead a person to their death, then so too can the lack of individuation. In general, those who commit *altruistic suicide* do so because they feel it is their duty (e.g., the followers of Jim Jones in Jonestown, Guyana, who committed mass suicide; Japanese kamikaze pilots). Durkheim (1951) divided *altruistic suicide* into three categories. The first is the suicide committed by men on the threshold of old age or stricken with illness. If a man feels that he is no longer useful in a community, then he must realize that it is time to let go. In many primitive cultures to die of old age was considered taboo. The second sub-category of *altruistic suicide* involves a wife killing herself because of her husband's death; the third category is that of followers/servants on the death of their chiefs.

When people decide to kill themselves in this manner it is because they feel they are obligated to do so. The relationship between the social levels of each person plays an important role in *altruistic suicide*. In these societies the individual plays a small role, and most people live similar lives. There is social prestige that is attached to suicide. Durkheim (1951) labeled the most altruistic type of suicide when a person kills himself for the joy of sacrifice because renunciation is considered praiseworthy.

Many of today's terrorists are willing to kill themselves because they feel so strongly about their cause, and believe that they will be rewarded in the "afterlife." These people are extremely dangerous to civil societies.

Anomic suicide occurs when periods of disruption unleash currents of *anomie*. Durkheim (1951) noted that during an 1873 financial crisis in Vienna, the number of suicides immediately rose for the next couple of years. (Stock market crashes are almost always accompanied by suicides.) The rate of suicides increased as life became increasingly difficult. In cases of economic disaster a declassification of persons is likely to occur, meaning that persons who were once in a high social class may be forced to become a part of a lower social class. All the advantages of their previous class standing become obsolete and they cannot adjust (Nisbet, 1965). The same can happen if the opposite occurs. If someone who never knew wealth and power suddenly obtains it, he may have difficulty handling his newfound prosperity. Many of today's big-dollar lottery winners have reported that their lives were ruined by their new economic fortune.

Durkheim made little mention of the fourth category of suicide, *fatalistic*, as it was only a footnote in *Suicide*. It is most likely to occur when regulation is excessive and is characterized by high degrees of external constraints. When these constraints are forced upon a society the people may feel suffocated and get restless. People believe that their lives are not going to get any better, or things will continue to get worse, which leads them to commit suicide. An example would be a slave who takes his own life because of the hopelessness associated with the oppressive regulation in his/her every action and behavior.

Religion

Durkheim's innovative perspective on religion and God is clearly outlined in his last major book, *The Elementary Forms of Religious Life* (1912). In this book, Durkheim argues that religious feeling, the spiritual, the sacred, and God are nothing more than collective representations of the human experience. *Religion* is the ultimate *nonmaterial social fact* that is associated with the *collective conscience*. In primitive societies religion is all-encompassing.

Religion arises from the need to explain and understand, and from sociability. Durkheim stated that religion was, at each moment of history, the totality of beliefs and sentiments of all sorts relative to the relations of man with a being or beings, whose nature he regarded as superior to his own.

Where *Suicide* focused on a large amount of statistics from varying sources, *The Elementary Forms* used one in-depth case study of the aboriginal Arunta tribe in Australia. Durkheim chose this group because he felt they represented the most basic, *elementary* forms of religion within a society. Durkheim wanted to show two things: the fact that religion was not divinely or supernaturally inspired and was in fact a product of society; and he set out to identify the common things that religion placed an emphasis upon, as well as what effects those religious beliefs had on the lives of the members of society.

The Arunta, a hunting and gathering tribe, participated in totemism. Totemism is a primitive form of a religious system in which certain things, particularly animals and plants, come to be regarded as *sacred* emblems (totems) of the clan. With totemism, an image or representation is placed on a totem pole. The images at the highest points of the totem were the most sacred. In addition to the physical aspects of totemism is the moral character. There are occasions when the members of the tribe come together at the totem and share a number of emotions, sentiments, and rituals.

Using the descriptions of ethnographic studies, Durkheim concludes that the Arunta religion is nothing more than the collective representations of the overwhelming power of society. In so doing, he is also saying the same thing about Judaism and Christianity (Garner, 2000). The general conclusion of *Elementary Forms* is that religion is eminently social, and serves as a source of solidarity and identification for the individuals within a society. Religion provides for a meaning of life, authority figures, and, most importantly for Durkheim, it reinforces the morals and social norms held collectively by all within a society. He did not dismiss religion as mere fantasy, for Durkheim recognized that it provides social control, cohesion, and purpose for people, as well as another means of communication and gathering for individuals to interact and reaffirm social norms.

In a comparison of religions from different cultures, Durkheim also concluded that a belief in a supernatural realm is not necessary or common among religions, but the separation of different aspects of life, physical things and certain behaviors into two categories—the *sacred* and the *profane*—is common. Objects and behaviors deemed *sacred* were considered part of the spiritual or religious realm, and were set apart from the *profane* or mundane, commonplace items. Durkheim (1973a) described "*sacred* things as simply collective ideals that have fixed themselves on material objects" (p. 159).

Morality

Some believe that we are born with the need for morality, others argue that it evolved over history. According to Wundt (Giddens, 1972), the true object of morality is to make man feel he is not a whole, but part of a whole—and how insignificant he is by reference to the plurality of contexts that surround him. Morality appears to us to be a collection of precepts, of rules of conduct. Violation of these rules sets forth consequences. Morality constitutes a category of rules where the idea of authority plays an absolutely preponderant role.

In *Moral Education*, a book first published in 1925, and likely taken from his lecture notes first developed at the Sorbonne, Durkheim articulates his view as to the role of sociology in investigating and reforming society and thought (Hadden, 1997). Morality, as with all social phenomena, can best be examined sociologically. Sociology, as a true science, must examine the criteria that make up morality. Durkheim states that art, by definition, moves in the domain of the unreal, of the imaginary. Morality, on the contrary, is the domain of action, and can only be grasped in relation to real phenomena; otherwise, it is lost in the void. To act morally is to do good to beings of flesh and blood. In order to feel the need to change, transform, and improve reality, we cannot abstract ourselves from it. On the contrary, we have to embrace it and love it, in spite of its ugliness, its pettiness, and its meanness (Giddens, 1972).

Moral ideas and sentiments are to be retained, according to Durkheim (1973b), but the historical bond with religion must be broken. He believed that educational institutions and the wider society should forge, and create, a new sense of morality, especially a morality that emphasizes the fact that inherent with freedom are rights, privileges, and duties.

Socialism

Durkheim remained throughout his life opposed to *socialism* and his sociology was an effort to construct a model of society essentially antithetical to that of Marx (Zeitlin, 1968). As Seidman (1983) notes, Durkheim did make mention of a version of a guild socialism, and a return to a socialism of the French tradition. But, Durkheim (1962) was not a fan of socialism as he describes "socialism as not a science, a sociology in miniature—it is a cry of grief, sometimes of anger, uttered by men who feel most keenly our collective malaise. Socialism is to the facts which produce it what the groans of a sick man are to the illness with which he is afflicted, to the needs that torment him" (p. 159)

Durkheim (1972) states that there are two very different ways of studying *socialism*. We can see it as a scientific doctrine on the nature and evolution of societies in general, and more specifically, of the most advanced contemporary societies. Socialism is wholly oriented toward the future. It is above all a plan for the reconstruction of present-day society, a program for a collective life. Because of socialism's utopian basis, there cannot be a scientific socialism. That is the very reason of Marx's failure.

In what sounds similar to ideas of *socialism*, Durkheim, who described the totality of moral rules as an imaginary wall, with the function of limiting and containing; believed that too much wealth so easily becomes a source of immorality. Through the power wealth confers onto persons, it actually diminishes the power of things to oppose them (Giddens, 1972). Thus, Durkheim seems to oppose persons with too much wealth because they are likely to become immoral.

Anomie

One of the prevalent themes of Durkheim's sociology is his concern with the decline of the common morality. Industrialization in particular, according to Durkheim, tends to dissolve restraints on the passions of humans. Where simple societies—primarily through religion—successfully taught people to control their desires and goals, modern industrial societies separate people and weaken their social bonds as a result of increased complexity and the division of labor. Durkheim believed that members of Western society are exposed to the risk of *anomie*. The word anomie comes from the Greek *anomia*, meaning "without law." Durkheim defined the term *anomie* as a condition where social and/or moral norms are confused, unclear, or simply not present. Feelings of normlessness lead members to deviant behavior. For Durkheim, anomie represents the primary pathology of modern society (Harcourt, 2001).

Individuals are confronted with *anomie* when they are not faced with sufficient moral constraint, or do not have a clear concept of what is and what is not acceptable behavior. For example, as Durkheim states in *Moral Education*,

> If the rules of the conjugal morality lose their authority, and the mutual obligations of husband and wife become less respected, the emotions and appetites ruled by this sector of morality will become unrestricted and uncontained, and accentuated by this very release; powerless to fulfill themselves because they have been freed from all limitations, these emotions will produce a disillusionment which manifests itself visibly. (p. 173)

Durkheim viewed *anomie* as a pathology. By thinking of *anomie* as a pathology, Durkheim was saying that deviant behaviors and the problems of the world could be "cured." Thus, the proper level of regulation, both in terms of issues of morality and civility, would guarantee a cohesive and smoothly operating society.

Functionalism

Durkheim's sociology was about society and culture, not individual action and motivation. He believed society and social structures are realities at a level above the individual human organism. He shares Comte's functionalist, evolutionary, and positive premises (Garner, 2000). The functionalist perspective views society as a sum total (the whole) of a large number (the parts) of persons, groups, organizations, and social institutions. Sociologists that utilize this perspective examine the role of society as it attempts to execute the necessary functions needed in order to maintain such needs as: national defense, internal social order, consumer production and distribution, food, clothing, and shelter demands from its citizens, and so on.

Consequently, the social structure is a complex system whose parts are said to be well-integrated and in a state of equilibrium when functioning properly. During periods of rapid social change, or with introduction of a new and dramatic force (whether social or natural), the social structure may be thrown out of equilibrium. When this happens, the various structures of society can become poorly integrated, and what were formerly useful functions can become "dysfunctional."

Functionalism, for Durkheim, is the idea that society is a system, and its parts (institutions) contribute to its stability and continued existence. His functionalist outlook did not include a value judgment, nor did he

imply that some societies were "better" than others; rather, that the parts of the system are interconnected and attempt to meet the demands of each particular society. When this occurs over a period of time and stability is met, the system is said to be functioning properly. His functionalist perspective was evolutionary in that he was interested in how societies change over time. He recognized that societies, as social systems, are not static, and are therefore subject to change at any time.

Durkheim's view on *functionalism* can be summarized with this quote from *The Dualism of Human Nature and its Social Conditions* (1914):

> A great number of our mental states, including some of the most important ones, are of social origin. In this case then, it is the whole that, in a large measure, produces the part; consequently, it is impossible to attempt to explain the whole without explaining the part—without explaining, at least, the part as a result of the whole. (p. 149)

Crime

Durkheim proposed that crime and deviance serve a *functional* role in society because they help to unite its members. From *The Division in Labor in Society,* Durkheim states, "Crime brings together honest men and concentrates them" (Giddens, 1972:127). All groups, organizations, institutions, and societies create laws and norms of expected behavior. When a law or major social norm is violated, it is met with a moral public outrage. The members of the community cling together in opposition to the violation, thus reaffirming that society's bond and its adherence to certain standards of expected behavior. Recognition and punishment of crimes is, in effect, the very reaffirmation of the laws and moral boundaries of a society. The existence of laws and norms are representations of a shared sense of morality within society. "We must not say that an action shocks the *conscience collective* because it is criminal, but rather that it is criminal because it shocks the *conscience collective*. We do not condemn it because it is a crime, but it is a crime because we condemn it" (Durkheim, 1984).

Punishing violators for their crimes reminds the nonviolators (society as a whole) not to risk deviating from the law, or they too risk sanctions. Punishment, then, helps to reaffirm the sense of morality within a community because it serves as a reminder to those who question authority and dare to deviate from the norm.

Durkheim believed that crime could also help to promote social change. Occasionally, a violation may not be greeted with public opposition, and instead may stimulate a re-evaluation of such a behavior on the part of the members of that society. Therefore, an activity that was once considered deviant, may be reconsidered and become part of the norm, simply because it gained support by a large portion of the society. In short, deviance can help a society to rethink its boundaries, and ignite social change.

Durkheim also examined the relationship between crime and law. He found that a society with mechanical solidarity is characterized by *repressive law*. In this close-knit type of society, members are very similar in their beliefs and share a strong sense of common morality. Consequently, a criminal is likely to be severely punished for violations of the law. On the other hand, a society with *organic solidarity* is characterized by *restitutive law*. In this more modern type of society, there is a greater concern with restitution (or making good) than severe punishment. There are few crimes committed that cause an outrage among societal members due to the lack of a strong common morality.

Dynamic Density

Closely related to the division of labor, *dynamic density* refers to the number of people in society and the amount of interaction that occurs among them. An increase in the number of people *and* an increase in the interaction among them (which is *dynamic density*) leads to the change from *mechanical* to *organic solidarity*. Durkheim believed that neither population increase nor an increase in interaction, when taken separately, is a significant factor in societal change. The increase in the number of people and an increase in interaction *together* bring about more competition for scarce resources and a more intense struggle for survival among the various components of primitive society (Ritzer, 2000a). The rise of the division of labor allows people and the social structure to complement, rather than conflict, with one another. This, in turn, leads to greater coexistence between individuals and greater efficiency on behalf of the social system.

Public Involvement

Durkheim's scholarly work is very impressive, but that was not the extent of his contributions to society. Always the crusader for a common morality, he possessed a strong commitment to society, was an active defender of Dreyfus, and a key figure in the reorganization of the French university system. He managed to combine scientific detachment with an intense commitment to morality. He abandoned his religious roots and preferred to be known as a Frenchman first and foremost. His nationalistic pride did not deter him from his goal of a liberal cosmopolitan civilization in which the pursuit of science was meant to serve the enlightenment and guidance of the whole humanity (Coser, 1977).

Relevancy

Durkheim enjoyed a social background that provided an opportunity for potential greatness. He came from a family that could provide relative economic security and received the best education. "He was rigorously educated in lower schools in France, at a lyceum in Paris, and then at the Ecole Normale Superieure in Paris" (Simpson, 1963:1). It was, however, Durkheim's taking proper advantage of his educational opportunities that prepared him to contribute so substantially to sociology, and his beloved society of France.

His theories are more coherent than any other classical sociological theory, and he applied his theoretical orientation in a wide variety of specific works. (Ritzer, 2000a). Durkheim was a man of character who attempted to mold events in order to put his cherished principles into practice (Coser, 1977). He founded and edited *L'Année Sociologique*, a professional sociological periodical. He provided the basic schematic for structural and functional analysis in sociology; and, insisted on the usage of empirical methodology, so that sociology could accurately claim itself as a science. Durkheim hoped that a scientific sociology would help to create a moral re-education in the Third Republic, and, at the same time, would help to replace religion, as the source of morality, with a secular morality.

With the advent of World War I, Durkheim felt obliged to help France in some way. He became the secretary of the Committee for the Publication of Studies and Documents on the War, publishing several pamphlets attacking pan-Germanism. Durkheim lost his son André, who died from war wounds, just before Christmas, 1915. André had followed his father to the Ecole Normale, and had begun a most promising career as a sociological linguist (Coser, 1977). Emile took the death of his son very badly.

He was able to write very little after this dramatic event, and eventually died on November 15, 1917, at the age of fifty-nine.

During his lifetime, Durkheim's works and contributions to society and social thought were very relevant and significant. His public involvement extended far beyond his academic achievements and include: serving on innumerable university committees; advising the Ministry of Education; helping to introduce sociology into school curriculum; and influencing Europe as well as many other parts of the world. Durkheim's ideas were taught in American universities by Talcott Parsons and Robert Merton. As Coser (1977) states, "He is, if not the father, then the grandfather of us all" (p. 174).

Durkheim's works and thoughts continue to be relevant and significant in the third millennium. Robert Merton expanded Durkheim's functional approach through his analysis of *manifest* and *latent* functions, utilizing the term *dysfunctional* as it applies to social systems, and the creation of *Anomie Theory*. Merton believed that too often, theorists look only at the manifest functions and not some of the underlying latent functions of behavior. Durkheim's study of elementary forms of religious life is a classic example of this, according to Merton. In his study of the Hopi Indian raindance, Merton expands on Durkheim's manifest acknowledgment that the Arunta practiced totemism, and that the symbols on the totem were in fact significant, in that they possessed a functional purpose. But, as Merton (1949) noticed, the Hopi raindance served a manifest function as a means of attaining the needed rain; but also, the latent function of the dance exercise itself, aiding in the maintenance of group solidarity.

As a functionalist, Merton examined the social structure and patterns of activity within organizations. He noticed that just because a system is set up and put into place, that does not guarantee it is working at peak performance or that it is *functional*. It may in fact have very negative or *dysfunctional* consequences on the organization or the persons who must deal with it. Bureaucracy, for example, is a system set up for specific procedural strategies that foster objectivity and the smooth operation of the organization. However, a bureaucracy, by its very design, is conservative (ritualism) and inflexible (formalism), therefore unable to cope with changes or flaws within the system (Merton, 1949). For example, if a courthouse is totally dependent on persons using computers to conduct daily business, it is rendered useless, or *dysfunctional* during an electrical power outage.

As initially developed by Durkheim, the concept of *anomie* refers to a condition of relative normlessness in a society or group. Indicators of *anomie* include: the perception that community leaders are indifferent to one's needs; the perception that little can be accomplished in a society that is seen as basically unpredictable and lacking social order; the perception that life-goals are receding rather than being realized; a sense of futility; and, the conviction that one cannot count on personal associates for social and psychological support. The success goal in American culture leads many to feelings of *anomie*. According to Merton (1949) it is the conflict between cultural goals and the availability of using institutional means—whatever the character of the goals—that produces a strain toward *anomie*.

Merton's *Anomie Theory* is a study of social deviance. In brief, he believed that society encourages all persons to attain culturally desirable goals (e.g. economic success) but the opportunity to reach these goals are not equal among the members of society. Structural barriers such as racism, sexism, and ageism may hamper one's opportunity to reach culturally determined goals. Persons feeling such social pressures, without the means to attain these goals legitimately, may adapt a number of deviant behaviors in order to avoid feelings of *anomie*.

In the following paragraphs a number of Durkheim's concepts and contributions are applied to today's society and their implications for the future. In his *Division of Labor*, Durkheim describes society as advancing from *mechanical* to *organic solidarity*, which develops out of differences in the economic and social structure. It is too simplistic to characterize societies into just two categories, but the basic premise in Durkheim's thinking is still relevant. Changes continue to occur in the economic, and consequently the political, institutions of societies throughout the world. Many of them have barely embraced industrialization, while others are well into post-industrialization. Computer skills, which are so critical in advanced modern societies, are nearly absent in developing nations. This fact alone guarantees a drastic *division of world labor*.

The division of labor provides a basis for *solidarity*, a concept that would seem to be always relevant. Immigrants to foreign countries nearly always bond together in ethnic communities, especially before becoming assimilated. Persons who share a characteristic that leads to discriminatory actions against them often unite in a form of *solidarity*. Environmental groups rally together in attempt to pass laws aimed at saving the planet from potential destruction. Examples of the application of *solidarity* are nearly endless.

The core of Durkheim's theory lies with the concept of *social fact*, especially with such *nonmaterial social facts* as the *collective conscience*, *collective representations*, and *social currents*. Durkheim was very concerned with what he perceived as the lack of morality in French society. It is safe to say that all societies today and in the future will wrestle with issues of morality. When religion is involved, there is generally little tolerance shown toward persons with opposing beliefs, resulting in persecution, conflict, and war (Delaney, 2000). The examples of this are nearly endless. In the United States, the "Religious Right" attempts to push their concept of morality onto others; from specific behaviors (e.g. outlawing abortion) to more general ones (family values). Religious differences in the United States are mild compared to many other countries. When there is a high degree of diversity in society, especially religious diversity, a shared *collective conscience* is nearly impossible. Durkheim emphasized the importance in worship of society, rather than of religion. He would surely have strong opinions with regard to the contemporary American debate over the Pledge of Allegiance. He would support the philosophy of separation of church and state, and agree with the position to remove the "Under God" phrase found in the pledge.

Today, it is becoming more common for people, especially among young people, to seek salvation in popular culture. Young people in such countries as Russia were raised without a religious environment and therefore do not even consider turning to religion for answers to life's spiritual questions, let alone for salvation. Instead, as many of their American peers, youths are turning to television and music. There is a certain fascination with celebrities (the "royals" of American culture) and people are intrigued by what they say and do. Television provides an outlet of pent-up emotions. Viewing television does not require one to read or write, it is an easy, mindless behavior to perform. Some celebrities, such as Oprah Winfrey, preach about morals and the ills of society. Trash television, such as the Jerry Springer show, are designed to boost self-esteem. Watching shows like Jerry Springer and Jenny Jones allows viewers to recognize

the fact that their lives are not as bad as the guests', and helps to restore the self-esteem of those on the "verge" of becoming future guests themselves! Watching sporting events and soap operas allow the viewers to "escape" for a while.

Music has been relatively important throughout much of human history. Recent decades have been characterized by the pop music of its time. During the 1960s much of the music was designed to stimulate people into action, whether it was an antiwar song, social protest, or a feel-good Beatles song. The Grateful Dead created a "cult" following that lasted for decades. The early 2000s have witnessed middle-class people embracing bands like Pearl Jam or Creed, pre-teens who love the music of Britney Spears, and urban youths who turn to rap idols such as Puff Daddy or Snoop Dogg. Music can be uplifting and spiritual and can fill an emotional void. There are a number of persons who have reached celebrity status in society.

Durkheim came to believe that the role of individuals would continue to grow in the future. Individualism was inevitable in modern society and there was no way of returning to the *collective conscience* style of society that dominated the past. The modern version of the collective conscience would be dominated by the *cult of the individual* (Chriss, 1993). These "cults of man," or the "cult of personality" would replace the role of religion in society. "In so regulating human behavior, these 'cults of man' would be performing the same function as religion in the traditional societies. The difference would lie in the focus of this regulation: the defense of the individual rights and liberties would be of paramount importance to the new cults" (Westly, 1983:7). The fact is, as the third millennium begins, there has been an increased emphasis placed on popular culture and many have found inspiration and strength in music and other outlets of the mass media. Pop culture and government can adequately fulfill the primary functions of religion. Through the "cults of the individual" the sacred becomes replaced by the profane.

Besides religion, the political institution of a given society will often dictate *social currents*. If the government is a repressive one, the citizens will have little say in the manner in which institutions and organizations are operated. In extreme cases, revolutions may result. Even in democratic societies *social currents* can be influenced by the governing political party and office holders. When a political party that has definite ideas on re-shaping society comes into power and is not kept in check by the other representatives of society, a new agenda can be forced unto the citizenry. Where *law* once provided a woman's right to control her own body and have a legal abortion, a new election may put into place representatives who can make such a behavior illegal. The *law*, along with the *division of labor*, and *dynamic density* are examples of Durkheim's *material social facts*.

Through the use of *empirical methodology*, Durkheim's study of *suicide* was evidence that sociology has a legitimate place in the social sciences. Not only did he establish that external social factors influence an individual's decision to commit suicide, he demonstrated that rates and patterns could also be ascertained. The New York State Parks Police in Niagara Falls have established a "suicide season" at the Falls. According to a pattern that emerges from statistics going back to 1856, the suicide season begins in the spring, then drops off drastically in October (Michelmore, 2000). In addition, statistics at Niagara Falls show that Monday is the most common day suicide is committed, and the most popular time is 4 P.M. Niagara Falls is second only to San Francisco's Golden Gate Bridge as the nation's most popular place to commit suicide (Michelmore, 2000). Persons may commit suicide when they experience *anomie*.

Many theorists today have extended Durkheim's original intention of the concept *anomie* and have applied it to the micro level. Individuals are often confronted with "feelings" of *anomie* when they find themselves in a dramatically new environment. The first-year student who is attending college hundreds of miles from home, who has yet to meet new friends, and is having a hard time navigating the campus that seems so imposing, may feel *anomie*.

The individual who starts a new job, who feels overwhelmed by the demands, and has no one to turn to in order to ask for advice may feel *anomie*.

In *The Division of Labor in Society*, Durkheim said that *crime* served a *functional* role in society because it helped to promote social change when a violation of a *law* caused such a public outrage that demands for change occurred. This happened when Rosa Parks refused to give up her seat to a white person, as law dictated at the time. Demands for the end of police brutality and laws to protect citizens during arrest often follow well-documented cases of abuse. Public outrage was so intense during the Rodney King arrest that a *social current* of mistrust was fueled among African Americans in Los Angeles, in 1992. The future will witness many new laws created in response to new *social currents* and new ideas of *morality*.

Durkheim's ideas of anomie combined with his thoughts on law are the roots of the "broken windows" philosophy in policing that is so popular in the United States at the end of the twentieth century and the beginning of the twenty-first century. This theory can be traced to James Q. Wilson and George L. Kelling's 1982 article, "Broken Windows." The basic premise of the broken windows approach states that, if minor forms of disorder, such as graffiti, littering, panhandling, and prostitution, are left unattended, it will result in neighborhood decline and encourage increased serious criminal activity. Contemporary examples of this policy in action include former New York City mayor Giuliani's implementing of an order-maintenance policing strategy emphasizing proactive and aggressive enforcement of misdemeanor laws against quality-of-life offenses such as graffiti, loitering, public urination, public drinking, aggressive panhandling, turnstile jumping (at subways) and prostitution (Harcourt, 2001). The city of Chicago enacted an anti-gang loitering ordinance prohibiting citizens from standing together in any public place "with no apparent purpose" (Harcourt, 2001). There is a very similar parallel between Durkheim's emphasis on legal regulation and the broken windows emphasis on order. Durkheim explains in the *Division of Labor* that social cohesion of modern society is at its optimal level when there is proper and sufficient legal regulation. Regardless of whether or not the "broken windows" philosophy continues as a popular form of policing, Durkheim's impact on the study of anomie, morality, and its relation to law and social order will remain of lasting concern for future generations.

The third millennium began with the continuous and growing importance placed by billions of people worldwide on the social institution of sport and leisure. Scholars and social thinkers often ignore the *social fact* that is sport. Games and sports represent a vital place and role in many people's lives. They provide for people an opportunity to escape from the daily routine. Durkheim's discussion of games is limited to a few pages in *The Elementary Forms of Religious Life* (1912/1995):

> It is well known that games and the principal forms of art seem to have been born in religion and that they long maintained their religious character. We can see why: while

pursuing other goals directly, the cult has at the same time been a form of recreation. Religion could not be religion if there was no place in it for free combinations of thought and action, for games, for art, for all that refreshes a spirit worn down by all that is overburdening in day-to-day labor (p. 385).

Games and sports, then, provide individuals with an escape and therefore serve an important function in society.

Games themselves can be stratified by levels of sacredness (Ward, 1998). Regular season games (the *mundane*) are not as important as playoff games (the *sacred*). The National Football League's championship game, called the "Super Bowl," has become an "unofficial" American holiday, and is viewed by over a billion people worldwide. World Cup Soccer and the Olympic Games only occur every four years, and therefore the intensity level among fans and participants increases dramatically and the games are deemed more important (*sacred*).

Sporting events help to provide for *group solidarity*. The ritual behaviors by both the athletes and the fans are numerous (see Delaney's *Community, Sport and Leisure*). The singing of the national anthem before the game is designed to inspire patriotism. Following the rules of expected behavior helps to reaffirm the *collective conscience*. Snyder (1991) argues that sport halls of fame, museums, and sites of sport memorabilia are extensions of Durkheim's notions of the *sacred* and *collective representations*.

It could be argued that Durkheim envisioned globalization. On *global solidarity*, Durkheim (1933) wrote:

> We have already seen that among European peoples there is a tendency to form, by spontaneous movement, a European society which has, at present, some idea of itself and the beginning of organization. If the formation of a single human society is for-

ever impossible, a fact which has not been proved, at least the formation of continually larger societies brings us vaguely near the goal. (pp. 405–406).

Emile Durkheim was, and remains, one of the greatest social thinkers of all time. His works will remain relevant well into the third millennium.

6

Georg Simmel
(1858–1918)

Georg Simmel, the youngest of seven children, was born March 1, 1858, in the heart of Berlin. The house he was raised in stood on the corner of Leipzigerstrasse and Friedrichstrasse, an area that Coser (1977) compares to Times Square in New York City. He was a modern man in a culturally active and vibrant environment, though he often felt as alienated as the "Stranger" he would later describe in one of his most brilliant works. Born a metropolitan, he would live and die a world-citizen (Spykman, 1966).

Facing anti-Semitism, Georg's paternal grandfather, born Isaac Israel, had changed his last name to Simmel in 1812 in order to become a German citizen. Simmel's father later converted to Catholicism and married a woman who was Lutheran. Georg Simmel was baptized as a Protestant (Pampel, 2000). He never identified with any of the religions of his family's background and never attended church services of any kind.

His father was a prosperous businessman and partner in a well-known chocolate factory that still manufactures candy bars in Germany today. While Georg was quite young, his father passed away. A friend of the family, and founder of an international music publishing house, was appointed

Simmel's guardian. Upon the guardian's death, Georg inherited a huge fortune, enabling him to live as an independent scholar (Giddens, 1969).

Georg Simmel (1858–1918) German micro-sociologist and founder of the "Formal School" of sociology.
Source: Courtesy of the Library of Congress

Simmel's mother was said to be very temperamental and domineering (Wolff, 1950). Georg's relationship with his mother was apparently very distant and he did not seem to have a sense of roots in any secure family environment. Feelings of marginality and insecurity plagued Simmel from an early age (Coser, 1977).

At the age of twelve Georg entered the Gymnasium (an academic high school), and after six years was admitted to the University of Berlin (Spykman, 1966). At the University of Berlin, he followed a regular course of study, concentrating mostly on philosophy, psychology, and history. Simmel was able to study with some of the most important academic figures of the day. These scholars included historians Theodor Mommsen, Johann Droysen, Heinrich von Sybel; the philosopher Eduard Zeller; the ethnologist Adolf Bastian; and, the art historian Herman Grimm (Coser, 1977).

Simmel's first efforts at a dissertation were rejected, and one of his professors commented, "We would do him a great service if we do not encourage him further in this direction" (Frisby, 1984:23). Despite this setback, Simmel received his doctorate in philosophy in 1881 with a dissertation (titled "The Nature of Matter according to Kant's Physical Monadology") on Kant's concept of matter. Simmel so loved Berlin that he refused to follow the example of most German academic men who moved from one university to another both during and after their studies. Instead, he stayed at Berlin, where in 1855 he became a private lecturer (*Privatdozent*) in philosophy. As a private lecturer he was dependent on student fees, in place of a regular salary. He lectured on a wide variety of subjects and theorists, including: logic, principles of philosophy, history of philosophy, modern philosophy, pessimism, ethics, psychology, Kant, Lotze, Schopenhauer, Darwin, and Nietzsche, among others. In spite of his marginality as a *Privatdozent*, Simmel was an extremely popular lecturer, not only among students, but with the cultural elite of Berlin. His lectures were described as clear, logical, artistic, and inspirational (Spykman, 1966).

During his fifteen years as a lecturer, Simmel was developing quite a reputation in German academic circles as well as internationally. He was especially popular in the United States, where his work was of great importance in the birth of sociology (Ritzer, 2000). Simmel's academic activities were not limited to teaching. His prolific writing included more than a hundred essays and a number of volumes of considerable size. Among the more critically acclaimed during this period were: "Moral Deficiencies as Determining Intellectual Functions" (1893); "The Fundamental Problems of Sociology" (1895); "Superiority and Subordination as Subject-Matter of Sociology" (1896); "The Persistence of Social Groups" (1898); and "A Chapter in the Philosophy of Value" (1900).

In 1900, Simmel received the title of *Ausserordentlicher Professor* ("professor extraordinary") at the University of Berlin. It was official recognition long overdue, but it was an honorary, rather than a remunerative, title. His new position did not give him full academic status and it kept him apart from the academic community. Furthermore, it failed to remove the stigma of an academic outsider (Ritzer, 2000). In spite of the support of such scholars as Max Weber, Simmel was unsuccessful for years in obtaining full academic recognition. It wasn't until 1914 at Strasbourg that Simmel finally received a position as professor (*Ordinarius*) of philosophy. He hated the idea of leaving Berlin, but financial reasons forced him to leave the place where he had worked and taught for nearly thirty years.

There were two primary reasons why Simmel's slow advancement in academic rank stood in contrast with his wonderful reputation as a speaker and thinker. First, being of Jewish descent, Simmel was victimized by anti-Semitism. Being a Jew in Germany has seldom been advantageous. Nineteenth-century Germany was not an exception. Berlin University was Prussian in its atmosphere, and the Prussian perspective of things was not likely to lead to a speedy promotion and official encouragement of Jewish teachers (Spylman, 1966). In a report written to the minister of education, Simmel was described as "an Israelite through and through, in his external appearance, in his bearing, and in his mode of thought" (Frisby, 1981:25).

The second reason Simmel had difficulty being promoted rests on the very nature of his works. Although his lectures attracted enthusiastic audiences of students and the cultural elite, his ideas were not welcomed by senior scholars in Germany who favored heavy topics and many footnotes. They believed he gave too much attention to superficial and frivolous topics like fashion, sociability, and everyday life; and, they particularly disliked his writing style, which was witty, ironic, aphoristic, and free of citations (Garner, 2000). He acquired a reputation as an "academic showman" (Giddens, 1969:137). Additionally, academic criticism centered around the fact that many of Simmel's articles appeared in newspapers and magazines, and were written for the general audience rather than academic sociologists (Rammstedt, 1991). His academic colleagues saw him as having a "destructive" rather than a "constructive" intellect. Consequently, while he was quite popular with the students and other members of the social community, his academic associates seemed to be a little "put-off" or even jealous of him.

When a failed attempt on the part of Weber to obtain a professorship for Simmel at Heidelberg in 1908 was realized, Simmel wrote to Weber stating that he believed that

some of his contemporaries viewed his (Simmel's) serious work as too critical, possessing even a destructive spirit, and that his lectures led one only to negation (Wolff, 1950). Simmel believed that his works were misunderstood. He believed that his work tended exclusively toward the positive, toward the demonstration of a deeper insight into world and spirit. Simmel even believed that it was part of his fate to be misunderstood, and he was convinced that the minister's (of education) "unfavorable mood" goes back to some such miscommunication (Wolff, 1950).

However, it would be a mistake to conclude that Simmel failed to have a support system that included his contemporaries. Simmel was very active in cultural events throughout Berlin. He attended meetings of philosophers and sociologists and was the co-founder, with Weber and Toennies, of the "German Society for Sociology." He was friends with two leading poets of Germany, Rainer Maria Rilke and Stefan George. Though he was discriminated against by a number of academic persons, Simmel enjoyed the friendship and support of such eminent academic persons as Max Weber, Heinrich Rickert, Edmund Husserl, and Adolf von Harnack (Coser, 1977).

Simmel was comfortable in many cultural circles. This sense of ease was enhanced by the financial security he enjoyed most of his life. Simmel and his wife, Gertrud, whom he had married in 1890, lived a comfortable bourgeois life. Gertrud was a philosopher in her own right who published work on religion and sexuality under the pseudonym Marie-Luise Enckendorf. Their home was a stage for cultivated gatherings where the sociability about which Simmel wrote so perceptively found a perfect setting (Coser, 1977).

After enjoying many years of success as a lecturer, Simmel moved to Strasbourg where he could fulfill a lifelong dream of becoming a full professor. Unfortunately, Strasbourg would become a source of many disappointments. First, he was deprived of practically every opportunity to lecture to students. Second, Simmel wrote of his displeasure at the lack of a true academic life in Strasbourg in a letter to Weber's wife: "We live . . . a cloistered, closed-off, indifferent, desolate external existence. Academic activity is = 0, the people . . . alien and inwardly hostile" (Frisby, 1981:32). The third disappointment was the biggest problem of all. A short time after he arrived in Strasbourg the war broke out, and with it came the complete demoralization of academic life. Strasbourg was a university at the borderline between Germany and France. The lecture halls were converted into military hospitals. The youth of Germany were sent to the front, and the faculty, with no students, contributed to the gruesome care of the dead and wounded. Simmel's effort to secure a chair position at Heidelberg failed. He would stay at Strasbourg and lecture to what few students were available until shortly before his death, on September 28, 1918.

Simmel felt the pain of war indirectly. He feared that the war threatened the very foundation of European culture and he despised the ethnocentric behaviors of the nation-states. He was equally displeased by the frenzied patriotism displayed by scientists and philosophers. He felt that many scientists and philosophers had given up their eternal calling and had become political propagandists (Spykman, 1965). Simmel's faith in European culture was shaken and because he saw himself more as a European than a German, he was pushed even further toward the edge of acceptability by his own countrymen.

Simmel never enjoyed a normal academic career and he died as a marginal figure in German academia. Although he had many students during his thirty years of teaching, he never established a "school of thought" in the traditional sense of the term. However, Simmel successfully left his lasting mark through a great number of publications. After his dissertation, his first publication, entitled *On Social Differentiation* (1890), centered primarily on sociological issues. *The Problems of the Philosophy of History* and the two volumes of the *Introduction to the Science of Ethics* were published in 1892–93. During this period Simmel sought to isolate the general forms or recurrent regularities of social interaction from the specific content of definite kinds of activity, such as political, economic, and aesthetic. Special attention was given to the problem of authority and obedience. In 1900, one of Simmel's most critically acclaimed works was published, *The Philosophy of Money*, a book as much about sociology as philosophy. Here he applied his general principles to a particular subject, economics; he stressed the role of a money economy in specializing social activity and depersonalizing individual and social relationships.

In 1908, Simmel produced his major sociological work, *Sociology: Investigations on the Forms of Sociation*. Much of this work had been published previously in various journal articles. Many of these articles were published in the United States, especially in *The American Journal of Sociology*. Simmel's sociology first became influential in the United States through the translations and commentaries of Albion Small (1854–1926), one of the first important American sociologists. Park and Burgess gave Simmel a prominent position in their classic *Introduction to the Science of Sociology* (1921). Spykman's (1925) *The Social Theory of Georg Simmel* provided further evidence of the enthusiastic reception for Simmel's work. *The Sociology of Georg Simmel*, translated by Kurt Wolff (1950), comprises Simmel's *Soziologie* (1908) and other works.

Intellectual Influences

There exists a wide variety of influences on Simmel's thoughts. Apart from his immediate teachers, the other formative influences included such divergent thinkers as Husserl, Marx, Weber, Hegel, Cohen, Goethe, Heraclitus, and Schopenhauer. Simmel addressed many of the same themes as the philosopher Friedrich Nietzsche, and openly shared Nietzsche's pleasure in contradictions, his aphoristic and unconventional style, and his combining of lightheartness and despair about the human condition (Garner, 2000). Heraclitus, for whom he had the most profound admiration, had a great influence on the formulation of his relativism, and there is too much similarity in Simmel's and Hegel's dialectic to attribute it to a mere coincidence (Spykman, 1965).

Simmel was well-versed in history, philosophy, and psychology. Unfortunately, he had an annoying habit of ignoring footnotes (or any other form of reference documentation). Consequently, it is difficult to distinguish his original ideas from those whom he read. Early in his career, Simmel was influenced by French and English positivistic thought and Darwinian and Spencerian evolutionary thought (Coser, 1977). He then turned to Kant and the neo-Kantians, a period when he produced some of his most substantial sociological work.

During his lifetime, Simmel published an estimated 200 articles and 22 books. These works covered a wide range of topics, including: morality, history, society, money, religion, art, philosophy; and the artists, writers, and philosophers themselves (Weingartner, 1962).

Darwin and Spencer

Simmel was clearly influenced by Spencer's evolutionary conceptions, especially his idea of differentiation. Evidence of this can be found in Simmel's works of the 1890s,

specifically in *On Social Differentiation* and in the *Introduction to the Science of Ethics.* According to Simmel, differentiation has the evolutionary advantage of saving energy in the relation between the organism and the environment (Coser, 1977).

He did not accept all interpretations of cultural evolution. In fact, Simmel was disturbed by current political attempts to implement Darwinian doctrines to support notions of superiority. Simmel was against the idea that all individuals and species were engaged in constant battles for dominance. However, Simmel did employ some modes of Spencerian and Darwinian reasoning to address the issues of the day. For example, in *Philosophie des Geldes*, Simmel argued that marriages engaged in for the sake of money (the tradition of the royals) lead to genetic mixtures, which biology has recognized as the cause of direct and deleterious racial degeneration. In another one of his 1890s' articles, *Einfuehrung in die Moralwisscenschaft* (1892), Simmel maintained that criminal dispositions were hereditary, and even protested against the preservation of the weak who will transmit their inferiority to future generations.

Simmel came close to Spencer's idea that societies evolve through stages, from primitive immersion in the group to autonomous individual growth in modern society. These beliefs were reinforced by many of the German thinkers during this era, including Adolf Bastian, a former teacher of Simmel's. In Germany, this type of evolutionary thought was referred to as "parallelism." Simmel was partly convinced of the optimistic and comforting belief in future perfectibility.

Kant and Neo-Kantian Thought

A discipline known as the Kant *Philologie*, concerned with the history, development, and works of Kant, has pre-empted a considerable portion of philosophical historiography since 1860. These studies began with immense commentary on the *Critique of Pure Reason*, produced in 1881–92 by Hans Vaihinger, known for his philosophy of the "As If" (which emphasis man's reliance on pragmatic fictions), and with the founding of the new journal *Kantstudien* (1896) and the Kant-Gesellschaft ("Kantian Society," 1904).

The fundamental question of Kant's philosophy, "How is nature possible?", was answered (by Kant) by saying that nature was nothing but the representation of nature. Thus, the notion of the realm of nature, the sensible world, is organized by human understanding in accordance with certain a priori principles of knowledge. Kant argued that man could never attain "true" knowledge of things in themselves, but only a knowledge that was mediated through certain fundamental mental categories, or "givens."

Like Kant, Simmel's philosophy is relativistic. Simmel distinguishes sharply between subject and object, between knowing mind and known world, between the organizing functions of the mind and the data of experience, between form and matter. But Simmel's relativism is much less severe than Kantian formalism. Simmel's relativism was something dynamic and functional. It was not primarily a formal structure, a doctrine; it was a mode of thinking, a thought form, a method of approach.

For Simmel, the truth is relative, not absolute. A single idea is true, is valid, only in relation to another idea, and a whole body of knowledge is available through experience in relation to the external world. The peculiar tendency of the human mind to accept notions of a truth from "significant others," (e.g. religious beliefs, rumors regarding other people) is proof of man's potential for infinite regression. Circular reasoning and dogmatic approaches to life hinder the discovery of the truth.

When Simmel asked himself in his famous essay, "How is society possible?" he used Kant's reasoning in explaining how nature was possible. Simmel viewed society as a result of the unity of reciprocal parts. He resolved that the fixed, the permanent, the substantial elements of society worked with social forces, movements, and the historical process of growth. With his emphasis on process and function rather than on product and content, he approaches Nietzsche and Bergson in their conception of life itself as the ultimate value (Spykman, 1965).

Simmel's approach to sociology primarily centers around the idea that society consists of a web, or a network, of patterned interactions, and it is the role of sociology to study the forms of these interactions as they occur and reoccur in different historical times and settings. In *Fundamental Problems of Sociology* (1895) Simmel states, "Society is merely the name for a number of individuals, connected by interaction."

Karl Marx

Simmel's idea of the dualism of life and objects of the mind, and the objectivation of the human mind come from Marx's idea of self-alienation. Simmel (1965) states that, "this dialectic is not a historical phenomenon of capitalism, but the general destiny of mature civilizations. The works of men lose the human coefficient and are established in autonomous contexts of their own. These intermediate layers of civilization threaten the genuine and natural unity between man and his values" (135).

Concepts and Contributions

Simmel's approach to sociology can best be described as a conscious attempt to reject the organic (analogy) theories of Comte and Spencer and the German historical description of events. He did not see society as a thing or an organism (organicist), nor merely as a convenient label for something that was an abstract creation (idealist). Society was the sum of all individual patterned interactions. Simmel did not believe that sociology was the science of everything human; its legitimate subject matter lies in the description and analysis of particular forms of human interaction. He believed that all human behavior is individual behavior, but much of it can be explained in terms of the individual's group affiliation and in terms of the constraints imposed upon him/her by particular forms of interaction (Coser, 1965).

Formal Sociology

Simmel—sometimes called the founder of the "formal school" of sociology—viewed society as a process that is real and not merely an abstraction, and built on this idea that the focus of sociology consists of a systematic analysis of social forms. His insistence on the forms of social interaction as the dominant focus of sociology was a decisive response to those historians and other representatives of the humanities who denied that a science of society could ever explain the novelty and the uniqueness of historical phenomena. Simmel never denied that particular historical events are unique because, when utilizing the sociological perspective (in 1959, C. Wright Mills would label this concept as utilizing the *sociological imagination*), one need not concern oneself with the uniqueness of events but, rather, with their underlying uniformities. Simmel justified this belief by pointing out that similar forms of socialization occur with quite dissimilar content, and similar social interests are found in quite dissimilar forms of socialization.

It cannot be denied that this is the case. There are similar forms of relationships between individuals in groups that are completely dissimilar in purpose and goal.

Superiority and subordination, competition, imitation, division of labor, personal bias, and countless other forms of relationships are found in all types of groups. A sociologist can always predict that the larger the group size the greater the probability of differences in opinions and power that will exist.

From Simmel's standpoint, the real world is composed of innumerable events, actions, interactions, and so forth. To cope with this maze of reality, people attempt to order it by imposing patterns, or forms, onto it. In fact, one of Simmel's dominant concerns was the *form* rather than the *content* of social interaction. Therefore, instead of a bewildering array of specific events, the individual is confronted with a limited number of forms. The sociologist's task is to do precisely what the layperson does, that is, impose a limited number of forms on social reality, on interaction in particular, so that it may be better analyzed.

For Simmel, *contents* represent the total array of everything that individuals bring with them in social interactions with others. Contents are seen as drives, interests, and purposes—phenomena residing in the individual (or the raw material of form). *Social forms* reflect common patterns and routines of behavior that individuals select from during social interactions (Pampel, 2000). Forms are supra-individuals, or interactional entities within which individuals are engaged and realize their interests. Simmel believes that forms cannot live independently of content (Larwrence, 1976). Forms indicate the way some infinite potentialities of life can be organized in such a manner that it attains structural stability.

The term *form* may not have been the best choice for Simmel, as he received a great deal of resistance in acceptance of its usage by other sociologists who viewed it dubious at best. Modern sociologists are more comfortable using terms such as social structure, role, or status in place of *form*. Simmel has also been criticized of imposing a sense of order where there may be none.

Simmel's approach to formal sociology can be defended on a number of fronts. First, he did reflect a number of real-life categories in his methodology. Second, he did not impose arbitrary and rigid categories on social reality but tries instead to allow the forms to emerge from social reality. Third, Simmel did not possess a strict theoretical orientation in which he tried to force all aspects of social life.

Social Types

In line with his methodological belief that categories of persons should be created in the study of human behavior, Simmel constructed a number of *social types* to complement his inventory of social forms. Among them were, "the stranger," "the spendthrift," "the mediator," "the adventurer," "the renegade," and "the poor."

The stranger, in Simmel's terminology, is not just a wanderer, a person who is here today and gone tomorrow; rather *the stranger* is a person with a fixed position within a particular spatial group. "If wandering is the liberation from every given point in space, and thus the conceptional opposite to fixation at such a point, the sociological form of the 'stranger' presents the unity, as it were, of these two characteristics" (Wolff, 1950:402). This phenomenon reveals that social distance within the group is based on spatial relations on one hand, but can be symbolic on the other. The stranger unites nearness of the group and remoteness concurrently.

In Simmel's description of *the stranger*, distance plays a central role. If the individual is too close with the other group members then he is not a stranger. On the other hand, if the individual is too far from the group then she has no contact with the group.

Being both near and far, the stranger is often called on as a confidant. Confidences entrusted to strangers run little risk of negative consequences, and yet allow for some relative feedback. Often, the stranger is more objective with group members because he is not tied to either of the conflicting parties. The stranger is bound by no commitments that could prejudice her perception, understanding, and evaluation. The stranger is not bound in action by habit, piety, or precedent.

The poor as a social type, is defined in terms of social relationships. The poor emerge only when a society recognizes poverty as a special status and then assigns others to assist them. Once the poor accept assistance, they are removed from their private status, and become a public issue. Society assigns them a negative status, a burden. Aid to the poor is often viewed as a requirement of society, more than a moral requirement to help the less fortunate. As Simmel (1908) explains, "the obligations we have toward the poor may appear as a simple correlate of the rights of the poor. Especially in countries where begging is a normal occupation, the beggar believes more or less naively that he has a right to alms and frequently considers that their denial means the withholding of a tribute to which he is entitled. Another and completely different characteristic—in the same category—implies the idea that the right to assistance is based on the group affiliation of the needy" (Levine, 1971:151).

Clearly, the poor are defined in terms of social relationships. The poor may feel that society owes them, and the non-poor may feel obligated to help or they may not. From a functional standpoint, Simmel felt that society must aid and support the poor so that they do not become active and dangerous enemies of society. Thus, aid to the poor is for the sake of society. Simmel recognized the poor in terms of *relative deprivation*, that is, people at all social-economic levels may feel poor compared to others in their group. Regardless of one's income, most people live on what they earn and always seem to want more money.

Dialectical Thinking

Simmel's sociological approach was guided by the dialectical approach. A dialectical approach is multicausal and multidirectional; integrates fact and value; rejects the idea that there are concrete dividing lines between social phenomena; focuses on social relations; and is deeply concerned with conflicts and contradictions. Simmel believed that "the world can best be understood in terms of conflicts and contrasts between opposed categories" (Levine, 1971:xxxv).

The forms of social life are constantly influencing individual decision and behavior. "The forms of social life impress themselves upon each individual and allow him to become specifically human. At the same time, they imprison and stultify the human personality by regressing the free play of spontaneity. Only in and through institutional forms can man attain freedom, yet his freedom is forever endangered by these very institutional forms" (Coser, 1977:184).

Simmel's (1904) fascinating and dualistic essay on *Fashion* illustrates a form of social relationship that allows those who wish to conform to the demands of society to do so. On the other hand, fashion allows those who choose to ignore current trends an opportunity to deviate and remain individualistic. The study of *fashion* is dialectical in the sense that the success and spread of any given fashion leads to its eventual downfall. That is, the distinctiveness of fashion is lost once large numbers of people come to accept it, from New York fashion runways to the K-Mart racks.

One of Simmel's primary interests was interaction (*sociation*) among conscious individuals, and his intent was to look at a wide-variety of interactions. For Simmel, *sociation* always involved potential opposite extremes: harmony involves conflict; attraction, repulsion; and love with hate. He believed that human relations are characterized by imperfect modes of *sociation* resulting in the potential of both positive and negative outcomes during interaction. Even couples involved in a "loving" relationship with one another, need to "blow off steam" (a safety valve) in order for loving relations to endure.

Social Geometry

Simmel's formal sociology is a clear effort to develop a *geometry* of social relations. *Social Geometry* or "Quantitative Aspects of the Group" is among Simmel's best-known works. Two of the geometric coefficients that interested him the most are social distance (e.g., *the stranger*) and numbers (e.g., *dyad* and *triad*). The role of distance in social relations can be summed as "the properties of forms and the meanings of things are a function of the relative distances between individuals and other individuals or things" (Levine, 1971:xxxiv). The value of something is determined by its *distance* from the individual. According to Simmel, an item will not be valuable if it is either too close and too easy, or too distant and too difficult, to obtain. Objects attainable only through great effort are the most valuable.

The basic principles of group structure and quantitative size (*numbers*) are best illustrated with Simmel's concepts and usage of the *dyad* and the *triad*. The numerically simplest structures that can still be designated as social interactions occur between two elements. The isolated individual is someone who does not interact with others. The dyadic group has a typical sociological form based on the fact that the most divergent individuals uniting for the most varied motives will show combinations of the same formation. Further, the dyadic characteristic holds true in the case of an association between pairs of groups (e.g., families) and other combination forms (e.g., organizations) (Spykman, 1965).

The strongest bonds are formed between two people, be they best friends, lovers, or married couples. Each member retains a high level of individuality, but they are aware of the fact that their social structure is immediately dependent upon one another. There is no independent structure within the *dyad*. Each member is directly responsible for any collective action; neither individual can deny responsibility by shifting the blame to the group; there is maximum involvement by both persons with a degree of intimacy; and, if either person departs, the group ceases to exist.

The *dyad* possesses unique characteristics that distinguishes it from other forms of *sociation*. The dyadic group, in contrast with all other groups of more numerous elements, is characterized by the fact that it does not attain a higher, superindividual life, so that the individual might feel independent of himself.

The simple addition of a third person to the dyad causes radical and fundamental changes to the group structure (form). This three-person group Simmel called a *triad*. The *dyad* has a closeness between the two members; the third modifies it entirely, but it is also further complicated by the fact that a further extension is not followed by a modification of corresponding degree (Spykman, 1965). The addition of a third element provides the opportunity for the development of an external superindividual and the internal development of divisions. The direct and immediate reciprocity found in the *dyad* is replaced by an indirect relationship that both reinforces and interferes with the immediate reciprocity. The new group is less dependent on the immediate participation of the elements; it absorbs less of the total personality; and it can continue its existence if one element leaves.

The dyadic group shows synthesis and antithesis. The entrance of a third element means transition, conciliation, and renunciation both of the immediate reciprocity and of the direct opposition (Spykman, 1965). The third becomes an intruder, but with whom will she join? The original *dyad* has an intimacy, which is the tendency of relations between two persons. Is the reason why the third person joined the group to weaken this intimacy, or to intensify it?

The third person may become the non-partisan arbitrator or mediator. In this case, the third element serves the group as a whole. The conciliator or arbitrator aims to prevent a disruption of the existing unity between the original two elements. The non-partisan can, however, also use his advantageous position for his own selfish interests. In such a case, his position becomes that of the *tertius gaudens*, Latin for "the third who enjoys." This previously unconnected non-partisan may spontaneously seize upon the opportunity that conflict between the other two offers. He may do this because the other two conflicting elements will compete for the third person's favor and therefore gain power of the group. Finally, the third person may implement a strategy known as *divide et impera*, Latin for "divide and rule." According to Simmel, this occurs when the third element intentionally produces conflict in order to gain a dominating position. The third person may do this in order to maintain power over the group, or if she has plans to ally herself with one of the original two members and then remove the other member.

Superordination and Subordination

According to Simmel, the most important form of relationship in the whole social world is the one between the leader and his followers, between the superior and his *subordinates*. It is a form of socialization critical for social life and the main factor in sustaining the unity of groups. Superiority and *subordination* constitute the sociological expression of psychological differences in human beings (Spykman, 1965).

The *superordinate* and the *subordinate* have a reciprocal relationship. The *superordinate* (e.g., boss, master, leader) expects the *subordinate* (e.g., employee, slave, follower) to follow the rules. Domination does not lie in the unilateral imposition of the *superordinate's* will upon the *subordinate* because of the reciprocal nature between the two. As Ritzer (2000) explains, "even in the most oppressive form of domination, *subordinates* have at least some degree of personal freedom" (270). The choices may be limited between submission and punishment and however little consolation the existence of this alternative may bring to the individual in question, it shows, nonetheless, that the superior–inferior relationship cannot be established without some active participation on the part of the *subordinate*. Thus, submission is not purely passive, but has an active aspect as well, and the resulting relationship is a form of *sociation*.

The sociological situation between the superordinate and the subordinate is completely changed as soon as a third element is added (Wolff, 1950). One might assume that an alliance between the *subordinates* would emerge because of their common form and thus jeopardize the power of the *superordinate*. But Simmel viewed this transformation of a numerical into a qualitative difference as no less fundamental if viewed from the master's standpoint. It is easier to keep two rather than one at a desired distance; in their jealousy and competition the master has a tool for keeping them down and making them obedient, while there is no equivalent tool in the case of *one* servant. Simmel summarized, the structure found in the triad is completely different from the dyad but not, on the other hand, specifically distinguished from groups of four or more members (Wolff, 1950).

Sociability

Simmel defined *sociability* as the "play form of *sociation*" (Martindale, 1988). *Sociability* is the association of people for its own sake and for the delight of interacting with others. The character of the gathering is determined by personal qualities and personalities of the participants. Interaction always arises on the basis of certain drives or for the sake of certain purposes. Interaction can be based on necessities, one's intelligence, wants and desires, will, creativity, and other elements that are a part of life. Interaction among large groups of people leads to the formation of a "society." Society, then, becomes a reality by form.

Sociability emerges as a very peculiar sociological structure. As such, Simmel (in *The Fundamental Problems of Sociology*) categorized many characteristics of *sociability*:

a. **Tact and Impersonality.** In the group setting there is seldom an external guide overseeing interpretations of proper behavior. Tact fulfills this regulatory function. Its most essential role is to draw limits, which result from the claims of others, of the individual's impulses, ego-stresses, and intellectual and material desires. Impersonality occurs when people are not acting socially. It is considered tactless because it interferes with sociability (social interaction).

b. **Sociability Thresholds.** Humans are a totality of dynamic complex ideas, wants, desires, and possibilities. According to motivations and relations of life and its changes, man makes himself a differentiated and clearly defined social phenomenon. Each person develops their own tolerance toward socializing with others, thus creating different sociability thresholds.

c. ***The "Sociability Drive" and the Democratic Nature of Sociability.*** As a foundation of law, Kant posited the axiom that each individual should possess freedom to the extent which is compatible with freedom of every other individual. Kant's law is thoroughly democratic. These democratic ideas are to carry over to society and assumingly social drives. One must note that the form of social drives varies from individual to individual.

d. ***The Artificial World of Sociability.*** The world of sociability is an artificial one, maintained only through voluntary interaction. Because of the often harsh reality of one's real life, it is easy to understand why persons often prefer the deceptive social world they have created and work so hard at maintaining.

e. ***Social Games.*** Many members of society will take part in interactions that attempt to outdo others, and resort to participating in social games. The seriousness of life often requires an emotional and physical outlet. Games are created and people actually "play society."

f. ***Coquetry.*** "In the sociology of sex, we find a play-form: the play-form of eroticism is coquetry" (Wolff, 1950). In general, the erotic question between the sexes is that of offer and refusal. Simmel believed that the nature of feminine coquetry (flirting) is to play up, alternately, allusive promises and allusive withdrawals—to attract the male but always stop short of a decision, and to reject him but never to deprive him of all hope. Her behavior swings back and forth between "yes"

and "no" without stopping at either. Despite these and many other potentially sexist remarks Simmel makes in this section, few would disagree that the very nature of coquetry makes it an element of sociability, played by both sexes.

g. ***Conversation.*** In brief, conversation is the most general vehicle for socializing. It is language that separates man from the other animals. Humans are capable of serious and frivolous conversation. Knowing how to master both is a huge asset in sociability.

h. ***Sociability as the Play-Form of Ethical Problems and of Their Solution.*** Individuals must function as a part of a collective in the world they live. They have their own personal set of ethics and values that often come in conflict with those of society. Sociability allows for the temporary shelter of these conflicts through participation in groups who share the same beliefs.

i. ***Historical Illustrations.*** A general conception of sociability is well-illustrated throughout time. For example, Simmel shows that in the early German Middle Ages, there existed the brotherhoods of knights.

j. ***The "Superficial" Character of Sociability.*** A simple fact remains, persons choose to form groups and societies for a wide variety of reasons, but at any time they are free to remove themselves. Thus, sociability has a very superficial character.

Secrecy

The secret is the hiding of realities by one or more persons from another person or persons. This can be done by either negative or positive means. According to Simmel, *secrecy* is one of man's greatest achievements. It represents an advancement from one's childish stage in which every conception is expressed at once, and every undertaking is accessible to the eyes of all. The secret offers a possibility of a second world alongside the manifest world; and the latter is decisively influenced by the former (Wolff, 1950).

In order for interaction to occur among persons, there exists the reality that these people must know at least some bit of information about each other. This is true whether we are talking about interactions with friends, family, colleagues, or less impersonal contacts. Over time we tend to know certain people very well, but we can never know them absolutely. We do, however, form some sort of unitary conception of other people through the bits of information we do have. Simmel (1906) sees a dialectical relationship between interaction (being) and the mental picture we create of others (conceiving) based upon the reciprocal relationship already established. In all aspects of life we acquire not only truths concerning others, but half-truths, false-truths, and flat-out errors of judgments.

The fact is, even if someone wanted to reveal *all* aspects of their personal life it would be impossible to communicate such a huge amount of information. There are times when people want to keep certain portions of their lives secret from others and intentionally hide information. In extreme cases they may even resort to lying. The intentional hiding of information takes on greater intensity when it clashes with the intention of revealing.

There comes a time when someone may confide previously hidden information with trusted others. In this case, they share information that is unknown to others. "Whether there is secrecy between two individuals or groups, and if so how much, is a question that characterizes every relation between them" (Wolff, 1950:330). Even

in the case where one of the two does not notice the existence of a secret, the behavior of the concealer, and hence the whole relationship, is modified by it. The secret contains a tension that is dissolved in the moment of its revelation. The secret is surrounded by the possibility and temptation of betrayal; an external danger of being discovered is interwoven with internal danger of giving oneself away.

It is easy to apply Simmel's concept of *social geometry* to the issue of *secrecy*. As for the element of *distance*, we tend to expect relative strangers to hold back information, but we are hurt and/or offended when it involves someone close to us. Thus, we can better accept lies from those who are distant from us. The lie of a lover is far more devastating than a lie from a movie celebrity or politician. *Secrecy* is also linked to the size (*numbers*) of society. In small groups, it is difficult to develop secrets because of the closeness of circumstances. In larger groups, secrets can more easily develop and are much more needed because of the many different characteristics of group members.

The Secret Society

The first internal relation typical of the *secret society* is the reciprocal confidence among members. It is required because the purpose of secrecy is protection. Of all the protective measures, the most radical is to make oneself invisible. *Secret societies* offer a very impressive schooling in the moral solidarity among members. Above all, is the oath of silence. The gradual initiation of a member into the *secret society* creates a hierarchy. With increased growth comes increased rituals. Features of the *secret society* include: separateness, formality, consciousness, seclusion, degrees of initiation, group egoism, centralization, and de-individualism.

Philosophy of Money

Simmel's magnum opus, *The Philosophy of Money* (1907) demonstrates that his theoretical scope rivals that of Marx, Weber, and Durkheim. *The Philosophy of Money* demonstrates conclusively that Simmel deserves at least as much recognition for his general theory as for his essays on microsociology. It is a difficult book that has daunted many would-be readers. Nevertheless, Simmel's insights about money are as valid today as they were a hundred years ago.

According to Simmel, economic exchange is best understood as a form of social interaction. His focus is exchange. Exchange is a universal form of interaction. In economics, not all exchange involves money, but money becomes a social tool. A society that uses money has replaced the barter system and, consequently, it reflects social evolution because of its acceptance of growth and rationalization. "The phenomena of the money economy are born primarily of that type of mental energy which is called intellect as distinguished from sentiment and feeling" (Spykman, 1965:232).

The use of money changes a society. The value of money is based on the faith (rationalization) that the currency can be used to purchase products. With the barter system the items offered for exchange are tangible, they exist, and are readily available. History has shown that people are reluctant to make such drastic changes in their economic culture. "The impulsive and emotional character of primitive people is undoubtedly due in part to the shortness of their teleological series" (Spykman, 1965:232).

In the economic realm, money serves both to create distance from objects and to provide the means to overcome it. Once we obtain enough money, we are able to overcome the distance between ourselves and the objects. The value of an object relates to the level of desirability and the degree of unattainability. In the process of creating value, money also provides the basis for the development of the market, the modern economy, and ultimately, the capitalistic society.

Like Marx, Simmel was concerned with capitalism and the problems created by a money economy. But Simmel saw the economic problems of his time as simply a specific manifestation of a more general cultural problem. Marx, as an economic determinist, viewed capitalism as the primary problem of society, and therefore subject to eventual change (for the better) through communism. Simmel viewed the economic structure as a part of the greater objective nature of society, which alienated man's subjective nature. The objective nature of society, including economics, was something inherent with human life and not subject to change.

Exchange

Simmel views exchange as the purest and most concentrated form of human interaction. Generally, all interactions can be viewed as exchanges. An interesting characteristic of exchange is that the sum of values is greater than it was before the exchange took place. Economic exchange, regardless of whether it involves material objects or labor, entails the sacrifice of some good or service that has potential value for others. Thus, to some extent, value attached to a particular object comes about through the process of exchange.

Value and exchange, according to Simmel, are inseparable. Value is put on the objects that are exchanged. Value is not always contained with the specific object, but is a product of comparison. The individual determines the value of something through comparison with something else.

Simmel conceives economic activity as sacrifice in return for a gain. The value of the gain is determined from the value of the sacrifice involved in order to obtain an object. Value is always situationally determined. The exchange is always "worth it" to the parties involved, at least at the actual instant that the exchange takes place. If a sacrifice is too high, then the value is too low and exchange does not take place.

Mass Culture

The term *mass culture* was not coined by Simmel, but his works reflect the concept. He believed central themes reflect social and cultural life in all epochs of history. Scholars must understand these *themes* to understand current culture.

Whenever life progresses beyond the animal level to that of the spirit, and spirit progresses to the level of culture, an internal contradiction appears. The whole history of culture is the working out of this contradiction. We speak of culture whenever life produces certain forms in which it expresses and realizes itself: works of art, religions, sciences, technologies, laws, and innumerable others (Etzkorn, 1968). Culture, having spirit, ceaselessly creates such forms which become self-enclosed and demand permanence. These forms are inseparable from life; they are fixed identities.

Like Marx, Simmel is concerned with the ineradicable dualism inherent in the relation between individuals and objective cultural values. An individual can attain cultivation only by assimilating to the cultural values that surround him. But, these values threaten to engulf and enslave the individual. Beyond the fetishistic character that Marx attributed to the economic realm of commodity production; Simmel indicates that these cultural contents have been created by people and they were intended by people, but they attain an objective form and follow an immanent logic of development, becoming alienated from their origin as well

as from their purpose (Coser, 1977). Thus, people come to reify social reality; and Simmel viewed social reality as "objective culture."

In the last years of his life, Simmel reflected on the drastic changes of the times— the phenomenon of *mass culture*. Simmel saw a tension between the way individuals experience and create culture ("subjective culture") and culture embodied in material objects and institutions ("objective culture"). He believed that the latter was growing rapidly, overwhelming the former so that individuals were crushed by the weight and force of culture that existed outside of their control (Garner, 2000).

One of the most well-known and influential works on the urban mentality was written by Simmel in an essay called "The Metropolis and Mental Life" (originally published in 1902–1903). Simmel described mental life as a combination of three basic traits: emotional reserve; an attachment to personal freedom; and a willingness to seek out and reward extreme individuality.

Emotional reserve, or indifference, is a self-protective device designed to shield the individual from the fast-paced tempo of urban life. Urban dwellers are bombarded by so many images, they must maintain a certain emotional distance from this sensory onslaught. Learning to react with one's mind rather than heart is a protective mechanism necessary in the metropolitan life.

Maintaining *an attachment to personal freedom* is described by Simmel as the emotional indifference that metropolitan persons exhibit toward one another. Caring for one's neighbor, which is such a critical element in some rural villages and towns, is viewed as pettiness in the urban setting. Unfortunately, for the urban dweller this individual freedom can create loneliness and despair.

The third trait of metropolitan life, *extreme individuality*, stems from the metropolitan need to do something drastic in order to attract social attention. Urban dwellers seem to almost be relieved when such individuals display their radical forms of behavior.

Relevancy

Simmel can best be described as a microsociologist who played a significant role in the development of small-group research, symbolic interactionism, and exchange theory. Simmel's grounding of sociology in some psychological categories is one reason why his sociology has proven attractive not only to symbolic interactionists, but social psychologists as well.

Simmel's main microsociological concern was with social process and the forms of interaction patterns in which individuals structure and restructure the social world. Simmel operated with a dialectical orientation that was demonstrated in a variety of ways. He was concerned with the conflicts that develop between individual culture and objective culture. His formal sociology and social geometry provided a schematic of an individual's social location, which would allow later investigators to locate and often predict the moves of social persons involved in webs of group relations.

At the macro level, Simmel paid little attention to social structure, often reducing them to little more than interaction patterns. His real interest at the macro-level resides with his work on objective culture. This concern was best illustrated in his essays of the metropolitan life. In *The Philosophy of Money*, Simmel discussed problems inherent with the capitalistic system, to problems of life in general.

The revival of interest in Simmel's thoughts, which has emerged in the English-speaking world since the 1970s, has brought to the forefront the attention of his contributions to cultural theory, in particular, his works on the concept of *spiritual life* (a

thinker must push beyond the confines of his era and anticipate the problems of the future); his works on "the crisis of culture"; and "the conflict of modern culture." Although Simmel does not use the concept "modernism," he identifies a number of contemporary cultural phenomena which would later be grounded under that term (Turner, 1990).

As the founder of the "formal school," Simmel successfully showed that society, as a process, is a real entity, and not merely an abstraction. Forms of interaction do exist, and are subject to systematic analysis. His insistence that the focus of study for sociologists should be on these *forms* of behavior provides a guideline for microsociology. It also provides a legitimacy for the discipline. For example, at the beginning of a semester a college professor can always predict what percent of the class will earn what letter grade. Who specifically will earn an "A" or "B" will be determined during the semester, but the form remains relatively constant for any professor who teaches consistently over a period of time.

On a daily basis most individuals interact with a variety of people in a variety of settings. Behavioral patterns are adjusted according to social environment. The college student may wake in the morning to the sounds of her roommate's stereo; join fellow dormmates at the dining hall for breakfast; attend classes with a number of other students and professors; go to work and interact with customers and co-workers; and finally get home in time to shower and dress for her date. These are just a few of the real-life categories and patterned interactions that will occur.

The creation of categories is not limited to forms of interaction, they are also applicable to *social types* of persons. The student who has moved hundreds of miles away from home to start her college studies, the young man who has crossed the country to start a new job, or the young child who finds herself at a new army base for the third time in five years, all share one common attribute—they are *the stranger*. Simmel's description of *the stranger* is not bound by physical distance; it includes the individual who is having a hard time blending in with the cultural environment. Add to this Simmmel's lucid insights regarding urban life, it is easy to see why so many people experience a level of social distance even when surrounded by thousands of people and a near-endless bombardment of stimuli.

Fontana and Frey (1983) apply the concept of *the stranger* in their brilliant article "The Placekicker in Professional Football: Simmel's Stranger Revisited." The placekicker in professional football often feels the effect of cultural marginality. He is both near and far from the group as shown by his predominant ethnic and cultural differences, his soccer (or other sports) background, along with the different methods of entry and socialization to football. Sometimes he may even go barefooted, a clear violation of the norm. His teammates usually shun him, and seldom associate with him, even on the playing field. With the rule changes that have occurred in the National Football League (NFL) over the past decades, it is the placekicker who has ironically come to dominate the game. The leading scorer on most NFL teams is the kicker (field goals and extra points after touchdowns). Thus, his kicking ability thrusts the kicker in a *superordinate* position within the team. His teammates, who do most of the work, become the *subordinates*.

One's self-interpretation of value is often in relation to their spatial location. Creative managers at Nortel Networks implemented a very simple and zero-cost strategical approach to the problem of social distance. Employee surveys indicated that workers were very upset with the reserved parking policy. The farther one had to park, the less important they were, and thus an indication of value to the company. When Nortel moved their global headquarters in suburban Toronto in 1997, general admission parking was initiated (Flaherty, 1999). It is presumed that the staff is happier, but top management will not be happy.

Simmel displays his mastery of the importance of *social distance* with his works on *social geometry*. The element of numbers is clearly explained with the concepts of *dyad* and *triad*. Students have an easy time understanding the significance of the simple addition of one person to an existing *dyad*. Many loving couples and best friends have been "split-up" because of a third person. Sometimes one may be victimized by the third person, other times one may be the third person. The third person may also serve a positive role, such as a mediator. Anyone interested in the field of counseling will serve such a role. For those individuals seeking power, learning how to use the *divide et impera* principle becomes an important tool in climbing the ranks.

The importance of numbers in group interaction has been applied to a number of scenarios in contemporary research. During the 1960s, two social psychologists, Bibb Latane and John Darley, noted how people in urban areas often ignore serious crimes that occurred around them. They concluded that the greater the number of persons in the group, the less personal resposibility any one person assumes (*diffusion of responsibility*). Thus, when 38 residents of an apartment complex in New York City (1964) did nothing in response to the screams of a young woman (Kitty Genovese) being repeatedly stabbed in an attack by a stranger, they all shifted intervention responsibility to the others (Baron and Byrne, 1997).

The diffusion of responsibility theory hypothesizes that when one person sees someone in need of help, the bystander's responsibility is clear; but with multiple witnesses to an emergency, the duty of assistance is spread equally among all the bystanders. For example, if a motorist has broken down in a isolated area, the first passerby is likely to offer assistance because they realize it could be some time before another motorist might driveby. Conversely, if a motorist breaks down on a busy interstate, numerous passerbys will ignore the disabled driver, and justifly their behavior because they do bear the brunt of solo responsibility.

Latane and Darley (1970) extended their study of the effect of group size on human performance. They showed that students working in groups produced less than those who worked independently. Groupwork was shown to reduce individual personal responsibility. This behavior is labeled *social loafing*, and results in reduced personal effort. Social loafing occurs because the relationship between one's effort and the group's outcome is less certain. Solutions to social loafing include:

1. Making the output or effort of each group member readily identifiable (Williams, Harkins, and Latane, 1981). You do this, you do that, and so on.

2. Increase members' commitment to successful performance (Brickner, Harkins, and Ostrom, 1986). Putting pressures on all members to work hard will offset temptations to engage in social loafing.

3. Increase the apparent importance of the task (Karau and Williams, 1993). We need to do well on this assignment in order to pass the course.

4. Strenghten group cohesiveness (Welson and Mustari, 1988). When individuals care about the group outcome, performance should increase.

Additional studies on the dynamics and processes of group behavior include *groupthink* and *group polarization*. Groupthink is a process whereby a group collectively arrives at a decision that individual members are privately at odds with, but do not contest. This generally happens in small cohesive groups with dominant leaders (Farley, 1998). Group polarization is a process in which a group moves toward a more extreme decision and course of action than any of its individual members preferred.

The group studies described in the previous chapters are but a glimpse into the theoretical tradition of Simmel's thoughts (though not in methodology, as he seldom engaged in experimental research).

Returning to the issue of power, another tool available for those who seek power involves learning other people's *secrets*. Knowledge always equals power. Knowing the right moment to reveal a secret is a demonstration of power. On the other, more honorable hand, being able to keep secrets and knowing with whom one can confide in, is also a sign of power. All these issues related to secrets influence social behavior.

Today, more than ever, most people work for someone else. Simmel's ideas of the *superordinate* (employer/boss) and *subordinate* (employee/worker) are easily understood in the context that one finds himself possessing one role or the other. In some work settings the employees enjoy relative autonomy. They may belong to a strong union or they are lucky enough to have an employer who truly values their contributions. In other work environments, the employees are not treated so graciously and they may actually dislike their boss and dread going to work.

Simmel's *philosophy of money* is still relevant today. When a monetary economic system replaces the barter system, that society is forever changed. Money may be an alienating force for some, but possessing it is the goal for most people in society. In fact, with the continuing trend of globalization, the formation of mega-societies such as the European Community, a uniform monetary system of *exchange* is the most logical solution.

Although most of Simmel's works are essays, his works are nonetheless substantial. It should be clear that students of social theory, and social thinkers in general, will continue to read the many important contributions that Simmel has provided to sociology.

Max Weber

(1864–1920)

Max Weber, son of Helene and Max Weber, was born on April 21, 1864, in Erfurt, Germany. He was the eldest of eight children, all of whom lived into adulthood except for two—Anna, who died in infancy, and Helene, who died at the age of four of diphtheria (Weber, 1988). Max himself was a sickly child, and continued to suffer from physical and mental torment throughout his life. As a child in 1866, he became ill with unilateral meningitis (Weber, 1988). The many medical problems that confronted the Weber children led Helene to be an extremely devoted mother.

The Webers were a prominent family of industrialists and civil servants with a considerable amount of political and social connections (Miller, 1963). Both of Max's parents descended from a line of Protestants, who had been refugees from Catholic persecution in the past. Weber's mother's family was originally a part of the Huguenot line, with her ancestors tracing back to Wilhelm von Wallenstein (Kassler, 1988). Weber's paternal grandfather had been a prosperous linen dealer in Bielefeld, where the family had moved after being driven from Catholic Salzburg because of their Protestant beliefs (Coser, 1977). While one of the sons took over to expand the business, another, Weber's father, went into politics.

Max Weber (1864–1920) German social thinker considered among the true masters of sociology.
Source: Courtesy of the Library of Congress

Max's mother, Helene Fallenstein Weber, was born in 1844 to Georg Friedrich and Emilie Fallenstein. Her father, who descended from a long line of school teachers and had been a teacher himself, fought in the war of liberation against Napoleon, and then settled down to a life of a Prussian civil servant. Helene was the youngest of four girls. She was a very religious woman, a Calvinist, who desired to become closer to God and placed all of her confidence in Him (Weber, 1988). In her mind, the physical aspect of marriage was a heavy sacrifice and a sin that was justified only by having children. This belief led Helene to desire becoming old so that she would be relieved of this "duty." Her husband, however, did not share Helene's intellectual and religious interests (Weber, 1988). The senior Weber, a politician, was most attentive to his political and social life, which caused a great deal of tension in his marriage.

The senior Max Weber, was born in 1836 to Karl August and Lucie Wilmans Weber. He married Helene in 1863, and in 1869 began an active career in politics. He was a lawyer, a Berlin municipal councilor, at times a member of the German parliament, later a member of the Prussian House of Deputies, a member of the National Liberal Party, and well-connected to eminent intellectual, industrial, and political figures in Berlin (Weber, 1988; Hadden, 1997). As a person very much a part of the political "establishment," the senior Weber enjoyed indulging himself and leading a life of leisure. His self-satisfied, pleasure-loving, and shallow life was fairly typical of German bourgeois politicians.

The Webers moved to Berlin in 1869 and settled in an upscale suburb (Charlottenburg) favored by academics and politicians. The Weber household entertained a number of notables from Berlin society. Among the houseguests whom Weber met at a young age were the historians Treitschke, Sybel, Dilthey, and Mommsen. The intellectual and political people who came to visit the Weber home served as an influence on Max. Weber learned to believe

that three great recent developments had occurred in Germany: that Germany had become a national state rather than a series of principalities, duchies, and kingdoms; that rapid industrialization was good; and that German imperialism had become a part of state policy (Miller, 1963). Unfortunately, his parents' marriage was showing obvious signs of trouble and increasing tension, which did not go unnoticed by the children. Weber's mother, with her strict religious commitments and Calvinist sense of duty, was in direct opposition with his father's hedonistic ethic.

Initially, the Bohemian lifestyle of his father was more attractive to the junior Weber. Father and son enjoyed each other's company and would often be found drinking and socializing with others. They also enjoyed duels. Later on, however, Max became closer to his mother's approach to life. Having to choose between such polarity in different parents caused a great deal of strain on Max's psyche (Ritzer, 2000).

As a student, Max received an orthodox, mainly classical education (Macrae, 1974). He was a good student, but his teachers complained about his lack of respect for their authority and his lack of discipline. On the plus side, Weber was an avid reader who by the age of fourteen was writing essays with references to Homer, Virgil, Cicero, and Livy. He had mastered an extensive knowledge of Goethe, Spinoza, Kant, and Schopenhauer before he entered college (Coser, 1977).

In 1882, at age eighteen, Weber entered the University of Heidelberg. Although intellectually prepared, Max was thin and socially shy. His shyness quickly disappeared when he joined his father's dueling fraternity. He became very active in dueling and drinking with his mates, and can best be described as "one of the boys." Drinking large quantities of beer with his fraternity brothers and proudly displaying dueling scars on his ever-expanding body had transformed Weber into a heavy-set Germanic boozer eager to take up an intellectual conversation or dueling challenge.

Identifying with his father's lifestyle was not limited to the realm of leisure. Weber had also chosen law as his academic pursuit. Despite his heavy partying, Max managed to maintain high grades and expanded his studies to economics, medieval history, and philosophy. After three terms at Heidelberg, Weber left for military service in Strasbourg.

During his time in Strasbourg, Weber came under the influence of his uncle, the historian Hermann Baumgarten, and his uncle's wife Ida, Helene Weber's sister. The Baumgartens became a second set of parents for Max, and their influence on his development would be instrumental in shaping the course of his future. Hermann treated Weber more as an intellectual peer, compared to his father who patronized him. Weber's own letters testified to the fact that Baumgarten was his main mentor and confidant in matters of politics and academics. His aunt Ida was a spiritually devoted Calvinist, who, contrary to Max's mother, was able to spark Weber's interest in religious readings. He began to appreciate the values and beliefs of his mother through the actions of his aunt. Weber even began to view his father as an amoral hedonist.

Weber's own moral behavior could be questioned when it becomes known that his first love was his cousin, Emmy, the Baumgartens' daughter. His engagement to her lasted six tumultuous years. Emmy suffered from frail health both physically and mentally, and was often confined to a sanitarium. Emmy was a lovely young woman, but she had inherited the nervous problems of her mother and grandmother which caused exhaustion and melancholia (Weber,

1988). After years of agonizing guilt, Weber ended the engagement.

With the completion of his military service, Weber returned to his parents' Berlin home, in the fall of 1884. His father wished to separate Max from the influence of the Baumgartens. The senior Weber provided financial support for Max while he attended graduate school at the University of Berlin. Except for one term at the University of Goettingen and short periods of further military service, Weber stayed at his parents' home for the next eight years. He developed a greater understanding of his mother and came to resent his father's intimidating behavior toward her.

Weber's doctoral thesis, *History of Commercial Societies in the Middle Ages*, an analysis of the impact of legal regulations on economic activities, was successfully defended in 1889. His tireless work habits allowed for the completion of his postdoctoral thesis (a requirement for a university appointment), *The Agricultural History of Rome in Its Relation to Public and Private Law* (Macrae, 1974). Weber became a lawyer and started teaching at the University of Berlin. In 1893, he became professor of economics at the University of Freiburg, moving from there to the chair of economics at Heidelberg, where he succeeded the renowned economist Karl Knies (Martindale, 1981).

Max Weber suffered continuous mental torment throughout his adolescence and into his twenties. He had become closer to his mother and learned to detest his father. Weber's inner turmoils and struggles all seemed to dissipate by 1893 when he married Marianne Schnitger, the twenty-two-year-old daughter of a physician (a cousin on his father's side). Marianne was born at Oerlinghausen on August 2, 1870. She was a very intellectual young woman who wanted to develop her own path in life, something that was not encouraged in rural areas. Here, the women were usually trained in domestic skills (i.e., cooking, sewing).

The Webers, being big city folks, took her in. Marianne formed a close mother–daughter type relationship with Max's mother Helene. She went to Berlin in the spring of 1892 to be trained for independent work and was very happy to be there (Weber, 1988). Although she had seen Max before, when Marianne saw him again a year and a half later, she knew she was in love. Max came to realize his feelings for Marianne when he did not enjoy witnessing her courtship with another man (whom Helene was also mothering and wanted to see the two become married). They wrote letters to one another, and before long became engaged. They were married in Oerlinghausen in 1893.

Marianne was most supportive of Weber's career and hosted many prominent intellectuals of the day in Heidelberg, just as Max's parents had in the Berlin of his youth. Max and Marianne enjoyed an intense intellectual and friendly relationship—but it appears that the marriage was never consummated. The prominent psychologist Sigmund Freud treated Max for impotency. Sexual fulfillment came to Weber only in his late forties, in an extramarital affair (Coser, 1977). Max and Marianne did, however, adopt his youngest sister Lily's four young children after she committed suicide (Weber, 1988).

From 1893 to 1897, Weber was a young teacher and politician. He was nervously irritable at times, and overloaded himself with teaching assignments and lectures and other tasks that left little free time for leisure (Weber, 1988). He reported for the Evangelical-Social Congress, joined the Pan-German Union, was a professor of economics (1894), a professor of political science (1896), and declined to run for election to the

Reichstag (1897) because he was interested in pursuing other things (Weber, 1988).

In July 1897, a major fight broke out between Max's parents. His mother wished to go on vacation alone to see her children, but his father wanted to join her and supervise the trip. He was jealous of all the close relationships that his wife had with others. When the family was all together, Max lashed out at his father and sided with his mother. Max accused his father of treating his mother unjustly and cruelly, and kicked his father out of his home. The two never reconciled and his father died the next month (Weber, 1988).

As one can imagine, this dramatic event led to more psychological problems for Max, who then suffered a series of nervous breakdowns. He resigned from the Pan-German Union and from teaching. Weber also suffered from insomnia, a sleeping disorder. He was institutionalized for a brief time in a sanitarium and was treated by a number of specialists, but to no avail. It took over five years for him to recover. During this period, Weber lived as a private scholar in semi-seclusion in Heidelberg. Weber's colleagues encouraged him to write about the university's restoration, which sparked his interest in writing again. Unexpectedly, in 1903, Weber became co-editor of the *Archiv fuer Sozialwissenschaft*, which became the leading social science journal in Germany. His editorial duties allowed him to reestablish contacts with academic colleagues and German socialites that he had lost during the years of his illness. He resumed his teaching duties during World War I.

In 1904 Weber delivered his first lecture in six and a half years while on a visit to the United States, a trip which aided his recovery and left him with an enduring fascination with America. His former colleague from Goettingen, Hugo Muensterberg, then at Harvard, invited him to read a paper before the Congress of Arts and Sciences in St. Louis. The lecture Weber delivered was on the social structure of Germany.

Between the years 1892 and 1905, Weber composed a series of essays and speeches that, according to Seidman (1983), addressed the failure of German idealism. These works dealt with the social and economic conditions in eastern Germany, and revealed Weber's materialist orientation. Seidman provides as evidence the strong influence of Marxist writings; Weber's examination of the changing economic foundations of Prussian political and cultural hegemony; and the political tone of the essays aimed to discredit the Prussian Junker class by means of a materialist critique. By utilizing a materialist analysis, Weber argued that recent historical developments pointed to the inevitable triumph of industrial capitalism and the bourgeoisie as the future of Germany. The Junkers are viewed as an historically obsolete, economically declining, and politically dangerous class with no value to Germany's future. In 1904 and 1905, Weber would actively attempt to politicize the German bourgeoisie.

As a note of historic relevance, in the 1870s Germany was unified under the controlling authority of Prussia, which implied the political and cultural dominance of the Prussian Junker class. The Junkers were originally a landed aristocracy. They had appropriated the peasants' land and were actively engaged in the economic affairs of the state. Eastern Germany was characterized by extremely large land estates organized along the lines of a feudal-manor economy. Since the Junkers' economic livelihood was directly tied to the productive side of the estate, the development of industrial and commercial capitalism was a major threat to their existence. The survival of the Junkers was dependent upon control of the economic sector.

Weber maintained that the spirit and practice of German liberalism never disengaged itself from the ideological hegemony of Prussian conservatism. Consequently, industrial capitalism in Germany was not founded upon the independent rationality of individualism operating in a competitive open market system; but rather through the controlling power of the state, with its policy of state enterprises, protectionism, and cartelization, which functioned as the guiding mechanism of economic progress (Seidman, 1983).

His many writings and speeches on social and economic organizations, religion, science, and politics rarely appeared as books during his lifetime. Some of them were inspired by the social currents of the time, while many others were historical in character. Weber's works gradually found their way into English translation. A complete listing of his works in English would take up a great deal of space; thus, a brief mention of his most significant publications is provided below.

The Webers' trip to America seemed to inspire Max, as his intellectual output was astonishing. In 1905, his classic *The Protestant Ethic and the Spirit of Capitalism* was published. In this work, Weber used religion, on an academic level, to explain why capitalism took place in some parts of the world, and yet failed to take hold in other parts. Weber published his studies of the world's religions in a global-historical perspective. These include: *The Religion of China: Confucianism and Taoism* (1916), *The Religion of India: The Sociology of Hinduism and Buddhism* (1916–17), *The Sociology of Religion* (1921). At the time of his death (June 14, 1920) he was working on his most important work, *Economy and Society*.

Before World War I, the Webers' home in Heidelberg had regained its status as a center of bourgeoisie and intellectual gatherings. When the war broke out, Weber, in accord with his nationalist convictions, volunteered for service. As a reserve officer, he was commissioned to run the nine military hospitals in the Heidelberg area. Initially, Weber felt the war was good for Germany, because it would help to unite it. He then became the first German (of any political position) to oppose it. He criticized the ineptness of German leadership and was particularly enraged by the increasing reliance on submarine warfare, which, he prophesied, would bring America into the war and lead to the eventual defeat of Germany.

In the last few years of his life, Weber became increasingly political. He wrote a number of major newspaper articles on politics, was a founding member of and active campaigner for the newly organized Deutsche Demokratische Partei; and served as an adviser to the German delegation to the Versailles peace conference. Proposals to make him a candidate for the Presidency of the Republic failed. In October of 1919, his mother Helene passed away. The following year, on June 14, 1920, Max Weber died of pneumonia.

Intellectual Influences

Max Weber had a thirst for knowledge and learning. He read the works of, and was influenced by, many that came before him. As an adolescent he read Greek and Latin classics: Homer, Virgil, Cicero, and Livy. Homer was a favorite of Max's because of the great naturalness with which all the actions were related. Weber enjoyed Homer because he wrote stories in which he did not present a chain of successive actions but describes the origin and the calm sequence of actions (Weber, 1988). Significant influences on Weber's works were supplied by the ideas of Comte, Marx, Nietzsche, and especially Kant and the neo-Kantians.

August Comte

The French sociologist Auguste Comte (1798–1857) was the person who coined the term "sociology." Comte believed in a "Hierarchy of Sciences." This theory proposes that each science is dependent upon the other, implying that the social sciences come about from preexisting natural sciences. The hierarchy goes from the simplest (which evolve the quickest) to the most complex forms of science. These are, from bottom to top: astronomy, physics, chemistry, biology, and sociology. The sciences above others rely on and borrow from the ones below, which makes the sciences higher on the hierarchy more difficult and abstract. Comte believed psychology to be a branch of biology, and that there could only be one science of society, with many natural sciences (Freund, 1968). Weber refuted this theory. According to him, "There can be as many sciences as there are different avenues to approach a problem, and we have no right to assume that we have exhausted all possible avenues of approach" (Freund, 1968:41). Weber believed that "a method must advance knowledge rather than be faithful to an imaginary ideal of cognition" (Freund, 1968:40–41). Clearly, Weber's methodological approach was influenced by ideas of Comte.

Nietzsche and Marx

The influence of both Nietzsche and Marx on Weber is especially evident in his sociology of ideas and interests. Weber believed that material and ideal interests directly govern individual conduct. Even world images are a product of created ideas one has. Social action is governed by the dynamic of individual interests. Weber placed greater significance on ideas than either Nietzsche or Marx, but he was affected by Marx's notion that ideas were expressions of public interests and served as weapons in the struggle of classes and parties (Coser, 1977).

Weber's historic materialistic orientation reveals a strong Marxist influence, and his theories of stratification and economic behavior have their roots in Marxian theory. They both agreed that modern methods of organization increased the effectiveness and efficiency of production, and that this new rationalized efficiency threatens to dehumanize its creators. However, Weber believed that alienation, the negative side of rationalization, was not limited to capitalistic social systems, and instead would be found in all social systems including socialism. Weber did not agree with Marx that the economic order was solely determined by the class struggle and the owners of the means of production. Instead, Weber emphasized that the character of political power and the effect of the military were also important factors in determining power relationships. Weber states that the charismatic leader as well as the economic producer were the engines of history (Miller, 1963). Additionally, *The Protestant Ethic and the Spirit of Capitalism* is, in part, a reaction to the Marxist metaphysical assumption that all the events of civilizations are reducible to a single cause, namely the economic order (Kasler, 1988).

Weber was also aware of Nietzsche's analysis of the psychological mechanisms by which ideas become rationalizations utilized in the service of private aspirations or power and mastery. Notions of *disenchantment* and *charisma*, though not directly tied to Nietzsche, were elaborated by Weber with the assistance of powerful stimulation from the author of *Beyond Good and Evil*. Weber's personal ethic of heroic stoicism was also inspired by Nietzsche. As Coser (1977) states, "there was much of *Zarathustra* in Wax Weber" (p. 250). Nietzsche and Weber were both worried

about the future of humanity and warned that the twentieth century would be filled with horror and tyranny.

As alluded to earlier in this chapter, Weber's historic materialistic orientation reveals a strong Marxist influence. His theories of stratification and of economic behavior have their roots in Marxian economics and sociology. Weber shared Marx's contempt for the abstract mystifications of the German idealistic philosophical tradition. Despite the fact that Weber came to regard Marx's economic interpretation of history as overly simplified, he remained respectful of Marx's intellectual prowess. Weber saw in Marxian revolutionary ideology the articulation of democratic ideals. Weber instructed his Munich students that all contemporary scholars owed a debt to the brilliance of Nietzsche and Marx. A large amount of Weber's work was influenced by these two brilliant thinkers.

Kant and the Neo-Kantians

"Weber tried to synthesize the Kantian and neo-Kantian, and idealistic and neo-idealistic tradition in Germany" (Martindale, 1981:377). Neo-Kantianism was a broad cultural movement focused on an intellectual critique of the currents of positivism, naturalism, and materialism which followed the aftermath of the decline of German idealism. In opposition to the viewpoint that deterministic currents of materialism and collectivist idealism dictated human behavior, the neo-Kantians affirmed the autonomy of individuals. In the tradition of Kant, the neo-Kantians assumed a critical posture toward all institutions, cultural forms, and traditions that suppressed autonomy (Seidman, 1983). The neo-Kantians, then, became critical of social domination, which in the eyes of many democrats provided the ethical and idealist underpinnings of a repressive government.

Weber strongly identified with the neo-Kantian movement. His Germany had a highly developed industrial economy, with a political structure dominated by the semi-feudal values of Prussian conservatism, patriarchal authoritarianism, and a highly developed formal legalism. The middle classes prospered economically while maintaining political indifference. The working class was completely excluded from the decision-making process. Weber was not happy maintaining the status quo and resented the continued political dominance of the Junkers. To Weber, the Junkers were the caretakers of the feudalistic traditions that hampered the emergence of a truly modern bourgeois class. Weber proposed a unified Germany where all people, including the working class, worked together toward the German national mission. He demonstrated in great detail the advantages of the rational, methodical ethic of work, which is the very foundation of the spirit of capitalism. Rational capitalism, to Weber, was an economic miracle.

He maintained a commitment to a critical and formal rationalism, moral individualism, and liberal-democratic values, ideas that are consistent with neo-Kantian beliefs. From the ideas of Friedrich Naumann—who stressed that the renovation of German liberalism can only occur if the bourgeois-liberal elements recognize that the workers must form the basis of future liberal organization—Weber conceived of the Protestant social reform movement.

The antipositivistic, neo-Kantian influence of thinkers like Rickert is seen in Weber's belief that reality is not reducible to a system of laws. He believed that no body of laws can exhaust a science of culture, nor can one ever expect to achieve complete predictability, since prediction is successful only within limited or closed systems. Society and culture are a result of an on-going *process*, and consequently, history is never predetermined, it moves toward unknown ends. Weber felt that there could be no objective ordering of the historical process (Mommsen, 1989). He regarded "historicism" as a "narrow-minded patriotism of the field" (Kasler, 1988:9). In response, Weber came to utilize the "ideal type" methodology to study society.

Concepts and Contributions

Max Weber is considered one of the "founding fathers" of sociology. "Weber was a man of enormous scholarly ambition, sporadic and volcanic energy, and wide learning. As a result, a great deal that he intended to complete, fill out, or refine was left in a kind of chaos of articles, treatises, schema, lecture notes transcribed by students, and so on . . . no man should be condemned merely for attempting in the intellectual sphere more than he could actually accomplish" (Macrae, 1974:4–5). His works are complex, varied, and subject to many interpretations.

Verstehen

Weber recognized that sociologists had an advantage over natural scientists in that they possessed the ability to *understand* the phenomena under study. Natural scientists cannot gain a similar insight of the behavior of an atom or a chemical compound. The German word for understanding is *verstehen*. Weber's sociology is primarily interpretative based on *verstehen*. He believed that sociologists must look at the actions of individuals and examine the meanings attached to these behaviors. For example, understanding *why* an individual did or said something—what meanings did they attach to the situation? Weber was interested in action and meaning; he thought it was important to understand how people give meaning to their actions.

Today, this goal is similar to techniques such as interviewing, focus groups, or ethnographic observation (Garner, 2000).

In its easiest translation, according to Weber, *verstehen* is a rational way to understand and study the world. His use of the term *verstehen* underscores some of the basic problems with his methodological thoughts. As Burger (1976) indicates, Weber was neither very sophisticated nor very consistent in his methodological pronouncements. Weber employed a series of definitions of *verstehen*:

1. *Deuten*, generally translated as "interpret."

2. *Sinn*, generally translated as "meaning."

3. *Handeln*, concrete phenomenon of human behavior, or "action."

4. *Verhalten*, a broad term referring to any mode of "behavior."

Weber's use of the term *verstehen* was common among German historians of his day and was derived from a field of study known as *hermeneutics* (Pressler and Dasilva, 1996). The German tradition of *hermeneutics* was a special approach to the understanding and interpretation of published writings. The goal was not limited to merely understanding the basic structure of the text, but the thinking of the author as well.

Utilizing this approach, for example, in his studies on the relationship between religion and capitalism, allowed Weber to learn what Hebrew prophets thought about God, or how Calvinists wrestled with the implications of predestination, by reading the words of Isaiah and Calvin (Garner, 2000).

Critics of the *verstehen* method claim that it is little more than "intuition," and that it represents a "soft," irrational, subjective research methodology. Weber vehemently denied this criticism, and countered that *verstehen* was a rational procedure of study involving systematic and rigorous research. In fact, Weber's very definition of sociology includes the *verstehen* approach. He describes sociology as a science concerning itself with the interpretive understanding of social action and thereby providing a causal explanation of both the course and consequence of such behavior (Swedberg, 1998).

Social Action

Weber conceived of sociology as a comprehensive science of *social action*. His initial theoretical focus was on the subjective meaning that humans attach to their actions in their interactions with one another within specific-historical contexts. By *action*, Weber meant meaningful, purposive behavior. Weber envisioned the study of society as the study of *social action* among humans. This perspective is in complete contrast to Durkheim's view of society as external structures that function apart from human purpose and will.

Weber treated the individual action as the basic unit, as an atom. He believed that sociology should reduce concepts to the understanding of action. Social acts are created by the actor. If the behavior is oriented toward others, it is a *social act*. *Social action* can be active or nonactive (failure to react). For example, if a construction worker whistles (active action) at a woman who walks by the construction site, but the woman ignores his behavior, she has demonstrated nonactive action. *Social action* can be past, present, or future behavior. Action can be nonsocial if it is oriented solely to the behavior of inanimate objects (e.g., an individual picking up trash at the beach). Active social action causes a reaction, whereas nonactive social action does not involve a reaction.

Social action does have its complications. Actors have subjective meanings that may be unique or different to others. In addition, meanings can change over time (for example, the term "gay" used to refer to feelings of happiness or giddiness; today the term is applied to homosexual behavior). Therefore, Weber believed, in order to fully understand the meaning of action, the researcher must incorporate the sociological method of *verstehen*.

Weber distinguishes between four major types of *social action*: zweckrational, wertrational, affective action, and traditional action. *Zweckrational* can be roughly translated as "technocratic thinking" (Edwards, 1997). It is defined as action in which the means to attain a particular goal are rationally chosen. It is often exemplified in the blueprints of an engineer who builds a bridge in the most efficient manner that allows passage over a body of water. Individuals who pursue a college degree in hopes of attaining a job that provides financial security are exhibiting Weber's zweckrational behavior.

Wertrational, or value-oriented rationality, is characterized by striving for a goal which in itself may not be rational, but which is pursued through rational means. The values come from within an ethical, religious, philosophical, or even holistic context—they are rationally "chosen" (Edwards, 1997). An example would be an individual seeking salvation through following the teachings of a prophet, or living a certain way of life in hopes of reaching "eternal salvation."

Affective action centers around the emotional state of the person, rather than in the rational weighing of means and ends. Sentiments are powerful forces in motivating behavior. Choosing a college strictly because one's girlfriend is enrolled at the same school is an example of *affective action*.

Finally, *traditional action* is guided by customary habits of thought, by reliance on what Weber called "the eternal yesterday" (Edwards, 1997). Many students attend college simply because it is traditional for their social class and/or family to attend—the expectation was always there, it was never questioned.

The central importance of Weber's work on *social action* is his idea that human behavior has become increasingly formally rational over the course of history. "Formal rationality" means careful, planned, and deliberate matching of means to ends; in formally rational action, human beings identify and use means that they believe are most likely to bring about a desired end. "All human beings engage in action, in meaningful behavior, but such behavior is not always formally rational. Only in modern societies does the mode of formal rationality pervade all spheres of action" (Garner, 2000:88). Weber used the term "disenchantment" to illustrate the point that in modern, rational society, certain modes of action once considered magical or miraculous were now easily explained scientifically.

From Weber's viewpoint, purposive rationality is viewed as fundamental for social action (Habermas, 1987). "Weber believed that if individuals are informed about the effects of different kinds of action, they will have a greater capacity to make decisions that are value-oriented but implemented rationally" (Ashley and Orenstein, 1985:210).

Ideal Types

At its most basic level, an *ideal type* is a concept constructed by a social scientist, based on his/her interest and theoretical orientation to capture the principle features of some social phenomenon. An *ideal type* is essentially a "measuring rod" whose function is to compare empirical reality with preconceived notions of a phenomena. *Ideal types* are *heuristic* devices used in the study of slices of historical reality.

An *ideal type* provides the basic methodology for historical-comparative study. It is not meant to refer to the "best" or to some moral ideal. The problem for comparative method is to get cases that can actually be compared. Weber's solution was the *ideal type*. As he conceived them, *ideal types* are hypothetically concrete creations (personalities, social situations, changes, revolutions, social institutions, classes, and so on), constructed out of their relevant components by the researcher for the purpose of instituting precise comparisons (Martindale, 1981). An *ideal type* is an analytical construct that serves as a measuring rod for social observers to determine the extent to which concrete social institutions are similar and how they differ from some defined measure. Weber's discussion of *social action* is an example of the use of an *ideal type.*

The *ideal type* involves determining the "logically consistent" features of a social phenomenon. The *ideal type* never corresponds to concrete reality but is a description to which researchers can compare reality. An *ideal type* of bureaucracy would be based on the immersion of historical data in order to compare it to some existing bureaucracy. "Ideal Capitalism" is composed of four basic features: Private ownership, pursuit of profit, competition, and laissez-faire.

To some extent *ideal types* are like stereotypes. But stereotypes are evaluative concepts, designed to close rather than to open analysis. Finally, *ideal types* are not averages based on some sort of arithmetic computations appropriate only to the investigation of quantitative variations along a single dimension (Weber, 1903). Average Protestants in a given area at a given time may be quite different from "Ideal Protestants."

Rationalization

The idea of *rationalization* lies at the heart of Weber's substantive sociology. Weber did not explicitly articulate the idea that the world is becoming increasingly dominated by norms and values of *rationalization*; rather it was a theme that one must extract from his specific studies. Weber's use of rationality is complex, multifaceted and was used most powerfully and meaningfully in his image of the modern Western world.

Weber believed that Western capitalistic civilization is unique; that it has properties not replicated by any other civilization. A general theme throughout Weber's works was the problem of the nature, causes, and effects of *rationality* on modern society. Only in the West, for example, has science, the most rational mode of thought, become the norm of thought and the guide of behavior. Weber noted that precise knowledge and refined observation appeared in India, China, Babylonia, and Egypt; but, Babylonian astronomy lacks a mathematical foundation, Indian geometry lacks the rational proof, medicine was developed in India but without a biochemical foundation, and a rational chemistry was absent everywhere except in the West. China lacked the historic method, Indian political thought had no systematic method or rational concepts, and only in the West had a rational jurisprudence developed (Martindale, 1981).

In his *Protestant Ethic and the Spirit of Capitalism* (1904–05) Weber's description of the contrast between the West and non-West extends to the arts and architecture. In music, for example, polyphonic sounds are widely diffused over the earth, but the rational tone intervals do not appear outside the West. In architecture, only in the West had the pointed arch and cross-arched vault been rationally employed for distributing pressure and creating many kinds of spaces. Further, while printing appears in China, only in the West does a literature designed only for print appear.

From Weber's perspective, the spirit of capitalism involves the rational and calculating pursuit of maximum profit. He argued that only in modern capitalism does the desire for unlimited profit combine with the efficient use of reason (Pampel, 2000). The popular writings of American Benjamin Franklin revealed his own spirit of capitalism, in that he hated wasted time and wasted money. This belief is easily illustrated in Franklin's belief that since time is money, those who spent time in leisure or relaxation were throwing away money (Pampel, 2000). Weber especially believed that Protestant beliefs encouraged the use of rational decision-making in pursuit of unlimited profit.

Contemporary social thinkers such as Stephen Kalberg (1980) have identified four basic types of rationality in Weber's work. These types of rationality provided Weber with the basic heuristic tools needed to scrutinize the historical realities of Western and non-Western societies.

The first type is *practical rationality*, which is defined as every way of life that an individual evaluates worldly activity and its effects on that person. It reflects a purely pragmatic and egoistic viewpoint when engaging in daily events. People who exercise *practical rationality* accept given realities and constraints in society and merely calculate the most expedient ways of dealing with the difficulties that they present. This type of rationality is in opposition to anything that threatens to alter the everyday routine.

Theoretical rationality involves a cognitive effort to master reality through such abstract means as logical deduction, induction, and attribution of causality; rather than, through action. This type of rationality allows individuals to transcend daily realities in a quest to gain enlightenment on such things as the "meaning of life."

Substantive rationality dictates courses of action based on a value system in which individuals' behaviors are limited. This type of

rationality is not limited to the West, and exists transculturally and transhistorically, wherever consistent value postulates exist.

The final category is *formal rationality*. Courses of action are dictated by universally applied rules, laws, and regulation. This type of rationality is critical for capitalism, for formalistic law, bureaucratic administration, and so forth, must be in operation for a rational enterprise to flourish. Universal laws and regulations characterize *formal rationality*.

According to Weber, *rationalization* is the product of scientific specialization and technical differentiation. In other words, a striving for perfection and refinement of the conduct of life (Freund, 1968). Similar to Marx's notion of alienation, *rationalization* as well as *bureaucratization* seemed, for Weber, an inescapable fate for future society. This notion is captured in Weber's description of the "Iron Cage." Instead of being able to roam and do what one pleases, bureaucracies consist of rational and established rules, and limited activity. These rules reflect the norms and values of society. Weber believed that the bureaucratization of the modern world caused its depersonalization.

Bureaucracy

According to Weber, *bureaucracies* are goal-oriented organizations designed according to rational principles in order to efficiently attain the stated goals. Offices are ranked in a hierarchical order, with information flowing up the chain of command, directives flowing down. Operations of the organizations are characterized by impersonal rules that explicitly state duties, responsibilities, standardized procedures and conduct of office holders. Offices are highly specialized. Appointments to these offices are rationally made based on specialized qualifications. All of the ideal characteristics of the *bureaucracy* are centered around the efficient attainment of the organization's goals.

In his *Economy and Society* (1925) Weber defined the bureaucracy ideal type by these characteristics:

1. Official business is conducted on a continuous basis.

2. Business is conducted in accordance with stipulated rules.

3. Every official's responsibility and authority are a part of a hierarchy of authority.

4. Officials do not own the resources necessary for them to perform their assigned functions, but they are accountable for the use of those resources.

5. Offices cannot be appropriated by their incumbents in the sense of property that can be inherited or sold.

6. Official business is conducted on the basis of written documents.

Weber described *bureaucracy* as an *ideal type* in order to more accurately describe their growth in power and scope in the modern world. He notes that as the complexity of society increases, *bureaucracies* grow. The *bureaucratic* coordination of the action of large numbers of people has become the dominant structural feature of modern societies. It is only through this organizational device that large-scale planning and coordination, both for the modern state and the modern economy, become possible. The consequences of the growth in the power and scope of these organizations is critical in order to more clearly understand our world.

In his historic examination of the origins of *bureaucracy*, Weber (1978) explains that the modern rational organization could not have been possible without two important developments: the separation of the household from the place of work, and the development of rational bookkeeping. The growth of *bureaucracy* is dependent on the social and economic preconditions that a money economy exists in order to provide payment of officials who work in the bureaucratic administration.

As Perrow (1986) summarizes, Weber's model of bureaucracy contains three groups of characteristics: those that relate to the structure and function of organization, those that deal with means of rewarding effort, and those that deal with protections for the individuals. In regard to the structure and functioning of the organization, Weber states that the business of the organization is conducted on a continuous basis; that there is a hierarchy of offices; and that this hierarchy entails a systematic division of labor. The second group of characteristics, dealing with rewards, addresses the issue of salaries, which are based on rank and what is deemed appropriate by the position one holds. Finally, Weber insisted that the rights of individuals should be protected to prevent arbitrary use of power.

Weber's (1947) core idea that bureaucracies found within organizations are designed to do something ("purposive activities") has been retained by most organizational analysts. His analysis and definitions of bureaucracy and organization have served as the basis for many other researchers (Hall, 1987).

It would be inaccurate to assume that Weber was a fan of *bureaucracy* just because he viewed it as a necessity in a rational society. Weber noted the dysfunctions of *bureaucracy*: It excludes emotion and personal involvement in favor of rational decision-making and it has led the modern world into a world that is often depersonal. Further bureaucratization and rationalization seemed an almost inescapable fate. In short, Weber viewed future society as an

"Iron Cage" (inescapable from *bureaucracy* and *rationalization*), rather than paradise.

Causality

Weber firmly believed in the *multicausality* of social phenomena. He expressed *causality* in terms of the probability that an event will be followed or accompanied by another event. Weber believed that it was not enough to simply record events as historians do; rather, sociologists should report the reasons for, and the meanings behind the action taken by the participants. Thus, Weber believed in both historical and sociological *causality*.

The notion of predicting human behavior is generally viewed as a difficult task; especially considering the many social influences and near limitless potential courses of action open to individuals. But Weber (1904) argued, for example, that human action is generally very predictable, except in the case of the insane. Humans enjoy routines and regular courses of action. They like the "feeling" of freedom, but even their leisure time arises precisely when it has been rationally calculated to fit their schedule.

Most researchers would agree that attaining *causal* certainty in social research is impossible. Weber believed that the best that can be done is to focus sociological theories on the most important relationships between social forces, and to forecast from that theory in terms of probabilities. For example, Weber disagreed with Marx's assertion of the absolute primacy of material conditions in determining human behavior. Weber's system invokes both ideas and material factors as interactive components in the sociocultural evolutionary process. He argued that Marx had presented an overly simplified theory that had emphasized just one *causal* chain, the one leading from the economic infrastructure to the cultural superstructure. This,

according to Weber, could not adequately take into account the complex web of *causation* linking social structures and ideas.

Weber (1904) attempted to show that the relations between ideas and social structures were multiple and varied, and that *causal* connections went in both directions. While Weber basically agreed with Marx that economic factors play a key role in understanding the social system, he gave much greater emphasis to the influence and interaction of ideas and values on sociocultural evolution.

Weber (1978) maintained that there were three primary topics of *causality*:

1. Human actions cannot be explained in terms of absolute "laws," such as cause and effect.

2. To grasp the meaning of human actions would require a different method from any known to, or required by, practitioners of social science (something beyond positivism).

3. The social scientist's own moral, political, or aesthetic values will enter into her conclusions in a way that those of the natural scientist's do not.

Weber had the view that the social researcher would have difficulty in attaining a value-neutral approach to social study. This issue is addressed next.

Values and Value Relevance

Weber believed that social scientists have a more difficult time than natural scientists in creating "laws" because inevitably the investigator's own values and interests interfere with judgment. Further, he believed that there is no absolutely "objective" scientific analysis of culture or social phenomenon. To illustrate this point, Weber insisted that a *value* element inevitably enters into the very selection of the problem an investigator chooses to study. This phenomenon is referred to as *value relevance*, meaning, the very selection reflects the investigator's *values*, because they will most likely study events that they are already interested in. *Value relevance* is extended to the macro level as well, in that the *values* of a society which the researcher is from influences/clouds decision-making and scientific study. In sum, *values*, according to Weber, play a crucial role before, during, and after the social research study.

One might think that Weber felt social scientists should *not* let their personal values influence their scientific research in any way. This is not completely true. While Weber was most adamant that teachers must control their personal values in the classroom, he believed scholars have a perfect right to express their personal values freely in speeches, in the press, and in their research. Students should be presented with the facts; attendees at a conference, or some other public gathering, expect to hear opinionated comments supported by facts.

It is important to remind the reader that Weber felt social scientists have at least one major advantage over natural scientists, that is, their ability to understand the social phenomenon under study. In regard to human action, researchers can do more than simply record protocols of recurrent sequences of events; they can attempt to understand the motives by interpreting human's actions and words. Unlike the positivists who insist on scientific, quantitative data to support their theories of human behavior; Weber believed that human behavior could best be understood through *verstehen*. Social researchers have access to the subjective (meaning, motivation, etc.) aspects of action, whereas the natural scientists do not. This schema is consistent with Weber's (1964) definition of sociology as the "science which aims at the interpretative understanding (*verstehen*) of social behavior in order to gain an explanation of its causes, its course, and its effects" (p. 29).

The social scientist is certainly capable of deriving facts from empirical study, but according to Weber (1964), this research cannot tell people what they "ought" to do. An empirical science cannot tell anyone what he "should" do—but rather, what he "can" do—under certain circumstances. Weber (1903–17) believed that the role of the social sciences was to help people make choices among various ultimate value positions. In his view, there is no way of scientifically choosing among alternative value positions; thus, social scientists cannot presume to make such choices for people. "The social sciences, which are strictly empirical sciences, are the least fitted to presume to save the individual the difficulty of making a choice" (Weber, 1903–17/1949:52). That is why Weber is fundamentally at odds with those who argue for a morality based on science. One might wonder, if not science, then what other criteria?

Types of Authority

Weber's discussion of authority relations provides another insight into the changing structure of the modern world. He wondered on what basis do men and women claim authority over others? Why do men and women give obedience to authority figures? Weber traced a parallel historical process in forms of authority and organization. He defined power as the ability to impose one's will onto another, even when the other objects. Authority is legitimate power, power that is exercised with the consent of the ruled. Weber's sociological interest in the structures of authority was influenced, at least in part, by his own political aspirations. Weber was certainly no political radical; in fact, he was often called the "bourgeois Marx" to reflect the similarities in the intellectual interests of Marx and Weber as well as their very different political orientations (Ritzer, 2000). Weber was nearly as critical as

Marx of the modern capitalistic system, but he expressed the need for a gradual change in society rather than revolting against it.

According to Weber, distribution of power and authority is the basis of social conflict. He stated that power is the probability that one actor within a social relationship will be in a position to carry out his own will despite resistance, regardless of the basis on which this probability exists. Whereas power is essentially tied to the personality of individuals, authority is always associated with social positions. Weber also stated, that while power is merely a factual relation, authority is a legitimate relation of domination and subjection. In this sense, authority can be described as legitimate power. Authority is a universal element of social structure, it both realizes and symbolizes the functional integration of social systems. If individuals in a given society are ranked according to the sum total of their authority positions in all associations, the resulting pattern will not be a dichotomy, but rather, like scales of stratification according to income and prestige (Dahrendorf, 1959).

In every association, the interests of the ruling group (maintenance of the status quo) are the values that constitute the ideology of the legitimacy of its rule, whereas the interests of the subjected group constitute a threat to this ideology and the social relations it covers. Employees obey superiors by custom and for material compensation but a belief in legitimacy is also necessary. "According to the kind of legitimacy which is claimed, the type of obedience, the kind of administrative staff developed to guarantee it, all the mode of exercising authority, will all differ fundamentally" (Weber, 1978:213). One's relation to power and authority reflects the desire to maintain the social system. Consequently, the dominate seeks status quo, and the subordinate seeks change.

Social class signifies conflict groups that are generated by the differential distribution of authority in imperatively coordinated associations. The elites will always be smaller in number, but more organized. The masses, as implied, will be larger in number, and far less organized. Classes, understood as conflict groups arising out of the authority structure, are in conflict primarily over the issue of power.

Weber uses an *ideal type* as an analytical tool in his discussion of authority relations. Weber proposed that there are three *types of authority* (legitimate forms of domination): rational-legal, traditional, and charismatic. All *types of authority* require an administrative staff characterized by efficiency and continuity (Dronberger, 1971).

Rational-legal authority is based on rational grounds and anchored in impersonal rules that have been legally enacted or contractually established. This *type of authority* has come to characterize social relations in modern societies. This is the *type of authority* found in the United States, characterized by *bureaucracies*. The authority exists in the position that one holds, not in the individual. The professor–student relationship illustrates this point. The professor has complete authority over the student in the classroom (class assignments, tests, term paper requirements, etc.), but no authority in social worlds such as nightclubs, ballgames, and so forth, because his authority is limited to the workplace. As another example, elected officials have the authority to make decisions for the district that they represent. The authority is in the "office," not the individual.

Traditional authority is a dominant type of authority in pre-modern societies. It is based in the sanctity of tradition, of "the eternal yesterday." Here, "loyalty is attached to the person of leader because he serves and is guided by tradition: attendant powers of control are handed down from the past . . .

persons exercising authority are designated according to traditionally transmitted rules . . . the object of obedience is the personal authority of the individual which is enjoyed by virtue of traditional statues . . . the group is primarily based on relations of personal loyalty" (Dronberger, 1971). *Traditional authority* is attained through inheritance or it may be invested by a higher authority (e.g. religious authority). An example of an inherited *traditional authority* would be monarchies (often referred to as "royalty"). Because of the shift in human motivations, it is often difficult for modern students to conceive of the hold that tradition held in pre-modern societies. There are still some societies ruled by monarchies even as humankind has entered the third millennium.

Charismatic authority rests on the appeal of leaders who claim that they possess extraordinary virtuosity. This type of authority is naturally unstable because it only holds up as long as the leader is alive, the leader maintains his/her charisma, and the people believe in the leader's virtuosity. Unlike the *rational-legal authority, charismatic authority* has no roots in anything legitimate or stable. The power *is* with the individual, not the political system. Weber believed that charisma was a revolutionary force. Charisma is by its nature unstable, it exists in its pure form only as long as the charismatic leader lives. In the long run, charisma cannot be routinized; inevitable the social system must be transmitted into either *tradition* or *rational-legal authority*.

Weber's typology of authority is important for many reasons, but particularly on the following two counts. First, he was one of the earliest political theorists who conceives of authority in all its manifestations as characteristic of the relation between leaders *and* followers, rather than as an attribute of the leader alone (Coser, 1977). Second, even though Weber never clearly defined charisma, its importance lies with his sociological approach in the understanding of "why" humans behave as they do.

Social Class and Inequality

Authority is equated to having power. Power differential is one of the distinguishing characteristics that gives rise to differentiated social classes. Weber's description of social class was similar to that of Marx, in that he defined a social class as a category of persons who have a common specific causal component of their life chances. Furthermore, this causal component is represented by economic interests (possession of goods and opportunities for income) and the conditions of the commodity or labor market (Gerth and Mills, 1946). Weber's theory of stratification differed from Marx in that he introduced an additional structural component to the formation of class, that of "status group" (Gerth and Mills, 1946).

A classification of this sort is based on consumption patterns rather than the process of production. Members of a status group come to identify one another based on lifestyles and by the social esteem and honor accorded to them by others. "Linked with this are expectations of restrictions on social intercourse with those not belonging to the circle and assumed social distance toward inferiors . . . . A status group can exist only to the extent that others accord its members prestige or degrading, which removes them from the rest of social actors and establishes the necessary social distance between 'them' and 'us'" (Coser, 1977:239).

As Weber came to recognize, those with money, over time, will eventually ascend to the top of the status position in society. Equally true is the reality that the economically poor will almost always find themselves at the bottom of the social prestige ladder. Social stratification then, will always consist of the "haves" and the "have-nots." There are individuals who bridge the gap between low economic status and yet possess high status (e.g., a priest, a successful community activist, etc.) but this is impossible for an entire social class of low economic status. The inequality that persons experience will be the result of the lack of power due to low economic status and/or low social prestige.

The Protestant Ethic and the Spirit of Capitalism

"Weber mused, there may be a suppressed political will waiting to be tapped and ignited. Perhaps a piercing intellectual jolt would unleash the stored-up critical energies of German liberalism. The jolt, of course, was the Protestant Ethic" (Seidman, 1983:218).

The Protestant Ethic and the Spirit of Capitalism was Weber's best-known work and marked the beginning of a Weberian sociology of worldview. Weber (1904–05) traced the impact of Protestantism—primarily Calvinism—with the rise of the spirit of capitalism. He investigated a causal relation between Puritanism and the psychological and cultural presuppositions of "spirit" of modern capitalist culture.

Weber came to believe that the *Protestant ethic* broke the hold of tradition when it encouraged men to apply themselves rationally to their work. Calvinism, he found, had developed a set of beliefs around the concept of predestination. It was believed by followers of Calvin that one could not do good works or perform acts of faith to assure a place in Heaven; you were either among the "elect" or you were not (Edwards, 1997). However, wealth was taken as a sign that you were one of God's "elect," thereby providing encouragement for people to acquire wealth. *The Protestant Ethic* fostered a reli-

gious spirit of rigorous discipline, encouraging people to apply themselves rationally to acquire wealth. Protestant asceticism used all its power against the relaxed enjoyment of possessions. It set limits to consumption, especially luxury consumption. It did, however, have the psychological effect of liberating the acquisition of goods from the restrictions of the traditionalist ethic (Weber, 1978).

Capitalism, was, in part, a result of the *Protestant ethic*. Capitalism grew from Calvinism. Calvinism stimulated hard work, a determination to succeed, and making money. In Germany, at this time, the Protestants were economically richer than the Catholics. The Catholics believed that those who give away "goods and materials" (charitable contributions of money, clothing, etc.) will be rewarded in Heaven. Since the Calvinists believed that only a select few get into Heaven, they must look for signs of grace to see if they are one of the few chosen. Economic success was seen as the primary sign.

Protestantism succeeded in turning the pursuit of profit as a moral crusade. Ideas such as "time is money," "be frugal," "be punctual," were all in the *spirit of capitalism*. This spirit allowed capitalists to ruthlessly pursue economic riches; in fact, it was their duty. Workers would cling to their work as if it were a life purpose willed by God. *The Spirit of Capitalism* legitimized an unequal distribution of goods as if it were a special dispensation of Divine Providence.

The Protestant Ethic helped to explain the growth of capitalism in the West, but Weber also wished to explain why capitalism did not grow in other societies. He found that several of these preindustrial societies had the technological infrastructure and other necessary preconditions to begin capitalism and economic expansion. The only force missing was cultural encouragement and approval to abandon traditional ways. Weber found that irrational religious systems inhibit the growth of a rational economic system. In China, Confucianism lead people to simply accept things as they were. Active engagement in a profitable enterprise was regarded as morally incorrect. Taoism was essentially traditional with one of its basic tenets being to not introduce innovations. This approach to life did not produce enough tension, or conflict, among members to motivate them to innovative action. In India, structural barriers of the caste system hampered social mobility and tended to regulate most aspects of people's lives. The Hindu religion, with its irrational belief of reincarnation, was completely opposite to the Calvinist belief in predestination. The Hindu merely gains merit for the next life. This idea system failed to produce the kind of people who could create a capitalist, rational economy.

While Weber does not believe that the *Protestant Ethic* was the only cause of the rise of capitalism, he believed it to be a powerful force in fostering its emergence.

Race Relations

Weber (1978) notes that if the degree of objective racial difference can be determined purely by physiological criteria, then the intensity of subjective feelings of attraction and repulsion between races might be measured accordingly. This keen insight into *race relations* was most likely developed in his observations of German attitudes toward the Jews. In his *The Sociology of Religion* (1921/1963), Weber termed the Jews "pariah people." He traced this role of "outsider" more to the desire of Jews to segregate themselves than to exclusion by the rest of society. Accepting the general position of Germans during this time, Weber argued that Jews needed to abandon Judaism in order to be assimilated into German society. Weber maintained a nationalist attitude supporting the assimilation of all minority groups, opposed to liberal ideas of pluralism.

To call Weber a racist would be a mistake, for he truly felt that minorities could reach higher levels of achievement in society if they were fully a part of it (assimilated). As discussed in chapter six, Weber was a longtime friend and supporter of Georg Simmel (a Jew who was discriminated against in his pursuit of a full-time teaching position), and as Abraham (1992) indicates, he was probably the most tolerant liberal thinker Germany could offer at that time.

If Weber's ideas on *race relations* were developed in Germany, they were most certainly reinforced during his only trip to the United States in 1904. Here he observed, "The Americans are a wonderful people. Only the Negro question and the terrible immigration form a big, black cloud" (Weber, 1926/1975:315). Weber's comments were prophetic. A few years after his visit, the tensions between blacks and whites erupted in a massive race riot. At the time of Weber's visit, millions of European immigrants were jammed into the crowded slums of northern cities and industrial towns. The bulk of Asian immigrants settled in the West, where they struggled against economic hardships, discrimination, and racism. Most of the black population was concentrated in the rural south, where they were subjected to violent abuse in the form of lynchings, brutal public beatings, vigilante raids by the Ku Klux Klan, and poverty (Kornblum, 1994). As Weber had noted, racial tensions were clearly evident throughout the United States.

Just fifteen years after Weber's American visit, a bloody riot broke out between whites and blacks in Chicago. Race riots have occurred throughout twentieth century America. As Jonathan Turner (1977) states,

American society has problems in assimilation and that racial and ethnic discrimination is operant in society. Parvin (1973) believes when groups of people become dissatisfied and frustrated with existing economic and political institutions there may come a point where the breakdown of law and order is preferred to its preservation. For an illustration of this point one needs only to recall the theme of the Los Angeles rioters of 1992, "No justice, no peace." The 1992 Los Angeles riot was the most costly in American history. Sixty people were killed, more than 2,300 injured, more than 6,000 arrested (87 percent of all arrestees were Black or Latino), and more than a half billion dollars of destruction occurred (Delaney, 1993).

Social Theory

Weber's works are so complex that he influenced the ideas of many others. Not only did he contribute various terms and concepts (still relevant today), and an elaborate methodology; he made substantial contributions to *social theory*. Specifically, Weber helped to influence such theories as structural functionalism, conflict, and symbolic interactionism. (Note: Weber did not use these terms, his studies and insights helped to create these *social theories*.)

In the 1920s, after Weber's death, American sociologist Talcott Parsons discovered his work (Macrae, 1974). In the early 1960s, Parsons, partly through a reconsideration of Weber's work, transformed his *structural functionalism* (Schlucher, 1981). According to Parsons, "Weber's thesis was that the development of Western modernity, of the system of modern societies, is not only of universal significance for the history of humankind but has also a specific direction and is in this sense not accidental" (Schluchter, 1981:70).

Conflict theory maintains that the social order that does exist in society is a result of coercion created by the people at the top of the social structure. Conflict theorists particularly emphasize the role of power in maintaining order within society. Weber believed that conflict underlies all social relations and determines power (Dronberger, 1971). Every society at every point is subject to a process of change. The possession of power is a critical element in *conflict theory*. As noted earlier in this chapter, power plays a critical role in Weber's works on the *types of authority*.

Symbolic interactionism is essentially a theory that suggests people interact with one another using symbols, and these symbols come to have meanings. Symbolic interactionists call attention to how social life is "constructed" through the everyday acts of social communication. Communication involves the use of symbols that, when put together, form words. Through the use of symbols such as communication, members of society are able to interact with one another. Effective use of symbols and communication is depended upon a shared understanding behind the meanings of symbolic interaction. *Symbolic interactionists* have warmly embraced Weber's use of *verstehen*. It was Weber who emphasized that social researchers must comprehend the "why" behavior occurred opposed to simply identifying "what" happened. The idea of *verstehen* (interpretive understanding), or using one's own experience to grasp a social phenomenon, is the *interactionists'* guiding principle (Goode, 1988).

Relevancy

Max Weber was a German social thinker who excelled in many different fields including sociology, economics, history, law, jurisprudence, and linguistics. He was a person of encyclopedic knowledge who displayed scholarly brilliance at an early age, quickly learned other languages as these provided access to materials helpful in his worldwide investigations. His areas of research ranged from studies of Polish farm workers to ancient religions and medieval entrepreneurs (Hadden, 1997).

"Max Weber has had a more powerful positive impact on a wide range of sociological theories than any other sociological theorist . . . Weber's work represents a remarkable fusion of historical research and sociological theorizing" (Ritzer, 2000:257). Weber's influence is traceable to the sophistication, complexity, and sometimes contradictory nature of his thoughts and actions. Anyone familiar with Weber's work will recognize him as an established historian, a scholar who made a deep study of the historical and social realities of many cultures and societies.

According to Stammer (1971), "Max Weber belongs, not to one particular university, one town, one country: he belongs today, even more than in his lifetime, to the whole scientific world" (p. 3). Furthermore, "In the opinion of some sociologists, Max Weber was the greatest social scientist of the first half of the twentieth century" (Martindale, 1981:389). Weber created the German Association for Sociology in 1909. He formed the starting point for the careers of many major sociologists of the mid- and late-twentieth century; among them Karl Mannheim, Hans Speier, Hans Gerth, Talcott Parsons, Robert Merton, and C. Wright Mills.

A full appreciation of the richness of Weber's work can be gained only through a knowledge of his empirical studies, in which the theoretical and methodological concepts (described in this chapter) were combined with a truly extraordinary scholarship to bring historical data into a new and sharper focus. Many of the significant trends in contemporary social science are extensions of work begun by Weber. Among these are stratification theory, the study of bureau-cracy and large-scale organization, the study of legitimate authority, the role of power, the sociology of law, the sociology of politics, the sociology of religion, and the sociology of music (Martindale, 1981).

Weber describes bureaucracies as goal-oriented organizations guided by rational principles in order to maintain efficiency. Offices are ranked in a hierarchical order, with information flowing up the chain of command and directives flowing down the chain of command. Operations of the organization are characterized by impersonal rules that explicity state duties, responsibilities, standardized procedures, and conduct of office holders.

George Ritzer has written a critically acclaimed book titled, *The McDonaldization of Society* (2000). In this book, Ritzer demonstrates the relevance of a number of Weber's concepts, especially *bureaucracy* and *rationalization*. Weber described the modern world as becoming increasingly rational—that is, dominated by efficiency, predictability, and calculability. For Weber, the model of *rationalization* was the *bureaucracy*, whereas for Ritzer, the fast-food restaurant serves as the paradigm of McDonaldization.

Despite the potential advantages of a *bureaucracy*, it often suffers from the *irrationality of rationality* (Ritzer, 2000). Weber worried about the "Iron Cage" syndrome, where actors become trapped by their own creations. Sociologists today have identified a number of other dysfunctions of bureaucracies: trained incapacity; decision-avoidance, ritualistic behavior, and failure to perform in a time of crisis. Ritzer believes that a *bureaucracy* is like a fast-food restaurant because they both create a dehumanizing work environment. In addition to dehumanization, other irrationalities of bureaucracies include: too much paper work and "red tape," an emphasis on quantity versus quality of product (over-quantification), human discontent toward the nonhuman technologies that replace them, and a number of other pathologies.

Ritzer chose McDonald's as his fast-food restaurant of study primarily because it had become the model of *rationalization*; and had routinized their procedures throughout the chain of stores worldwide. As the third millennium begins, the *irrationality of rationality* (as so prophetically predicted by Ritzer), has become so pronounced that new movements against the rationality of the McDonald's model are beginning to form.

It is interesting to note that in 2002 McDonald's was sued by a very irrational person who claims not to have realized that eating greasy food will cause one to gain weight. McDonald's acted rationally by announcing that it will adjust its method of cooking french fries in an attempt to reduce the caloric-fat count in its delicious-tasting product. The move may turn out to be irrational if sales decline.

In his book, *The Work of Nations*, Robert Reich, an economist and Secretary of Labor during President Clinton's first administration, builds on the work of Weber. Reich believes that rational calculation is now leading away from *bureaucratization* toward new forms of organization, such as the "global web." He argues that rational calculation is a constant in modern society, while bureaucratization was only one historical method for implementing formal rationality (Garner, 2000).

Anyone who works for, or comes in contact with, large organizations—including fast-food restaurants, government offices, college administrators, the telephone company, and so on—realizes that *bureaucracies* are still very evident; and even though they may be transforming or evolving into some other form, they are still a source of frustration for many humans.

Weber contributed a great deal to sociological theory and methodology. His con-

cept of *verstehen* is still utilized today. It is popular with social researchers who are interested in understanding "why" certain behaviors occur. Potentially, it allows for a great deal of insightful information into the character of human behavior; and this type of information will always remain relevant to social researchers, social thinkers, and social control agents. His insights into *social action* reveal his initial theoretical focus on the subjective meaning that humans attach to their interactions with one another. People behave (nearly all the time) in a manner that is calculated to meet some sort of desired outcome. *Social action* is behavior directed toward another, all social relationships are mutual to each other. The *values* that people hold play an important role in their relationships. Consequently, understanding *(verstehen)* the values of others come into play during social interaction. The more one knows about the other (including their values), the more likely their behavior can be predicted. Every individual lives with this reality on a daily basis, and is very unlikely to ever change.

Weber's methodological approach is enhanced by his firm belief in the *multicausality* of social phenomena. That multiple social forces affect persons all the time is impossible to argue with; the more variables the researcher can control, or "allow" for, the more likely she is to accurately predict human behavior. Weber firmly believed, however, that "laws" of human behavior are impossible to create. Many researchers disagree with Weber's conclusion and strive to create such "laws." This is a debate that will surely continue throughout the third millennium.

The difficulty that social researchers have in creating laws is greatly impacted by what Weber described as *values* and *value relevance*. Social researchers work with certain biases and therefore complete objectivity is impossible. Scientists will always be involved in research that others label as unethical or immoral. Many people condemn genetic engineering and cloning; but if the researchers value the advancement of scientific knowledge, they are maintaining their values. Social researchers are also involved in this controversy, as they examine the social implications of such technologies. Weber had correctly pointed out that advancements in technology affect the social system.

Weber's analysis of the *types of authority* and the role of power remains a foundation in conflict theory. Modern society is characterized by a *rational legal authority*. Through his brilliant work found in *The Protestant Ethic* and *The Spirit of Capitalism*, Weber demonstrated that certain cultural barriers, especially those based on religion, hampered the growth of a rational economy system. Thus, while the West was experiencing mass industrial growth and enjoying economic wealth, other societies remained primitive. The relevance of this topic is exemplified by the growing phenomenon of *globalization*. The third millennium begins with a great disparity between the economic rich countries and the developing poor nations. Without a change in cultural attitudes, the financially poor societies will never develop their full economic potential and risk further polarization.

Weber's ideas on social class and inequality continue to assist sociologists today. His attempts to identify and explain the variables that give rise to social class stratification have inspired many social thinkers in this area; especially with regard to the "haves" and the "have-nots" concept. Members of similar social groups (whether it is based on religion, race, ethnicity, social prestige, or economic status) generally create a "we" category in order to identify themselves as a community. "Through social interaction and group participation, a sense of 'we-ness' is created, where the term 'we' becomes an extension of their identity. Sports fans will use the term 'we won the game.' An ethnic group, such as the Irish, might state: 'We have long been oppressed by the English'" (Delaney, 2002b:172). Ethnic and racial groups often attempt to maintain their distinctive "we-ness" (Shibutani and Kwan, 1965). By so doing, external groups come to view the group by their "they-ness" (Rose, 1981). Consequently, by establishing a "we" group, a "they" label is also created. In reality, these "we–they" categories are often similar to the "haves–have-nots" labels. Studies in race and ethnicity relations reveal how members of the dominant, or majority, group (the "haves"), utilize prejudice and institutional racism as a means of maintaining power and control over the subordinate groups (the "have-nots") (Delaney, 2002b). The subordinate group serves as a scapegoat to be blamed for societal problems.

Max Weber, a brilliant thinker, is one of the "Founding Fathers" of sociology. "His *detached concern* for the trials, the tragedies, and the occasional successes of social action made him an as yet unsurpassed master of the art and science of social analysis" (Coser, 1977:260).

8

Charles Cooley
(1864–1929)

Charles Horton Cooley was born in 1864 on the Ann Arbor campus at the University of Michigan. He was the fourth of six children in his family. The Cooley family had its roots in New England and were direct descendants of Benjamin Cooley, who settled near Springfield, Massachusetts, before 1640. Charles' father, Thomas McIntyre Cooley, came to Michigan from western New York. Thomas Cooley was born into a large family of farmers and, hoping to raise his level of social prestige, felt that he needed to acquire an education and move west. Thomas Cooley was an ambitious, energetic, outgoing man who started a career as an editor and real estate operator, and then finally became a lawyer. Thomas would go on to become a justice of the Supreme Court of Michigan, dean of the University of Michigan Law School, and the first Chairman of the Interstate Commerce Commission. He achieved recognition for the high caliber of his legal thinking and became well-known nationally for a number of legal treatises. Thomas Cooley achieved his goal of attaining social prestige as the family was very well-off financially and were respected members of Michigan's legal and social elite.

The young Charles Cooley was none of the things his father was and found it difficult to live up to the "grandness" of his father. As

Charles Cooley (1864–1929) American sociologist who influenced social psychology and symbolic interactionism.
Source: Courtesy of the Library of Congress

a child, Cooley was prone to illness that may have been caused by the strained relationship with his father, as doctors determined that many of his ailments were psychosomatic. Among other things, Charles suffered from a speech impediment. Whereas his father was "larger than life," he was sickly, shy, introverted, tended to stay to himself, and preferred reading and introspection to the life of social interaction expected of a social elite. He was keenly aware of his obligation not to embarrass the family and to maintain some level of contribution to society.

In 1880, Cooley entered the University of Michigan. He did his undergraduate work in engineering, a subject that he did not particularly like. He did, however, take a number of courses in history, philosophy, and economics. After earning his bachelor's degree in mechanical engineering, Cooley worked in Washington for two years as a surveyor for both the Interstate Commerce Commission and the Census Bureau. While at the Census Bureau, "he collected and analyzed statistics on street railways . . . his first research undertaking" (Sills, 1968:378).

Throughout his college years and after, Cooley remained an avid reader and especially enjoyed the works of Charles Darwin and Herbert Spencer. It was his independent readings, rather than formal courses of instruction, that guided Cooley's life course. After some time spent in travel and study in Europe, Cooley returned to Michigan to continue his studies. While he was a graduate student, he met and later married Elsie Jones, whose father was a dean at the university. Elsie was very energetic and outgoing. They had three children, who would become subjects of observation for their father in his quest to understand the development of self.

It was as a graduate student, in 1892, that Cooley started teaching and in 1894 he earned his Ph.D. in political economy, with a minor in sociology. He had developed a strong interest in sociology, but there was as yet no department of sociology at Michigan.

As a result, the questions for his Ph.D. examination came from Columbia University (Ritzer, 2000). His dissertation, *The Theory of Transportation* (1894), was a theory on the role of transportation, with the basic assumption being that population growth was related to the amount of expansion of roads and railways in those areas. "His thesis, *The Theory of Transportation*, is a pioneering study in human ecology, still highly regarded" (Sills, 1968:378). This was the first of many theories that began the great contribution of Cooley to the discipline of sociology. Thus, he began his career in the study of social structures, but would later become almost solely interested in the study of society on the micro level, especially an interest in the social-psychological aspect of sociology.

During Cooley's lifetime, the United States was undergoing an exceptional social-economic transformation. The industrial revolution altered all aspects of society. "Industrialization ushered in giant corporations, sprawling factories, sweatshop labor and the ubiquitous automobile. A huge wave of immigration was altering the face of the nation, especially the cities, where a majority of Americans lived . . . . With bigger cities came bigger fears of crime, vice, poverty, and disease" (Bailey, Kennedy, and Cohen, 1998:662). This enormous social change ushered in the Progressive Era of the early 1900s and the philosophical movement of pragmatism. "The concept of pragmatism held that truth was to be tested, above all, by the practical consequences of an idea, by action rather than theories. This kind of reasoning aptly expressed the philosophical temperament of a nation of doers" (Bailey, et al., 1998:583).

Throughout his teaching career at Michigan, Cooley was concerned with social upheaval and with the many social problems and issues of the day, but clearly preoccupation with the self—his own self—remained his primary concern. Having managed to assert his independence (primarily from his father's considerable shadow), Cooley was content to lead a sheltered, relatively uneventful existence in Ann Arbor. Cooley spent his entire career at the University of Michigan, where he devoted himself to work that derived mostly from self-examination and the observation of the behavior of those dearest to him, his children.

Cooley served as instructor of sociology from 1895 to 1899. In 1899, he became assistant professor. Rising through the ranks quickly, Cooley became an associate professor in 1904 and three years later was appointed full professor. Cooley's sickly demeanor and nervous approach to undergraduate teaching did not go over very well with undergraduate students. Graduate students, however, were inspired by his in-depth analysis often revealing his very being. Graduate students considered it an honor to attend his seminars and admitted that they were influenced by his approach throughout their lives (Coser, 1977). Cooley did not care much for the mundane activities of academia—the committee meetings, required social gatherings, the pettiness of faculty politics, and so on—preferring, instead, the scholarly pursuits of active research and publication.

Cooley declined many offers to join more prestigious departments of sociology, including one from Franklin Giddings to join Columbia. His chose instead to complete his career in Ann Arbor. Cooley had friends in high places at Michigan and this allowed him certain freedoms that might not be found elsewhere. For example, he had no trouble teaching his "controversial" theory of evolution course, as many other evolutionary theorists were facing censorship at various American campuses during this time. Cooley recognized such pressures on radical thinkers, stating, "The head of a department

(whatever his own views) will seldom choose a man whose opinions, or whose mode of expressing them, are likely to discredit the department with the general administration. This does not bar radicals, if they are men of tact, but their radicalism seldom survives their success" (Cooley, 1927:185).

Despite having to deal with the petty jealousies of colleagues at Michigan, Cooley enjoyed a protective administrative environment without which he may never have been able to become the productive scholar that he was. The university also provided an audience to test his ideas. Cooley did have a few close friends among the faculty. He belonged, with John Dewey, to a small social group called the Samovar Club. Members met to drink hot chocolate and discuss Russian literature. He was also close enough to George Herbert Mead, who later taught at Michigan, to share ideas with him. Cooley helped in the founding of the American Sociological Association; he wrote entries in his journal on the meetings, which he attended religiously for twenty-five years, and was appointed president in 1918.

Cooley's publications include: *Personal Competition* (1899); *Human Nature and the Social Order* (1902); *Social Organization* (1909); *Social Process* (1918); and the posthumous *Sociological Theory and Social Research* (1930). Cooley was pleased with the steadily expanding sale of his books. Following the end of World War I, there was a jump of a hundred percent in the sale of *Social Organization* alone (Coser, 1977). *Social Organization* remained Cooley's best-selling book. The fact that overall book sales continued to rise was evidence to the author that he had reached his contemporaries and, equally important, the younger generation as well. "In comparison with some of his contemporaries in sociology, he wrote very little, but his books were carefully written and have had a lasting influence" (Martindale, 1981:322).

Intellectual Influences

The avid reader that he was, Cooley was exposed to many different philosophies and was influenced by the writings of many scholars. He was more deeply influenced by historians, psychologists, philosophers, and those well-versed in literature than by sociologists. He was immensely impressed with the writings of the great thinkers including, Goethe, Thoreau, and Emerson. "As his own nature was serious and somewhat introverted, he was attracted particularly to philosophers of idealism, introspection and reflectiveness" (Devine, Held, Vinson & Walsh, 1983:121). Cooley also enjoyed the works of de Tocqueville and James Bryce. The patriotic Cooley enjoyed Byrce's writings on democracy, especially his analysis of American democracy. Among his contemporaries, he enjoyed Gabriel Tarde in France, Lester Ward, and Franklin Giddings in America.

The social thinkers who had the greatest influence on Cooley were: William James, James Baldwin, Charles Darwin, and Herbert Spencer.

William James and James Baldwin

Talcott Parsons (1968) indicates that, "Cooley's major theoretical reference point was the work of William James . . . . It was Cooley, along with Mead, who harvested the fruits of James's innovations in philosophy and psychology" (p. 59). Coser (1977) maintains that chronologically speaking, the influence of James on Cooley came relatively late, and Cooley's overall approach was shaped before reading the work of James, a Harvard scholar.

Cooley's distinctive views on the nature of the self, and his elaboration of the concept of the *looking glass self*, owe a debt to both James (psychologist and philosopher) and Baldwin (psychologist and philosopher).

During the 1890s, when Cooley attempted to provide a genetic explanation of the origin and growth of personal ideas, he made a careful study of both Baldwin and James. The experiments and studies of Baldwin, published in 1895 under the title *Mental Development in the Child and the Race*, left their mark on Cooley's *Human Nature and the Social Order*. Cooley borrowed much of the data from Baldwin's case studies and from his general social-psychological orientation as well (Coser, 1977).

His debt to James is even more significant. Cooley applied to society the kind of approach that James had applied to the self. It is not surprising that Cooley's conception of the *self* corresponds very closely to what James called the *social self*. "James argued that consciousness does not consist of a joining together of bits and pieces of ideas but that it flows like a stream and that every conscious state is a function of the entire psycho-physical context" (Coser, 1977:320). Thus, the mind, as a biological unit, and one's sense of self are shaped by social factors. "The personality of a friend, as it lives in my mind . . . is simply a group or system of thoughts associated with the symbols that stand for him" (Cooley, 1902:84).

A person's own self represents some of his or her ideas—a notion that would be meaningless without the basic distinction, made by James, between the "I" and the "me." The *social self,* according to James, is a core of ideas adhering to the self with such words as "I," "me," "mine," "myself." The self consists of those things individuals come to see as belonging distinctively to them. Cooley (1902) explains that the core of the self is formed by an instinctive self-feeling. Imagination and habit, operating on instinctive self-feeling, create the social self. "Imagination cooperating with instinctive self-feeling has already created a social 'I' and this has become a principal object of interest and endeavor" (Cooley, 1902:167). Further, "habit has the same fixing and consolidating action in the growth of the self that it has elsewhere, but is not its distinctive characteristic" (Cooley, 1902:155).

Charles Darwin and Herbert Spencer

Charles Darwin shocked the world in 1871 with his publication of *The Descent of Man,* wherein he applied his evolutionary framework to humans. Cooley was very interested in Darwin's views on evolution and the interrelatedness of nature. This interest led Cooley in search of his own theory on the process of nature. Cooley admired Darwin for his sense of the complex interrelationships that governed the natural world. Cooley's holistic philosophy, his stress on interactions and interrelations, and his rejection of all types of atomistic interpretation in the study of man were deeply influenced by the works of Darwin.

Cooley had less enthusiasm for "social Darwinist" evolutionary thinkers, including Spencer. He agreed with Spencer's general conception of the progressive nature of life, but not his specific views of society. He did not care for Spencer's dogmatic approach to reasoning and his disregard of individual personality. This is easy to understand, as Cooley was a social reformer and progressivist, while Spencer was an uncompromising utilitarian individualist. Cooley also rejected Spencer's focus on the use of scientific methods and processes in the study of the social sciences. Instead, the method of pragmatism practiced by James appealed to him. "As a method, pragmatism hovered close to life, refusing to close the process of thought prematurely, taking its cue from facts of life, willing to be led to new conceptions of purpose as deeper facets of human emotion and expectations were discovered" (Stumpf, 1994:388).

Despite his philosophical differences with Spencer, Cooley acknowledged that it was the writings of Spencer that were the inspiration for his interest in the field of sociology. Cooley (1930) states that, "Nearly all of us who took up sociology between 1870, say, and 1890, did so at the instigation of Spencer" (p. 263).

Concepts and Contributions

Compared with his contemporaries, Cooley's contributions were initially viewed as limited and unassuming. However, as the third millennium begins, students are becoming more exposed to his works, rather than those of Ward or Giddings. Cooley's contributions to theories of the middle range and social interactionism have endured the test of time.

The Organic View of Society

The theory of society as a living growing organism, a biological idea utilized by Spencer, is not quite the viewpoint of Cooley. His sociology is holistic in the sense that he believed that all processes of the social system are interrelated. Cooley's *organic view of society* is that, "All nature, all life, human life, and social life are interrelated, interdependent, and interconnected unities" (Hinkle, 1967:11). Cooley (1918) believed that the whole society lives and grows through the interaction with all the rest of the parts (social processes) through vast reciprocal activity.

All social processes are constantly in motion with interdependent parts that are affected by the interaction and interrelatedness of all the other parts within the whole. Cooley asserted that one cannot study one part without taking into consideration the effects of the other parts. Also, within the context of his *organic view of society*, public opinion is an important element in establishing social consensus and, as such, public debate is a necessary element in any democracy. Cooley's *organic view of society*, as well as his notion of consensus, and endorsement of gradual rather than revolutionary change within society, are functionalist in character. It is important to note that Cooley's organistic views differ from those of Spencer. Spencer viewed societies as analogous to living organisms in a biological sense, a view that Cooley rejected. "Accuracy demands that Cooley's organicism not be misstated. His organicism is equitable with holism. It does not seriously and essentially involve biological analogies" (Hinkle, 1967:13).

It is Cooley's *organic view of society* that led him to his primary objection to Spencer's utilitarian individualism. The individualistic approach that was so dominant in America and England at the time created a belief that those who worked hard deserved the riches that they attained, and those who had difficulty surviving and progressing in society must suffer from some sort of defect. The "weak" would eventually die off. Cooley (1918) insisted that society was an organic whole with interdependent parts. Therefore, any harm to some of the parts would effectively hurt the whole society.

The organic point of view is witnessed in the concepts of the primary group, human nature, and the looking-glass self—often referred to as the *triadic relationship*. These concepts are mutually related and dependent, and Cooley's views on social interaction require that they be; one cannot survive without the others. The looking-glass self is dependent upon the primary group for its sense of self and socialization; there would be no primary group without the looking-glass self. Human nature is formed within the primary group and has an effect on the looking-glass self. All pieces are in constant motion, interacting, interrelating, dependent upon one another to remain whole.

The Primary Group

His holistic view of social life led Cooley to focus his analysis on the explanations of groups and social organizations. He hoped to explain how man is linked with society. Cooley's foremost contribution to the theory of groups rests with his contribution of the *primary group*. "By primary groups, I mean those characterized by intimate face-to-face association and cooperation . . . . The result of intimate association, psychologically, is a certain fusion of individualities in a common whole, so that one's very self, for many purposes at least, is the common life and purpose of the group" (Cooley, 1909:23). These associations are primary in several senses, but chiefly in that they are fundamental in forming *human nature*. A closer examination reveals that Cooley (1909) was trying to show that even though we are instinctively and initially bound to our natural self, in the end our true goals are aimed to help the whole.

Cooley's idea of the *primary group* was influenced by William Graham Sumner's distinction between the "in-group" and the "out-group." What draws one to a particular group involved a moral unity. Ferdinand Toennies had distinguished between *Gemeinschaft* (a type of society or social setting characterized by intimacy, closeness, strong emotion, cooperation, and common values and beliefs) and *Gesellschaft* (a type of society or social setting characterized by formality, emotional reserve, superficial relations between individuals, and a lack of universally agreed upon values and beliefs).

For Cooley, *primary groups* are intimate, face-to-face groups that play a key role in linking the individual to the larger society. The *primary group* is relatively small, informal, involves close personal relationships, and has an important role in shaping the self. *Secondary groups* (or relationships) involve a collectivity whose members relate to one another formally and impersonally.

The fundamental properties of the *primary group* include:

1. Face-to-face association
2. Unspecified nature of associations
3. Relative permanence
4. A small number of persons involved
5. Relative intimacy of participants

Primary groups are such groups from which individuals receive their earliest and most basic experiences of social unity. They are the source of the individual's ideals, which derive from the moral and ethical unity of the group itself. Cooley (1909) stated that the most important *primary groups* are the family, the playgroup of children, and the neighborhood or community group of elders. Furthermore, these are the basic human stages in regards to *primary group* succession.

Primary groups are especially critical for children. First and foremost, it is within the *primary group* that children develop a sense of self. "The self develops in a group context, and the group that Cooley called the primary group is the real seat of self-development" (Reynolds, 1993:36). Secondly, they provide the initial source of socialization and interaction with the larger society. Cooley (1909) insisted that they are fundamental in forming the social nature and ideals of the individual. *Primary groups* provide children with their first experience of interacting in the social world. Successful socialization occurs when the child learns to behave and interact "properly" in the larger society.

Primary groups include individuals with whom we form our closest relationships and, because of this, individuals learn to share their expectations with one another

(Meltzer, Petras, and Reynolds, 1975). These close relationships give individuals a sense of "we" or belonging; an element that is critical to their sense of self. As Cooley (1902) explained, "The group self or 'we' is simply an 'I' which includes other persons . . . one identifies himself with a group and speaks of the common will, opinion, service, or the like, in terms of 'we' and 'us'" (p. 209). The group self or "we" can only be understood in relation to the larger society, just as the "I" can only be understood in relation to other individuals in the *primary group*. Although these relationships can change, the bond for a "common spirit" remains, which makes it difficult to sever ties with our *primary groups* (Cooley, 1909). Interestingly, Cooley believed that in order for individuals to grow, new *primary groups* must be sought out.

Human nature also develops through interactions in *primary groups*. Cooley (1909) explained *human nature* as "the nature which is developed and expressed in those simple, face-to-face groups that are somewhat alike in all societies; groups of the family, the playground, and the neighborhood" (p. 30). *Human nature* involves such concepts as sentiments and sympathy, love, resentment, ambition, vanity, and feelings of social right and wrong. Cooley concluded that *human nature* cannot develop without *primary groups*, which once again underscores the importance of primary group interaction, especially play groups for children. *Primary groups* are not to be assumed as always linked by love and harmony alone; rather, they are often characterized with competitiveness.

The concepts of *primary groups* and the *looking-glass self* are closely intertwined in Cooley's thought. In short, it is within the *primary group* that the *looking-glass self* emerges and that the ego-centered child learns to take others into account, and thereby becomes a contributing member of society.

The Looking-Glass Self

The looking-glass self is one of the most interesting and important concepts that Cooley articulated upon; and it is the third element of his *triadic relationship*. It is influenced by the work of William James's *social self* and his argument that the social self arises reflectively in terms of the reaction to the opinions of others on the self. The *social self* is "any idea, or system of ideas, drawn from the communicative life, that the mind cherishes as its own (Cooley, 1902:179).

The theory of the *looking-glass self* is based on the idea that individuals are interested in their own appearance because it belongs to them. We are thereby "pleased" or "displeased" by whether or not our appearance is as we would like it to be. In our imaginations we perceive in another person's mind their impression of our appearance and character, then we are affected by this perception. Cooley outlines three key principles of the *looking-glass self* theory:

1. The imagination of our appearance to the other person.

2. The imagination of their judgment of that appearance.

3. Our resulting self-feeling, such as pride or mortification.

Therefore, an individual's self-image mirrors the imagined reactions of others to our appearance, demeanor, and behavior. We must think of everybody as a mirror because, as we look at others, we are in a sense looking at ourselves. In short, we see ourselves as others see us. Cooley (1902) illustrated the reflective nature of self by comparing it to a looking glass, "Each to each a looking glass, reflected the other that doth pass" (p. 183).

The concept of the *looking-glass self* is especially important when applied to children. Cooley described in great detail in *Human Nature and the Social Order* (1902) that a child's personality is plastic and malleable. Through observation of his own children, Cooley explained how this sense of self is developed. Children become aware of the existence of others in their presence and learn that their actions will cause reactions in others, especially their mothers. Children learn that they can manipulate their environments to get the response they are looking for, which gives them a sense of power and control. For example, a child who wants to get out of her crib will cry loudly until someone responds to the temper tantrum and picks her up from the crib. It is through this sense of power and control that a sense of self begins to emerge. The *primary groups* are particularly important in relation to the *looking-glass self* because they involve the individuals one most trusts and respects.

The child obtains an identity primarily from the significant others in his life. An identity develops when the child realizes that his or her picture idea or image of self "reflects" other people's picture of him or her. In Cooley's terms, what is reflected are the imaginations of others concerning the individual (Reynolds, 1993). Cooley explained that it is not "mere mechanical reflection" that moves us to feel pride or shame, but, rather, an imagined vision that another person has of our appearance or character. If people (especially primary group members) laugh and tease a child, that child is likely to develop a negative self-identity. If a child is constantly being told how smart and attractive she is, then she is likely to see herself in such a manner and develop a positive self-identity.

Of course, the messages that individuals receive from others are a matter of interpretation and depend on how one perceives such messages. Our interpretation of self and how we appear to others varies on the person who is doing the judging. We generally care far more about the opinions of significant others than we do of strangers.

Even within this context Cooley (1964) elaborated that, "we are ashamed to seem evasive in the presence of a straightforward man, cowardly in the presence of a brave man, gross in the eyes of a refined man and so on" (p. 124). It is this assumption of another's feelings that leads us to behave differently. People learn to behave differently based on the social environment. It is appropriate to yell and scream at a football game, for example, but not during most church services. The child learns distinctions such as these during early childhood socialization.

James and Cooley both identified the importance of the environment on behavior. We learn to act as society (others) wants us to act, not as we might want to. Two youths cannot play catch with a football during church services just because they want to, the negative reactions of others will be enough to stop inappropriate behavior in those properly socialized. Society itself is an interweaving and interworking of mental selves. Through socialization, society is internalized in the individual psyche; it becomes a part of the individual self through the interaction of many individuals, which links and fuses them into an organic whole. Cooley argued that a person's self develops through contact and interaction with others. By identifying a sense of self, individuals are able to view themselves as any other social object. Cooley (1964) stated that there can be no isolated selves, "there is no sense of 'I' . . . without its correlative sense of you, or he, or they" (p. 182).

The Self and "I"

Charles Cooley and George Mead pioneered the development of a microsociological tradition in theory. Strongly influenced by pragmatic philosophy, both social thinkers charted a self that forms in interaction, through language and other types of communication. *The self* is formed in society; it is flexible and changing; and it responds to experience. Society and self are dialectical processes; the self is formed in interaction with others, but, at the same time, society is composed of many individuals with distinct selves. There is a biological basis to the *self*, but it becomes a human self only through interaction with others (Garner, 2000).

The idea of *self* is related to what Cooley described as the "*I*," elements in which we all envelop. Cooley (1902) utilized two analogies in his attempt to illustrate the self. The first analogy stated that, "the 'I' is like a central colored area on a lighted wall" and the second analogy is that the "'I' concept is like that of a nucleus of a living cell, not altogether separate from the surrounding matter, out of which indeed it is formed, but more active and definitely organized" (p. 180). These analogies indicate that indeed each of us is a part of the whole, and yet each of us is unique to the surrounding environment. With the former example, we can see that the lighted wall is everyone around us (society), while the individual, or the "I," is indicated by the central colored area. In the same general context, Cooley's living cell analogy is used to show that every living organism (society) consists of different cells (individuals) that perform specialized tasks.

In *Human Nature*, Cooley attempted to explain how the use of pronouns such as "I" and "me" explain the development of a person's self-feelings. Cooley refers to the pronouns of the first person to have "a substantial, important, and not very recondite meaning, otherwise they would not be in constant and intelligible use by simple people and young children" (p. 169). The word "I" is used every day and without a reflection on what the word "I" means. Cooley explains in great detail the wide-variety of social contexts in which the "I" is utilized.

"I" is Used to Describe One's Feelings
Cooley started by explaining that the "I" can be used to describe one's feelings. He did not believe that "the feeling aspect of the self" is the most important, but he did find it to be the most instinctual. Cooley described the use of "I" as an important function that is found in the history of the human race and it is an important plan in the survival of any race. Cooley illustrated that at birth we all become attached with the vague notion of "I." Over time, and through experience, becoming associated with or rather incorporated with the term "I," we begin to become familiar with it. This happens through our senses, muscular or visual. As we grow into mature persons the content behind the term "I" extends. As the mind grows, so does the sentiment behind the first person pronoun. What content a person puts behind "I" is impossible to say. Cooley (1902) used the example of fear (a learned behavior) to try and explain what the "I" is. "Very much as fear means primarily a state of feeling or its expression, and not darkness, fire, lions, snakes, or other things that excite it, so 'I' means primarily self-feeling, or its expression, and not body clothes, treasures, ambition, honors and the like with which this feeling may be connected" (p. 172). Individuals learn (among nearly limitless other things) to fear different objects and they also learn how to express their feelings within the context of "I." As in, "I was so afraid that I was going to fail that test, I could not sleep all night."

"I" in Relation to the Body   Cooley stated that when we use "I" in conversation or literature it is normally in response to the material body, but really the word "I" is referring to the opinions, feelings and desires being expressed by the person and having no thought about the body. Cooley conducted a research project in which he classified the first one hundred "I's" in Shakespeare's *Hamlet*. The word "I" was used in connection with perception fourteen times; with thought, thirty-two times; with wish, six times; as speaking, sixteen times; as speaker to, twelve times; in connection with action, nine times; vague or doubtful, ten times; and in reference to bodily appearance, once. Cooley (1902), concluded that "Shakespeare's characters are seldom thinking of their bodies when they say 'I' or 'me' and in this respect they appear to be representative of mankind in general" (p. 177).

"I" in Relation to Habit   Cooley stated that "habit and familiarity" are not enough incitement for an idea to connect onto the self. The idea of phases and habit have been thrust upon the individual by circumstance and not by choice. Cooley tried to explain the fact that the perceptions of the self and "I" come from habit that becomes fixated in the mind. After a while the concept of "I" can not be changed.

"I" in Inanimate Objects   Cooley described how as individuals we perpetuate "I" into inanimate objects. By nature, we call any inanimate object "I." This can best be illustrated with games and sports. When playing golf a person may say, "I'm on the green from my tee shot." Or a child who is flying a kite might say, "I'm higher than you." In reality your body and mind are not being hit by a club nor flying in the sky. As individuals, we often have a difficult time separating ourselves from the things we do.

"I" as It Relates to Society and Others   The "I" relates to our own self-feeling. Our self-feeling is a product of our interactions with others within society. Cooley explained that there is a correlation between one's self-feelings and purposeful activity. He used an example of a boy who makes a boat and then invites his friends to look at his creation. If they mock his boat, the boy will be disappointed, and if they praise the boat the boy will be proud. Cooley explained that as soon as the boy turns his attentions to a new project, his feelings will fade and, in time, he will feel indifferent toward the boat. This is similar to the person who plays the same musical compact disk (CD) over and over again, until eventually, the CD is no longer played.

These feelings accompany us into our adult life. Cooley stated that throughout life, the appreciation and disapproval that we receive for all of our work will diminish over time. "Cooley's person reflects upon the self through the viewpoint or perspective of another. Thus, self-awareness does not cause the person to reflect or operate upon idiosyncratic elements . . . but instead, upon the values or needs of the social milieu" (Fry and Wickland, 1980:47–48). Cooley explained that one's self-feeling has its roots in where it feels most comfortable. We are all drawn to what we know.

"I" as It Changes to "We"   "The group self or 'We' is simply an 'I' which includes other persons" (Cooley, 1964:209). Cooley explained that those who share a common bond take the pronoun "I" and change it to "we," as in the *primary group*. Individuals may also use the term "we" in connection with others that they do not know, for example, when one refers to a baseball game and says, "We lost on a bad call." Even though he or she is not on the team, they still feel a bond to it.

"I," Self-Feeling, and Love   Cooley explored the influence of love on human development by examining its effect on the "I" and self-feeling. He described how love tends to lessen the individuality of the person, and yet it can also be a powerful binding force. He made a distinction between a healthy love and a disinterested love. In a healthy love, each partner shares equally in the relationship. In disinterested love, one individual brings more to the relationship,

while the other diverts their time and attention from the other person. Cooley explained that when love is not equally reciprocated, as if "love closes," the self becomes hardened. In order to protect one's self-feelings they may become arrogant and mean. Cooley (1902) offered advice from Henry David Thoreau, who suggested that instead of closing up, one should break loose. Cooley (1902) added, "No matter what a man does, he is not fully sane or human unless there is spirit of freedom in him" (p. 188). Cooley was clearly an advocate for love. He believed that when a person is passionate about someone else they want to "mean" something to them. Everyone wants to feel important and necessary, but it is most important to feel "wanted" by the person that one desires, or loves. Further, Cooley stated that there are no other feelings that say "mine" so fiercely (e.g., "She is my girlfriend.").

"I" and Children   Cooley placed a great deal of importance on the study of children, especially in terms of human development. He is famous for studying his own children. Cooley called his second child M. when referring to her in research. He described how his children learned their pronouns "I" and "my." Cooley detailed the complications with the understanding and the comprehension of pronouns. His second child M. understood what belonged to her. If you asked her where her nose was, she would have no problem saying, "Here is my nose." Yet confusion existed in understanding how someone else could say, "Here is my nose." Another problem that involves pronouns and children is the possessiveness behind pronouns. Cooley referred to his first child as R. Cooley noticed of his children, "It was extremely common to see R. tugging at the end of a plaything and M. at the other, screaming 'my,' 'my'" (p. 190). Child M. cannot distinguish between "me" and "my," she sees the toy as an extension of herself.

Cooley also described a situation where a toy is not even in sight or reach but one child will ask, "Where is my toy?" There is no separation of his, hers, and mine. It all belongs to the child.

Cooley further explained that pronouns and one's self-feelings are intertwined, even at an early age. Cooley again used his own children to explain. He said that even during the first week, his daughter M. would cry for things she wanted. Screaming and crying would be her way to express her feelings and her wants. It is the language of a child before she learns to use "I" and "me." The child observes others saying "me" and "mine" and connects these feelings with things that they want or feel that they should have. Cooley (1902) stated, "The first person pronoun is a sign of a concrete thing after all, but that thing is not primarily the child's body, or his muscular sensations as such, but the phenomenon of aggressive appropriation, practiced by himself, witnessed by others, and incited and interpreted by a hereditary instinct" (p. 191). Parents teach their children about possessiveness by claiming things as mine, his, or hers. When children claim things, or desire things, parents respond to the demands—it is part of human nature.

Cooley showed that the first-person pronouns are learned. When a child uses his feelings, connects them and there is a subsequent reaction by others, he has learned a form of communication. This communication, according to Cooley, is initiated by some sort of instinctual emotion. Through conversation, a child learns the appropriate use of the first-person pronouns.

Utilizing research on his own children, Cooley showed how some children connect with their feelings earlier than others. Cooley indicated that R. was much slower at learning pronouns than sibling M. He sometimes called his father "me." Cooley explained this by the child's shyness. He believed that his child either had little social feeling or had problems asserting his social feelings. M. on the other hand, had no problem asserting herself. Cooley felt that this was because M. felt the need to protect what was hers from her big brother. M. therefore was more comfortable in asserting her self-feeling. Cooley observed the inevitable progression of R. When R.'s mother would take things away that were dangerous (e.g., a knife) to R., she would claim that it was "hers." R. would then want to claim something that was his, therefore expressing his self-feeling. He then learned to communicate his "my" and "mine" by example.

Cooley's work with the first-person pronouns provides an in-depth insight into the growth of human development. Humans have the ability to communicate what is theirs, how they feel, and how they want to express what belongs to them. Cooley's insights strongly indicate that through interaction, humans are raised to claim what is theirs. Individuals' own inner self-feelings make them aware of what belongs to them. The use of first-person pronouns allows individuals to express and explain themselves.

Sympathetic Introspection

Although Cooley had a background in statistical process as well as scientific methods, he chose to forego these traditional systematic methods in his sociological studies. He did not believe the scientific method and the use of empirical data were beneficial in the study of the social sciences. Instead, he preferred a qualitative approach.

Cooley and Mead both rejected the behavioristic view of human beings, a view that people simply respond to given stimuli. They believed that since people possess a consciousness and a sense of self, the focus of study should center on this aspect of social reality. "Cooley urged sociologists to try and put themselves in the place of the actors they were studying, to use the method of *sympathetic introspection*, in order to analyze consciousness. By analyzing what they as actors might do in various circumstances, sociologists could understand the meanings and motives that are at the base of social behavior" (Ritzer, 2000:50). He employed self-analysis, observations of his own children, autobiographies from his students, books, and so on, in the formulation of his analysis.

Sympathetic introspection is a concept similar to Max Weber's *verstehen*. *Verstehen* is a German word that translates as "understanding" in English, and reflects Weber's emphasis that the study of human behavior must be centered upon attempts to investigate the subjective meanings actors attribute to their actions. Cooley agreed with Weber's subjective focus. *Sympathetic introspection* is "a methodology that did not settle for observations of external behavior, but attempted to tap the meaning and interpretations of the participants" (Meltzer, Petras and Reynolds, 1975:10). To understand society one must understand the social facts, which according to Cooley are, "those human bonds whose existence depends on the ideas society's members have of one another" (Reynolds, 1993:35). Cooley believed that it is through *sympathetic introspection* that these bonds can be explained and understood. Cooley described material facts as nonmental facts and although important, "these material facts are not nearly as important as those human bonds" (Reynolds, 1993:35).

Sympathetic introspection can be applied to Durkheim's *altruistic suicide*. Altruistic suicide occurs when individuals are highly integrated into their group, that is, they feel a strong connection and commitment to that community. From Cooley's perspective, Durkheim's theory provides the material fact of the individual's strong commitment to the group, but it fails to provide the reason for this strong commitment. Through the use of *sympathetic introspection* a researcher would be able to determine why the social bond existed between the individual and the group. Consequently, the real explanation for this type of suicide might involve the reasons why an individual was highly integrated into the group, not the simple fact that the individual was integrated into the group.

Critics of Cooley's *sympathetic introspection* methodological approach to the study of human behavior point to the lack of any scientific credibility. Although Mead will improve on Cooley's methodology, Coser (1977) states that he must be reckoned among the pioneers in sociological method.

Social Process

Cooley's social theory was much different than that of many of the other major social theorists. Cooley, as well as Mead, did not view society as an external, coercive structure that exists beyond and prior to individual action, as the French theorists in the tradition of Comte and Durkheim had. Nor did Cooley give much attention to class structure, status inequalities, political action, and large-scale historical change, the primary concerns of Marx and Weber. Cooley's view of society and culture is relatively accepting, uncritical, and, in fact, he had relatively little to say about structures. From his holistic and organic view he conceived of social life as a mass of reciprocal behavior that was not necessarily sensitive to structural barriers.

Cooley did, however, offer astute insights into *social process*. Through *primary group* participation individuals receive their earliest and most basic experiences of social unity. They are the source of individual's ideals, which derive from the moral unity of the group. Communication allows for the spread of these ideals between actors of the group and subgroups. Communication becomes a key ingredient in cementing social bonds. The unity of social mind (ideals) and social structure is social organization.

Social organization is partly coextensive with public consciousness or public opinion. Public discourse is critical in order to attain mutual understanding of one another's points of view. The social mind, then, constantly forms itself into wholes, consciously and unconsciously represented by fashions, fads, new technologies, traditions, customs, institutions, and so on, which spread and generate more varied structures of differentiated thought symbols.

Consequently, Cooley saw public opinion as "an organic process," with communication as the key. Communicated differences are the lifeblood of public opinion and represent an important element in establishing social bonds and consensus. Consensus is not simply a mere aggregate of separate individuals, but an organization, a cooperative product (structure). Even conflict is conceived as necessary and healthy, for it forms the framework of a new emerging form of consensus. The ability to communicate one's opinion in a public forum is critical in a democracy. Cooley was a passionate defender of the virtue of democracy, for he viewed it as a mode of governance that arrives through moral unity and not through the suppression of differences.

Relevancy

The works of Charles Horton Cooley have inspired many social thinkers. He was a man of introspection who enjoyed the simple things in life. He liked long walks with friends and camping. He did not enjoy surprises or unpredictability in his own life, which is ironic since he insisted on allowing for a multitude of explanations when explaining human behavior in his research

studies on others. He felt contentment living in Ann Arbor, Michigan, and enjoyed teaching at the University of Michigan. For it was here that his confidence grew and he was able to become his own man and step outside of his father's considerable shadow.

Cooley is known for a wide range of ideas and is remembered today mainly because of his insights into the social-psychological aspects of social life. Cooley had an interest in consciousness and the development of self, but he refused to separate them from the social context. This is best exemplified by his concept that is still discussed today, the *looking-glass self*. Through the use of this concept, Cooley came to understand that people possess consciousness and that it is shaped in continuing social interaction (Ritzer, 2000).

The *organic view of society* as proposed by Cooley expressed his holistic approach to the study of sociology. This approach was in direct opposition to the utilitarian-individualistic approach preferred by Spencer. The debate in the legitimacy of one orientation over another continues today, and will throughout the third millennium. There will always be social thinkers who will see the merits of either technique.

One of Cooley's most significant contributions to future social thought involves his works on the *primary group*. The rapid growth of globalization in the early 2000s has left many people disenchanted, detached, and lacking in the spirit of community. Humans are social creatures, and as such will always need to bond with their fellows. Individuals search for an immediate group that provides them with communal unity. The socialization process is most effective when communicated by primary group members onto the individual. Socialization is the process by which one internalizes the expectations of others, particularly significant others. Through socialization children learn how to respond appropriately in various social contexts; they learn social skills that are necessary to function in society; they learn the roles and expectations of others; and they develop a sense of self. In short, we become "human" through socialization.

To illustrate the relevancy of the primary group, especially in terms of the socialization process, one needs simply to study children who were raised in social isolation. These children are often referred to as "feral children." In a "typical" case, a child is born and raised with little, or no, adult supervision. The child might be imprisoned in an attic or basement, they are given enough food to survive, but without human love, compassion and simple interaction, the child will not develop language or social skills. In Norco, California, Riverside County sheriff's deputies found a six-year-old girl, Betty, wearing only a diaper and chained to a bed in a house filled to the ceiling with trash and feces. When authorities attempted to emancipate the girl, she curled up and cowered in a corner, unable to speak, moaning and making small sounds. The girl's mother had her daughter chained to the bed off-and-on for five years (Williams, 1999).

A six-year-old feral boy in Moscow, Russia, spent two years (during the mid-1990s) living with a pack of stray dogs after being abandoned by his parents. The boy, Ivan, would approach adults and ask for food, which he would share with the dogs. The dogs would leap to defend the boy if adults tried to harm him. They also found warm places to sleep, something that can be difficult when you are on your own in a place where winter temperatures reach 22 degrees below zero Fahrenheit. On several occasions social workers attempted to separate the boy from the dogs, but such was the bond between them that the efforts were unsuccessful. After tricking the dogs with a meat bait, the authorities were able to "rescue" the howling and biting child.

These two stories of feral children indicate how important primary group association is, especially for young children who need to develop a wide range of social and biological skills. Ivan, the Moscow boy, was able to maintain some of the language he learned through his parents (before they abandoned him) by asking (communication) adults for food. The human brain functions biologically; but to become human, the brain needs to be stimulated to learn and develop socially. This can only occur through the socialization process and primarily through primary groups.

Stories of feral children represent an extreme; in most cases children are provided with a relatively loving, trusting, nurturing environment in which their human development progresses through normal stages. In other cases, children are exposed to any number of dysfunctional elements that may physically or emotionally scar them for years. Consequently, the field in the study of child development has flourished, as many "experts" attempt to guide families through the developmental process. After the family, peer groups grow in importance for the child. They are exposed to fellow classmates at school, and friends they play with in their neighborhood. The normal course of development causes some old friends to be abandoned as others enter one's life. Entering college, geographic relocation, starting a new job, getting married, are all factors in one's changing primary group affiliation. Not all bonds are broken; some people maintain close relationships with long-time friends, and most people remain relatively close to their family of orientation. Surely, the importance of the primary group, and the need to study its relationship with, and the impact on, individuals will continue through the third millennium.

The relevance of the effect of the *looking-glass self* can be illustrated with the example of the practice of "tracking" and "ability grouping" of students in elementary through high school. After all, Cooley felt that the concept of the *looking-glass self* is especially important when applied to children. In many schools, students are placed into groups based on their teachers' assessment of their abilities. When they are placed in classes with different content or different levels of content, this practice is called tracking. When students are grouped within classes on the basis of ability, it is called ability grouping (Farley, 1998). More than half of all U.S. elementary schools use some type of ability grouping, although a number of schools are moving away from it. When students are "on track" they begin to see themselves as others evaluate them. The students evaluated with high ability are encouraged to enroll in classes that will prepare them for college and professional careers. They will have a strong sense of self and are generally more confident and likely to succeed. All of this is because their imagined interpretations of the judgments by others resulted in a positive self-feeling.

For the students who were "tracked" with a negative evaluation of ability, the expectations to succeed are lowered, and they are often placed in remedial courses, which is supposedly for their benefit. Unfortunately, a negative stigma has been attached to these students. Placement in such courses usually reinforces the idea to the student that they are stupid, or losers. If these messages are unchanged, then the imagination of the judgment of their appearance will lead to a negative self-image.

Cooley and James both acknowledged the importance of the environment on behavior. Few environments place a greater emphasis on the sense of self, or the presentation of self, than the world of gangs. Among the most treasured values among gang members is to never "punk-out." Always be cool, always be ready to defend yourself and your set. Anderson (1994)

refers to this phenomenon as the "code of the streets." Based on his observations of ghetto streets over several years, Anderson found that gang members rejected "middle-class values" and instead maintained a commitment to the code of respect. Respect is defined as being treated right, or with proper deference (the precise definition is not consistent). If a gang member has been "dissed," or disrespected, he must retaliate physically and with violence if necessary. The code of the street is a subcultural adaptation to the lack of faith in the judicial system, police treatment, and the strong disapproval from the larger society. Thus, the negative judgment of their behavior, which resulted in negative self-feelings, led to the creation of the code of the streets as a way to attain positive feedback from their primary group—the gang.

Self-image influences many aspects of one's life. Self-esteem has been linked to success in business and in one's personal life, and the lack of it has been linked to substance abuse, unemployment, suicide, and a host of other personal and social problems. There are countless programs designed to enhance children's, and adults', self-esteem. It has reached a point where some parents are reluctant to criticize or punish their children in fear of harming their fragile egos. Self-esteem is used as an explanation for every imaginable personal problem. Psychologists act as if by simply improving one's self-esteem, social problems will disappear. "Where even the vilest act can be explained away as an unfortunate but inevitable result of a poor self-image, our capacity to distinguish between good and evil seems to be in jeopardy" (Hewitt, 1998:xii). The role of self-esteem is indeed a debated subject area.

Ancient man had little time to be concerned over how he "looked" or his table manners, but undoubtedly, he did not like being "dissed." Therefore, one can conclude that issues of self-esteem and a sense of self have been important since the dawn of civilization, and will continue to be so until the end of time.

Cooley's use of the *sympathetic introspection* method in the study of human behavior inspired the field of symbolic interactionism and the qualitative paradigm. Qualitative methods attempt to uncover the subjective nature of human behavior that allows researchers to explain "why" behavior occurs. Most sociologists promote sociology as a science, and therefore implore that researchers must use the quantitative methods of science. Quantitative methods are the objective, logical tools of science that provide facts and figures describing observable patterns and events in social life. American sociology is especially quantitative. The advent of supercomputers has enhanced this trend dramatically in recent years. The quantitative–qualitative debate is an ongoing one that will continue into the third millennium.

As a final comment on the relevancy of Cooley's concepts and contributions to the future, an examination of the importance he places on communication and public discourse reveals his commitment to democracy. He was a passionate defender of democracy. Freedom of speech is critical in a democracy. Individuals must be given opportunities to express themselves in public, and, today, via the media (e.g., news editorials, opinion writing, talk-radio, internet chatrooms, etc.). A wide variety of outlets must be made available. Unfortunately, the number of companies that control over half of all U.S. media outlets has dropped from 50 in 1983 to just 6 in 1999 (*Buffalo News*, 2000). The trend toward a centralization in power in communications must be watched carefully. The framers of the Constitution deemed this so important that the First Amendment guarantees the freedom of speech, the rights of the press, and the right of people to peacefully assemble. These rights are critical for all Americans, today and in the third millennium.

Cooley was a man of idealism and optimism, for which he was often criticized. This criticism was based on the fact that Cooley lived an idyllic life far removed from the enormous social changes taking place in the United States. Karl Marx was criticized for his utopian societal beliefs that would come about from the proletariat revolution, but, unlike Cooley, he experienced firsthand the effects of the immense social changes taking place. One might ask, "So what?" He was the prototype of what today is often derisively called an "armchair sociologist" (Coser, 1977). Cooley provides hope to all those sociologists who are not out there in the "trenches" collecting hard empirical data, that it is possible to advance the social sciences while sitting in one's armchair. His theories on primary groups and their relationship to the development of self as well as basic human social development remain applicable. His research method of sympathetic introspection is commonly used today, and most likely will continue so in the third millennium.

George Herbert Mead

(1863–1931)

George Herbert Mead was born on February 27, 1863, in South Hadley, Massachusetts. Mead came from a religious and educated family that encouraged his intellectual development. When Mead was seven, the family moved to Oberlin, Ohio. George's father, Hiram Mead was a minister in the Congressional Church and taught homiletics (the art of preaching) at Oberlin Theological Seminary (Miller, 1973). Hiram Mead benefited from the progressive education for which Oberlin was known (Farganis, 2000). Oberlin was founded in 1833 by a militant Congregationalist reformer, the Reverend John Jay Shipherd, and was one of the first American colleges to admit Blacks. In 1841, it became the first coeducational college to grant a bachelor's degree to women (Coser, 1977). Oberlin was one of the primary stops along the route of the Underground Railroad that helped thousands of southern Black slaves to escape to the north and to Canada.

George's mother, Elizabeth Storrs Billings, came from a family background in which intellectual achievement was greatly valued (Coser, 1977). When her husband died, Elizabeth taught at Oberlin College to make ends meet and later became the president of Mount Holyoke College (Miller, 1973). Mead's

only sibling Alice, born four years before him, married Albert Temple Swing, a minister from Fremont, Nebraska (Miller, 1973).

George Herbert Mead (1863–1931) American pragmatist, philosopher, social scientist, and primary founder of symbolic interactionism.
Source: National Library of Medicine

169

There is little information on Mead's childhood except that the family spent a few summer vacations on a farm in New England (Miller, 1973). His mother saw to it that the young George would go through his daily regimen of prayer, study, and good works. It was her dream that George would follow in his father's footsteps in the Chritian ministry (Shalin, 2000). Mead entered Oberlin College at the age of sixteen and was described as a serious, cautious, quiet, mild-mannered, and kind-hearted person (Miller, 1973). Academically, he was interested in literature and poetry, as well as English and American history.

Oberlin College was not nearly as progressive in its academic thinking as it was in displaying a sense of social conscience for the oppressed members of society. Challenging the narrow theological dogmatism of the college was strongly discouraged. Memorization of "truths" consistent with Christian theology was encouraged over intellectual debate. Mead's son recalls that while George was at Oberlin, "Questioning was discouraged, ultimate values being determined by learned men in the dogmas and passed on to the moral philsophers for dissemination" (Wallace, 1967:398). For a mind as thirsty for stimulating conversation and knowledge as Mead's, this was surely difficult, as he found throughout his lifetime that the best expression for his brilliant, encyclopedic mind came in the form of conversation.

Socially, Oberlin College did not allow dancing or drinking. Many students were active members of the Anti-Saloon League, a group founded in Oberlin that preached on the evils of alcohol. Concerned over potential interaction among men and women coeds, the college maintained separate library hours for males and females (Pampel, 2000). Mead's negative reaction to Oberlin's excessive theological agenda led him to lose his faith in the Christian ethics. "The son of many generations of Puritan theologians had lost his faith in the dogmas of the church" (Coser, 1977:342). Mead once remarked that he spent 20 years trying to unlearn what he learned the first 20 years of his life (Schellenberg, 1978). He had pushed himself in Christian ideology, for the sake of his mother, for as long as he could, and confessed to his best friend, Henry Castle, that, "her happiness is bound up in me" (Shalin, 2000:303).

In 1881, Hiram Mead died, leaving very little in financial support for his family. George found a job as a waiter to pay his way through college, and his mother taught at the college. In 1883 Mead graduated from Oberlin, and accepted a job to teach at a primary school. Several teachers had just resigned from the school because they were unable to cope with a large number of students who were terrorizing classmates and teachers. Mead stood up to the rowdy students and began expelling large numbers of them from school. The Board of Trustees failed to support Mead and discharged him after just four months (Miller, 1973).

For the next three years Mead alternated between jobs as a tutor and as a surveyor for a railroad in Minnesota and Canada. He had long abandoned his one-time dream of starting a literary paper in New York, but he continued to read widely during his spare time. Mead's thirst for an intellectual outlet for his energetic mind was beginning to get the best of him. He began to write to his college friend Henry Castle. Castle came from a wealthy, well-educated family that had extensive land holdings and political influence in Hawaii (Baldwin, 1986). While at Oberlin, Mead and Castle often discussed issues related to life, God, poetry, and evolution. The two friends came to favor modern secular beliefs over religious doctrines. It is most likely Castle who had the greatest influence over Mead's reexamination and eventual break from his theological tradition (Wallace, 1967). His future interest in psychology would be shaped, at least in part, by a conscious effort to avoid direct confrontation with his past theological values (Schellenberg, 1978). Mead was also becoming acquainted with the new developments in the natural sciences, and in particular was impressed by Darwin's work on the evolution of species (Pampel, 2000).

In 1887, Castle had been admitted to the graduate program in philosophy at Harvard University, and persuaded Mead to give graduate school a try. They would live as roommates and continue their philosophical discussions. Mead found his philosophy courses stimulating but too abstract and isolated from the real world (Pampel, 2000). At Harvard, Mead's philosophical interests lay in the romantic philosophers and Hegelian idealism, as taught by Josiah Royce (Baldwin, 1986). Mead also studied under William James, whom he worked for, and tutored his children (Miller, 1973). Both Royce and James left a permanent mark on Mead's life and outlook (Coser, 1977). His exposure to advanced philosophy further eroded Mead's remaining Christian beliefs (Pampel, 2000).

Unhappy with the abstract nature of philosophy, Mead decided to change his course of study to physiological psychology. Psychology was still just a branch of philosophy at that time, but Mead deemed it more practical and scientific to the obscure thought of many of the philosophers he studied. For his second year of graduate school, Mead accepted a scholarship to study in Germany, the location of the world's most renowned specialists in physiological psychology (Pampel, 2000). Mead first went to Leipzig to study with Wilhelm Wundt, whose conception of the "gesture" would greatly influence his later works

(Coser, 1977). Also at Leipzig, Mead studied under Stanley Hall, the American physiological psychologist who sparked Mead's interest in that discipline (Farganis, 2000). In 1899, Mead went to Berlin to study both psychology and philosophy taught in the tradition of Simmel (Pampel, 2000). Coser (1977) speculates that Mead was taught by Simmel himself, although he was never able to confirm this.

In 1891, while Mead was in Berlin, Henry Castle brought his sister Helene with him to visit George. Over a period of just a few months, Helene and Mead became very close, fell in love, and were married on October 1, 1891. He quit graduate school (never earning a graduate degree) to accept a lecturer's teaching position at the University of Michigan, teaching philosophy and psychology (Scheffler, 1974).

At Michigan, the young and idealistic Mead hoped to combine scholarship and social action, a tradition he learned and embraced while in Germany. His colleagues included Charles Cooley, James Tufts, and the young philosopher John Dewey. Dewey served as a role model for Mead, as he was already active in social involvement and academic success. Dewey had published his first book at age 27, and his second book at age 29. This work ethic would follow Dewey throughout his life. Mead and Dewey quickly realized their similar interests and became lifelong friends. Dewey's daughter would state, some time later, that the Meads and Deweys remained friends until their death (Strauss, 1964).

In 1893, Dewey received an offer to become the chair of the department of philosophy at the University of Chicago. Although Dewey had known Mead for just one year, and George did not have a graduate degree, Dewey insisted that he be allowed to bring Mead to Chicago with him as condition of his employment. Further, despite the lack of any publications, Dewey was even able to secure the position of assistant professor for Mead at Chicago. Mead would remain at the University of Chicago for the rest of his life.

The extraordinary growth of both the city of Chicago and the University of Chicago provided Mead and Dewey with a wonderfully exciting intellectual environment. The city of Chicago was little more than a small log fort in 1833, and had become a major city just six decades later (Faris, 1967). At the time of Mead's appointment, Chicago was primarily a meat-packing center occupied by numerous slaughter houses. Chicago boasted the first steel-framed skyscraper; reversed the flow of the Chicago River; and, as a result of massive and rapid migration along with the attendant disorganization of many slum districts, laid claim to numerous social problems. It was the perfect place for applied academic study and social reform.

The University of Chicago had just opened prior to the arrival of Mead and Dewey, through an endowment funded by such industrialists as John D. Rockefeller (Pampel, 2000). It opened its pseudo-Gothic doors in 1892 under the presidency of William Harper, a professor of Bible at Yale University, with the idea that it would compete with the older eastern universities such as Harvard, Yale, and Princeton. Harper was an aggressive president who ruthlessly raided eastern universities, offering twice the normal salary and light teaching loads, in hopes of attracting the most brilliant scholars. The original faculty included eight professors who gave up college presidencies to teach at the University of Chicago (Coser, 1977).

The city of Chicago had become a practical social laboratory for social thinkers, especially sociologists. Mead's greatest contribution to sociology and the so-called "Chicago School" of thought rests with his development of social psychology. Influenced strongly by Dewey and the environment of the university, Mead began to evolve a philosophy of social life that combined a number of academic interests. His philosophy aimed to combine thought with action, science and progress, and the individual and community (Pampel, 2000). Mead and Dewey were heavily involved with the philosophical school called pragmatism. "In essence, pragmatism extends the scientific methods of the natural sciences to all areas of intellectual life" (Pampel, 2000:179).

During the early years at Chicago, Mead remained in the public shadow of Dewey. When Dewey accepted a position at Columbia (leaving because he felt that the University of Chicago was not providing enough support for his educational experiments), Mead did not assume the eminent position once held by his friend. One reason was his limited publications. Mead experienced great difficulty putting his ideas in writing, but that never stopped his creative thoughts. His lectures were eagerly greeted and well-attended by students. He never used notes and possessed a powerful style of presentation. Mead seldom looked directly at the students, and discouraged questions and discussion. He never entered the classroom until after the bell rang, left immediately at the end of class, and took measures to avoid contact with students interested in asking him questions. Despite this, his students loved his lectures (Pampel, 2000). Most of Mead's major works were published by graduate students from notes taken in class.

Mead expanded on Wundt's theories of the gesture by emphasizing the importance of social factors in the evolution and development of communication, role taking, mind, and self. Between 1910 and 1920, Mead worked on integrating Einstein's theory of relativity with his own thinking, attempting to bring unity to the entire scientific and pragmatic worldview. He eventually pieced together an evolutionary cosmology that integrated all the sciences and resolved philosophical problems in terms of emergence—beginning with the emergence of the solar system and planets, then dealing with the evolution of life and increasingly higher levels of animal awareness, and culminating in human mind, self, and society (Baldwin, 1986). During the last years of his life, Mead turned increasing attention toward macrosocietal issues and international relationships; thus formulating his unified theoretical perspective (Baldwin, 1986).

In early 1931, after teaching at the University of Chicago for nearly forty years, Mead became embroiled in a bitter conflict between the department and the president of the university. So great was the bitterness that Mead wrote a letter of resignation from his hospital bed, indicating his desire to not only leave the university, but Chicago as well. Upon his release from the hospital the next day, April 26, he died suddenly at the age of 68. At his memorial service, James H. Tufts said, "He was the most interesting conversationalist I knew. He was informed and informing" (Miller, 1973:39). His close friend Dewey stated, "His mind was deeply original—in my contacts and my judgment the most original mind in philosophy in America, of the last generation . . . . I dislike to think what my own thinking might have been were it not for the seminal ideas which I derived from him" (Scheffler, 1974:150).

Intellectual Influences

There were numerous influences on Mead's thoughts as he possessed a wide-variety of interests. He was knowledgeable in philosophy, psychology, history, biology, and sociology. Mead was familiar with mathematics and mathematical rationality, and enjoyed music and poetry. His family's background in religion exposed him to Puritan Christianity and theological dogmatic thinking.

William James

The properties of Mead's social psychology and symbolic interactionism can be traced, at least in part, to William James. In his brilliant *Principles of Psychology* (1890), James called for the re-examination of the relations between individual and society (Martindale, 1981). Although James was a product of his time and accepted the instinct theory that was so prevalent, he began to believe that there were other aspects beyond biology that tended to modify behavior. His works on *habit* were of special importance as James recognized that habit reduces the need for conscious attention. If an individual is capable of forming new habits, then he is also capable of modifying his behavior. James (1890) believed that the individual acquires a new nature through habit.

A second critical aspect of James's psychology was his rethinking of the role of "consciousness." He noted that consciousness always involves some degree of awareness of the person's self. The person appears in thought in two ways, "partly known and partly knower, partly object and partly subject . . . . For shortness we may call one the *Me* and the other the *I* . . . I shall therefore treat successively of (a) the self as known, or the *Me*, the 'empirical ego' as it is sometimes called; and of (b) the self as knower, or the *I*, the 'pure ego' of certain authors" (James, 1890:176).

The empirical self, or *me*, is the sum total of all the person can claim as one's own; their feelings, emotions, actions of self-seeking and self-preservation. People possess as many social selves as there are individuals who have images of them in mind. The self as knower, the *I*, or pure ego, is a much more complicated subject matter (James, 1890). The *I* refers to the sense of self that a particular person possesses at any given specific moment in time.

In the tradition of James, Mead (1934) argued that consciousness must be a product of the dynamic relationship between a person and her social environment. Mead stated that it is an erroneous idea that, "'Mental' phenomena [are] conditioned [to] reflexes and similar physiological mechanisms—in short, to purely behavioristic terms" (p. 10). Every individual is constantly involved in a succession of interactions with others, all of which influence and shape one's mind. Consciousness is continuous, subject to the vast array of stimuli presented to it from the social environment.

Mead was clearly influenced by James in his works on the development of self. Mead even used the same terminology of the "I" and "me" in explaining the structure of the self. Mead reasoned that the self consisted of an "I" which is capable of understanding the social "me." Further discussion on Mead's usage of the "I" and "me" follows later in this chapter.

German Idealism

Learning from the ideas of Fichte, Schelling, and Hegel, whom Mead called "the Romantic Philosophers," Mead understood the German idealistic tradition tended to generalize, and made a philosophical doctrine of the notion of the life process (Coser, 1977). The Romantic idealists utilized the self–not-self process in experience, and identified this process with the subject–object process. This subject–object process was similar to James's analysis. Mead learned from the German tradition that there is no consciousness that is not conscious of something; therefore, the subject and object are inevitably interrelated. There cannot be a subject without the object being aware of it, just as there cannot be an object without it being a subject. "Mead took the idea that the development of the self requires reflexivity—that is, the ability of an individual (the subject) to be an object to himself as a result of 'taking the attitudes of others who are involved in his conduct'" (Adams and Sydie, 2001). This idea would greatly influence Mead's concept of the generalized other.

Mead came to view the German idealists as preoccupied with the relations of the self to its objects. He felt that Fichte was too concerned with moral experiences. He believed that Schelling and Hegel focused too much attention on the aesthetic experience, and experience of thought, respectively (Coser, 1977). Above all, Mead found fault with Hegel for not having formulated adequate concepts of the individual and of the future. Hegel's philosophy is thus incapable of grasping individuality in its concreteness (Joas, 1985).

Having studied in Germany, Mead was most directly influenced by Wilhelm Wundt, where he became impressed by Wundt's theories of language and the gesture. Wundt was the heir apparent of the German idealistic tradition. He was able to relate German idealism to the social sciences through his psychophysical parallelism (Martindale, 1981). In the introduction to Mead's *Mind, Self, and Society*, Charles Morris clarifies the distinction between Darwin and Wundt's conception of the gesture by explaining that Wundt helped to separate the gesture from its internal emotional implication and regard it in a social context. In the tradition of Wundt, Mead viewed the gesture as the transitional link to language from human action. The gesture preceded language and mediates the development of language as the basic mechanism that allows for the "sense of self" to arise during the course of ongoing social interaction. Thus, Mead came to argue that the gesture can *only* be explained in a social context. Years later, a more mature Mead (1934) would come to describe a gesture as those phases of the act which bring about the adjustment of the response of the other.

From Hegel, Mead took the idea that consciousness and society were dialectically emergent phenomena (Adams and Sydie, 2001). Mead replaced Hegel's "Spirit" with a concept of a "unified world" that emerges through the realization of universal human potential. He believed that social development was dependent on individuals becoming aware of their "opposition to one another" and working through such oppositions (Mead, 1938).

Charles Darwin and Evolutionism

As with many of the early social thinkers, Mead was raised in a religious family. However, an analytical mind that seeks the truth and supports the validity of science is bound to find the fallacies inherent with religious dogma. Research has clearly shown that as a person's level of education increases, their religiosity decreases. The primary influence on Mead's final abandonment from the theological shackles of his youth was Charles Darwin (Coser, 1977). The fact of evolution presented by Darwin was enough evidence for Mead to conclude that the religious doctrine that he was raised to believe was false. Darwin's influence on Mead extended to his philosophical and psychological beliefs as well.

For Mead, the key figure for a new beginning in philosophy was Charles Darwin. Darwin's model of an organism in an environment, to which it must adapt in order to survive, provides the means for the understanding and discovery of all behaviors, humans included. The knowledge of human behavior rests with the awareness of all the conditions set by nature on the organism's reproduction of itself. In addition, the organism must be able to deduce the subject's behavior within the external world that is separate from itself (Joas, 1985).

As for Darwin's influence on psychology, Mead (1934) stated, "One of the important documents in the history of modern psychology, particularly for the psychology of language, is Darwin's *Expression of the Emotions in Man and Animals*. Here Darwin carried over his theory of evolution into the field of what we call 'conscious experience'" (p. 15). Darwin showed that there are a number of acts that express emotions. The part of the organism that most vividly expresses emotions is the face. Darwin studied the muscles themselves in order to determine whether such changes in the face might actually express emotions such as anger. Darwin studied the blood flow in fear and in terror in order to determine if changes in the blood flow itself causes a change in emotions. Darwin theorized that there must be some rhythm of circulation in blood flow that corresponds to various emotions.

According to Mead (1934), Darwin discovered a greater validity in the acts or gestures of behaviors themselves. For example, dogs exhibit attitudes (gestures) of anger and intent to attack (act) with their teeth. "The attitude, or in a more generalized term, the gesture, has been preserved after the value of the act has disappeared" (Mead, 1934:16).

Mead vehemently disagreed with the psychology of Darwin that assumed emotion was a psychological state, a state of consciousness, and that this state could not itself be formulated in terms of the attitude or the behavior of the form. Mead found no evidence for the prior existence of consciousness, and concluded that consciousness is an emergent form of behavior. The social act is a precondition of the conception of consciousness.

Darwin taught Mead to think in terms of process (evolutionary process) instead of fixed forms. Mead (1936) came to realize that process will shape form. The organism has one form now, but it will have another form later, dependent on the conditions under which it is exposed. For Mead, the evolutionary process was a pragmatic, scientific approach to problem-solving. "Evolution is the process of meeting and solving problems" (Mead, 1936:143). Thus, the primary influence of evolutionary thought on Mead was the recognition that there are no fixed structures; instead, there exists changing forms through a continuing process.

Darwin's general idea of evolution was very important to Mead, but it was his idea of random variations that Mead found most intriguing. As Mead (1934) interpreted Darwin's idea that constant pressure leads to the selection of which variants are better adapted to the conditions under which selection occurs, Mead concluded that it was this randomness that allows for the unpredictability and indeterminism in the course of human evolution.

American Pragmatism

A critical influence on Mead's intellectual thinking was *pragmatism*. Although Mead would become one of the key figures in the development of pragmatism, he was initially introduced to pragmatic philosophy by John Dewey, William James, and James Baldwin. Mead (1938) viewed pragmatism as a "natural American outgrowth." It reflected the triumph of science in American society and a belief in the superiority of scientific data and analysis over philosophical dogma and other forms of inferior beliefs. Pragmatists reject the idea of absolute truths and regard all ideas as provisional and subject to change in light of future research (Ritzer, 2000). For pragmatists, truth and reality do not simply exist "out there"—they are actively created

as humans act in and toward the world (Shalin, 1986). Truth is determined by humans' adaptations to their environments, therefore revealing the transitive character of both truth and consciousness.

Pragmatists believe that human beings reflect on the meaning of a stimulus before reacting. The meaning placed on various acts depends on the purpose of the act, the context in which it is performed, and the reactions of others to the act (Adams and Sydie, 2001). Mead's notion of the act as social was directly influenced by Dewey and Cooley. Dewey believed that reflexive action(s) leads to the construction of such issues as morality. Thus, Mead came to view even issues such as ethics and morality as socially constructed, and not fixed entities. Different cultures are easily explained by the realization of the fact that people with different life experiences come to different interpretations of events and impose different meanings on acts.

The collaboration of ideas between Dewey and Mead was mutually beneficial. On the one hand, close examination of Mead's social psychology reveals many influences from Dewey. On the other hand, as Charles Morris (1934) states in the "Introduction" to *Mind, Self, and Society* in regard to both Dewey and Mead, "Neither stands to the other in the exclusive relation of teacher to student; both . . . were of equal though different intellectual stature; both shared in a mutual give-and-take according to their own particular genius. If Dewey gives range and vision, Mead gave analytical depth and scientific precision" (p. xi).

Behaviorism

Mead (1934) defined behaviorism as simply an approach to the study of the experience of the individual from the point of view of his conduct (behavior). His version of behaviorism was not consistent with the way in which it was used by his contemporaries, especially John B. Watson. The behaviorism of Mead's time was borrowed from animal psychology and applied to humans (Ritzer, 2000). Watson represented the attempt to account for socio-psychological phenomena in purely behavioristic terms (Martindale, 1981). Mead criticized Watson for ignoring the inner experiences of consciousness and mental imagery.

However, Mead did believe that inner experiences could be studied by behaviorists, as long as a social-behavioristic approach was utilized. This social-behavioristic approach would lead to the development of *symbolic interactionism*. Instead of studying the mind introspectively, Mead focused on the act (the social act). Acts are behaviors that respond to stimuli. In a variation of the stimulus–response relationship described by behaviorists and exchange theorists, Mead described a stimulus–act relationship. The difference being, the inner consciousness responds to the stimulus before the individual responds, thus creating an *act* that takes in account the existence of the mind and free-will.

Concepts and Contributions

George Herbert Mead is generally described as the founder of modern symbolic interactionism. He is usually described as a social-psychologist who explained the emergence of mind, consciousness, and self through human symbolic interaction. Beyond that, Mead developed a philosophical system that allowed him to construct a social theory that unifies all facets of society and social experience—subjective and objective, macro and micro (Baldwin, 1986).

As an American and influenced by the American values of liberty, equality, and individualism, Mead's experiences differed greatly from those of the Europeans who helped to create the field of sociology. American history is very different from that of Europe's history of feudal structures with a monarchy, an aristocracy, and serfdom. The American Bill of Rights was designed to limit the power of the central government so that no such past European political structures could exist in the United States. The values of freedom and individual effort contributed to the development of market capitalism relatively free from government control (Pampel, 2000). American values, concerns, issues, and ways of thinking left their marks on early American sociology as it developed a practical, can-do attitude toward the world (Garner, 2000). This attitude led to the formation of pragmatism.

As Shalin (1992) explains, for much of the twentieth century, the Europeans rejected pragmatism and dismissed it as a crude expression of Anglo-Saxon utilitarianism. Even the European thinkers sympathetic to the new American intellectual current found it inferior to the continental philosophical tradition. By the 1960s, European thinkers such as Jürgen Habermas began to acknowledge the validity of pragmatism and its counterpart, symbolic interactionism (Shalin, 1992).

Pragmatism

Morris (1934) explains in the "Introduction" to *Mind, Self, and Society*, "Philosophically, Mead was a pragmatist; scientifically, he was a social psychologist. He belonged to an old tradition . . . which fails to see any sharp separation or any antagonism between the activities of science and philosophy, and whose members are themselves both scientists and philosophers" (p. ix).

Pragmatism is, in essence, the extension of the scientific method to all areas of intellectual inquiry, including psychology, sociology, and philosophy. All ideas and theories are tested on their ability to solve problems and provide useful information. Thus, an idea can be evaluated in terms of its consequences. Mead's version of pragmatism should not be confused with the everyday vulgar usage of "being pragmatic" in reference to any practical, matter-of-fact viewpoint or behavior. Mead and the Chicago-school philosophers integrated a philosophical system that is designed to advance all facets of human knowledge and improve the human condition by the rigorous application of scientific methods (Baldwin, 1986).

Pragmatism provides an intellectual justification for social action, therefore integrating consistently with the American respect for problem-solving, progress, and democracy. Mead felt that all ideas and theories should be tested in the real world for their consequences; those that make society better, help solve problems, and work in the real world are judged valid and valuable. Unlike most philosophers, Mead rejected isolated thinking, and the lack of application, as a means of relating to the real world. Rather than debates about "truths," the American pragmatic approach stressed by Mead would concentrate on testing the ideas in the real social world (Pampel, 2000). For example, in the debate over the existence of God, a question that, despite centuries of religious and philosophical debate, has failed to be answered empirically, pragmatists would concern themselves with issues of: Does the belief in God make for a better society, encourage moral action, or improve human lives?

The pragmatic philosophy sees human beings as active and purposeful creatures. Yes, humans are biological creatures, but they are also social beings capable of developing an active, coping self in society (Garner, 2000). Humans are not fixed beings, they are products of their environment capable of learning and changing.

Symbolic Interactionism

Ironically, the most important thinker associated with the Chicago School and *symbolic interactionism* was not a sociologist but rather a philosopher, Mead. It must be made clear that there was no such field as symbolic interactionism per se when Mead first started teaching social psychology at Chicago. It was Herbert Blumer, following in the tradition of Mead and Cooley, who coined the term *symbolic interactionism* in 1937. It was Mead's students who put together their notes on his courses and published *Mind, Self, and Society* posthumously under his name, which had primary influence on Blumer and the development of symbolic interactionism.

Mead believed that human beings have the capacity to think and decide on their own how they should act in given situations, and that they react on the basis of their perceptions and definitions of the situations in which they find themselves (Cockerham, 1995). Mead did not ignore legitimate social forces that strongly influence or limit alternate plans, such as being born into an economically lower-class family, or losing one's job due to economic downsizing. But the symbolic interaction approach suggests that people cope with the reality of their circumstances according to their comprehension of the situation (Cockerham, 1995).

Mind, Self, and Society

Mead's *Mind, Self, and Society* represents his attempt to understand individual social experiences in relation to society. He argued that there can be no self, no consciousness of self, and no communication, apart from society. Mead felt that social experience is the sum of the total dynamic realities observable by the individual who is a part of the ongoing societal process (Kallen, 1956). Society must be understood as a structure that emerges through an ongoing process of communicative social acts and through interactions between persons who are mutually oriented toward each other (Coser, 1977).

Mead (1934) viewed the *mind* as a process and not a thing, as an inner conversation with one's self, which arises and develops within the social process and is an integral part of that process. The mind reflects the human capacity to conceive what the organism perceives, define situations, evaluate phenomena, convert gestures into symbols, and exhibit pragmatic and goal-directed behavior.

The mind, or mentality, resides in the ability of the organism to respond to the environment, which in turn responds, so that the individual can control responses to stimuli from the environment. The mind emerges when the organism demonstrates its capacity to point out meanings to others and to itself (Strauss, 1956). Mead feels that the human animal has the unique capacity of controlling his responses to environmental stimuli and isolating those responses during the very act itself. This ability is the product of language (Miller, 1973). Language becomes the mechanism of control during the reflection process of interaction between the organism and the environment.

The concept of *self* is a critical issue in Mead's works. The *self* involves the process whereby actors reflect on themselves as objects. Thus, the self has the rare ability to be both object and subject. The self is something which has a development; it is not initially there at birth, but arises in the process of social experience and activity. The developmental process of the self is not biological, but rather it emerges from social forces and social experiences. Even the human body is not representative of self until the mind has developed and recognizes it as such. The body can simply be there as an existent structure in the real world, but the self has

the characteristic that it is an object to itself; and that characteristic can then distinguish itself from other objects and from the body (Pfuetze, 1961).

Language represents the developmental process from interpreting gestures to the capability of utilizing symbolic communication and interaction. Sharing a language allows people the ability to put themselves in the role of the other and to understand why they act the way that they do. It is this reflexivity that allows for the development of self because the persons are able to consciously adjust and modify their own behavior (Mead, 1934).

In regard to *society* Mead (1934) states, "Human society as we know it could not exist without minds and selves, since all its most characteristic features presuppose the possession of minds and selves by its individual members; but its individual members would not possess minds and selves if these had not arisen within or emerged out of human social process in its lower stages of development" (p. 227). Mead believed that the behavior of all humans have a basic social aspect to them. The experience and behavior of the individual is always a component of a larger social whole or process. The organization of human experience and behavior is *society*. Because humans have the ability to manipulate their environment, a wide-variety of human societies may exist.

The "I" and the "Me"

Mead is the earliest of the social thinkers to examine the socialization process from the interactionist perspective. He believed that human behavior is almost totally a product of interaction with others. The self, which can be an object to itself, is essentially a social structure that arises from social experience. A baby is born with a "blank slate," without predispositions to develop any particular type of personality. The personality that develops is a product of that person's interactions with others.

According to Mead, the self is composed of two parts: the "I" (the unsocialized self) and the "me" (the socialized self). Both aspects of the self are part of an individual's self-concept (Cockerham, 1995). The self is a product of the dialogue between the "I" and "me." The "I" is the spontaneous, unsocialized, unpredictable, and impulsive aspect of the self. It is the subject of one's actions. The "me" develops gradually through interaction and internalization of the community; it monitors the "I" (Cockerham, 1995). The "me" is the part of the self that is formed as the object of others' actions and views, including one's own reflections on one's self (Garner, 2000). When an individual fails to conform to the norms and expectations of society, she is under the influence of the "I."

The "me" is the judgmental and controlling side of the self that reflects the attitudes of other members of society, while the "I" is the creative and imaginative side of the self (Pampel, 2000). The "me," then, represents the organized set of attitudes that one assumes and that one introjects on their private self, and the "I" represents the organism's response to other's acts, behaviors, and attitudes (Pfuetze, 1965). The "me" has a self-control aspect, in that it acts to stabilize the self, while the "I" is associated with change and reconstruction of the self. The combining of the "I" and the "me" leads to the creation of individual personality and the full development of self (Pfuetze, 1954).

The "me" is the aspect of self that attempts to seek conformity to the expectations of others in the community. This does not imply that the "me" represents morality or pro-social behavior; as the norms the "me" seeks to conform to may be deviant or criminal by society's standards. A gang member's "me" personality will assimilate

to such behaviors as robbery, selling drugs, and acts of violence against the innocent law-abiding citizens. The emergence of the self as a product of multiple interactions with others reveals that the social environment plays the most significant role in the creation of personality.

Mead believed that we are never totally aware of the "I" aspect of ourselves and that is why we periodically surprise even ourselves by our own behavior. We see and know the "I" only after the act has been carried out. Consequently, we know the "I" only in our memories (Ritzer, 2000). The self appearing as the "I" is the memory image of the self who acted toward himself and is the same self who acts toward other selves. Additionally, the processes that go into making up the "me," whom the "I" addresses, is the experience that is induced by the action of the "I" (Reck, 1964). The differences in our memory presentations of the "I" and the "me" are those of the memory images of the initiated social conduct and those of the sensory responses thereto. The "I" of introspection is the self that enters into social relations with other selves. It is not the "I" that is implied in the fact that one presents himself as a "me." And, the "me" of introspection is the same "me" that is the object of the social conduct of others (Reck, 1964).

Development of Self

The development of self is critical for the creation of consciousness and the ability of the child to take the role of the other and to visualize her own performances from the point of view of others. To understand the formation of the self, Mead studied the activities and socialization of children. Mead (1934) noted that newborn babies do not have a sense of themselves as objects; instead they respond automatically and selfishly to hunger, discomfort, and the various stimuli around them. Very young babies do not have the ability to use significant symbols; and therefore, when they play, their behaviors are little different from those of puppies or kittens, who also learn from imitating their parents. Through play and as children grow, they begin to learn to take the role of others, "A child plays at being a mother, at being a teacher, at being a policeman; that is, it is taking different roles" (Mead, 1934:150).

In his theory of the *development of self*, Mead traced patterns of interaction that contribute to the emergence of the social self during childhood (Pampel, 2000). To learn the role of others, the child must come to understand the meanings of symbols and language. Much of this learning takes place through various forms of play. The development of self takes place through a number of stages; and although many reviewers of Mead's stages of development concentrate on just two stages (the play and game stages), it is more useful to identify two additional stages.

1. **Imitation Stage.** At the most basic level of play, infants develop an emerging awareness of other people and physical objects. Babies learn to grasp, hold, and use simple objects like spoons, bottles, and blankets. As their physical skills further develop, they learn to play with objects by observing and imitating their parents. For example, the parent might pick up a ball and throw it, then coax the child to do the same thing. The infant is capable of understanding mere gestures, and until they learn to speak, they are capable of little more than imitating behavior. However, even imitation implies learning, as babies discover that some behaviors are positively rewarded and other behaviors bring punishments (Pampel, 2000).

2. **Play Stage.** At this stage of development the child has learned to use lan-

guage and the meanings of certain symbols. Through language the child can adopt the role or attitude of other persons. They not only *act out* the roles of others, their imaginations allow them to pretend to be that person (Pampel, 2000). They can dress up and "play" (act) mom, a firefighter, a wrestler, their pet dog, or even a cartoon character. While at play, the child will act in the tone of voice and attitudes of whom he is "playing" and in doing so, "he calls or tends to call out in himself the same response that he calls out in the other" (Mead, 1964). The child has learned to take the role of specific others. Although lower animals also play, only humans "play at being someone else" (Aboulafia, 1986:9). By role-playing the child learns to become both subject and object, an important step in the development of self (Ritzer, 2000).

3. **Game Stage.** At this stage the child must now be capable of putting herself in the role of several others at the same time, and to understand the relationship between these roles. As Mead (1934) states, "The fundamental difference between the game and play is that in the latter the child must have the attitude of all the others involved in the game. The attitudes of the other players which the participant assumes organize into a sort of unit, and it is that organization which controls the response of the individual" (p. 154–5). Mead used the game of baseball to illustrate his point. When the ball is hit, the fielder must make the play, but he must also know the role of his teammates in order to understand such game complexities as where to throw the ball if there are already runners on base, and so forth.

Understanding the roles of others is just one critical aspect of the game stage. Knowing the rules of the game mark the transition from simple role taking to participation in roles of special, standard-ized order (Miller, 1973). Abiding by the rules involves the ability to exercise self-control and implies that the individual has learned to function in the organized whole to which she belongs (Mead, 1934). The game is viewed as a sort of passage in the life of a child from taking the role of others in play to the organized part that is essential to self-conscious-ness. Learning the diverse roles in organ-ized games helps the child to understand the more general workings of social life (Pampel, 2000).

4. **Generalized Other.** The generalized other develops from the successive and simultaneous use of many roles. The generalized other is a kind of corporate individual or a plural noun; it is the uni-versalization of the role-taking process (Pfuetze, 1954). At this stage of develop-ment of self individuals come to take the attitude of the whole community, or what Mead called the "generalized other." At this point the individual not only identifies with significant others (specific people), but also with the atti-tudes of a society, community, or group as a whole. The generalized other is not a person; instead, it is a person's conscious awareness of the society that he or she is a part of (Cockerham, 1995).

The ability of individuals to adopt the attitude of the generalized other is what allows for diverse and unique per-sons to share a sense of community. The self-revealed is not "I" but the empirical self "me." The "me" develops through communication and participation as the person takes on different roles and en-ters the perspective of the community (Pfuetze, 1954). It is through associations with others in different places through-out the community (such as work, school, church, ballgames, etc.) that the

many "selves" of an individual person-ality are awakened, developed, and cor-related into a moral community.

The development of self is depend-ent on interactions with others within the community. These interactions help to shape the individual's personality. Whereas the play stage requires only pieces of selves, the game stage requires a coherent self (Ritzer, 2000). Embracing the standards of the community is ac-complished by recognizing the general-ized other. The awareness of the generalized other enters a person's thinking and influences how that person will act in certain situations. In this man-ner, the generalized other exerts control over individual behavior. The individual may have any number of generalized others in their life, including family, friends, gang, political party, national al-legiance, and so on. Some of these gener-alized others are more important than others, but nonetheless, are taken into account when a person decides what is relevant in choosing from courses of ac-tion.

The Act

Mead's analysis of *the act* reveals his social-behaviorist approach to the stimulus–re-sponse process. The response to a stimulus is not automatic because the individual has choices of behaviors in which to react. Mead (1982) states, "We conceive of the stimulus as an occasion or opportunity for the act, not as a compulsion or a mandate" (p. 28). In *The Philosophy of the Act* (1938/1972) Mead iden-tifies four basic and interrelated stages in the act.

1. **Impulse.** The impulse involves "gut" reactions or immediate responses to certain stimuli. It refers to the "need" to do something. If the individual is

thirsty an impulse will tell them to drink. Reactions to this impulse still involve a level of contemplation and decision-making. If the immediate environment does not offer something to drink (nothing at home) then the individual must now decide whether or not to leave the environment (go to the store) to find a drink, or decide to put off the decision to drink until later (wait for roommate to come home with groceries). The environment may provide a source to secure a drink (soda machine) but still put up obstacles in attaining it (machine is out of order). The impulse, like all other elements of Mead's theory, involves both the actor and the environment (Ritzer, 2000).

2. **Perception.** The second stage of the act is *perception*. The individual must know how to react to the impulse. People will use their senses as well as mental images in an attempt to satisfy impulses (Ritzer, 2000). Because people are bombarded with potentially limitless stimuli, they must choose among sets of stimuli that provide the characteristics most beneficial to them and ignore those which do not. After all, it is the act of perceiving an object that makes it an object to the person; perception and object cannot be separated from one another. They are dialectically related to each other (Ritzer, 2000).

3. **Manipulation.** Once the impulse has been manifested and the object has been perceived, the individual must take some action with regard to it (Ritzer, 2000). The individual conforms himself to the environment or perhaps conforms the environment itself in order to satisfy the impulse. Tired of waiting for his overdue roommate and feeling very thirsty, the individual decides to go to the store and purchase a beverage.

4. **Consummation.** At this, the final stage, the individual has followed through on a course of action and can consummate the act by satisfying the impulse (drinking the beverage). Mead viewed the four stages of the act as interrelated. He also viewed the act as involving one person, while the *social act* involves two or more persons.

The Social Act

A social act may be defined as one in which the stimulus (or occasion) sets free an impulse (found in the very character or nature of its being) that then triggers possible reactions from those found in the environment (Reck, 1964). Mead restricted the *social act* to the class of acts that involve the cooperation of more than one individual, and whose object as defined by the act, is a social object (Reck, 1964). The basic mechanism of the social act is the *gesture*.

According to Thayer (1968), the importance that Mead placed on gestures were influenced by Darwin's *Expression of Emotions in Man and Animals*, in which Darwin describes the physical attitudes and physiological changes as expressive of emotions (the dog baring teeth for attack). This suggested an evolutionary biological origin of the gesture of language, which Mead found appealing (Thayer, 1968). However, he objected to Darwin's subjectivistic psychological theory that emotions are inner states and gestures are the outward expressions of these ideas and meanings (Thayer, 1968).

Mead emphasized the importance of the *vocal gesture* because the individual who sends a vocal gesture can perceive that vocal signal much the same way as the listener does. That does not guarantee that the listener will respond in the manner in which the sender anticipated (Baldwin, 1986). Verbal gestures represent signs, which, being heard by the maker as well as other parties to the social act, can serve as a common sign to all parties to the social act. The mutually understood gesture becomes a *significant symbol* (Martindale, 1981). Common gestures allow for the development of language, which consists of a number of significant symbols. Only humans developed to the point of being able to use language and develop significant symbols. Symbols allow people to communicate more easily. The development of symbolic communication leads to inner conversation with the mind, and reflective intelligence (Baldwin, 1986). The tendency for the "same" responses, of a significant symbol, lead to organized attitudes which we arouse in ourselves when we talk to others (Reck, 1964).

Communication through vocal gestures has a special quality, in that we cannot see our own facial gestures, but we can hear our own vocal gestures. Because we can hear our own vocal gestures they potentially carry the same meaning for both the listener and the speaker. They also provide the speaker with an opportunity to answer himself as he hopes the listener does (Pampel, 2000). Thinking about responses appropriate in social settings is what Mead called the *generalized other*.

Mental Processes of Intelligence and Consciousness

Mead (1934) defines *intelligence* broadly as the mutual adjustment of the acts of organisms. Humans exhibit a different form of intelligence from other animals in that they have the capacity to understand and use significant symbols. Through the use of symbols humans can carry on conversations with themselves (Mead, 1934). This self-communication allows for reflective intelligence, which in turn, allows humans the ability to inhibit action temporarily, to delay their reactions to a stimulus (Mead, 1934). Reflective intelligence is central to the devel-

opment of a self-concept, self-control, role-taking, empathy, and numerous other social-psychological phenomena (Baldwin, 1986). It is also important for transmitting social customs and creates opportunities for social change.

Humans also have the ability to use reason which allows the individual to choose among a range of actions. In short, Mead (1934) states, "Intelligence is largely a matter of selectivity" (p. 99).

Mead's analysis of the evolution (from the irrational Greek thinkers, to religious dogma, through to the Enlightenment) of knowledge regarding *consciousness* and *intelligence* provides strong support for the hypothesis that the scientific method was superior to all other means of attaining knowledge (Baldwin, 1986). Consciousness was on a continuum from low levels of feeling in simple organisms to high levels of symbolic thought in humans.

There is an ambiguity in the word "consciousness." It might be used in the sense of "awareness," or "conscious of," and to assume that it is coexistent with experience and lodged in the brain. Mead firmly believed that consciousness is explained in terms of social process, and is subject to change from external stimuli found in the objective world—the environment. An environment arises for an organism through the selective power of an attention that is determined by its impulses that are seeking expression (Reck, 1964). Thus, consciousness is created through "awareness" and becomes "emergent" through social interaction (Reck, 1964).

Language

For Mead, language has its origins in gestures (Thayer, 1968). Gestures are important in the very nature of communicative behavior and they provide the basic explanation in the creation of selves (minds). The most important characteristic of the gesture is its social properties, that is, how it affects and coordinates behavior between two or more individuals (Thayer, 1968). As described earlier in this chapter, the ability to communicate through language represents the developmental process in the development of self. Members of a community that share a common language possess the ability to take the role of the other, thus providing the means for a better understanding in the other's behavior.

Mead felt that the structure of one's language has a great impact on one's train of thought. He believed that language is a social institution that is influenced by a wide-variety of social groups and societies. The economically poor will speak a different language from those of the wealthy class, and the mentality of farmers is different from that of a city person. Thus, language is subject to symbolic interpretations and meanings held by certain persons, in certain places, at certain points in time.

The behavior of the individual can only be understood if one understands the behavior of the whole social group that he is a member of. Individual's actions are influenced by the larger community, their social acts go beyond themselves, and implicate the other members of the group (Strauss, 1956). According to Mead, language does not play a role in the formation of society. The formation of language is an effect of the existence of society. Society is formed through social grouping and interaction among individuals. Initial interactions were limited to gestures (facial and vocal), over time they advanced to symbolic interactions and the inevitable creation of language. In short, the social group is formed first, and then language is formed (Strauss, 1956).

The process of the development of language begins with the realization that society is made of individuals. These individuals come in contact with one another and during these social acts individuals use gestures. Gestures become known as symbols or acts (past, present, or future). Within the community there is a shared meaning of these gestures or symbols. Each symbol signifies a certain meaning. Following facial gestures is the formation and use of vocal gestures. When vocal gestures are put together in some meaningful manner they create language. Thus, language is the grouping together of significant vocal gestures that have understood and shared meanings between individuals. The definition of language is the significant vocal gestures that elicit the same response and meaning in the speaker as it does in the listener (Joas, 1985).

The primary contribution of symbolic interaction and language is that it provides for the means of *communication* between community members. The essential aspect of communication is that the symbol should arouse in one's self what it arouses in the other individual (Farganis, 2000). The symbol must have a degree of universality to any person who finds himself in the same situation (a contemporary example would be the universal symbol for handicapped persons). There is a possibility of communication any time individuals share the same language.

Science and Social Progress

Mead and Dewey's pragmatic thinking reveals that they confidently accepted the unity of science and progress as much as they accepted the unity of thought and action (Pampel, 2000). They believed that science provides a clear and effective way to test ideas on how to improve future society (Pampel, 2000). Scientific analysis eliminates bias and dogmatic thinking. For Mead, the use of reason and science was clearly superior to that of the Christian evangelistic thought that he was exposed to in his youth. Science and democratic social action was far more valuable than unreasoning faith and prayer.

Darwin's theory of evolution greatly impacted Mead's thinking of science and progress. Mead believed that the evolutionary principles that Darwin attached to his studies of various species also apply to social organization and societies. Evolutionary thinking allows individuals to use their intelligence to adjust to the problems they face in everyday life (Pampel, 2000).

A proponent of science, Mead did not agree with positivist science. The fundamental mistake of the positivist theory of science is, in Mead's eyes, that it regards all events as instances of laws, and that means it conceives of all surprising facts, those which run counter to expectation, as instances of scientific laws that have not yet been ascertained (Joas, 1985). For Mead, the conceptual objects of science do not replicate an ultimate reality which causally determines the subjective phenomena of our perceptual world. Rather, they are inevitably referred to the world of our actions and immediate experiences. This is true in three ways (Joas, 1985):

1. The problem that requires a scientific solution itself makes the appearance in the world of our immediate experiences; it is linked to the observation of anomalies.

2. The testing of an hypothesis must rely on immediate experiences . . .

3. . . . which, cannot be dispensed with even by those theories that claim to effect a general reconstruction of theories themselves.

Like science, history is, for Mead, a progressive process that can never be completely planned and is essentially unpredictable, since it is the result of intentional action and of causal determination.

Two main strands of his writing indicate Mead's *worldview* perspective. First, he advocated analyzing all ideas via the scientific method. Second, he was strongly opposed to a mind–body dualism in all its forms because it split the world into two irreconcilable parts (Baldwin, 1986). Mead's scientific method included "empirical cosmology." Traditional philosophical cosmologies included nonempirical metaphysical assumptions. For Mead, science is a problem-solving system that works toward unity, without expecting to reach a final static state.

A central theme of Mead's writings is that the world of knowledge is an organic whole in which all the parts affect each other to produce a dynamically fluctuating system. His key method of approach was to organize all topics in terms of evolutionary processes, developmental processes, and other types of processes. For this reason, Mead has been described as a *process philosopher*. He believes that the temporal dimension cannot be excluded from the real; the real is not timeless, but consists of acts, happenings, and events (Baldwin, 1986).

According to Mead, both mechanism and teleology are merely postulates. They are dogma. Mead explained that internal conversation that we carry on in our heads is the "mechanism of thought"; and describing oneself objectively, as if looking at oneself from the role of others, is the "mechanism of introspection" (having an internal conversation with oneself). Mead advocated an objective, scientific approach to human conduct, placing humans in nature rather than above nature. At various points, Mead described his form of objective psychology as "behavioristic psychology" (Baldwin, 1986). It is important to note that at this time, the term "behaviorism" had just come about and there was no consensus on its meaning, just as today there is great ambiguity in the term *postmodernism*.

Ethics

Solving moral problems requires, according to Mead, creative intellectual effort and consideration of all values relevant to the given situation. For Mead, the value relation is an objectively existing relationship between subject and object; but it is not equated with a cognitive relation (Joas, 1985). Value-relations and cognitive relations are distinctly different. Their differences, however, do not lie in a merely subjective character of evaluation as opposed to ascription of objectivity to cognition, but rather, in their correlation to different phases in an act.

Many of Mead's scattered articles and theses can be grouped around the notion of universal morality. His analysis of the functions of "punitive justice," which in his judgment is not therapeutic but does serve to stabilize the structure of domination in a society, belongs just as much in this thematic complex as do his articles on patriotism as an ethical and psychological problem (Joas, 1985). Ethical universality is possible only through the human capacity of role-taking, aided by communication, which leads to the concept of sociality. Moral problems can be solved rationally by exploring values held by different individuals.

Mead wrote about philanthropy from the point of view of ethics. Charity implies both an attitude and a type of conduct that may not be demanded of whomever exercises it. Whatever the donor's inner obligation may be, the recipient on his side can make no claim upon it. Yet the inner obligation exists and in part limits the charity itself, for the donor cannot fail in her other commitments because she has answered the appeals of charity too generously (Reck, 1964).

Obligation arises only with choice: not only when impulses are in conflict with each other, but when within this conflict they are valued in terms of their anticipated results. We act impulsively when the mere strength of the impulse decides. The kindly impulses that lead us to help those in distress may breed beggars and organized charity (which attempt to bring reason into action). That the

recognition of an obligation is at the same time the assertion of a right is tantamount to the individual's identifying himself with those who make the claim upon him, for an obligation is always a demand made by another or by others (Reck, 1964).

Social Theory

According to Joas (1985) Mead's theories provided a convergence of two very different philosophical and scientific traditions: the dialogical approaches of linguistic theory in the German tradition of hermeneutic humanities, and the approaches to a generative theory of grammar that followed upon the great strides made by Noam Chomsky toward an investigation of human language which is both universal in orientation and empirically fruitful. Mead himself assigned his theories to behaviorism and its focus on the act and human responses to external stimuli. He was also a leading figure in the formation of pragmatism (Ritzer, 2000). The primary elements of Mead's micro theory have been clearly discussed throughout this section of the chapter.

Mead's approach to macro theory is based in large part on evolutionary models, but it is significantly different from evolutionary views used by more idealistic social scientists. The process of social evolution involves a bilateral relationship between people and their environment; and increasing use of reflective intelligence and science should allow humans to gain ever greater control of the whole process. By criticizing society's faults and cooperating with others to develop more functional alternatives, we can hasten the evolution of better social conditions and more functional relations with the ecological systems.

Mead analyzed several social institutions, including science, economics, religion, criminal justice, democracy, and other forms of government. Mead's method of macro-analysis involved drawing on all empirical disciplines such as history, and so forth. Mead's macro theories are completely compatible with his views on biology and social psychology, and all elements of his theoretical system are fully integrated. Society is needed for the emergence of minds and selves from the biological substrate, and minds and selves are essential for the complex types of social organizations produced by our species (Baldwin, 1986).

There is noticeably less detail and precision in macro facets of Mead's theoretical system than in the micro. This is due to his early heavy orientation toward micro-level concerns, and because of his background as a philosopher.

Relevancy

George Herbert Mead was a philosopher, social scientist, and humanistic individual. He was a person of great vision, with the skill for synthesizing an enormous breadth of knowledge in an elegant, unified system. He developed a philosophy of science and beautifully integrated social theory in such a way that they are as important today as they were in his own time (Baldwin, 1986). Mead's theory combines macro- and micro-social processes, mental and physical events, academic and practical concerns.

Mead examined the development of the mind and the self, and regarded the mind as the natural emergent from the interaction of the human organism and its social environment. Within this biosocial structure, the gap between impulse and reason is bridged by the use of language. By conquering language, Mead believed humans become aware of their roles in life; this awareness allows for the emergence of the self. Intelligence, he believed, develops over time. His social theories remain relevant today.

The potential for the development and elaboration of Mead's form of pragmatic so-

cial science is enormous. Mead's general approach could unify the many subdivisions of sociology. Mead's pragmatic social science has both theoretical elegance and practical utility. Mead's theory is also adaptive in that it allows for social change. Mead himself was dedicated to both intellectual work and social reforms; and his theory reflects his strengths in both areas. We can benefit from, and elaborate upon, both facets of his work (Baldwin, 1986).

Societies of the West have long accepted the validity of the pragmatic approach and will certainly continue to value this scientific method in the third millennium. This is especially true with regards to business and commerce. Pragmatism provides an intellectual justification for such social action as globalization. Pragmatists realize that humans are not "scripted," biological beings or limited by predetermined courses of social actions; they are social beings capable of developing and modifying both themselves and society.

From a sociological perspective, Mead's greatest contribution to social thought lies with his ideas on symbolic interactionism. Considered one of the "Big Three" sociological theories (along with conflict and functionalism), symbolic interactionism has maintained a steady and powerful presence within the discipline. With its brilliant insights to microsociological behavior symbolic interactionism will remain a dominate theory in the future.

Mead was the most important early figure associated with the "Chicago School" approach to sociology. Although the term symbolic interactionism would not arise during his lifetime it was his influence that lead to its creation. The Chicago School tradition was strengthened by the brilliant works of Erving Goffman (1922–1982) and Herbert Blumer (1900–1987). Blumer and Goffman would both leave the University of

Chicago to teach at Berkeley, and they attempted to develop a center of symbolic interactionism at Berkeley (Ritzer, 2000).

As stated earlier in this chapter, it was Blumer who coined the term "symbolic interactionism" in 1937; he also established the three basic premises of the theory. According to Blumer (1969), the first premise of symbolic interactionism is that humans act on the basis of the meaning that they attribute to any course of action. For example, if someone observes another person drowning in a partially frozen lake will they attempt to help the victim? The course of action taken by an individual will be determined by how one interprets the situation. If the individual views such an attempt as futile and determines that the risk will surely endanger his own behavior, he may choose not to venture out onto the lake. Another person may view the situation completely differently: that inaction is morally wrong and to do nothing while witnessing another human being dying is not proper behavior and consequently risks his own life to save the victim.

Second, symbolic interactionism stresses that meaning develops out of the social interactions we have with other humans. Thus, the person who risks his own life to save a drowning victim is deemed heroic by those who would encourage such behaviors; while the person who did not risk his own life in a perceived futile attempt to save the drowning victim is looked upon as sensible by those who interpreted such an attempt as foolhardy.

The third premise of symbolic interactionism emphasizes the interpretive process. That is, people do not automatically accept everything others tell them, they continue to reevaluate their knowledge and experiences and are therefore capable of reshaping their perceptions of events and chance their "normal" course of action. The individual who viewed any attempt to rescue the drowning victim as futile might change his course of action if he realized that victim is his own child.

Canadian-born Erving Goffman, who received his Ph.D. from the University of Chicago, developed a distinctive approach to symbolic interactionism through the publication of a series of books that led to a dramaturgical model in the study of human social behavior. His version of symbolic interactionism is therefore known as *dramaturgy*. Goffman's best-known work is *The Presentation of Self in Everyday Life* (1959). Goffman compared human social action to that found in the world of the theater. He was especially influenced by Shakespeare's *As You Like It*:

> All the world's a stage
> And all the men and women merely
>   players;
> They have their exits and their entrances;
> And one man in his time plays many
>   parts.

As Coser (1977) explains, Goffman transformed a rather vague analogy into a powerful dramaturgical vision. He attempted to illustrate and analyze the complicated ways in which individuals construct images of their selves in encounters with significant others. Goffman referred to humans as *actors* who *perform* roles in the social *settings* making use of *props* in order to gain the *audience's* approval. "When an individual plays a part he implicitly requests his observers to take seriously the impression that is fostered before them. They are asked to believe that the character they see actually possesses the attributes he appears to possess, that the task he performs will have the consequences that are implicitly claimed for it, and that, in general, matters are what they appear to be" (Goffman, 1959:17). The theater analogy extends to Goffman's idea that actors perform on a *stage* that consists of both the front and back regions. The front stage is characterized by the visible aspects of the performance and contains the physical objects (props) used to make the performance appear more believable. The front stage consists of the setting, appearance, and manner (Goffman, 1959). The actor then, is expressing *presentation of self*. The back stage is an area where the actor can prepare herself for her upcoming performance. Thus, the backstage can be viewed as the person the actor *really* is; while the front stage is the person the actor *wants* the audience to see.

Application and relevance of these concepts to contemporary and future life is nearly endless as the tenets of dramaturgy fall within the domain of all micro-interactions that persons have. The student (actor) who wants to be perceived by the professor and her classmates (audience) as an intelligent individual will demonstrate evidence of knowledge in assigned materials by participating (perform) in classroom (setting) discussion and will take diligent notes (props). When people interview for a job, they will present themselves in such a way as to show that they are the best candidate for that position. The individual (actor) behaves (performs) in a manner that is conducive of behavior expected at that work environment (setting) and will dress appropriately (props) for the occasion in order to impress the interviewer (audience). The young man who meets his girlfriend's parents for the first time while picking her up for a date will attempt to say and do all the right things in order to maintain peace and harmony. Consequently, he (actor) will arrive at his girlfriend's house (setting) on time and dressed cleanly and neatly (props), greet her parents (audience), and make polite conversation (performance) while he assures them that he has great respect for their daughter.

In all these cases the actor's behavior has been shaped by front-stage performances in which the actor was attempting to provide a positive presentation of self. Backstage insights might reveal something entirely different. The student who presented herself as studious may have simply read two or three pages of assigned reading shortly before class in order to participate in a limited fashion and the notetaking might have been unrelated to class lecture notes. The individual on the job interview may have made false claims on his application and was responding to questions in the interview simply to maximize an opportunity to get the job even though they had no real intentions, or capabilities, of following through on such job expectations. And the young man may had said all the "right" things to his girlfriend's parents, attempting to demonstrate that his intentions were most honorable, when, in fact, they might have been most devious.

Mead's ideas, then, not only directly shaped the creation of symbolic interactionism, they also indirectly lead to the formation of dramaturgy. Symbolic interactionism and dramaturgy are part of what is collectively known as the sociologies of *everyday life*. Douglas (1980) explains that the sociology of everyday life is a sociological orientation concerned with the experiencing, observing, understanding, describing, analyzing, and communicating about people interacting in concrete situations. The sociologies of everyday life include: symbolic interactionism, dramaturgical analysis, labeling theory, phenomenology and ethnomethodolgy, and existentialism. Since symbolic interactionism and dramaturgical theory have been previously explained a brief description of the remaining theories follow.

Labeling theorists, according to Douglas (1980), agree with the symbolic interactionists that people must share a symbolic universe, that they are taught to do this, that this influences their actions, and that of course, all of this must de done through so-cial interaction. Labeling theorists generally believe that the most important labelers are the official agencies of control, such as teach-ers, the police, and the courts.

Phenomenologists are much more con-cerned with the way individuals construct in their own consciousness the meanings of things. They see the social world as ulti-mately made up of many more individual constructions than do the symbolic interac-tionists, dramaturgists, or labeling theorists. They are primarily concerned with how so-cial meanings are constructed.

Ethnomethodology, which was origi-nally derived from phenomenology, is the most unique of the everyday theories in that it is predominately concerned with the analysis of social accounts (e.g., body lan-guage and linguistic statements), especially with the analysis of the ways in which indi-viduals speak to each other in everyday life and how they appear to be rational. It is the study of linguistic accounts of behavior.

The existential theorists differ from the phenomenologists and other interactionists in viewing perceptions and feelings (anxiety, dread, love, hate and envy) as the ultimate goals and wellsprings of social meanings and actions. They see the social world as filled with conflict; individuals who are alone because of self-constructions of reality; and one where emotional needs of individu-als are dominated by modern institutions.

Mead's specific ideas of the development of self; distinctions between the "I" and "me"; the social act; the mental processes of intelligence and consciousness; gestures and language are all a part of his symbolic inter-actionist approach. They reflect his primary attention to micro-orientations. Mead demonstrated how human mental processes are part of the larger social process and the importance of human beings' ability to com-municate through the use of symbols. Such a

distinctive human capacity allows individu-als to have inner conversations with them-selves and allows for actors to take the perspective of the other. The use of symbols has been expanded in recent years in an at-tempt to create universal symbols that have a shared meaning in regard to native language. These symbols include the universal handi-cap designation. The use of universal sym-bols is an important first step in creating a single human species' language. A universal language by the end of the third millennium would make for a most useful and beneficial goal for humankind.

Mead's theory continues to be influen-tial in contemporary symbolic interaction-ism, social psychology, and sociology (Ritzer, 2000). His works continue to attract theorists throughout the world and will un-doubtedly continue to do so for some time. Ritzer (2000) explains that perhaps his great-est weakness as a theorist is his limited work at the macrosocietal level and his somewhat ambiguous and inconsistent use of some of his concepts, especially intelligence. However, since many contemporary theo-rists have attempted to bridge these limita-tions, the reputation and brilliance of Mead's work will continue far into the future.

The Adlers (2000) have extended Mead and Cooley's theoretical work with their concept of the *Gloried Self*. The gloried self emerges when individuals become the focus of intense interpersonal and media attention, leading to their achieving celebrity status. The gloried self reveals the creation of a sometime unintended self-identity, even in the face of considerable resistance, as a result of the actor becoming a "public person." The role of the media is an increasingly impor-tant variable that was foreign to earlier social theorists (for the obvious reason of it's recent development). The media are responsible for the creation of the *medial self*. Print and video coverage of "celebrities" has led to the development of such people as athletes as "human-interest" stories. The public is not only overwhelmed with information provided by the media on these individuals during the season they participate in their sport, the media now present specials on their personal lives during the off-season.

Delaney (2001) has attributed the demise of the sports hero to the overwhelming role of the media. Delaney believes that sports fans now have too much knowledge of their sports heroes and consequently the mystique has disappeared. For as quickly as the media love to create a "hero status" of persons, they are equally quick to destroy their very creations by reporting the increasingly large number of deviant behaviors many athletes engage in.

George Herbert Mead was a gifted social theorist who was more comfortable with the accomplishments of others, especially his students, than he was interested in having the spotlight shine on his own contributions. As Coser (1977) explains, he was proud and happy to have gifted students and encouraged and guided their careers while impressing them with his classroom lectures. This is clearly evident in the fact that it was his students and colleagues who published most of Mead's works posthumously.

10

Thorstein Veblen

(1857–1929)

Thorstein Bunde Veblen, the son of Norwegian immigrants, was born on a Wisconsin farm July 30, 1857. He was the sixth of twelve children born to Thomas Anderson Veblen and Kari Bunde Veblen. His parents were peasants who worked hard as children of tenant farmers in their native country. Veblen's paternal grandfather had been duped out of his right to the family farm and had fallen from the honored status of farm owner to that of a disgraced tenant (Coser, 1977). Veblen's mother's father had a near similar plight, having been forced to sell his farm in order to meet lawyers' fees. He died at a young age, leaving Kari an orphan at the age of five (Coser, 1977).

Veblen's parents emigrated to America and first settled in Wisconsin. They suffered a parallel fate to that of their parents in Norway, being driven off their Manitowoc, Wisconsin, farm by land speculators. When Veblen was eight years old, his family moved to a larger farm on the prairie lands of Whelling Township in Minnesota. Even here his parents were forced to sell half of their land in order to pay usurious interest rates. "Hatred of tricksters, speculators, and shyster lawyers ran deep in the family tradition and found characteristic expression in much of Veblen's later writing" (Coser, 1977:276).

Thorstein Veblen (1857–1929) American social scientist whose theories are grounded in economic considerations.
Source: CORBIS

In Minnesota, Veblen grew up in a frontier settlement with his siblings who continued to speak Norwegian at home while they learned English in school. Through hard work and frugality, the family became quite prosperous as efficient farmers. Compared to most native American farmers, the Veblen children were beneficiaries of better educational opportunities. As Mitchell explains in *What Veblen Taught* (1947), "An intellectual drive seems to characterize the family. An elder brother of Thorstein became a professor of physics and one of his nephews . . . a distinguished mathematician" (p. xi).

Thomas Veblen was a well-respected, intelligent man who minded his own business and refused to take part in the religious quarrels that dominated the community. Thorstein took after his father. His compulsive independence, fights with other boys, teasing of girls, and general harassment of the elderly were often viewed as unsettling among the members of the community. As Thorstein reached adolescence he transformed his behavior into sarcasm and creative wit. By the time of his confirmation, Veblen had made it clear he no longer believed in his Lutheran faith. "Thorstein was personally out of step with the political and Lutheran religious orthodoxy around him, and his keen mind handled this maladjustment through wit, sarcasm, and criticism" (Adams and Sydie, 2001).

The new-found wealth of the Veblen family allowed Thorstein the opportunity to consider higher education. His father agreed that the road to self-improvement was through education (Coser, 1977). At age seventeen Veblen entered the academy of Carleton, a Christian evangelical school that was predictably strict and coercive toward free-thinking and -acting behavior. Carleton placed an emphasis on teaching the classics, moral philosophy, and religion. The natural sciences were not valued. As one might imagine, Veblen was not well-suited for Carleton. Despite this reality, Veblen entered Carleton College at age twenty, and graduated at twenty-three with the class of 1880 (Veblen, 1947).

While at Carleton, Veblen met his future first wife, Ellen Rolfe, the niece of the president of the College (they eventually married in 1888). Perhaps the only professor to impress Veblen while at Carleton was John Bates Clark, who later (at Columbia University) was to win fame as one of the foremost economic theoreticians of his generation (Veblen, 1947). Clark's ideas were mildly socialist and appealed to Veblen.

Immediately after graduation, Veblen accepted a teaching position at Monona Academy in Madison, Wisconsin. The religious atmosphere at this Norwegian school was too oppressive for Veblen's liking and because of theological disputes (e.g., the idea of predestination) he decided to leave at the end of the school year. Interestingly, the school closed permanently at the same time. When his brother, Andrew (father of the future famous mathematician Oswald Veblen) decided to study mathematics at Johns Hopkins University, Thorstein decided to accompany him. Veblen declared philosophy as his major and economics as a minor.

The social climate of America would begin to have an impact on Veblen as he headed east. The Civil War and general agrarian unrest and radicalism of the midwest had piqued Veblen's curiosity. He was introduced to the works of such social thinkers as Kant, Mill, Hume, Rousseau, Spencer, Huxley, and Tyndall. At Johns Hopkins, Veblen took three courses with George S. Morris, but he was not impressed with the Hegelian philosophical slant presented in the lectures.

After just one year at Johns Hopkins, and failing to receive a scholarship, Veblen decided to transfer to Yale University. He was eager to study philosophy under Reverend Noah Porter, president of Yale. At this point in time, philosophy at Yale (as with most universities) was still taught from a religious bias, and Veblen's agnostic tendencies were not congruent with the philosophical teachings as presented. Veblen constantly challenged his professors and fellow (mostly divinity) students, who were preparing to teach the gospel. He tried to distance himself as much as possible, but this survival technique cultivated an aura of aloofness (Coser, 1977).

The intellectual atmosphere at Yale was to soon stimulate Veblen beyond what he originally had hoped. William Graham Sumner, a sociologist who taught the ideas of Spencer and Darwin, raged epic battles against Noah Porter, a man still deeply consumed by religious transcendentalism. "A month before Veblen left Yale, Sumner was victorious and the whole curriculum of Yale was revamped. Science won over religion" (Coser, 1977:279). Veblen was highly impressed with Sumner, and although in later years he would disagree with his conservative economics, he was nonetheless attracted to his willingness to take a stand on major issues and express an independence of mind and thought. Veblen managed to maintain a friendship with Porter as well—an important point, because he would supervise Veblen's dissertation.

In 1884, Veblen earned his doctor's degree after successfully defending his dissertation, "Ethical Grounds of a Doctrine of Retribution." Later in the same year, he published a paper, "Kant's Critique of Judgment" in *The Journal of Speculative Philosophy* (Veblen, 1947). Veblen seemed destined for immediate success in academia; he had strong letters of support from Sumner and Porter, and a Ph.D. from an Ivy League school. Unfortunately, as Ritzer (2000) explains, he fell victim to discrimination because of his agnosticism and his Norwegian background (immigrant status). Adding to his difficulties are the facts that the job market was tight, and Veblen was the type of person who had difficulty "selling himself" (Veblen, 1947).

Disappointed, Veblen moved back to Minnesota, claiming to be in poor health. His brothers were inclined to believe that he was simply loafing (a slacker)—a sin by Norwegian standards. He kept himself busy by reading everything that he could acquire, some writing, and a bit of nondescript office work (Veblen, 1947). As mentioned earlier, in 1888, he married Ellen Rolfe. Her father, the president of Carleton College was dismayed that she would marry a son of Norwegian immigrants. Even so, he gave the newly-weds one of his farms in Iowa. Veblen began to pursue academic positions a little more seriously. He and his wife shared a passion for the radical agrarian movements (e.g., labor unrest) and read Edward Bellamy's socialist utopia, *Looking Backward* (1888). Veblen began to view economics as the answer to this specific social problem.

Veblen decided that it was time to continue his studies, this time at Cornell. He entered Cornell as a graduate student in the social sciences in 1891. While there he published a paper, "Some Neglected Points in the Theory of Socialism" in *The Annals of the American Academy of Political and Social Science*. The publication was in the tradition of the evolutionary theories of Spencer, but at the same time it argued for the abolition of private property (Coser, 1977). Shortly thereafter, Veblen published a number of technical papers for *The Quarterly Journal of Economics*. Veblen's mentor, economics professor J. Laurence Laughlin, had just been asked to take charge of the department of economics at the newly founded University of Chicago. Laughlin was so impressed with the quality of Veblen's papers that he secured a special university grant to award a fellowship to Veblen so that he might join him at Chicago. Suddenly, Veblen found himself in the company of perhaps the most stimulating group of scholars ever assembled.

William Rainey Harper, president of the University of Chicago, extracted large sums of money from the university's founder, John D. Rockefeller, in order to attract a first-rate faculty to Chicago. Veblen was among the many professors to benefit from the diverse and multitalented faculty. It should be noted that Veblen was merely a tutor his first three years at Chicago, and was finally promoted, at the age of 38, to instructor. In fact, during his stay of more than a decade at the university, he never attained a higher rank in the faculty than that of assistant professor (Veblen, 1964).

Veblen taught courses on agricultural economics, socialism, and the history of economic theory (Veblen, 1947). His teaching methods were unorthodox and he seemed to deliberately discourage students from taking his courses. He often mumbled through his lectures but always displayed his wit—which was something that his students would come to admire a great deal. His students never knew exactly what to expect in the classroom. He hated grading student papers so he usually gave them either a "C" or "B" grade, or whatever his mood of the moment dictated. He was especially susceptible to women, who were very attracted to Veblen, and stories often circulated about his affairs. The many scandals left his wife understandably upset. He often left love letters from his female admirers in his pockets. Veblen realized that the college frowned upon this behavior, but his attitude was akin to, "what am I to do, if I am pursued, and I am not the pursuer" (Coser, 1977).

Professionally, Veblen eventually became the editor of *The Journal of Political Economy*, which Laughlin had founded immediately after his arrival. His level of academic production increased tremendously while at Chicago. He made many lucid contributions to his own journal. In 1898, he published his first critique of economic theory, "Why Is Economics Not an Evolutionary Science?" in *The Quarterly Journal of Economics*. His first, and most widely read book, *The Theory of the Leisure Class,* was published in 1899. His next book, *The Theory of Business Enterprise* (1904) provided a systematic critique of American business. It was not as well received as *Leisure.* Conservatives disliked it because he criticized the free-enterprise system, and radicals disliked it because he rejected Marxism.

Despite his growing fame and notoriety, the increased awareness of his crumbling marriage due to his extramarital affairs was causing a strain among Chicago administrators. Veblen had taken a trip to Europe in 1904 with a woman other than his wife. The college asked him to sign a paper declaring he would have no further relations with the woman involved. He refused, stating that he could make no such promises. In 1906, Veblen took an associate professorship at Stanford University. The undergraduates at Stanford were very unsupportive of Veblen. They disapproved of his general appearance and boring teaching style. Making matters worse, Veblen continued with his womanizing. His wife had left him twice because of his cheating. Eventually, the scandalous behavior led to his resignation from Stanford in 1909. He was offered the secretaryship of the Smithsonian Institution, but Stanford University officials insisted on "hounding him and thus were instrumental in preventing it" (Veblen, 1964). Finding an academic position was now becoming quite difficult, as Stanford insisted on "black-balling" his every move.

Finally, in 1911, a former student, H. J. Davenport, and "the best friend Veblen ever had" came to his rescue and convinced the president of the University of Missouri to offer Veblen a position in its School of Commerce, of which Davenport was the dean (Veblen, 1964). His appointment was at the lower rank of lecturer. Veblen was also divorced in 1911. In 1914 he would marry a former student and divorced mother of two, Anne Fessenden Bradley. She was a dedicated wife and helped Veblen with his writings. While at Missouri, Veblen published his third book, *The Instinct of Workmanship*. Shortly after the beginning of World War I, he published his *Imperial Germany and the Industrial Revolution*. This book was followed by *An Inquiry into the Nature of Peace* (1918). Also in 1918, he published his tirade on the structure and operation of the American university, *The Higher Learning in America*. Other books that followed were generally collections of previously written articles. These books include: *The Vested Interests and the Common Man* (1919), *The Place of Science in Modern Civilization* (1919), *The Engineers and the Price System* (1921), and *Absentee Ownership and Business Enterprise in Recent Times* (1923).

The last years of Veblen's life were spent on the fringes of academic life. His constant search for an academic position worthy of him led to many different career paths. In 1918, he had moved to New York City to become an editor of *The Dial*, a magazine founded by Ralph Waldo Emerson. His savage attacks on the established order gained him many new admirers. His editorship lasted just one year. By 1926 Veblen returned to Palo Alto, California and lived in a shack town. The money he had invested in various stocks and in the raisin industry became worthless. On August 3, 1929, Veblen died, "just before the Depression that many felt his work anticipated" (Ritzer, 2000:339).

Intellectual Influences

As with most social thinkers, Veblen was influenced by the ideas of a wide variety of social thinkers. Among the intellectual influences on Veblen were Karl Marx, Herbert Spencer, Charles Darwin, Edward Bellamy, Immanuel Kant, American pragmatism and psychology, and anonymous authors of the Icelandic sagas. No thinker operates in a vacuum, he borrows liberally and synthesizes freely—and Veblen plundered here and there (Rosenberg, in Veblen, 1963).

Karl Marx

Veblen presented a number of lectures on Marx and Marxist socialistic economics at Harvard University (April, 1906) and published them as a series of articles in *The Quarterly Journal of Economics* (1906 and 1907). In these publications it becomes clear that Veblen did not regard himself as a Marxist (Veblen, 1963). In fact, he makes many non-Marxist and anti-Marxist statements. As Adams and Sydie (2001) explain, "had Veblen been more optimistic about the ability to change society, he might have been a Marxist. But in various writings Veblen raised the same criticisms of Marx as others were making: History is goalless, not goaloriented; the poor do not become increasingly miserable; and there is not likely to be a growing reserve army of unemployed workers" (p. 246). Veblen argued against the validity of the doctrine of increasing misery and the Hegelian philosophical postulates; and without these ideas, the Marxist doctrine becomes groundless (Veblen, 1963).

Veblen questioned the very concept of the existence of economic laws, especially those proposed by Marx. For example, why does a worker have the right to the total value of his or her labor? And why should deprivation lead to a proletarian revolution? Veblen argued that it would be those who create and maintain the industrial arts, the technologists and engineers, that would lead a revolution against the business class, if such a revolution were to occur. The workers would merely follow, and not lead a revolution as Marx believed. Furthermore, Veblen rejected Marx's unscientific Hegelianism and teleological optimism.

Despite his overwhelming criticism of Marx, Veblen was indeed greatly influenced by him. Many of Veblen's technological explanations of evolution have their roots in Marx's historic economic analysis. Veblen's discussion of the business and industrial class is influenced, at least in part, by Marx's notion of alienation. It should be clear that Veblen's model of social stratification is essentially a two-class system (the business and industrial classes). Veblen was also influenced by the Marxist ideas of Engels, Antonio Labriola, Werner Sombart, and Gustav Schmoller. Veblen's institutional economics is very similar to the methods of German historical economics (Coser, 1977).

Herbert Spencer and Charles Darwin

Veblen viewed economics from an evolutionary framework. He borrowed from the ideas of Spencer and Darwin to declare that humans engage in an evolutionary struggle with the natural environment for an increasingly efficient adaptation. "The evolutionist doctrine of Darwin and Spencer provided Veblen with his general method as well as with his overall view of the story of mankind" (Coser, 1977:291). Veblen believed strongly in Spencer's survival of the fittest principle and applied it to his analysis of industry. Those businesses that were most "fit" will survive, while the unfit will perish. The survival of the fittest principle also helped Veblen to explain how social institutions change and develop (because they are adapting to the changing environment). He correctly noted that selective adaptation can never catch up with the progressively changing situation, or environment; and, that each

successive move tends to obsolescence as soon as it has been established (Veblen, 1899). Thus, change is constant. It should be noted that Veblen's former teacher, Sumner, had adopted and taught Spencer's laissez faire doctrine, but Veblen rejected the individualistic conclusions of Spencer.

Veblen often spoke of economics in terms of pre-Darwinian and post-Darwinian science. In "The Evolution of the Scientific Point of View," Veblen explains, "the characteristic feature by which post-Darwinian science is contrasted with what went before is a new distribution of emphasis, whereby the process of causation, the interval of instability and transition between initial cause and definitive effect, has come to take the first place in the inquiry; instead of that consummation in which causal effect was once presumed to come rest" (Veblen, 1961:37). Furthermore, the process of change is continuous and has no final term.

Darwin's biological explanations stimulated Veblen's theory of cultures. "Cultures are complexes of prevalent habits of thought with respect to particular relations and particular functions of the individual and of the community . . . . The biological view of man's evolution suggests that habits of thought are formed by the activities in which individuals engage. The activities that occupy most hours are likely to exercise most influence in making the mind" (Veblen, 1947:xxi). Because economic factors greatly influence one's behavior, they also impact habits of thought. These ideas eventually lead to Veblen's *science of wealth* approach in his study of community and industry (Veblen, 1947).

Edward Bellamy

As stated earlier, Veblen and his wife enjoyed Bellamy's novel *Looking Backward* (1888). The socialist utopian ideas appealed to Veblen. Unlike most utopians and reformers, Bellamy advocated making the machine process work in cooperation toward the goal of achieving a socialist state, rather than fighting the inevitable machine process (Dorfman, 1934). Veblen was pleased with this brand of utopian thought because it did not advocate the reactionary behavior of going back to an agrarian society. Bellamy attacked the (then) current economic system because it caused such economic interruptions as depressions, mass unemployment, and the privatization of land and capital. Bellamy encouraged a system of nationalized industry, a utopian scheme where no leisure class of property, nor competitive emulation exists. All industrial processes would be linked and run by an "efficient industrial army" (Coser, 1977). Although Americans today would have a difficult time accepting Bellamy's vision of society, his book sold more than one million copies by the year 1900. Bellamy's ideas would surface throughout Veblen's works, and are especially evident in his *Theory of the Leisure Class*.

Immanuel Kant

Early in Veblen's career, he read many of Kant's works. As stated earlier in this chapter, Veblen published a paper, "Kant's Critique of Judgment." Veblen's treatise *The Nature of Peace and the Terms of Its Perpetuation* was consciously modeled after Kant's *Perpetual Peace*. This book, along with its companion piece, *Imperial Germany and the Industrial Revolution*, reflects Veblen's ideas on war and peace. Veblen describes the causes of international conflict. He wrote that industrial techniques had advanced so far that no part of the earth was secure from aggression. He also foresaw that each country would react to this reality and common menace by arming itself "defensively" against any possible attack. Veblen used the term *competitive preparedness* for the penulti-

mate stage (Veblen, 1963:9). The term used in contemporary society is "cold war." Veblen worried that cold war could, at any time, lead to hot war but the apocalypse could also be averted. To that end strong measures must be taken. He proposed a sort of "world community" and promoted "insubordination" among traditionally submissive peoples. Toward this end, he also encouraged that all merchant shipping should be conducted under neutral colors as a step toward the unification and pacification of mankind (Veblen, 1963).

Pragmatism and Psychology

American pragmatism was the prevailing intellectual thought during Veblen's primary academic years. He had attended Charles Peirce's lectures at Johns Hopkins and was a colleague of John Dewey and George H. Mead at the University of Chicago. American pragmatism was greatly concerned about such issues as *self* and *self-esteem*. As Veblen would describe it, acquiring self-esteem is sometimes demonstrated through leisure class activities. Frank Boas, was serving as the curator of Chicago's Field Museum during part of the time Veblen, was making a name for himself because of his law of "conspicuous waste." Veblen applied this concept in his *The Theory of the Leisure Class* by using the term "conspicuous consumption."

William James had an influence on Veblen as well. James stated that all perception is apperception (all perceptions come with a bias) and every scientific inquirer sees what his mind is prepared to see, and preparation of the mind is the result of previous experiences and the thoughts to which they have given rise (Veblen, 1947). For example, Darwin's vision was clarified, long after he sifted through the massive amount of notes he had written from his observations, and he came upon the idea of *natural selection*.

Veblen possessed a different view of economics than his predecessors because his mind was equipped with later psychological notions. Veblen valued psychology because it provided an alternative view of economics. He applied the instinct-habit psychology of Darwin and James to explain a wide-range of human activities. This type of analysis points to Veblen's contribution to social psychology.

Concepts and Contributions

It is somewhat difficult to organize Veblen's concepts and contributions in a consistent logical flow because he lacked a systematic discourse. He was often a marginal person in the academic world and held positions primarily in economics departments. He did not mind challenging prevailing social thought or certain codes of ethical and moral behavior. Often he was a satirist, and yet he produced a body of social theory of enduring significance. Veblen's most famous and lasting contribution to social thought rests with his discussion on the leisure class.

The Theory of the Leisure Class

To say that Veblen was critical of the *leisure class* would be an understatement. The *leisure class* was a term used by Veblen to describe those persons who engaged in nonproductive economic behavior; they were similar to the business class (to be discussed later in this chapter). The leisure class was "guilty" of participation in wasteful consumption. In order to impress others, members of the leisure class engaged in *conspicuous consumption* (purchasing items not necessary for basic survival) and *conspicuous leisure* (nonproductive use of time). Veblen theorized that not only were members of the leisure class directly harm-

ing the economic stability of society, they served as models for members of the other classes to emulate, resulting in a society consumed with wasting time and money.

Individuals are driven to such "wasteful" behaviors in an attempt to gain some level of self-esteem. In order to gain or hold esteem, merely possessing wealth or power is not enough. Veblen argues that wealth or power must be put into evidence for esteem to be awarded. Veblen states (1947),

> not only does the evidence of wealth serve to impress one's importance on others and to keep their sense of his importance alive and alert, but it is of scarcely less use in building up and preserving one's self-complacency. In all but the lowest stages of culture the normally constituted man is comforted and upheld in his self-respect by "decent surroundings" and the exemption from "menial offices" (p. 230).

Thus, Veblen while recognizing why persons participate in leisure class activities, he is also critical of it, believing that leading a good productive life should be enough for one's positive self-esteem.

Leisure activities provide a subjective value and are a part of a reflex of utility as a means of gaining respect from others. From the time of Industrialization most city people had few opportunities to organize sports. It was the people of great wealth that maintained highly publicized "lives of leisure" (Veblen, 1899). Among the working classes, sports participation seldom went beyond the role of spectatorship. Rules against assembling (due to the fear of riots) in large crowds were suspended when people participated in controlled commercialized spectator events. Sports were gaining a new found focus at the beginning of the twentieth century. Whereas the wealthy had often used sports (e.g., polo or horse racing) to reinforce status distinctions between themselves and the masses, the working class were viewing sports as an opportunity to enter the ranks of the rich and powerful (Coakley, 2001).

Veblen feared this change. He asserted that sports was inherently immoral and degrading and that it represented either arrested human development or the incapacity of people to reach full spiritual development and maturity (Nixon and Frey, 1996). In his view, sports manifested a "predatory temperament" that led to exploitation, excessive aggression, hostility, and a variety of behaviors designed to create inequality during competition (Veblen, 1899). Veblen worried that granting someone status as a result of exploitation and nonproductive behavior compromised the value of routine labor (Phillips, 1993). In his mind, sports were exploitative, in part, because the primary goal is to defeat the opponent—often at any costs.

One final point regarding the importance of Veblen's *The Theory of Leisure the Class* is its focus on *consumption* rather than production. This book marks a shift in social theory away from a narrow focus on production matters and a shift in attention toward consumption issues (Slater, 1997).

Conspicuous Consumption

The primary reason for Veblen's disdain of the leisure class was a result of their *conspicuous consumption* behavior and attitude toward life. Nixon and Frey (1996) describe *conspicuous consumption* as "a public display of material goods, lifestyles, and behavior in a way that ostentatiously conveys privileged status to others for the purpose of gaining their approval or envy" (p. 211).

Throughout most of human history, there existed a two-class system, those with wealth and/or power and those without. As the economic system grew and became more complex the social structure changed with it. As Veblen (1899) explains, "In the sequence of cultural evolution the emergence of a leisure class coincides with the beginning of

ownership" (p. 22). Modern societies are characterized by a multilayer stratification system. Working class persons are envious of the wealthy because of their material success. As workers' incomes surpass a basic subsistence level, they have purchasing options. Veblen believed that the pursuit of owning material goods and general decision-making over economic spending options should be made wisely.

During the aristocratic age, or what Veblen (1899) called "the age of barbarism," wasteful styles of competitive behavior were limited to the wealthy. That alone bothered Veblen, but now, with modern industrial economic social systems, members of the whole social structure were challenging the ideal of decency. In *The Theory of the Leisure Class*, Veblen states that those people who live above the subsistence level do not use the surplus, which society has given them, primarily for useful purposes. Instead of seeking to expand their own lives, to live more wisely, intelligently, understandingly, they seek to impress other people with the fact that they have a surplus. Veblen called the ways and means for creating such an impression *conspicuous consumption*. Behaviors associated with *conspicuous consumption* include spending money, time, and effort quite uselessly in the pleasurable pursuit of inflating one's ego and self-esteem.

According to Veblen, the Chinese noblewomen's tradition of binding of the feet was an extreme example of a willingness to suffer conspicuous consumption in the pursuit of self-esteem. The agony that these women willingly accepted as a badge of honor, a behavior that served no redeeming value, revealed their "vulgarness," and made them no better than the peasants. Veblen reveals an amazing sense of foresight by using the motor car as an example of conspicuous consumption in the modern era. In *Leisure*, Veblen states that cars are not selected primarily for use, comfort, or transportation, but instead to maintain one's status in the community. The make, the model, the gadgets (today we would call them "extras"), the upholstery, are what matter the most. Veblen noted that families were known to have gone without milk for the children in order to buy gasoline for the car (Veblen, 1899).

Closely associated with the idea of conspicuous consumption is *conspicuous leisure.* Veblen describes *conspicuous leisure* as living a lifestyle where the pursuit of leisure and the appearance of privilege are used in order to gain approval or envy. It is a self-esteem enhancement technique. Those who engage in *conspicuous leisure* are attempting to present evidence, in a public forum, of their ability to survive without having to work. According to Veblen (1899) examples of this would include: the knowledge of dead languages and the occult sciences; of correct spelling; of art; participation and spectatorship of sports; and spending time at dog and horse races. Employing servants is the ultimate demonstration of wasting time among the leisure class. It is time wasted in the care and maintenance of a person who has the ability to pay for such a waste of time.

Capitalist Waste

A by-product of conspicuous consumption and leisure is *capitalist waste.* Veblen believed that members of all social classes engage in waste. He also felt that few people intentionally seek to waste time or money. Instead, people find it necessary to consume conspicuously because cultural norms dictate such a behavior. In industrial societies it is a cultural norm to spend money. In America, consumption is critical for economic success. It becomes a sense of duty (Veblen, 1899). Veblen stated that conspicuous consumption is not limited to acts seen publicly, but even in those things consumed in total privacy. This would include the many self-indulgences that individuals afford themselves

(e.g., taking a bath with scented perfumes surrounded by highly priced scented candles in order to "enjoy" the cleansing function). Veblen concludes that conspicuous consumption has reached the point where the "habits of the mind" have pervaded nearly every domain.

Veblen describes the "habits of the mind" as having three primary characteristics (Ashley and Orenstein, 1985):

1. They occur without rational reflection.

2. They appear to be in congruity with and, in fact, form the basis of commonsense understanding among people.

3. They are resistant to change and tend to persist for a time even after the material conditions (forms of labor activity) that gave rise to them have disappeared.

In modern society, managers of large enterprises became known as "captains of industry." Veblen saw these people as the new aristocracy, uncontrolled by government but controlling a larger portion of the world's resources. As captains of industry they often act benevolently, as befits their wealth and position. They are capable of doing "good things" (Veblen, 1904). They will often donate money toward treasured passions (e.g., Andrew Carnegie's building of libraries). But as Marx had already noted, the good capitalist, while doing nice things for the public, in order to keep the "have-nots" docile, does not allow humanitarian motives to interfere with making a profit (Adams and Sydie, 2001). Veblen believed that the capitalists are guilty of a great deal of waste, sometimes deliberately, and other times indirectly. He believed that they engage in *sabotage*, or the destruction of goods and resources. This destruction is both direct (e.g., through war) and indirect (e.g., *obsolescence*). Veblen recognized that capitalists would realize far greater profit if they could build into the economic system the need to constantly replace material items with newer, upgraded models of the original product—planned obsolescence.

Veblen's overall view of modern society, spearheaded by capitalists and their waste, destruction, and sabotage of industry, along with the growing number of people who willingly participate in conspicuous spending and leisure class activities, was clearly a negative portrayal. His writings often reflect his cynical view on the nature of industrial society.

The Industrial System and the Business Enterprise

The masses are best served by an *industrial system* that maximizes output at a low cost. The capitalists, or the *business enterprise*, is best served by a moderate output at an inflated price. As Marx had already noted, conflict between these two groups is inevitable.

Using a Marxist perspective, Veblen believed that a clash between *business* and *industry* was inevitable. The business enterprise, led by the "captains" of industry, focus on making profits for their companies; but to keep profits high, they often engage in efforts to limit production. This action obstructs the functional operation of the industrial system and negatively affects society as a whole. Society would be better served if industry was run at optimal levels. Veblen was basically stating that the leaders of industry were the cause of many societal problems and that industry should be led by those people who best understood the industrial system and were concerned with the general welfare of society. Engineers were among those who Veblen felt were suited for this role.

In *The Theory of Business Enterprise* (1904) Veblen stated that the motive of business is pecuniary gain, with the method essentially purchase and sale. The goal and usual outcome is an accumulation of wealth (Veblen, 1904). Veblen stated that the business enterprise is coextensive with the development of machinery. He attempted to support his theory of the business enterprise by tracing the historical development of business from premodern times; especially through his analysis of the shipping industry. He felt that the study of shipping was important because, "shipping was the only considerable line of business which involved an investment in or management of extensive mechanical appliances and processes, comparable with the facts of the modern mechanical industry" (Veblen, 1904:21).

The early leaders of business tended to be entrepreneurs who were designers, builders, shop managers, and financial managers. Veblen believes that they *earned* their money more so than modern business leaders. These early business leaders were more speculative buyers and sellers, and less financier strategists. But, since the advent of the machine age, the circumstances of business had changed.

> Instead of investing in the goods as they pass between producer and consumer, as the merchant does, the business man now invests in the processes of industry; and instead of staking his values on the dimly foreseen conjunctures of the seasons and the act of God, he turns to the conjunctures arising from the interplay of the industrial processes, which are in great measure under the control of business men (Veblen, 1904:22).

Modern business leaders can now almost exclusively concern themselves with financial matters. Consequently, in Veblen's view, modern business leaders are not earning their income, since finance makes no direct contribution to industry. For example, modern corporations, as a type of business, are primarily concerned with making sales and profits, rather than finding ways to maintain quality of workmanship and a fully employed society. He did, however, note that modern business leaders were responsible for dramatically increasing the productive capacity of industry.

According to Veblen, the *industrial system* is composed of three coordinated factors of production: land, labor, and capital (Veblen, 1921). "The reason for this threefold scheme of factors in production is that there have been three recognized classes of income: rent, wages, and profits; and it has been assumed that whatever yields an income is a productive factor" (Veblen, 1921:27). Veblen goes on to say that this scheme has existed since the eighteenth century (industrialization). In *The Place of Science in Modern Civilisation* (1919/1961), Veblen described these three factors in terms of economic laws that take place "naturally" or "normally" (p. 280).

The threefold scheme of coordinate factors in production is notable for what it omits—the *industrial arts*.

> It assigns no productive effect to the industrial acts, for example, for the conclusive reason that the state of the industrial arts yield no stated or ratable income to any one class of persons; it affords no legal claim to a share in the community's yearly production of goods. The state of the industrial art is a joint stock of knowledge derived from past experience, and is held and passed on as an indivisible possession of the community at large. It is the indispensable foundation of all productive industry, of course, but except for certain minute fragments covered by patent rights or trade secrets, this joint stock is no man's individual property. For this reason it has not been counted in as a factor in production (Veblen, 1921:28).

Veblen (1921) acknowledged that with the rapid advancement of technology, the *industrial arts* could no longer be ignored when discussing factors in economic production. Veblen (1923) defined the *industrial arts* as the accumulated knowledge of ways and means (p. 63). The *industrial arts*, then, may be viewed as an historically developed product of technological knowledge, continuously subject to change as innovation and inventions are introduced to industry.

The industrial arts are a fact of collectivism, of group life activities; and thus, technological knowledge is held and carried forward collectively by the community (Veblen, 1947). The industrial arts are a product of past knowledge and subject to constant change as new elements of insight and proficiency are continually being added and worked into the greater body of technological knowledge. However, the industrial arts are not always available to all members of the community. As Veblen (1947) explained, "in a more advanced state of the industrial arts, where ownership and the specialization of industry have had their effect, trade secrets, patent, and copyrights are often of substantial value, and these are held in segregation from the common stock of technology" (p. 178).

The industrial system is controlled by the captains of industry, and as previously described, their primary concern is to restrict production to the point that maximum profits are realized. The primary pursuit of profit is harmful to society, especially for workers who lose jobs (due to production limitations and cost saving measures) and consumers who pay higher than necessary costs for products and services. Despite the fact that profit is the major goal of business, technological improvements in production had made industry so efficient and effective that the American economic system flourishes.

Economic Theory

Veblen was an economist. As Ritzer (2000) states, "If Veblen was identified with any field during his lifetime, it was economics (he was offered the presidency of the American Economic Association, but refused the position)" (p. 327). In his essay "Why is Economics Not an Evolutionary Science?" Veblen (1898) presents a "cumulative causation" approach to his study of social, economic, and political behavior. Veblen was critical of the economics of his day and the idea of natural laws governing human behavior. Veblen (1919/1961) stated, "economics is helplessly behind the times, and unable to handle its subject-matter in a way to entitle it to standing as a modern science . . . probably no economist to-day has either the hardihood or the inclination to say that the science has now reached a definitive formulation, either in the detail of results or as regards the fundamental features of theory" (p. 56).

In a series of articles, originally published in three installments in *The Quarterly Journal of Economics* (1899 and 1900), Veblen provided an historical analysis of economic theory. Among these articles was "The Preconceptions of Economic Science" where Veblen (1947) stated, "economic science in the remoter past of its history has been mainly of a taxonomic character, later writers of all schools show something of a divergence from the taxonomic line and an inclination to make the science a genetic account of the economic life process, sometimes even without an ulterior view to the taxonomic value of the results obtained" (p. 39). He felt that this divergence from the established canons of theoretical formulation reflected the progressive movement in science. Objective thinking reflects an evolutionary framework and often challenges the "matter-of-fact" habit of the mind. An evolutionary method and ideals are the antithesis to the taxonomic methods and ideals of pre-evolutionary days.

In "The Beginnings of Ownership," an article that first appeared in *The American Journal of Sociology* (1898), Veblen states that in accepted economic theories the ownership of productive labor belongs to the person who produced it. To this end, Veblen (1964) suggested that both the socialists and the classical economists (the two extremes of economic speculation) are substantially as one. "With the socialists it has served as the ground of their demand that the laborer should receive the full product of his labor. To the classical economists the axiom has, perhaps, been as much trouble as it has been worth. It has given them no end of bother to explain how the capitalist is the 'producer' of the goods that pass into his possession, and how it is true that the laborer gets what he produces" (Veblen, 1964:32). Veblen (1964) explained that debates over ownership of productive labor and possession of property have existed throughout human history.

Veblen viewed the emerging utility economics theory as a mere variant of classical economic theory. He argued that it was static, hedonistic, rationalistic, teleological, and deductive theory which accepted natural rights concepts (Ritzer, 2000). Veblen believed that teleological and deductive theories failed to explain social change in economic life. Only those economic theorists who were willing to abandon doctrines and maxims resting on natural rights and utilitarianism could call themselves scientists. Veblen (1898) argued that modern sciences are evolutionary in nature. Furthermore, he felt that current economics was not an evolutionary theory, and therefore, it was not scientific. He acknowledged that current economic theory was supported by empirical data (a necessary requirement for any discipline to call itself a science) but its research fell short of being science. Veblen (1898) stated that economics must consistently combine the enumeration of data with a narrative account of industrial development, leading to an elaborate body of knowledge in order to be a science. Evolutionary sciences, on the other hand, already possess a close-knit body of theory. Evolutionary theory allows for change. "It is a theory of a process, of an unfolding sequence" (Veblen, 1919/1961:58). Veblen argued that the social sciences must adopt the evolutionary framework.

Evolutionary Theory

Veblen's analysis of human society was rooted in the historic tradition. Veblen (1914) described early human history as a "savage society" (primitive) characterized by peace and cooperation. During this era, humans focused on the well-being of the immediate community. As time went on, humans became more competitive and predatorial. This later stage was known for its "barbarism" character, highlighted by its competitiveness and warlike character. During this period, human attention shifted toward self-interest and the use of industrial arts to gain an economic advantage over others. The stage of barbarism was replaced by handicrafts and the machine age. Material interests begin to dominate human behavior. Ownership of the means of production becomes the cornerstone of the modern industrial society. The thirst for raw materials and precious resources lead many societies into warfare. These predatory societies accumulated property as a symbol of success. Ultimately, the modern societies that possess the industrial arts begin to dominate. But, these societies must be of sufficient size, for it follows that "a large and widely diversified industrial scheme is impossible except in a community of some size—large enough to support a number and variety of special occupations" (Veblen, 1947:181).

Veblen (1947) noted that modern societies claim to be superior, and in some ways this claim is accurate. However, "the claim is that the modern culture is superior on the whole, not that it is the best or highest in all respects and at every point. It has, in fact, not an all-around superiority, but a superiority within a closely limited range of intellectual activities, while outside this range many other civilizations surpass that of the modern occidental peoples" (p. 3). The truth of the matter is that modern society has proved itself best capable of fitting into the changing environment. Furthermore, Veblen (1947) stated that modern civilized peoples are more capable of an impersonal, dispassionate insight into the material facts with which mankind has to deal. A civilization that dominated by this matter-of-fact insight will prevail against any cultural scheme that lacks this element.

Veblen noticed that social systems and social institutions also gradually evolve over time. The influence of Spencer and Darwinist ideas are evident in Veblen's *Evolutionary Theory*. He believed that social institutions must adapt to the changing environment. He was particularly interested in the role of technology and how it affects society in general, and industry specifically. As Spencer had articulated, Veblen believed that the "fittest" survive while the "unfit" risk dissolution. The evolutionary perspective is utilized in Veblen's theory of social change. Social change in society was directly related to the "state of industrial arts," or the level of technology available to a society (Veblen, 1904). Veblen noted that while the level of technology available to a society is crucial in determining its culture, the effect of technology is not always immediate. The effect of technology on society can be delayed and indirect. In other words, new technology does not automatically generate new political systems, religious beliefs, and moral attitudes. Instead, it modifies existing social institutions and norms and values of society. As Veblen (1899) explained, "Institutions are products of the past process, are adapted to past circumstances, and are therefore never in full accord with the requirements of the present" (p. 90).

Social change itself can polarize society. Those involved with the new technology have a "vested interest" in seeing change in society. Meanwhile, those who have a "vested interest" in the old way of doing things will want to maintain the established social institutions even when they are no longer in accord with emerging technological advancements. Veblen believed that technology represents progress, and in the end, technology will erode and reshape old institutions to adapt to the inevitable change. After all, failure to adapt to innovative, technological advancements ultimately leads to dissolution. Veblen notes that some individuals and institutions lag in their adaptation. Additionally, in periods of transition between the old ways and the new emerging social order, social conflicts are likely to surface.

Veblen's evolutionary framework was not unilinear. He was very aware of the fact that some cultures borrow the technological arts from other societies, and therefore skip the trial and tribulations of developing such technologies themselves. Thus, some societies can skip certain stages in evolutionary development. Technological arts that are borrowed are "ready-made." As an example, Veblen described how the Germans borrowed British machine technology (during Industrialization), after it had reached its more advanced state, and were able to apply them to the fullest in an environment unimpeded by vested interests (Coser, 1977). Veblen (1915) presented a similar scenario in an article "The Opportunity of Japan." He described modern Japan as a near perfect society to embrace industrialization because the people are "imbued with a sense of loy-

alty to their rulers" and the rulers would benefit by borrowing technology in a more advanced state than when Germany borrowed it from England.

Cultural Lag and Cultural Borrowing

In contemporary sociology, most students are introduced to the term *cultural lag* by the ideas of William Fielding Ogburn. Ogburn's (1922, 1942) theory states that a cultural lag occurs when one part of culture changes before, or in greater degree than, other correlated parts do; thereby causing a gap between the parts that had never existed previously (e.g., the use of e-mail has created a gap between those who use it and those who do not). This theory is most often applied to the adaptation of new technologies to existing social institutions. Veblen had also utilized this term.

Two key concepts of Veblen's evolutionary theory are *cultural lag* and *cultural borrowing*. When describing the advancements of the industrial arts in the modern world, Veblen often spoke of the capitalists who possessed a "vested interest" in maintaining current social institutions so that they may hold onto their power position. Those capitalists who introduce technology find it in their best interest to aid social change, especially in the political and economic institutions. Ultimately, true technological advancements cannot be stopped, and those who fail to embrace the changing environment risk, at the very least, lagging behind as society moves forward. In *The Theory of Business Enterprise* Veblen (1904) described the various business conceptions and business methods that developed in Europe during the sixteenth and seventeenth centuries. England would first usher in the Industrial Revolution. As their technology continued to grow, so too did their presence as a global power. Other continental countries soon learned the need to embrace industrialization. Veblen argued that even captains of industry that introduce new technology can be guilty of cultural lag when they purposely limit production in order to maximize profit.

Cultural borrowing brings with it many advantages. As discussed earlier, the borrowing of technology, after the original creators of such technology have learned to fully maximize its usage, involves all the benefits without all the original costs. For example, as new machines are created, certain safety risks, that were not foreseen, begin to reveal themselves. Once the machine has been redesigned for safety concerns and maximum output it has reached its highest value. Duplicating the finished product ensures the elimination of the errors found inherent with the original design.

Veblen (1914) also believed that the borrowing of certain cultural ideas excludes the moral and "spiritual" baggage often felt by the original culture. Unencumbered by such ritual restrictions the borrowing culture simply utilizes whatever benefits the borrowed ideas possess. Thus, *cultural borrowing* assists in industrial efficiency. The borrowers are in a position of intellectual advantage which leads to technological proficiency (Veblen, 1915/1942). Veblen acknowledged that cultural borrowing can have negative aspects as well. Primarily, the borrowing society may not be suited for the utilization of new technologies. The new technology may be so huge that it consumes the borrowing society.

Human Nature: Class, Gender, and Race

Much of Veblen's theory and ideology is centered on the wealth of industrialists and the general distress of the masses. He considered societies and their institutions to be imperfect and he was often pessimistic about the future. He believed that many human behaviors were ingrained. In fact, Veblen (1914) believed that instincts were at the core

of most human behaviors and that humans engage in "tropismatic action"—behavior that involves no conscious thought processes. This type of behavior becomes habitual, and ultimately institutionalized. However, because humans possess an advanced form of intelligence they are capable of breaking from the chains of tradition. Innovation and invention lead to technological advancements and social change, and in turn, begin to shape and alter culture. Consequently, even if human instincts exist, social forces will always modify and affect behavior.

Thus, any descriptions of *class, gender, and race* are subject to change. This can be encouraging news for those people who face economic deprivation, oppression, racism and sexism, because human behavior is alterable.

Veblen's theory of *class* begins with the claim that humans possess an instinct of workmanship—a need to work, create, to do something (Veblen, 1914). Early human history witnessed daily struggles for basic subsistence and survival. The need for status would serve to stimulate the desire to create a surplus. Accumulation of any desired item brings automatic status to the owner within the community. The item in question is irrelevant because the possessor of the wealth is not going to use it for useful purposes, but is going to use it to impress others. Thus, accumulation itself becomes the goal. As industrial society arose, the accumulation of property becomes the symbol of success.

Lower-class workers were forced to work in factories and other forms of manual labor in an effort to stay above the subsistence level. They generally worked long, hard hours for relatively little pay. The wealthy began to consider manual labor to be distasteful, and sought to avoid work altogether in order to engage in conspicuous leisure. An important feature of conspicuous leisure involves manners and decorum, for as Veblen (1899) stated, good breeding requires time and application; and these were behaviors that the lower classes could not afford to invest their time on. The wealthy not only wasted their time on conspicuous leisure, they also engaged in conspicuous consumption; by showing off their status the wealthy purchase overpriced, and functionally, unnecessary items (fancy clothing and automobiles).

These behaviors (among many others) reflect the nature of the industrial society. The wealthy are consumed by the desire for greater wealth and status, often at the cost of productive efficiency. As Veblen (1904) stated, "prosperity now means, primarily, business prosperity; whereas it used to mean industrial sufficiency" (p. 178). Veblen warned that when the wealthy class becomes so consumed with leisure pursuits, they risk losing their instinct for self-preservation. "Leisure and accumulation, then, eventually lead to the weakness and stagnation of this class, especially as they are supplanted by the new rich, or 'nouveau riche' " (Adams and Sydie, 2001:250). Pareto said much the same thing in his "Recirculation of the Elites" thoery.

In *The Theory of the Leisure Class*, Veblen explored the role of *gender* in society. He noted that at the beginning of human history both man and woman shared equally in the drudgery of life, but as time went on, poor women began to feel the burden of hard tasks more and more (1899:13). The biological facts of pregnancy and nursing certainly limited primitive women's mobility, while the tribe could survive if the male was gone for a period of time. In early hunter–gatherer societies the gender division of labor became heightened. Activities such as hunting, warfare, religion, and sports were being reserved for men. Not surprisingly, the activities of war, hunting, government, religion, and sports were treated as honorific (Phillips, 1993). According to Veblen (1899)

the predatory nature of hunting and fighting came to define the masculine role, while women were left to do more mundane, albeit more productive, things. The idea that hunting was the universal domain of activity reserved for men is outlined in G. P. Murdoch's (1935) review of "appropriate" tasks for women and men in 224 preindustrial societies.

Routine work was considered unworthy of the best men. They were driven by the possession of various trophies. The predatory stage of human development was characterized by men showing off their possessions as trophies. Aggression becomes a valued character trait in men. Veblen argued that throughout the barbarian stages of culture the seizure of female captives and the appropriation of women was primarily a demonstration of trophies. He noticed that among the modern industrial wealthy class, the woman of the highest value was one with small hands and a narrow waist; characteristics of little value in productive work activities. Thus, for wealthy families, a woman who did not have to work became evidence of pecuniary strength (Veblen, 1899). Exhibition of pecuniary strength was further demonstrated by her style of dress. The wealthy woman engaged in conspicuous consumption by purchasing ridiculously high-priced dresses and accessories in order to show others her habitual idleness (Veblen, 1894).

Veblen did not assert that current gender roles were as they should be. He acknowledged that the sentiment of women's rights was at the forefront of social issues. He agreed that women should not have to live their lives vicariously through men, and modern industrial society should free women to expand their gender roles.

Many of Veblen's biases are evident in his discussion of *race*. His evolutionary theory included references to the Negro population of the South as "low in economic efficiency, or in intelligence, or both" (Veblen, 1899:322). He argued that there are individual and racial differences in instincts. The Europeans (and their colonies) had an advantage because of their "hybrid" stock—racially mixed, while "lower cultures," because of their racial homogeneity, are disadvantaged compared to Europeans. The instincts of Europeans are better equipped to adapt to the changing environment. In his article, "The Blond Race and the Aryan Culture," Veblen (1919/1961) stated,

> that the blond type or types of man (presumably the dolichocephalic blond) arose by mutation from Mediterranean stock during the last period of severe glaciation in Europe . . . . Since this blond mutant made good its survival under the circumstances into which it was so thrown it should presumably be suited by native endowment to the industrial and climatic conditions that prevailed through the early phases of the neolithic age in Europe; that is to say, it would be a type of man selectively adapted to the technological situation characteristic of the early neolithic . . . (p. 477).

Higher Education

The academic environment is presumed to cherish higher values and the legitimate purposes of education: science and scholarship. And yet, Veblen noticed that many of his colleagues embraced neither one. How frustrating for professors who have colleagues that do not embrace this very foundation of higher learning. Veblen (1918/1957) saw little hope for an educational establishment that was distracted from its only legitimate purposes. Religion no longer held the dominant position in academia, but was to be replaced by business. In his mind, one was as much an impediment as the other. Veblen felt that the goals of business, which are driven by economic concerns, were in contrast to the goals of education, learning, and scholarship.

Ideally, the classroom should be small in size and occupied by serious students only. However, during the twentieth century, the university system had taken on the task of educating large numbers of undergraduates. Veblen recognized the value of educated students to the community, but he felt that such a task should not be taken on by the university, it should be left to the secondary, professional, and technical schools. To cope with the increasing numbers of students, the university system employed several techniques to ensure standardization and general control.

Veblen was especially upset over the introduction of a large number of extracurricular activities on college campuses designed to cultivate the habits of thought and life. Among the activities that Veblen (1918) disliked were sports, fraternities, and clubs. He felt that all these activities were leading students toward career choices in business. Veblen feared that some day in the future, student activities would become a chief criterion for choosing a college, rather than the pursuit of scholarship and the advancement of science. Veblen was disappointed with the university administration, especially the governing boards. Of those serving on governing boards, Veblen asserted that they had little true understanding of higher education and ultimately interfere with scholarship and science. Board members and academic heads of universities were becoming driven by economic issues instead of academic concerns.

Relevancy

Thorstein Veblen is not a social thinker in the ranks of Marx, Durkheim, Weber, or most of the other previously discussed theorists, but many of his ideas and contributions remain relevant as the third millennium begins. His theory of the leisure class remains in academic discourse. His insights into the industrial system and the business enterprise have led to discussion in such areas as conspicuous consumption, cultural lag, and cultural borrowing, concepts that are applicable today.

The impact of the sports and recreation industry on today's society would most likely startle Veblen. If not surprised, Veblen would surely be displeased. He believed that leisure activity participation was counterproductive and a waste of valuable time. Many modern social thinkers, especially sport sociologists, would disagree with such an assessment. According to a 2002 Clemson Univeristy research report, sports and recreation is a $160 billion industry. Major League Baseball salaries alone topped $2 billion in 2002 (Blum, 2002). In addition, many professional sports teams are now owned by "captains" of industry (e.g., Robert Murdoch owns the Los Angeles Dodgers, George Steinbrenner owns the New York Yankees). Veblen might have to reconsider his disbelief in the validity of sports and leisure participation as a productive pursuit if he were to consider the following thoughts and ideas.

Those who participate in sports and leisure are not simply engaged in nonproductive economic behavior. Friendships are formed based on shared activities (Hamid, 1993). Leisure-centered groups offer some of the same membership advantages that are provided by ethnic clubs (i.e., rituals; beliefs and outlooks on society and community; norm expectations; and anomie and alienation reduction). Social interaction plays an important function in an individual's life. Everyone wants to feel that they fit into a group or society. Individuals want to experience a sense of unity with their fellows. Consequently, by joining together in groups, the individual becomes a part of the whole. The group provides them with a distinctive identity based on their membership (Lee,

1993). As Delaney and Wilcox (2002) explain, "the sense of identity that sport provides for so many people cannot be underestimated. The commitment, loyalty, and passion that so many fans have for sport is the reason it has existed for so many centuries. The trend of increased commercialization of sport *may* someday bring an end to *professional* sports as seen today, but sport itself will always be a fixture of society" (p. 213).

Today, leisure activity may be viewed as one of the most telling indicators of who a person really is; even more so than one's occupation (Delaney, 2001). This is often true because work is something that most people do in order to earn a living, while sport and leisure participation is done voluntarily. Stone (1955) argues that sport's role in American industrial society may have the latent function of bringing continuity into the personal lives of many Americans. Sports-based loyalties formed in adolescence and maintained through adulthood serve to remind one that there are some areas of stability in a social world seemingly consumed by rapid social change.

Delaney (2001) states, "sport is as much a part of American society as are other social institutions such as family and religion. Sport is such a pervasive activity in contemporary America that to ignore it is to overlook a social phenomenon that extends into a multiple of social arenas, from education, economics, art, the mass media, and community, to international diplomatic relations. It has been said that sport is a microcosm of society. Sport reflects the mores, values, and general culture of a society" (p. ix). The study of sport and leisure is even more important today than it was in Veblen's era. It is likely that Veblen's criticism of sport was really an attack against the wealthy. "Veblen enjoyed the irony of discussing 'savages' and the 'modern upper class' in the same sentence, so one cannot be sure how much of his criticism of sport was serious theory and how much was intended as a put-down of the rich. It would seem unlikely that a particular spirit of exploit survived from savage origins of European society up to the present" (Phillips, 1993). Veblen's less-than-complimentary description of the role of sport is oversimplistic and it is false to conclude that leisure pursuits are merely nonproductive behavior.

Veblen (1899) observed that the American upper-class industrialists of the late-nineteenth century were a leisure class who distinguished themselves from the masses by the means of *conspicuous consumption* and *conspicuous leisure*. Conspicuous consumption is the public display of material goods, lifestyle, and behavior, in such a way as to show off to others one's privileged status for the purpose of gaining approval or envy. Examples of this type of behavior are numerous in all-advanced industrial societies. Hospital wings, university buildings, monuments, statues, stadiums, churches, and other such structures are built with elaborate design and serve the ultimate function of public display of wealth and privilege among those who can afford to sponsor such construction. Individual consumers have found a wide-variety of methods to flaunt their privilege. Among the most obvious examples are: luxurious mansions; automobiles that are high in cost and low in practical function (e.g., sports cars, SUV's); overpriced "designer-label" and "brand-name" clothing and fashion; five-dollar "fancy" cups of coffee; "upgraded" versions of computer software that offer very little improvement from the most recent version; and cell phones. Even in economically poor societies, such as the oil producing nations of the Middle East (e.g., Kuwait, Saudi Arabia), the rulers choose to reside in extravagant castles and live lavish lifestyles; consequently separating themselves from the masses.

Conspicuous leisure is public involvement in expensive or extravagant leisure pursuits to convey the appearance of privilege or status for approval or envy. As described earlier in this chapter, sports and leisure have become a major economic industry. Clearly, a large number of people are participating in and/or serving as spectators of the sports industry. Many middle-class people purchase season tickets to their favorite sports team in order to cheer for their team, but also, to convey to others that they have the both the time (luxury) and the means (finances) to do so. As the sports industry became more lucrative the level of enticement and perks offered to wealthy season-ticket holders increases. The wealthier season-ticket holder can enjoy "luxury box" seating, equipped with private bathrooms, television screens, waitress/waiter service, private entrance into the stadium, and other such perks that vary from stadium to stadium.

Many people "belong" to health clubs so that they can work out and increase their general "fitness." The irony of such membership activity often escapes those people who drive to the gym just to ride a bike or use a "stairmaster." Why not run to the club? The answer lies primarily with the fact that some people simply want to be "seen" at the club. The fact that people have the time to work out under such conditions often implies conspicuous leisure. Many other leisure pursuits (e.g., surfing, rafting, skiing, snowboarding) are associated with the basic premise that the participant has both the time and money to spend on leisure. This is not meant as a criticism of such behavior; in fact, the activities describe above are worthwhile pursuits from a contemporary perspective. Veblen would disagree. But, perhaps if Veblen had been born a hundred years later, his outlook on leisure participation would be much different.

Other forms of *conspicuous leisure* exist separate from the sportsworld. Mundane behaviors such as tanning (sunbathing), traveling, attending concerts, dancing, playing video games are all examples of conspicuous leisure. It takes many hours a week in the sun to attain the "perfect" tan. Even those who use tanning salons must take the time to go there and pay the cost to use the radiant bulbs. And why do people in such places as Buffalo feel the need to be tanned in February? It is often a way of demonstrating a lifestyle choice, to impress others, and perhaps suggesting that they just returned from an exotic vacation. Certainly, traveling and vacations imply a level of leisure. Many people cannot afford to travel to the seven continents of the world. Those who accomplish such a feat clearly have both the time and the means. Most people have attended at least one concert in their life, but others are known for taking large segments of their life off to travel with their favorite band while they are on tour. One such famous group of people are known as "Deadheads." Deadheads are the die-hard (are there any other kind?) fans of the Grateful Dead rock band. These legions of fans would take weeks, months, and in some cases years off from their "normal" routines to travel with the band, raising money in a variety of creative ways to support this life of leisure. Today, fans of the band Phish are the closest to the Deadheads. And while it is true that many Deadheads were known for their dancing, those who go to nightclubs on a regular basis to dance, and be seen, are quite a different category of people. Those who enjoy night-clubbing live a lifestyle that screams independence from daily, routine, grind-it-out professional behavior. To be in a position to sleep all day and dance and drink all night implies a leisure lifestyle.

Finally, there is perhaps no other activity that serves so little purpose as playing video games. It serves no productive function whatsoever and would have surely driven Veblen to madness! There are few productive people who can afford to waste time, es-

pecially in such a trivial manner as playing video games.

Many of Veblen's ideas related to the *industrial system* and the *business enterprise* are relevant today. The new "captains" of industry are the giant corporations and oil companies who are slowing devouring their competition and utilizing every imaginable technique to maximize profits. Oil-producing nations will often cut back on production, either because the market is too saturated or as a political tool used as a threat against its enemies (especially during times of warfare). The business enterprise will create various products and advertise them as a "limited edition." This technique supposedly increases the value of the item because the purchaser can "brag" to others that they possess something that most others do not (potentially creating envy). The "captains" of industry, guided by their prime directive of maximizing profits are not concerned with the effects certain decisions that devastate the workers. They make such business decisions as "downsizing" and "cutbacks." Large portions of the labor force are laid off work; they now have difficulty paying their mortgages and putting food on the table, but the industrialists make higher profits. A willingness to cut back on profits would keep the labor force employed, and society as a whole would benefit. Veblen noted long ago that the industrialists were not making the positive contribution to society that it could, or should.

Through an evolutionary framework, Veblen's economic theory proposes the validity and value of *cultural borrowing* and describes the effects of *cultural lag*. Cultural lag is related to the survival of the fittest principle. As outlined in chapter three (Herbert Spencer), those who fail to embrace the new technologies of a culture risk making themselves obsolete. College graduates realize the value of computer skills in the job market. Failing to possess a certain level of computer-skills knowledge automatically disqualifies candidates from most jobs. *Cultural borrowing* plays an important role here as well. The college student of today does not have to build and design a computer, they are already available for purchase. The advantage of each new generation is that they have access to all the industrial arts that preceded them. We do not have to learn how certain technologies were developed, we simply need to learn how to utilize the new technologies. So many cultural items are borrowed that *cultural diffusion* (the spread of cultural items from one society to another) surrounds us. Archaeological evidence suggest that many cultural items have spread worldwide from a common source, creating some similarities among very diverse societies (Murdock, 1935). Food is an excellent example of cultural borrowing and cultural diffusion. Throughout the United States a wide variety of ethnic foods are available. Most people enjoy such a diversity in choice. Some people would be surprised to find out the origins of some of their favorite foods. Spaghetti, for instance, originated in China and was adopted by Italians after Marco Polo's travels in the thirteenth century.

Veblen's theories are grounded by economic considerations. He realized that the industrial arts had reached a high level of efficiency and that the industrialists were driven by the pursuit of profit rather than making society as a whole better. The industrial need for raw materials and the political influence held by the captains of industry would influence modern societies toward acts of aggressiveness, with no region of the world too remote to escape the influence of the dominant cultures. Veblen foresaw that each country of the world would find a way to defend itself from possible military (and cultural) attack. Those societies that feel threatened must react aggressively or risk dissolution. The only other possible solution is to embrace the reality of change and employ the methods of cultural borrowing and diffusion.

Karl Mannheim

(1893–1947)

Karl Mannheim (1893–1947) German-born social thinker who created the sociology of knowledge.
Source: Courtesy Henk Woldring

Karl Mannheim was born on March 27, 1893, in Budapest, Hungary, of Jewish middle-class parents. Budapest, a Central European city, was dominated by German cultural influences (Mannheim, 1952). Mannheim was heavily influenced by the stimulating intellectual community that surrounded him. He benefited from the insights of Jewish and non-Jewish intellectuals alike. He spent his formative years in Hungary and Germany during a period of extraordinary social and intellectual unrest. This period was characterized by the First World War and the chaos of a revolution and a counterrevolution immediately following it (Mannheim, 1952).

The only son of a Hungarian–Jewish father and a German–Jewish mother, Karl was born with a heart defect and would suffer from poor health his whole life. He would die from a heart attack at the relatively young age of fifty-three. Mannheim attended school at the Budapest humanist *Gymnasium* and then proceeded to start studying philosophy at the University of Budapest. Just before he began his studies at the University, Mannheim met Georg Lukacs. "At that time, Lukacs had not yet made his conversion to Marxism, but he had already established a substantial reputation as the author of several important works in philosophy, aesthet-ics and literary criticism" (Bailey, 1994:46). Lukacs led a small group of intellectuals known as the *Szellemkek* or "sprites" (ghosts, spirits), by virtue of their deep concern with problems of the "spirit" (*szellem*). From 1915 to 1918 Mannheim was an active member of the Lukacs Sunday Circle group, and it was here where many of his ideas on the state of culture first surfaced. The group discussed issues of cultural malaise and decline, while trying to find some hope for cultural renewal (Bailey, 1994).

In between the time that Mannheim first met Lukacs and was active with the Sunday Circle group, Karl was involved with the Budapest Social Scientific Society. Philosophically, this society was more positivistic in outlook than the Lukacs group, but Mannheim managed to actively participate in both groups for some time. Mannheim was also a member of a student society, the Galileo Circle, a group energized by reformist ideals, positivism, and the philosophy of William James. By the time Mannheim left for Germany he was well immersed in the ideas of positivism (something he would reject later in life) and reform-oriented ideas (Coser, 1977).

In 1912, Mannheim left Budapest for Germany, to attend the University of Berlin. At Berlin, Mannheim studied under Georg Simmel, and was very impressed by him. Mannheim was most impressed by Simmel's philosophical ideas rather than his formal sociology. Many of Mannheim's earliest published writings reveal a strong influence from the ideas of Simmel. For example, in 1917, the Lukacs group organized a series of public lectures and seminars with a theme of the "Free School for Studies of the Human Spirit." Mannheim was chosen to give the inaugural lecture. This address would later be published as "Soul and Culture" (1918) and reveals influences from Simmel's writings on "the tragedy of culture" and Lukacs' *Soul and Form* (Bailey, 1994). In brief, Simmel promoted the idea that it was up to the present generation of intellectuals to lead society through the crisis of political uncertainty.

Mannheim received his doctorate in philosophy in 1918. His dissertation, entitled "The Structural Analysis of Epistemology" (published in German in 1922), is a study of societal structures and intellectual diversity (Mannheim, 1953). His dissertation reveals hints toward his future focus, the study of knowledge. Meanwhile, Hungary was experiencing a revolution (in 1918) led by a bourgeois-socialist regime, under the leadership of Mihaly Karolyi. Their reign and power were short-lived, as they were replaced in early 1919 by Béla Kun's Communist party. Lukacs had recently become an active member of the Communist Party and was able to secure a teaching position (philosophy lecturer) for Mannheim at the University of Budapest. Although Mannheim was basically apolitical, his friendship and association with Lukacs linked him to the Communist Party in the eyes of the public. Kun's regime was also short-lived and replaced in mid-1919 by a counterrevolutionary, fascist, anti-Semitic regime led by Admiral Miklós Horthy. Because Mannheim was Jewish and linked to the Communist Party, his life was suddenly in real danger. The life he once enjoyed with the company of many, mostly Jewish, intellectual groups was now threatened by fascists.

Mannheim stayed in Hungary until 1920, when, after several intermediate stops, he ended up at the University of Heidelberg. It was here that Mannheim began to focus on sociology. Until this point in time he had considered himself a philosopher. Mannheim met many intellectuals and increased his intellectual horizons. "While in Germany, he was influenced by the blossoming academic atmosphere: he attended lectures by the philosopher Martin Heidegger, studied with Alfred Weber, and was influenced by the Neo-Kantians and by Edmund Husserl, the founder of phenomenology" (Farganis, 2000:191). Alfred Weber was the brother of Max who, along with Max's wife Marianne, had started the "Weber group" in 1921. Alfred was a noted scholar himself, and he would succeed Georg Lukacs as Mannheim's mentor (Ritzer, 2000). Mannheim eagerly joined the "Weber group."

On a personal level, 1921 was significant for Mannheim as well. In March he married Juliska Lang, the daughter of a very wealthy Budapest family. Her family did not approve of the marriage because they did not want her to marry someone who was employed in a field that paid relatively poorly. The couple were fellow students at both Budapest and Heidelberg. Juliska was an intellectual herself, with a Ph.D. in psychology. She would hold a professorship position at the University of Amsterdam. Karl's interest in psychology and psychoanalysis, especially in his later life, was, of course, inspired by his wife. Juliska would help Karl with his academic essays, and after his death saw to it that much of his work was published. Karl and Juliska never had any children.

Mannheim taught as a *Privatdozent* (private scholar/lecturer) at the University of Heidelberg for many years. Interestingly, this was the same marginal position occupied by Simmel for most of his academic life. Mannheim now felt this was the appropriate time to apply for German citizenship; he was successfully naturalized. Mannheim successfully published a number of his essays during the early 1920s, among them: "The Distinctive Character of Cultural-Sociological Knowledge" (1922), where he criticizes Marx for falling into the relativist paradox; "A Sociological Theory of Culture and Its Knowability" (1924), where he speaks highly of Marx and his "positivist" focus on the socio-economic realm; "Historicism" (1924) (to be discussed later in this chapter); "The Problem of a Sociology of Knowledge" (1925), his first explicit state-

ment on the sociology of knowledge; and, "Ideological and Sociological Interpretation of Intellectual Phenomena" (1926), where Mannheim ceases to identify with Marx's attempt to provide a causal account of meaning (Bailey, 1994; Mannheim, 1952).

Mannheim was appointed as professor of sociology and economics at the University of Frankfurt in 1927. He would stay there until he was forced out by the Nazis in 1933. In his six years at Frankfurt, Mannheim would develop some of his best-known works, especially, *Ideology and Utopia* (1929). The famous Institute of Social Research in Frankfurt (the "Frankfurt School") was in the same building as the sociology department. The Frankfurt School was home to such brilliant sociologists as Theodor Adorno and Max Horkheimer, social theorists who would be instrumental in forming "critical theory." Mannheim did not like the pro-Communist stand of the School, but he did agree with their anti-Nazi stand. The "critical" theorists were disappointed that Mannheim did not take a more active political role in his approach to academia, but Karl had always tried to remain somewhat distant from active participation in politics.

Overall, Mannheim was very happy during the Frankfurt years. He enjoyed teaching at one of the more liberal universities in Germany, and he was a popular professor whose classes were always full. It is fair to assume that Mannheim would have liked to stay at Frankfurt, but this was not to be the case, as a major political force came to power in Germany in January 1933. This power was Adolf Hitler and the Nazi party. Because he was Jewish, Mannheim feared imminent danger, and within months he fled to England. Mannheim arrived in London in May 1933, and he had already secured a teaching position at the London School of Economics. He remained a refugee until he was naturalized as a British citizen in 1940.

In 1945 he became a full-time sociology professor in the London School of Economics and Political Science, a position he held until his death in 1947 (Mannheim, 1936).

The move to England signified a very important time in Mannheim's life, both personally and academically. The emigration from Hungary to Germany had been easy for Mannheim; the cultures and intellectual atmospheres were equally stimulating and therefore presented no real obstacles for successful transition. But the move to England would be far different. It was truly a foreign society to Mannheim. Academically, Mannheim's very preoccupation with the ideas of utopia and a sociology of knowledge designed to assist in the political organization of society now seemed meaningless and pointless in light of Nazism. The move to England was so dramatic to Mannheim that most sociologists describe him in terms of the "German" Mannheim and the "British" Mannheim. "Before 1933, Mannheim's work was characterized by a faith in the essential beneficence of the historical process. His writings in the sociology of knowledge were premised on the assumption that history carries the truth in its progress" (Bailey, 1994:61). Mannheim's belief that society is historically progressing was shattered by Hitler's political victories. Mannheim had warned in *Ideology and Utopia* that man's utopian impulse was disappearing and was in danger of extinction. The events of 1933 convinced him that utopia was merely an illusion.

The "British" Mannheim abandoned Marxist ideas and began to embrace a Durkheimian sociology that values stability, democratic planning and social reconstruction. Mannheim rarely published articles in academic journals in England, and instead concentrated on publishing books. They include: *Rational and Irrational Elements in Contemporary Society*, published in 1934; *Man*

and Society in an Age of Reconstruction (1940), *Diagnosis of Our Time* (1944) *Freedom, Power, and Democratic Planning* (1950), *Essays on Sociology and Social Psychology* (1952), *Essays on Sociology and Social Psychology* (1953), *Essay on the Sociology of Culture* (1956), and *Systematic Sociology* (1957). The "English" Mannheim's writing style had "softened" and it became far more readable to its audience. Mannheim taught at London for twelve years. He passed away on January 9, 1947, shortly after the end of World War II.

Intellectual Influences

As described previously in this chapter, Mannheim was clearly influenced by a large number of theorists, his contemporaries and predecessors alike. He was an active participant in a wide variety of social academic groups. He claimed three different citizenships, and lived through the turmoil of both world wars. Among the more significant intellectual influences on Mannheim, and those to be discussed in this section, are Lukacs, Hegel, Simmel, Weber, Marx, and positivism.

Georg Lukacs

Georg Lukacs was one of Mannheim's earliest influences. Lukacs was the leading figure of the *Szellemkek*, the intellectual group that Karl was a member of for many years. Rempel (1965) states that Lukacs was the source of two major influences on Mannheim:

1. He demonstrated the general value of the sociological method in all fields of history.

2. He showed that Marx was the only one who truly grasped Hegel's idea of self-alienation. (p. 15)

Bailey (1994) explains that "from Lukacs, Mannheim learned that the relation between socio-economic base and ideological superstructure could be conceived as a reciprocal, dialectical relation, rather than as a mechanical, causal relation" (p. 53). In general, Lukacs' work in the historic framework would influence Mannheim's work in *historicism*.

Lukacs had a direct impact on Mannheim's works as well. Specifically, many of the central ideas of Lukacs' *History and Class Consciousness* reappear in Mannheim's *Ideology and Utopia* (Bailey, 1994). Lukacs' *History* represents an attempt to demonstrate the intellectual superiority of Marxism over all Bourgeois philosophical attempts. "For Lukacs, the central focus of Marx's original method had been 'the dialectical relation between subject and object in the historical process.' Through a materialist transformation of Hegel's idealist dialectic, Marx had developed the fundamental premise that the realm of sociohistorical reality is constituted through a dialectic of subjective and objective forces" (Bailey, 1994:9). Lukacs analyzed Marx's *fetishism of commodities* to reveal the dialectical character of the Marxian critique of political economy. Lukacs' theory of reification, "Reification and the Consciousness of the Proletariat" attempts to show the continuous spread of reification throughout all spheres of social-capitalist development.

G. W. F. Hegel

Hegel is perhaps the origin of both Marxism and historicism and consequently served as an influence on the work of Mannheim. Hegel spoke of the historical conditioning of the human spirit, on dialectical relationships between historical phenomena, and "process thought." All these elements are used in Mannheim's work (Coser, 1977). From Hegel,

Mannheim "derived the conception of history as a structured and dynamic process . . . and seeing facts and events not as isolated phenomena and occurrences but in relation to the dominant social forces and trends" (Zeitlin, 1968:283). From Hegel (and Marx) Mannheim came to view history as a structured and dynamic process. Mannheim's work on historicism was clearly influenced by Hegel.

Georg Simmel

Simmel had a direct effect on Mannheim due to the fact that Karl was a student of Simmel's for a year in Berlin. Mannheim was interested more in Simmel's philosophical ideas than he was in his sociological concerns. Mannheim was influenced by Simmel's use of the distinction between objective and subjective culture, especially in terms of how culture is transmitted to each historical actor (Coser, 1977). Mannheim felt that the objective culture surrounds and dominates the actor. Mannheim notes, however, that the objective culture can only continue through the devotion and collaboration of the next generation of actors. Consequently, each generation can, and should, strive for cultural renewal and seek ways to escape the burden placed on it by the previous generation. Mannheim's "Soul of Culture" articulates distinctions between objective and subjective culture.

Max Weber

For Mannheim, utilizing the historic method to study behavior must be accompanied by some explanation and understanding as to why human acts always seem to involve specific purposes, motives, and values of the actors concerned. In short, he felt that *understanding* requires a concern with the mind. Thus, Mannheim was looking for the meaning of interrelationship behaviors and interactions, and applied interpretive understanding in the tradition of Max Weber. For Weber, human conduct was always "meaningful" whether individuals realized it or not (Zeitlin, 1968). *Verstehen* was important for Weber because the social sciences have the advantages of asking the subjects *why* they are behaving the way that they are.

In the *Protestant Ethic and the Spirit of Capitalism* Weber came to explain the role between religion and economic industrial development. He used a systematic approach to explain the revolutionary transformation of industrial society and tied it to a specific variable, the *spirit* of industrialization and Calvinism (Neisser, 1965). Weber even suggested that Calvinists have a "calling" (vocation) to live a certain lifestyle. Mannheim attempted to use this Weberian approach to explain how knowledge was spread. His "sociology of knowledge" remains one of Mannheim's most lasting contributions to sociology.

Karl Marx

The greatest single influence on Mannheim was Karl Marx. Mannheim, like Max Weber before him, has been described as a "bourgeois Marx" (Zeitlin, 1968). Early in his academic life, Mannheim first became introduced to the works of Marx through Lukacs. At that time Mannheim was largely influenced by Marx's positivistic ideas. Following the end of the Hungarian Soviet Revolution, Mannheim redirected his attention to "revolutionary Marxism." In light of the social climate of revolutions and counterrevolutions, Mannheim felt that Marxist ideas seemed more relevant than ever before. "Marx's basic prophecy, the advent of the proletarian age after the final collapse of capitalism, seemed on the point of being realized, not only in Russia but also in Central Europe" (Mannheim, 1952:3).

Mannheim maintained a lifelong effort at applying Marxian methodological principles to the study of man, society, and history. Mannheim accepted Marx's idea that there was a correlation between the economic structure of society and its legal and political organization (Zeitlin, 1968). Marx's "utopian" visions of a world dominated by Communism radically challenged the traditional outlook of society, and it proposed replacing a meaningless world with one of equality (Mannheim, 1952). Marx would directly influence Mannheim's utopian views. Mannheim's view on *historicism* are tied to Marx's idea that ways of thinking are tied to ways of doing. An individual's "way of doing" was influenced by social structures; and for Marx, the economic structure dictates one's choice of behavior. Mannheim came to believe that ideas are not merely "from the inside" of an individual, they are in response to determinants emanating from the outside social structures. Mannheim's sociology of knowledge was influenced by Marx's "theory of ideology." Marx believed that ideologies are distortions of reality that reflect the interests and values of the ruling class (the capitalists) (Ritzer, 2000). Zeitlin (1968) adds that Mannheim's sociology of knowledge links the political, legal, philosophical, and religious institutions to the economic institution, in the spirit of Marxism.

Positivism

It was during the time of his involvement with the Budapest Social Scientific Society and the Galileo Circle, a group comprised of social reformers who embraced progressive literature, that Mannheim accepted the idea of positivism. Social theorists who believe that the social world can be studied in the same manner as the natural world, via the establishment of laws, are referred to as positivists. They seek to find social laws that allow for the prediction of future social events. To establish a "law" positivists look for determining causes of events and behavior. The positivist technique is the truest scientific approach in sociology. Given that Mannheim wanted his sociology of knowledge to be scientific (opposed to philosophical), with a commitment to empirical research, one might conclude that Mannheim was a positivist. However, he was also committed to understanding the "meaning" of behavior, and therefore, his sociology of knowledge was more accurately a form of interpretive sociology.

His preoccupation with methodological pluralism led him to reject the positivistic conclusion that meaning could be reduced to empirical explanation. In his "The Problem of a Sociology of Knowledge" (1925), Mannheim refers to positivism as "an essentially deluded school" because it emphasized only one type of data collection—the empirical method used by the natural sciences—and because it assigns no value to philosophical interpretation. For these reasons, as the years went by, Mannheim tended to be very critical of positivism. Still, he valued positivism because, in his view, Marx was a positivist, and Mannheim assigned credit to Marx for being the founder of the sociology of knowledge. Second, he recognized the validity of empirical data to support theory. And third, he wanted to do some type of science, and positivism is the closest thing to doing science in sociology.

Concepts and Contributions

Karl Mannheim lived an exciting life and was exposed to a wide variety of events and academic influences. He was as much a product of his physical environment as any of the social thinkers discussed so far in this book. The "German" Mannheim produced perhaps the most important works for sociological theory: the sociology of knowledge, historicism, and his ideas on ideology and utopia. But, with the advent of World War II, the "English" Mannheim abandoned many of his works in progress (in some cases, never returning to them) and instead, shifted his focus toward a diagnosis of his time, social reconstruction, and issues pertaining to rationality and irrationality.

The Sociology of Knowledge

Mannheim's greatest contribution to sociological theory is generally accepted to be his *sociology of knowledge*. The *sociology of knowledge* is grounded "within Marxist thought concerning the relationship of ideas to their historical context" (Farganis, 2000:192). Marx believed that the ruling class ideas dominate society and that the masses tend to support these cultural ideas because of *false consciousness*. Marx also believed that *true consciousness* would arise when the proletariat comprehends the objective reality of society. Mannheim argued that ideas come from multiple sources (e.g., generations, status groups, schools, etc.), but concluded that the most significant source of cultural ideas lies with social class (Ritzer, 2000). Bailey (1994) warns that interpreting Mannheim's work is complicated enough but adds that translation problems adds to the difficulty. "The English edition of *Ideology and Utopia* (1936) and *Man and Society in an Age of Reconstruction* (1940) are quite different books in comparison with the German originals (1929 and 1935 respectively). In both cases material has been added . . . [and] there were also significant shifts in language and meaning" (p. 42). Mannheim also makes it clear that he never worked out all the aspects of this theory, as his attention to more pressing issues would arise with the advent of the Nazis coming to power in Germany.

In "The Sociology of Knowledge," found in *Ideology and Utopia* (1936), Mannheim writes that, "the sociology of knowledge is one of the youngest branches of sociology; as theory it seeks to analyze the relationship between knowledge and existence; as historical-sociological research it seeks to trace the forms that this relationship has taken in the intellectual development of mankind" (p. 264). Mannheim had attempted to accomplish many things with this theory, but his primary goal was to determine the link between thought and action. Mannheim believed that thought was not an isolated activity but actually an activity that is set in a sociological context. In other words, the way one thinks is dependent on more than just that person, it is also dependent on the society in which one grew up, as well as the thought processes of those who came prior.

The "social climate of the times" that one is raised in binds people of the same *generation* together. A generation of people do not all necessary come into contact with one another, rather they are similar in structure to that of a social class—they share certain social characteristics. Mannheim's *generation* for example was characterized by living through two world wars and multiple social disturbances caused by revolution. Contemporary American culture is well-familiar with the term "Baby Boomers," a name given to a generation of people born in a (roughly) twelve-year period immediately following the conclusion of World War II. This generation of people all share a number of common experiences, social outlooks, and represent a distinctive phase of the collective historical process.

"The sociology of knowledge is closely related to, but increasingly distinguishable from, the theory of ideology, which has also emerged and developed in our own time" (Mannheim, 1936:265). According to Mannheim, the study of ideology involves uncovering the "deceptions and disguises" of politics and special interest groups in order to determine their true role in society. The sociology of knowledge is concerned more with the varying ways in which objects present themselves to the subject according to differences in social environments. Mannheim realized, of course, that individuals are capable of thinking, but he insisted that all ideas and sentiments that motivate an individual to behave are not explained solely on the basis of one's own life experience. Mannheim (1936) explains, "the principal thesis of the sociology of knowledge is that there are modes of thought which cannot be adequately understood as long as their social origins are obscured" (p. 2). To explain what he meant by this, Mannheim used the analogy of language. He said that one cannot understand language based on observing just one individual, because, although she speaks that language, it is not just hers. The language belongs to those who surround her and those who came before her.

Mannheim viewed all knowledge as a product of the social structure that surrounds an individual as well as the historical evolution that the knowledge has gone through on its way to becoming what it is. Thus, all knowledge is learned, and it is a product of that which has evolved throughout history. Mannheim states that, "one of the greatest achievements in the evolution of man [was] when, with slow but unbroken progress, he learned to record his own history" (Mannheim, 1940:147). The idea that all knowledge is socially dependent is grounded in the German tradition of *standortgebunden* (Baum, 1977). Mannheim believed that knowledge must evolve, it cannot remain stagnant. He stated that all things change and all things are seen from a certain perspective. Perspective "signifies the manner in which one views an object, what one perceives in it, and how one construes it in his thinking" (Mannheim, 1936:272). His ideas on perspectivism are an integral part of the sociology of knowledge. What one sees at any given time is not simply an individual perspective, it is the product of past events and current interactions. This notion reflects Hegel's idea on reification, in that, we come to view certain things as "real" when society tells us it is real.

Neisser (1965) describes the sociology of knowledge as a *historical science*, "in the sense that the influence of social factors on the development of knowledge has undergone and will continue to undergo historical changes" (p. 18). Utilizing the historical method, Mannheim identifies stages of human evolutionary development. As articulated by Neisser (1965), during the "Early phases" (stage 1) of evolutionary development, "Apeman and paleolithic man possessed skills that they could not have acquired without some thinking. Knowledge begins in this period at the latest" (Neisser, 1965:34). Throughout most of human history, including or excluding the Neanderthaler, humans remained at the primitive level of hunting and gathering, using crude tools. The domestication of animals and the use of agriculture preceded the highly developed civilizations of Sumer and Egypt by only a few thousand years.

The second stage in the development of knowledge is referred to as the "later phases of practical knowledge" and is characterized by an extension of knowledge, the development of town life, city economy, and the eventual transition to city-states and followed by a system of commercial capitalism. Some parts of the world remained isolated and their knowledge level increased much more slowly. Success transitions could only be possible through the development of new types of military and political organization. Military organization implies the possession of relatively advanced knowledge, but it also required special leadership qualities.

Societies must extend their practical knowledge, especially if they are in threat of predatory invasions. Technologically advanced societies have routinely destroyed one-time dominant cultures throughout history. For example, the city-state power of the Aztecs were no match for the imperialistic Spanish explorers, and they were wiped out during the Spanish invasion. Europeans took advantage of their advanced level of technology to colonize much of the world. This colonization is also responsible for the spread of knowledge; especially in terms of improving architecture, agriculture, bookkeeping (recorded history), and increasing the general level of education (literacy).

The final stage of development is the "practical knowledge in industrial capitalism." Industrial capitalism represents rapid improvement in technological skills. Among the many benefits of the industrial capitalism is the fact that production levels increased dramatically, a great deal of manual labor was replaced by machines, a middle-class developed, entrepreneurs became interested in the further development of the methods of production, and individual levels of technology increased tremendously.

As sociologists have come to realize, Mannheim's *sociology of knowledge* is multifaceted and a complete analysis of this work would require far more space. Mannheim had correctly identified that social processes influence the process of knowledge. He distinguished two ways that one acquires knowledge. The first is "from the inside" (individual meanings) and the second "from the outside" (the reflection of a societal process in which the individual is a part of). Mannheim clearly demonstrated that social process does not merely play a peripheral role in the evolution of knowledge, it is the critical element of the development of knowledge. In short, Mannheim argued that knowledge and *how one thinks* are *historically* determined, connected to both time and social circumstance.

Historicism

In Mannheim's essay *Historicism* (1924) the influences of Hegel and German idealism predominate. Mannheim's *historicism* reflects both German idealism in general, and German historiography (which is called *Historismus* in German) specifically. German historicism explains that society is what it is because of its history. "Each society, each culture, is in some way an historically produced totality, and the social scientist must try to understand the lives of the people in it in concepts generated by their own self-understanding and interpret the details of this society, or this culture, in terms of its totality" (Baum, 1977:28). From this perspective, the goal of the researcher is to remain value-free when conducting social research (in the tradition of Weber), and not to introduce their own predefined ideas and categories in their study.

The social scientist is to respect the group, or culture, under study, and because it recognizes a plurality of truths (people from different strata will have different ideas of "truth"), historicism will lead to relativism. This statement introduces two important points. First, the reality that within the socio-historical totality, different social groups and strata will possess distinctive "styles of thought." Meaning the views of any particular group only represent a portion of the knowledge found in the totality; and each viewpoint represents a "perspectivistic" condition. Second, Mannheim denied the existence of perspectivistic character of all sociohistorical knowledge because the relativistic approach implies that all views are of equal worth; and therefore, none can claim to have absolute "truth."

In his essay *Historicism*, Mannheim declares that his doctrine of historical knowledge is a function of the theoretical "standpoints" produced by history itself, and not relativism. He argues that historic knowledge remains controllable, so long as it concentrates on finding facts. The "truth" will come out if the sum parts of the society and culture are all a part of the fact-finding process. Mannheim (1952) states that truth is an object itself. He firmly believed in the truth of history. For Mannheim, historicism was the legitimate successor of religion; it was an intellectual movement that seeks the "truth" that religion pretends to provide. It was no mistake that Mannheim used such concepts as "movement," "process," and "flux," in his descriptions of the sociocultural reality. It was a part of his grand desire to find the truth, to reveal the hidden elements found in social institutions, and to unveil the processes that lead to social stability and social change.

Ideology and Utopia

In *Ideology and Utopia* (1936), Mannheim is concerned with "how one actually thinks." In the Marxist tradition, that human's social existence determines their social consciousness, Mannheim stated that individuals act against one another in diversely organized groups, and while doing so, they think with and against one another. Thus, one's social position impacts their behavior. If one is in an advantageous position they will want to maintain the status quo; if one is in a less-fortunate social position, it would be in their best interest to support social change. *Ideology* is commonly thought of as a set of ideas, doctrines, and opinions that justifies the social structure (it can be thought of as a philosophy or *Weltanschauung*). Mannheim used the term *ideology* to characterize the ideas that support the status quo.

It attempts to control the future by reshaping the past. He used the word *utopia* to describe the complex web of ideas that favored social change. It is oriented toward the future. He believed that both sets of ideas advance historical interests (Farganis, 2000).

Mannheim made a distinction between two types of ideology, particular ideologies and total ideologies. *Particular ideologies* involve systems of knowledge that hide and distort the truth. These social systems may deliberately lie to the public, such as the tobacco industry which attempts to convince people that smoking is medically safe. *Total ideologies* are systems of knowledge tied to the social/historic place and time that one resides in (Adams and Sydie, 2001). Examples of total ideologies could be "conservative thought," and "bourgeois-liberal" (Mannheim, 1936). American contemporary examples of total ideologies would include "religious-right" and "liberal-left." Mannheim believed that the only way a researcher could understand the *total* conception of an ideology is to examine it sociologically. Mannheim's discussions on ideology are deeply tied to its Marxist origins, but it was not a term that Marx coined. It is generally acknowledged that Antoine Destutt, a French philosophe, was the first to use the word "ideology" in 1796 (Carlsnaes, 1981).

The *utopian mentality* is described by Mannheim as a state of mind that "is incongruous with the state of reality within which it occurs" (1936:192). He describes *utopia* as a type of ideology, but distinguished it by saying that it transcends the immediate situation (it departs from reality). Mannheim stated that, "every period in history has contained ideas transcending the existing order, but these did not function as utopias; they were rather the appropriate ideologies of this stage of existence . . ." (1936:193). Mannheim provided the bourgeoisie idea of

"freedom" as an example of utopian thinking because it called for the realization of a new social order. He described wishful thinking as the state of mind in which the imagination finds no satisfaction in existing reality and seeks refuge in wishfully constructed places and periods. Myths, fairy tales, other worldly promises provided by organized forms of religion are all expressions of what is lacking in actual life. Wish-fulfillment takes place through projection into time and/or space.

Mannheim (1936) explained that changes in the configuration of the Utopian mentality went through four stages. The first stage of the utopian mentality is the *Orgiastic chiliasm of the Anabaptists*. At this stage, the lower classes of the postmedieval period gradually become aware of their own social and political significance; but they were still far removed from "proletarian self-consciousness" (p. 212). The "spiritualization of politics," which may have begun during this point in history, more-or-less affected all the social currents of this time. *Chiliasm* joined forces with the active demands of the oppressed strata of society. A millennial kingdom stood against the church that made every effort to paralyse this union. Thomas Munzer and the *Anabaptists* transformed activistic movements of these social strata and attempted to change society.

The second stage, the *Liberal-Humanitarian Idea*, is characterized by the conception of utilizing rational thought to offset evil. This represents the importance of the *idea* in human mental development. The bourgeoisie and the intellectuals are instrumental at this stage. The utopia ideas of liberal humanitarianism also arose out of the conflict with the existing social order. Stage three, *The Conservative Idea*, has no real utopian value. It comes about in reaction to the previous liberal stage of development, maintaining the status quo, and embracing those things found in the past that still exist in the present highlight the values of this period. It is a period devoid of concern for new ideas. The conservative mentality has no predisposition toward theorizing. This is in accord with the fact that humans do not theorize about actual situations in which they live as long as they are well-adjusted to them. The conservative mentality, as such, has no utopia. It consists of habitual and often reflective orientations toward events.

The final stage of the utopian mentality is the *Socialist-Communist Utopia*. From the tradition of Marx, the goal is the overthrow of the existing social structure, and the creation of a classless society. The utopian element in socialism represents not merely a compromise, but also a new creation based on inner synthesis of the various forms of utopia that have arisen hitherto.

The influence of Lukacs' *History and Class Consciousness* is found throughout Mannheim's *Ideology and Utopia*. For example, both Mannheim and Lukacs stressed that forms of thought are relative to one's social position and that truth is conceived in largely pragmatic terms. Bailey (1994) provides a detail account of the similarities and differences between their two works.

As a final note, a few years after the publication of *Ideology and Utopia*, Mannheim began to lose faith in the ability of the sociology of knowledge to provide the basis of a scientific society (science of politics). Because of the events of 1933, Mannheim seemed to completely lose interest in the sociology of knowledge, and would instead concentrate on social planning and reconstruction.

Diagnosis of Our Time

As a sociologist, Mannheim was interested in social change, and with the advent of the Second World War, European societies were facing powerful social forces designed to alter the world forever. During such radical times the forces for peace and social stability also came to the forefront. In *Diagnosis of Our Time* (1943), a collection of essays that were written (except chapter five) in wartime, Mannheim presented a sociological analysis of the current time. The essays found in this book originated as lectures. For example, "Diagnosis of Our Time" was first presented at the conference of the Federal Union at Oxford, January, 1941; and "The Crisis in Valuation" was used during a series of lectures on "The War and the Future" beginning in January, 1942 (Mannheim, 1943).

In chapter one, "Diagnosis of Our Time," Mannheim believed that society had been taken ill, and questioned "how do we cure this disease?" He stated, "We are living in an age of transition from laissez-faire to a planned society. The planned society that will come may take one of two shapes: it will be ruled either by a minority in terms of a dictatorship or by a new form of government which, in spite of its increased power, will still be democratically controlled" (Mannheim, 1943:1). The feared dictatorship that Mannheim worried about was, of course, a reference to Hitler and the Nazi regime. The alternative form of power (which seems to exist today) would involve strong independent nations linked together by a common call to democracy. Mannheim predicted that if his diagnosis is proven true, diverse nations such as Germany, Russia, Italy, Britain, France, and the United States would share a common path toward a planned society. Although Mannheim goes on to state that his conclusion should not be treated as a prophecy, it became one nonetheless.

Mannheim predicted that specific "Social Techniques" would need to arise in order for any central government and its masses to agree on the future direction of their society. These techniques include a series of inventions and improvements in the fields of economics, politics, military, and other social issues. For example, Mannheim stated that a new military technique that allows for a greater concentration of power in the hands of few, armed with more powerful weapons, would replaced the armies of the past that were armed with simple rifles and guns. "A man with a rifle threatens only a few people, but a man with a bomb can threaten a thousand" (Mannheim, 1943:2). The implication here (and something that has been realized today) is that this change in military technique contributes a great deal to the probability of a minority rule (e.g., the Taliban's minority rule in Afghanistan).

Mannheim noted that social techniques themselves are neither good nor bad in themselves, it depends on the use that is made of them by human will and intelligence (Mannheim, 1943). The same is true for the idea of social planning. It is neither inherently good nor evil, it depends on the planners and the leaders. A planned society designed to provide education, health care, and social benefits is a "good" society; whereas a society ruled by a dictator who abuses his power at the expense of the masses is an "evil" society. A planned society is only as good as its leaders. The masses are seldom fully aware of the large picture, especially in terms of economics and politics. Mannheim used the example that only a few people were aware of the approaching chaos and the crises in the system of valuations. They noticed that medieval society was vanishing, but the disintegration was not yet completely apparent because of the Philosophy of Enlightenment. The secularized systems of Liberalism and Socialism were also developing. "No sooner had we made up our mind that the future would resolve itself into a struggle for supremacy between these two points of view than a new system of valuation emerged, that of universal Fascism. The basic attitude of the new outlook is so different from that of the previous systems that their internal differences seem almost to vanish" (Mannheim, 1943:12). In short, what is usually found in any one social environment are often very contradictory philosophies of life—religion, morality, politics, and economics.

Planned Social Reconstruction

The "English" Mannheim was academically focused on analyzing current society in hopes of reconstructing it for the better. He felt that, "no longer did it behoove the scholar to stay in his academic tower when all of civilization threatened to fall into the abyss of fascism" (Coser, 1977:437). In *Man and Society: In an Age of Reconstruction* (1940), Mannheim describes the world as one consumed by a growing crisis. In the German edition of *Man and Society*, Mannheim dedicated it to "My Masters and Pupils in Germany" (Mannheim, 1940). He was acknowledging those who had experienced in their own lives the tremendous age of transformation. Mannheim was now showing a commitment to *applied* sociology. He used his theory of rationality to describe the modern world and attempted to address specific problems.

Correcting the ills of society would be difficult. As Mannheim noted, "The main problem in the remaking of man is to transform his thought and action. Just as obstacles always arise in changing from one economic system to another, from one political opinion to another, so we meet with the same resistances when we have to think or act in a new way" (Mannheim, 1940:147). Since this problem exists at the large-scale macro level, the solution would be much more challenging. He was careful to point out that a planned society must not suppress individuals' criticism of society, for complete suppression would produce far more negative results. A society must not become so static that it loses its dynamic quality; and individual expressionism remains a stimulant to innovation and change. A rational approach to society should not involve complete control over irrational "charm." Mannheim viewed such things as creativity and spontaneity as charms of the irrational form.

Mannheim was convinced that society was passing into a new stage. "Unless we realize this, we shall lose the boundless opportunities which a co-ordination of social techniques would put into our hands" (Mannheim, 1940:265). To plan for freedom, a deliberate and skillful handling of these techniques must be employed. A planning authority must use empirical data in order to make rational-scientific decisions on judgments that affect society. Mannheim used taxation as a prime example of a technique that should be based on a logical system. Fair taxation remains an issue of debate today. Paying one's fair share is the "rational" procedure, but that is not always the reality, as the wealthy and the elites tend to find ways of avoiding paying a proportionate amount of tax compared to middle-class citizens.

Another specific example of Mannheim's *planned reconstruction* of society involves the economic policy of laissez-faire. He did not view laissez-faire as a viable alternative in the modern world because this type of system invites chaos. Mannheim argued that large, modern societies must have some economic controls and planning. It was no longer a choice between laissez-faire and planning, but a choice between rational and irrational forms of planning.

Rationalism and Irrationalism

Mannheim (1940) argues that a society in which the rational habits of thought are unevenly distributed is bound to be unstable and subject to chaos. It will most likely be characterized by disorganized and irrational

mass movements if no new techniques are developed to control the wave of irrationality. The old leaders will be declared incompetent and the masses will seek qualified leadership. The modern world attempts to present as many rational devices and courses of action as possible. The trick in proper rational leadership is to provide stability while simultaneously allowing for acceptable levels of irrational behavior.

The concepts of *rational* and *irrational* are indispensible in sociological analysis. Mannheim suggested that sociologists use the words "rational" and "irrational" in two forms, the "substantial" (thinking) and "functional" (action) rationality and irrationality.

Mannheim (1940) describes *substantial rationality* as a "thought which reveals intelligent insight into the inter-relations of events in a given situation. Thus the intelligent act of thought itself will be described as 'substantially rational'" (p. 53). On the other hand, everything else that is false or not an act of thought at all (e.g., drives, impulses, wishes, and feelings) are called *substantially irrational*. For a series of actions to be *functionally rational* it must be organized in such a way that they lead to a predetermined goal, are calculable, and efficient. Mannheim uses the "common soldier" as an example of someone who abides by a system (military) where he does not "think," he follows orders (actions). The monotony of training assures that there are no "freethinkers" among the ranks of the military; they are to act, not think. Societies held together by tradition are said to be rational because they are accountable for a series of actions. *Functional irrationality* can be viewed simply as "everything which breaks through and disrupts functional ordering" (Mannheim, 1940:54). Nonproductive behavior such as committing acts of violence would be an example of functionally irrational action. Critics of this idea can easily point to the fact that even violent behavior often serves a purpose that is not immediately evident.

The importance of making distinctions between the types of rationality lead Mannheim to this conclusion: "The more industrialized a society is and the more advanced its division of labour and organization, the greater will be the number of spheres of human activity which will be functionally rational and hence also calculable in advance" (Mannheim, 1940:55). Individuals in modern societies have far more opportunities to act purposely. This type of rational activity allows for the phenomenon of self-rationalization. *Self-rationalization* involves an individual's systematic control of her impulses; something which is critical if she hopes to have every action guided by rational, calculated behavior that leads to a predetermined goal.

One could argue, then, that the processes of rational and irrational behavior can be applied to both the societal planning level (macro), and the individual planning level (micro).

The Intelligentsia

Mannheim wished to explain the role of the elites, or *the intelligentsia*, within the planned society framework. Are the bearers of intellectual culture members of the aristocratic "society" of the elites, or are they members of the masses, considering the fact that they are dependent upon individual patronage? In *Ideology and Utopia* (1936) Mannheim explains that the *intelligentsia* are not a class (i.e., they have no common interests, they cannot form a separate party); they are in fact, *ideologues*. They are a "classless aggregation," or an "interstitial stratum," and they are not "superior" to others; but they are capable of doing something (action) that most members of other strata cannot—their academic training has equipped them to face

the problems of the day in several perspectives, and not just one, as most people are equipped (Mannheim, 1952). Mannheim emphasizes that the *intelligentsia* possess the *potential* ability to adopt a variety of perspectives toward any given social issue or phenomenon, that does not mean that they will always do so. After all, the intelligentsia are not devoid of class interest. Mannheim borrowed Alfred Weber's term "relatively unattached intelligentsia" to imply that intelligent people are still a part of everyday life and prone to self, as well as, class-interests.

The *intelligentsia* can assist in the reconstruction of society. They can help modify and create new social policies designed to assist the rational transformation of society. The *intelligentsia* also possess the unique ability to attach themselves to the various levels of the social strata. They can impress the elites with their knowledge and help implement change, and they can also identify with the lower economic classes because they are generally found among their economic ranks.

Sociology of Education

Perhaps the most important role of the *intelligentsia* is their ability to educate the next generation. Mannheim felt strongly about the role of education as a way of dealing with the crisis of transformation. He was influenced by Wilhelm Dilthey's view of education as the "planful activity of grown-ups to shape the mind of the younger generation . . ." (Mannheim, 1962:16). Mannheim explains that the word "education" "derives from *educare* which refers to the bringing-up of children physically and mentally. It is a word of such wide reference that at times it is, of necessity, vague" (1962:15). It was the responsibility of the community, the group of people in which the child lives, to raise the next generation. The community's cultural values, objects, and artifacts help to link the child with society. Education, then, serves a primary role of assimilating the next generation to the cultural norms of society. All the different groups that the child is exposed to, the family, the village, the nation, are all responsible for educating the next generation based on the prevailing standards and ideas.

In *An Introduction to the Sociology of Education* (1962) Mannheim suggests that, "In studying education we try to create scope for reflection; and, secondly, to establish the study of education as a coherent body of facts and principles so that the work done in schools and elsewhere should be built upon foundations which are as nearly scientific as possible" (p. 3). The study of education involves the coordinated efforts to provide answers to questions from a variety of subject areas. Consequently, Mannheim insisted that the field of education would be best served through an integrated approach. He felt that the present course of education had become too specialized.

To overcome overspecialization, Mannheim argues that both teachers and students must become more knowledgeable about sociology, because only sociology offers the comprehensive perspective of social events and issues. He felt that teachers should know the social worlds of their students in order to better teach them. Students at secondary schools and colleges and universities were urged to take an introductory level course in sociology so that they would be better prepared for college and social life. He insisted that both students and teachers must increase their level of "social awareness." Social awareness is critical if democracy is to survive. An integrative educational system would lead to integrative behavior among the educated. Because sociology emphasizes utilizing multiple perspectives in the study of social behavior, it is the most highly valued educational subject.

Mannheim (1962) concludes, "No educational activity or research is adequate in the present stage of consciousness unless it is conceived in terms of a sociology of education" (p. 159). The primary contribution of the sociological approach to the theory and history of education is that it draws attention to the fact that educational goals and techniques are socially constructed.

Relevancy

Mannheim made many significant lasting contributions to the field of sociology. The relevancy of his sociological work is evident in many social arenas. He is generally credited with creating a major subfield of sociology, namely, the *sociology of knowledge*. Mannheim freely admitted that his sociology of knowledge was at times inconsistent, and contradictory; but still, he shed much light on the subject. He attempted to show how social process is interrelated with thought, and although he was never truly able to come up with a complete synthesis, he did come close. Working within the historical framework, Mannheim demonstrated how ideologies originate from many sources; all of which are products of past and present behaviors. In contemporary society there are many examples that reflect cultural and socioeconomic differences. The wealthy are used to a certain privileged lifestyle that include many comforts not afforded to lower-class members: fine dining, expensive wine at dinner, luxury vacation trips, new automobiles, access to all the latest technological innovations, and so on. Raised in such an environment one begins to expect that lifestyle as the norm. Children from lower economic classes learn to value "simpler" comforts: cooling off at an open fire hydrant on a hot summer's day, picnics at a lake, going to a ballgame, and so forth. Expectations and reality are directly tied to one's socio-economic environment.

Mannheim's ideas on *ideology* and *utopia* are really contemporary versions of the study of social stability and social change. An ideology reflects the dominant feelings, attitudes, and beliefs of society that are commonly agreed upon. In contemporary American society there exist strong feelings of nationalism, a general support for the tenets of democracy, a thirst for material success, needs for psychological support, and the search for a meaningful existence while on Earth. These ideals represent a portion of our ideology. To protect its ideology, the American government has financially invested a great deal of the federal budget toward national defense. The strength and reach of America's ideology extends to nearly every point of the globe; and closely nearby will exist an American military presence. There also exists conflicting ideological perspectives than that of the prevailing one found in the United States. External threats to our ideology are confronted by combination of a strong American military and a dominance found in economic commerce and political power.

Utopian ideas are a type of ideology, but they transcend the immediate reality. The utopian perspective involves concepts such as myths, wishful thinking, and dreaming of a reality that is assumed to be better than the one found in the present situation. Marx's view of Communism is often described as utopian because the idea of a society in which all members are perceived as equal, more or less, and share equally in the scarce resources has been proven to be naive at best. People who are not happy with their present situations tend to be preoccupied with utopian ideas, the "what ifs" of social reconstructive behavior. "What if" I win the lottery? Many people have played the "What if I win the lottery" game with their friends and families. It almost seems reassuring to the "economically unsecured" individuals to dream of a world that would exist if they had the financial independence that comes with winning a large lotto payoff. That is why social research has shown that it is the economically lower-class persons that spend the largest amount of money on the lottery. The odds of winning are terrible. The wealthier persons realize that, and therefore spend less money on the lottery. Then again, the wealthy have less incentive to spend money on the lottery due to their relative financial security.

Mannheim's works on the *diagnosis of our time, planned social reconstruction*, and *rationalism and irrationalism* received less notoriety than his earlier works, but are nonetheless relevant to contemporary and future society. Having lived through both world wars and viewing up close and personal the devastating results of such vile warfare, Mannheim's focus on social reality was clearly influenced by the "climate of his times." Utopian ideas were merged with reality. He dreamed of a better society, but grounded his *utopian* ideals in a realistic *planned reconstruction*. A rational reconstruction of society based on a common call to democracy was Mannheim's vision of an international global community. Evidence of this logic exists throughout the countries of "The West." The nations of Europe have merged into the European Community (EC). The euro serves as the symbolic linkage among the diverse nations that make the parts of this greater whole. This common currency and relative ease of travel between the EC countries is only the beginning of the advantages to such a planned sociopolitical union. The logic behind this merger is realized immediately, especially in terms of the economic impact on the world's markets.

Planned reconstruction in the form of urban renewal has been going on in the

United States for decades. Unfortunately, simply planning the reconstruction of society does not guarantee its successful outcome. Many plans that had the best intentions have failed miserably, and our cities are filled with examples of urban decay. Political in-fighting often causes the "evils" of irrational thinking to take hold. In the Buffalo–Niagara region, home to the Peace Bridge that crosses into Canada, it was decided in the late 1990s that a new bridge was needed due to increased traffic. Politicians debated over the "type" of bridge to build. Should it be a twin-span bridge or some type of "signature" bridge with a cosmetic-tourist attraction style? The debate lingered, and four years later, there was still no decision made.

The fact is, all societies, democratic or authoritarian, utilize planned social reconstruction; it is the primary function of government. Mannheim hoped to show how his theory of planned reconstruction could benefit society. He is to be commended for attempting to demonstrate the applicability of theory to everyday social reality.

As the third millennium begins, the value of education is perhaps more evident than at any other time in history (although an argument could be made that the need for literate people during Industrialization was dependent on education and therefore this was the most critical point in history for education). Today, education is often promoted as the answer to all of society's problems. If there is a drug problem in society, then we need to educate people on the effects of taking drugs. If there are race-relation problems in society, then we need to educate people on the value of multiculturalism or assimilation. Undergraduate college students are being told by their professors that, in most academic majors, they most likely need to go to graduate school to find a job in that field. More women than men are graduating from college; this will be important in breaking down the "glass ceiling." In short, few people question the validity of a quality education.

The questions become: Are students receiving a quality education? Are there problems in the field of education? How should teachers teach, and how should students learn? It was issues such as these that Mannheim addressed in his *An Introduction to the Sociology of Education*. No one ever gave full credit to (then First-Lady) Hillary Clinton and her approach to raising a child, "It takes a village." One can trace this reference back to Mannheim and his approach to education—that it takes the community—because the child is raised in town, village or city. The student is a part of the greater community, and therefore it takes the entire community to properly raise and educate her. Mannheim felt that the school held a responsibility to the community in which it resides. "The school must take vitality and relevance from the life of the society in which it is set and it must regard itself as doing work which is unique in that it teaches children that it is reasonable and necessary for them to run counter to some of the currents that they feel in the society around about them" (Mannheim, 1962:25). In other words, the school must get involved with the immediate geographical area and demonstrate a leadership role in the community. I involve my students with the "service learning" technique. Students must do work in the community as volunteers in such various projects as: tutoring inner-city children, working at a gang-rehabilitation program, cleaning the environment, or working at a nursing home. The institution itself can give back to the community by investing funds directed toward social services (e.g., day-care programs), physical repairs (e.g., sidewalk repairs), gentrification programs, and a number of other options.

Mannheim discusses the fact that schools have locations, and buildings, with some sense of definiteness and permanence; and in fact, they can become landmarks themselves. He finds curious the idea that in some places of the world (during his lifetime)—in some schools in Australia, New Zealand, Canada, and elsewhere—there were "radio schools" where children learned from their own homes, forming groups separated by perhaps hundreds of miles, but united by a common program. He envisioned the "possibilities of the 'television school' [which would] force us to reconsider what a school is" (Mannheim, 1962:134). Mannheim seems to have predicted the advent of "Distance Learning" or "Instructional Television," an approach to education adopted by many colleges across the United States. In light of its relation to the radio schools of the past, one might ask, is this distance-learning approach to education progressive or reactionary? Distance learning is a hot topic area in the field of education, with many people who promote it, and many more people who fear losing their jobs (and the sense of community that the traditional school provides) because of it.

Mannheim also discussed the problem of the school curriculum. He argued that, "A curriculum should no longer be a collection of innumerable haphazard arrangements of the past nor the result of bargaining and compromise between departments whose only aim is to expand like imperialist Balkan states at the expense of their neighbors" (Mannheim, 1962:143). Schools at all levels are constantly revising their core curriculum, and Mannheim would surely be disappointed to see that the political nature of colleges is as bad as it ever was. In-fighting and disagreements are the norm among academic departments and individual colleges found in the system. Students are also weary of changes to the curriculum. They enter college in "catalog year" and can generally either abide by the rules of that curriculum, or go by the rules of the new one. Nearly all students who attend college for four years can expect at least one change in the curriculum.

The sociology of education proposed by Mannheim concluded with a call to activism among the educators. He stated, "In a bygone age the bankers were the respectable people. In a democratically planned society the teachers will have to play one of the noblest parts. This they can only achieve by regarding their work as a serious attempt to understand and to contribute to the life of the community" (Mannheim, 1962:155). Nearly all college professors understand the importance of contributing to the community. Decisions on tenure usually include teaching and scholarship, but also involve service to the community.

Karl Mannheim contributed a great deal to the fields of sociology and social thought. What might serve as a curious last impression of his relevancy is the fact that he contradicted himself and was at times inconsistent in his own thinking. We are all products of our times and environments. When his environment of Germany was rocked by the Nazi regime's coming to power in 1933, he was forced to flee for his life. His very belief in society and his views of mankind were changed in light of the chaos of war. This is surely something that everyone can relate to; the fact that in light of new evidence, or a drastic change in one's personal or social life, one comes to reevaluate current beliefs and path of life. Everyone will notice inconsistencies in their own behavior and ideas as their own life moves on. Perhaps at one point in time, one might have viewed labor unions in a negative way because they perceived them as little more than a third party interfering with the proper dialogue between employee and employer. Then later in life, the same person finds himself being victimized by management, and lacking the influence and power of a strong union to represent him in his cause, loses his job. The person may now wish he had a union to support him.

The institutional structure of society is not the only social aspect of human life that is subject to planned reconstruction. People reconstruct personal perspectives on their outlook of life due to new information. They reconstruct their vision of past events, and they are generally capable of reconstructing their present situations.

Talcott Parsons
(1902–1979)

Talcott Parsons, the youngest of five children, was born in 1902 in Colorado Springs, Colorado. He came from a religious family that valued education. His father was a Congregational minister and professor at Colorado College. His mother was a progressivist and a suffragist (Camic, 1991). When his father was dismissed by Colorado College, he moved the family to New York City, where he worked for a year at the YMCA in order to support his family. He would later become president of Marietta College in Ohio.

While in New York, Parsons spent his last two years of high school at the Horace Mann School for Boys. The school was designed to place exceptional students, who planned academic and professional careers, into top colleges. Talcott was accepted into Amherst College, which was earning a reputation as a leading liberal arts college in the nation. Amherst fostered an intellectual environment that was perfectly suited to Parsons. He began his career as a biologist and later became interested in economics and sociology. Parsons had a broad interest in the role of politics in society and had become sympathetic to the Russian Revolution and the British Labor Party (Camic, 1991). "In his junior year, a course on institutional economics completed his conversion from biology to social science" (Adams and Sydie, 2001:346). His early exposure to biology, with its focus on

the importance of the interdependence of an organism's parts, would tremendously influence his sociological outlook on social behavior (Wallace and Wolf, 1991).

Talcott Parsons (1902–1979) American sociologist, structural functionalist, and grand theorist.
Source: Harvard University News Office

235

He graduated from Amherst in 1924 and a year later entered the London School of Economics. At London, he studied with Bronislaw Malinowski, L. T. Hobhouse, and Morris Ginsberg. Parsons accepted Malinowski's view of societies as systems of interconnected parts. Malinowski believed that all individuals have psychological needs, and that societies provide ways of fulfilling these needs. A greater influence would come from L. T. Hobhouse, who incorporated social philosophy and various social institutions (e.g., religion, economics, politics) into a sociological framework. This prompted Parsons to accept the importance of institutional economics in the study of sociology. The following year he received a scholarship from the University of Heidelberg, where he first learned of the works of Max Weber, especially *The Protestant Ethic and the Spirit of Capitalism*. Weber had spent a large portion of his academic career at Heidelberg, but had passed away five years prior to Parsons' arrival. Weber's widow held meetings at her home on the works of her deceased husband Max; and Parsons regularly attended. As evidenced by his doctoral dissertation (1927), "The Concept of Capitalism in German Literature," Parsons was greatly influenced by Weber. While Parsons was working on his dissertation, he was teaching at Amherst.

Upon the completion of his dissertation, Parsons was appointed as a nonfaculty instructor of economics at Harvard University. In fact, from the period of 1927 to 1936, his rank was lower than that of an untenured assistant professor (Camic, 1991). Not only did his ascension through the ranks of academia start slowly (he was finally tenured in 1939), it was marked by switches to various departments at Harvard. Because of his strong interests in sociology, the obvious choice was to start Parsons in the sociology department. He was given a three-year position as a fac-ulty instructor and joined Carle Zimmerman and Pitirim Sorokin as inaugural faculty in the department of sociology. This was not a happy period for Parsons as he did not get along with Sorokin, the department chair. Sorokin allowed personal differences in academic styles between the two to jeopardize Parsons' career. Remembering the way that Colorado College wrongly dismissed his father years earlier, and upset over President Meiklejohn's firing by Amherst, Parsons' anxiety and bitterness toward the politics of academia were understandable (Adams and Sydie, 2001).

After leaving the sociology department, Parsons would work with Gordon Allport and Henry Murray, of the psychology department; and Clyde Kluckhohn, of the anthropology department, would join Parsons in 1945 to establish the Department of Social Relations. This department would become famous for its interdisciplinary collaboration in the behavioral sciences and served as a model for similar departments at other institutions. Parsons worked as chair of the department for its first ten years and remained active in the department until its dissolution in 1972. A year later, Parsons retired as Emeritus Professor. He continued teaching as a visiting professor at such universities as Pennsylvania, Rutgers, and UC Berkeley. Parsons died in May 1979.

During the early 1930s, Parsons conducted research on the sociology of medicine. In 1937, he published *The Structure of Social Action*. In this book, Parsons unifies a set of concepts of the determinants of human behavior into a "general theory of action." He would refine this original theory in his works *The Social System* and *Toward a General Theory of Action*, both published in 1951. *The Structure of Social Action* was well-received by the academic world, but again, Sorokin (an acclaimed theorist in his own right) was less than supportive of Parsons. Parsons gathered support among other professors on campus and was finally promoted to assistant professor in 1936, but still without tenure. Parsons began to receive offers from other colleges that truly appreciated his value to a sociology department specifically, and to the university in general. He stayed true to his course, worked hard, and rose above those who might try to hold him back. The academic world appreciated his work, even when those closest to him did not. In 1949 he was elected president of the American Sociological Association. Parsons published more than 150 books and articles. His publications in the 1950s and 1960s secured his reputation as a lasting giant in the field of sociology. His more significant publications beyond those already mentioned include: *Essays in Sociological Theory* (1949, 1954), *Working Papers in the Theory of Action* (1953), *Essays in Sociological Theory* (1954), *Family, Socialization and Interacting Process* (1955), *Structure and Process in Modern Societies* (1960), *Social Structure and Personality* (1964), *Societies* (1966), *Sociological Theory and Modern Society* (1967), and *Politics and Social Structure* (1969).

In light of the civil crisis in the United States during the 1960s, the seemingly conservative nature of Parsons' structural-functionalist approach seemed to lose its validity by the end of the decade. Variations of conflict theory and postmodernism began to dominate macrostructural analysis. However, functionalism has not disappeared. Among the many contributions that Parsons has left the field of sociology is his influence on graduate students, especially in his early years of teaching. His most famous student was Robert Merton, who is a highly acclaimed theorist in his own right. Merton adopted the functionalist approach but incorporated the reality of the dysfunctional aspects of social action and social systems. Kingsley Davis and Wilbert Moore

were two other early graduate students of Parsons who both contributed to the central themes of structural-functional theory. Parsons would have a positive influence on a number of significant students throughout his career.

Intellectual Influences

Parsons created one of the most dominant sociological theories, structural-functionalism. He knew from the time as a young student that his focus would be on macro issues, and because of this he showed little interest in microtheoretical approaches. Somewhat curiously, he ignored the works of Marx.

General Academic Influences

As an American who studied both in the United States and Europe, Parsons was exposed to a variety of ideas. His interest in macroanalysis would draw him closer to European perspectives, for they were the ones currently focused on macro issues. Parsons states in the introduction to *Essays in Sociological Theory* (1954), "Karl Mannheim once stated that one of the principal differences between European and American sociology lay in the concern of the Europeans, especially on the Continent, with the diagnosis of the larger social–political problems of their time, a trait of sociology which connected it with the philosophy of history, while American sociology had been much more concerned with specific and limited empirical studies of phases of our own contemporary society" (p. 12). There is little, or no, evidence to suggest that he was influenced by the emerging tidal wave of symbolic-interactionism and American pragmatism that were being spearheaded by Mead, Cooley, Blumer, Dewey, and others. In his first book, *The Structure of Social Action* (1937), there are only a few references to established American sociologists. (Among them: Merton, Homans, Sorokin, Veblen.) Years later, in *Essays in Sociological Theory* (1954), Parsons compliments Mead and Cooley for their insight about problems of intimate interaction; but he criticizes them for failing to develop a solid program of detailed research. However, it was at Amherst that this one-time natural scientist was converted to the social sciences in a philosophy course where he first heard of the works of such people as Cooley, Sumner, and Durkheim. Durkheim would go on to have a more significant influence on Parsons than either Cooley or Sumner. Parsons was also exposed to the works of Veblen in an economics course.

At the London School of Economics, Parsons studied with Hobhouse, one of the first leading authorities on the evolution of morality; with Ginsberg, an expert on the economic institutions of preliterate societies; and with Malinowski, who was a pioneer of structural-functional analysis in anthropology. Parsons' attempt to integrate all the social sciences into a science of human action is a direct influence from Malinowski. The two most important theorists that Parsons was exposed to were Max Weber and Emile Durkheim. In "Christianity and Modern Industrial Society" Mannheim (1963) explained how his ideas were "shaped as they were by European experience under the influences in particular of Max Weber and Durkheim" (p. 34).

Emile Durkheim

Parsons valued broad comparative studies and found that the two most important programs of research in the last generation were conducted by Max Weber and his comparative study of religion, and of Emile Durkheim in his study of suicide rates (Parsons, 1954). Parsons described Durkheim's study on sui-

cide as, "intermediate between the broad comparative method and what might be called the 'meticulous' ideal of operational procedure" (Parsons, 1954:16). He criticized Durkheim's crude attempt at statistical method, but marveled at his ingenuity in working out a variety of significant combinations of data. Durkheim's study revealed differences in suicide rates based on one's religion that held up internationally; differences between rates in armed forces and in the civil population of the same nations; and variations of rates as they relate to the business cycle. Durkheim demonstrated that theory supported by empirical data provided a sense of legitimacy in sociology's claim to be a science.

Durkheim is also famous for his study of the aboriginal Australian society (found in *The Elementary Forms of the Religious Life*, 1915) where he emphasized and documented the "pan-religionism" of most primitive societies. Primitive societies are permeated with religious sentiments and activities ruled by the prominence of religio-magical belief systems and the prevalence of ritual activities. Parsons (1966) noticed from Durkheim's study that *sacred* items, like kinship, were not only prominent, they were also elaborately structured. Parsons came to see the whole sociocultural system as linked to the kinship system. Furthermore, he interpreted the sacred significance of totems as being linked to the organization of clans as kinship units. "The totemic references are so formed as to symbolize the integration of the social unit within the total order of the human condition . . ." (Parsons, 1966:38). Thus, from Durkheim, Parsons came to see the validity of a structural, functioning system linked together through need (kinship) working toward the greater good of the whole society. Durkheim's ideas also influenced Parsons' *evolutionary theory*, to be discussed later in this chapter.

Max Weber

The greatest influence on Parsons would be Max Weber; he wrote his dissertation "Concept of Capitalism" based primarily on Weber's *The Protestant Ethic and the Spirit of Capitalism*. Parsons was exposed to Weber's works while he studied in Europe and he was the one who later translated Weber's works into English for American sociologists. Parsons felt that Marx's reductionist approach to explaining social structure and social action tied nearly exclusively to the economic realm as overly simplistic and not realistic. He favored Weber's unwillingness to simplify explanations of the complexity of the social system. "Weber essentially established certain broad differentiations of patterns of value-orientations, as we would now term them . . . . He showed how these . . . patterns 'corresponded' to the broad lines of differentiation of the social structures of the societies in which they had become institutionalized" (Parsons, 1954:15). Parsons felt that Weber's analysis marks the first major development in the systematic discrimination of major types of value systems and their link to social structures, since Toennies' famous distinction between *Gemeinschaft* and *Gesellschaft*.

Parsons learned of Weber's "problems of meaning" and of the "ideas" behind the cultural symbolic interpretation of "representations" (e.g., concepts of gods, totems, the supernatural), which form ultimate realities, but are not themselves such realities. Thus, behavior is influenced by the social system. Parsons (1966), agreeing with Weber, concluded that, since the social system is made up of the interaction of human individuals, interactions are affected by the social environment. Interactions are a part of the greater action system and need to be incorporated into any grand theory. As Weber before him, Parsons wanted to describe convincingly logical types of social relations applicable to all groups, small and large. Parsons would create a system (a general theory) of social action to include all its aspects. His first attempt at this systematized scheme appears in *The Structure of Social Action* (1937).

Concepts and Contributions

Parsons attempted to generate a grand theory of society that explains all social behavior, everywhere and throughout history, with a single model—structural functionalism or, more simply, functionalism. Naturally, his theory is often quite abstract, but it is nonetheless very elaborate. Although abstract theorizing is currently out of favor in contemporary sociology, Parsons' analysis of social systems and social action remains a must read for students of sociological theory.

Functionalism

Once the most dominant theoretical position in sociology, *functionalism* views society as having interrelated parts that contribute to the functioning of the whole system. For example, a university is a social system of many parts. There exists specific buildings and personnel to address a variety of tasks. Professors teach and conduct office hours within academic buildings; coaches teach and train athletes in athletic facilities; administrators conduct bureaucratic functions in their offices; maintenance workers have sheds and garages to store their equipment; and so on throughout the system. Many diverse people with specific functions contribute to the functioning whole of the system. Functionalism is a macrosociological theory because of its focus on large-scale social patterns and social systems. Functionalism has two basic assumptions:

1. **Interdependent parts** Society's social institutions (e.g., religion, politics, military, economics, education, sports and leisure, etc.) are all linked together; a change in one institution inevitably leads to changes in other parts. In order to function properly, the system will seek equilibrium, or stability. Equilibrium allows for a smooth running system.

2. **General Consensus on Values** Members of society must have a general agreement on issues of right and wrong, basic values, and morality issues, in order for the system to function properly. If people lose faith in society (the system) they will seek change. Rapid change within the system is something the functionalist approach is not geared to handle.

It would be incorrect to assume that the functionalist approach ignores social change. It explains social change as a result of such variables as population growth (due to migration and increased child birth rates) and increased technology (e.g., computers and the fact that they influence all social institutions). Functionalists are so aware of social change that they often wonder how society maintains itself at all. Parsons' functionalist theory is centered around a *homeostatic* model of society; that is, society's institutions attempt to restore themselves to a state of *equilibrium* (Kornblum, 1991). There is no implied implication of success, as the society's social system may not necessarily be properly built to deal with dramatic changes. Consequently, the social system is designed to minimize conflict. The government, with legitimate authority, is equipped to create and enforce laws in an attempt to maintain stability within the greater system.

The structural-functional approach of Parsons was a lifelong development and re-

flected the era in which he lived. The post-World War II era was highlighted by a great prosperity among many Americans. The 1950s was a decade of relative societal calm and an increasing economic boom. "Structural-functional sociology mirrored these real-life developments. It emphasized societal stability and the match between institutions like the economy, the family, the political system, and the value system" (Garner, 2000:312). The basic premise of functionalism—stability or equilibrium—is a sound one; after all, in order for any society to last a long time, there must be some sense of social order and interdependence among the various institutions. With its commitment to stable social institutions, the 1950s were the perfect years for Parsons' structural-functional theory to dominate sociological thought.

Parsons believed that sociological theory must utilize a limited number of important concepts that "adequately grasp" aspects of the objective external world. In this manner, these concepts correspond to concrete phenomena. As Turner (1978) explains Parsons' theoretical approach, "theory must, first of all, involve the development of concepts that abstract from empirical reality, in all its diversity and confusion, common analytical elements. In this way, concepts will isolate phenomena from their imbeddedness in the complex relations that go to make up social reality" (p. 40). Thus, Parsons' theoretical framework is grounded in empirical research of concepts created by the ideas and actions of those under study. In "The Role of Ideas in Social Action," Parsons (1954) explained that his theory of action is an analytical one, and any analysis of ideas must be conducted on an empirical, scientific basis. Parsons used his analytical concepts throughout his writings, and were first presented in his brilliant book, *The Structure of Social Action*.

Social Action Theory

In the preface to *The Structure of Social Action*, Parsons (1937) made clear his commitment to empirical research as a guiding force behind his theory. "This body of theory, the 'theory of social action' is not simply a group of concepts with their logical interrelations. It is a theory of empirical science the concepts of which refer to something beyond themselves . . . True scientific theory is not the product of idle 'speculation,' of spinning out the logical implications of assumptions, but of observation, reasoning and verification, starting with the facts and continually returning to the facts" (p. v). Parsons acknowledged the subjective nature of human activity and therefore wished to make it clear the distinction between the concepts of *action* and *behavior*. For Parsons, behavior seems to imply a mechanical response to stimuli, whereas *action* implies an active, inventive process (Ritzer, 2000). Parsons (1937) insisted that in order to qualify as an action theory, the subjective aspect of human activity cannot be ignored.

Parsons' *social action theory* begins with a biological-sociological conceptualization of the basic unit of study as the "unit act." "Just as the units of a mechanical system in the classical sense, particles, can be defined only in terms of their properties, mass, velocity, location in space, direction of motion etc., so the units of action systems also have certain basic properties without which it is not possible to conceive of the unit as 'existing' " (Parsons, 1949:43). Parsons then elaborated his meaning of the concept, an "act." He stated that an *act* involves the following criteria:

1. It implies an agent, an "actor."

2. For purposes of definition the act must have an "end," a future state of affairs toward which the process of action is oriented.

3. It must be initiated in a "situation" of which the trends of development differ in one or more important respects from the state of affairs to which the action is oriented, the end.

4. There exist alternative means to the end, in so far as the situation allows alternatives. In cases where there are no alternative choices (e.g., a prison inmate has few choices of action), a "normative orientation" of action will exist (Parsons, 1949:44).

Parsons (1937) explained that an act is always a process in time, and that the concept "end" always implies a future reference to a state (or situation) that does not exist yet. Actions consists of the structures and processes by which human beings form meaningful intentions and, more-or-less, successfully implement them in concrete situations (Parsons, 1966).

Social action is performed by an *actor*. The actor can be either an individual or a collectivity (Wallace and Wolf, 1991). Parsons' *theory of social action* involves four steps. First, Parsons believed that actors are *motivated* to action, especially toward a desired goal (e.g., college degree). Parsons referred to a "goal" as the time of the termination of the actor's action in which the desired "end" has been reached. Second, the actor must find the *means* to reach the desired goal (e.g., college fund created by the student's parents, student loans, personal computer). Next, the actor must deal with *conditions* that hinder reaching the goal (obstacles that impede a student from reaching a college degree might include proper intellect, time to study, personal crisis, etc.). And finally, the actor must work within the *social system* (e.g., administrative rules and procedures, taking tests, and all the required courses). Working within the social system is often quite challenging.

Social System

In *The Social System* (1951), Parsons attempted to further articulate his social action theory by integrating the role of structure and processes of social systems on the actor. "Analyzing social systems involves developing a system of concepts that, first of all, captures the systemic features of society at all its diverse levels and, second, points to the modes of articulation among personality systems, social systems, and cultural patterns" (Turner, 1978:46). Parsons described a system as a "complex unit of some kind with boundaries, within which the parts are connected, and within which something takes place" (Adams and Sydie, 2001:350). Systems have parts, or subsystems. The *social system* is an arrangement between parts/elements that exists over time, even while some elements change. For example, the social system of a university continues even as students, professors, and staff come and go. This reflects the reality of the organizational nature of social systems. Organizations, like social systems, are designed to function even as people leave; thus, people are replaceable, while the social system is capable of maintaining itself.

Not all social systems are designed equally, some are much more complex than others. Still, a number of general assumptions of the social system can be made:

1. Systems are made of order and the interdependence of parts.

2. The system, and all of the subsystems, strive for equilibrium (normal activity, self-maintaining order).

3. Systems are generally static, or move in a progressively deliberate matter.

4. A disruption in the "normal flow" of one subsystem can cause a disturbance throughout the whole system.

5. Systems have boundaries, which may involve actual physical space, or time and distance.

In Parsons' later years, he took an interest in the field of *sociobiology*, where he analyzed the differences between a biological system and a social system. He identified four such distinctions, which can be briefly summarized:

1. **Growth** Biologically, individuals grow to a certain point and then growth stops. A social system may be static for some time, and then grow, or it may continue to grow for an extended period of time.

2. **Spatial.** Biological systems are clearly bounded (e.g., one's internal organs are bounded within the physical body), while social system boundaries are not so fixed, or limited (e.g., United States territory extends beyond the mainland borders).

3. **Time.** A biological unit has limits, mortality; whereas a social unit can survive for centuries (e.g., nation states, organized religions).

4. **Parts/Subsystems.** A biological system is often very specialized and dependent on the proper functioning of the whole for its very survival. A major breakdown in one area can lead to the destruction of the unit (e.g., heart failure will lead to the death of the biological unit). Within social systems, parts are easily replaceable and the system moves on (e.g., sport franchises dissolve, but the league survives).

With these general descriptions of social systems, Parsons placed social actors into the mix. For Parsons (1951), a social system is a mode of organization of action elements relative to the persistence or ordered processes of change of the interactive patterns of a plurality of individual actors. The role of the actor allowed Parsons (1951) to create three distinct units within the social system. First, he reiterated that the most elementary unit of a social system is the "act." The act becomes a unit in a social system so far as it is part of a process of interaction between its author and other actors.

Second, Parsons stated that for the purpose of a more macroscopic analysis of social systems, it is convenient to make use of a higher order unit than an act; namely, the "status role." (Status refers to a structural position within the social system, while a role is what the actor does in such a position.) Since a social system is a system of processes of interaction between the actors, it is the structure of the relations between the actors (as involved in the interactive process), which is essentially the structure of the social system. The social system is a network of such interactive relationships. Each individual actor is involved in a plurality of such interactive relationships with one or more members of the social system. Therefore, it is the participation of an actor in patterned interactive relationships that plays the most significant unit (or role) of the social system. This participation is influenced by one's "location" in the relationship, which is referred to as one's "status" (e.g., a private in the armed forces has far-less status than a general). Parsons (1951) pointed out that the statuses and roles, or the status-role bundle, are not, in general, attributes of the actor, but are units of the social system; though possessing a given status may often be treated as an attribute.

The third unit of the social system is the actor himself. After all, it is the actor who holds a status, or performs a role, and therefore is always a significant unit. The actors themselves are a composite bundle of statuses and roles.

Parsons explained in the Preface of *The Social System* that within the frame of reference of action, such a conceptual scheme must focus on the delineation of the system of institutionalized roles and the motivational processes organized about them. With that in mind, Parsons introduced functional requisites for each of his categories of action (personal, social, cultural, and behavioral)—systems levels.

Systems Levels

Parsons argued that social systems must be structured in such a way as not to impede the action. The system must find a way to integrate and motivate the cultural diversity of actors into a certain kind of ordered system. The coordination of diverse actors stabilizes the system. Through the method of collaboration, actors are united in a solidary system with shared goals. Every organization depends on this voluntary sharing of action for the smooth operation of the social system. Parsons' general theory of action and his analysis on the structure of society allowed him to organize four distinct *systems levels*: social, cultural, personality, and behavioral.

1. **Social Systems.** The fundamental starting point in a discussion of systems levels is the concept of a *social system* of action—the interaction of individual actors. The process of interaction between actors, then, is seen as a type of social system. Of the four systems levels, *social systems* is the topic that Parsons wrote the most on. A social system consists of a plurality of individuals interacting with each other, where during the course of interaction, roles and rules are determined. People who properly perform their role and follow the rules of the system generally benefit from it. Rules, norms, and expectations help to maintain the system and allow for social action within a guiding framework. A fundamental property of social action is that it does not consist of only ad hoc

"responses" to particular situational "stimuli," but that the actor develops a system of "expectations" relative to the various objects of the situation. In other words, the actor learns to adapt to the system's needs in order to best secure her own role within the system.

2. **Personality Systems.** Actors do not always act in a manner that best fits the needs of the social system. Individual personality (defined as the organized system of orientation and motivation) traits often surface that may be structured only relative to their own need-dispositions and the probabilities of gratification or deprivation contingent on the various alternatives of action that may be available (note: this analysis possesses an Exchange Theory element to it). Parsons (1951) even stated that actors have a tendency to seek "optimization of gratification" (or as B. F. Skinner said, man is a pleasure-seeking animal).

3. **Cultural Systems.** Action that is not self-directed is generally in response to *cultural systems*. Humans usually act in such a way that their activity has "meaning." Recognizing "symbols" and behaving symbolically is a result of cultural influences that have value and meaning to the actor (e.g., nationalism, religious beliefs, sport team loyalty). Actors develop a normative aspect toward social action, to the point where cognitive orientation is readily taken for granted. Individuals create priority setting devices that are mandated by cultural expectations. For an example, when a ship is sinking out to sea, the American cultural expectation is "Women and children first" (for the lifeboats), indicating a survival bias against adult males and reflecting a cultural value of women and children. The *cultural system* develops as a result of the socialization process,

where actors have learned the differences between right and wrong, good and evil, and issues of morality; and therefore, they have learned how to act "properly" within the social system. Ritualistic practices become cultivated, institutionalized, and lead to societal priorities.

4. **Behavioral Systems.** Parsons did not write much about *behavioral systems*. They reflect the physical aspect of the human being. The idea is that at birth we are simply behavioral organisms; only as we develop as individuals do we gain a personal identity. This work set the tone for his future work on sociobiology. In *The System of Modern Sociology* (1971), Parsons discussed specifically the central nervous system and motor activity.

Parsons spoke of the importance of integrating all four systems through the socialization process. Actors need to internalize needs/values/cultural preferences in order to help maintain the social system (society). The civilizing process of socialization would control biological instincts and urges (superego versus id) so that they would not come to the forefront (e.g., learning not to belch in public, even though you may feel better, maintaining proper hygiene, etc.). Parsons believed that the socialization process allowed the *id* (pleasure-seeking, biological instincts) to properly develop into the *superego* (as a reflection of society). He believed that nearly all people do develop through this process. Individuals learn to channel their needs through socially approved means.

Pattern Variables

In an attempt to make his abstract theory of action more explicit, Parsons created/formulated *pattern variables* which categorize expectations and the structure of relationships. Pattern variables allow for comparison between relationships. Parsons had three primary thoughts in mind when developing these variables: They should be general enough to permit the comparison between relationships of different cultures; they should show relevance to action frames of reference; and, they should be relevant to all social systems. These five *pattern variables* were, "phrased in terms of polar dichotomies, which, depending upon the system under analysis, would allow for a rough, categorization of decisions by actors, the value orientations of culture, or the normative demands on status roles" (Turner, 1978:48). The five pattern variables are:

1. **Affectivity—Affective Neutrality** The issue here is whether the actor can expect an emotional component in the relationship/interaction situation. A newlywed couple should expect a great deal of affection in their relationship. The sales clerk–customer relationship is a neutral one because it is an objective sale situation.

2. **Diffuseness—specificity** This refers to a range of demands that may be expected in the relationship. If the relationship is a close one between actors then there exists a potential for a wide range of demands and expectations (diffusion). Close friends expect a lot from their friends; a minimum requirement would include loyalty and trust. The relationship between most students and their professors is generally limited to classroom situations and office hours (specific).

3. **Universalism—Particularism** This is an interesting dichotomy in that issues of morality often come into play. The primary concern is: Does the actor treat the other on the basis of a general norm, or does someone's particular relationship with the other cause particular action? In other words, is everyone being treated fairly, or are some given a priority status? Someone who works at the Department of Motor Vehicles is supposed to treat all customers equally. But, if she erases traffic violations for her boyfriend, she has acted in a particular fashion. If people are to meet a minimum requirement for a specific job (universalism) exceptions should not be made based on some other criteria (particularism).

4. **Achievement—Ascription** These pattern variables deal with quality of performance. Do actors interact with others on the basis of who they are (achievement: earning a college degree, paying one's "dues"), or on the basis on some inborn quality over which the actor has no control (ascribed: race, gender, age)? If someone is judged simply on ascribed characteristics the quality of performance evaluation is compromised.

5. **Collectivity—Self-Orientation** The issue here relates to the motivation of the actor. Is the behavior directed toward a particular person, or is action directed toward the collectivity? Self-interest action often overrides a commitment to the group or specific others.

These five dichotomies represent, for Parsons, the universal dilemmas of action. George Homans (see chapter thirteen) proposed that his five basic psychological propositions could explain all social behavior. The criticism is the same for both Parsons and Homans: Can these five categories of behavior really explain all courses of action?

AGIL (Functional Imperatives for All Action Systems)

The four functional imperatives for all social systems is the next major contribution of Talcott Parsons. They are meant to further articulate his pattern variables. In

1953, Parsons collaborated with Robert Bales and Edward Shils to publish *Working Papers in the Theory of Action*. It was in this book that the conception of functional imperatives would arise and come to dominate the general theory of action. Three years later, Parsons, along with Neil Smelser, published *Economy and Society* to further outline these imperatives (Turner, 1978). The experiments of Parsons and Bales (on leadership in small groups) were the source of the data used to develop their classification scheme. Wallace and Wolf (1991) indicate that the subjects used in these studies were almost all white, upper-middle- or upper-class, Protestant males; and therefore suggest that the data lack generalization credibility.

The functional imperatives are based on Parsons' hypothesis that process in any social system is subject to four independent functional imperatives, or "problems," which must be met adequately if equilibrium and/or continuing existence of the system is to be maintained (Parsons, 1956). In short, these are tasks that must be performed if the system, or subsystem, is to survive. Over the years, the function imperatives have come to be known simply as *AGIL*, based on the first letters of the four functional imperatives.

1. **Adaptation** Social systems must secure sufficient resources (e.g., raw materials, technology) from the environment and distribute them throughout the system. Thus, the system must show that it can adapt to changes in the system and/or environment. It may involve the manipulation of the environment (e.g., building dams to control flooding) in order to secure the desired resources that are deemed necessary in order to reach the goal(s) of the social system. The responsibility of this functional imperative rests with the economic institution of a society.

2. **Goal Attainment** The social system must first clearly establish its goal(s). This need may seem obvious, but goals do vary from one social system to the next. If it is a business, the primary goal is most likely to maximize profits. However, if the business is a nonprofit organization, its primary goal will be to collect resources in order to distribute them to those deemed worthy, or deserving. In order to reach the stated goals, the social system must mobilize resources and energies, while establishing and maintaining priorities. The primary responsibility for this function is the political system (government).

3. **Integration** This function involves the regulations and coordination of actors/subsystems within the greater social system in order to keep it functioning properly. The system must coordinate, adjust, and regulate relationships among the various subgroups. This is accomplished by the legal system, or the prevailing court of laws. In its attempt to reach goals, the system must often fight to maintain equilibrium and stability; consequently, it is important to keep deviance to a minimum.

4. **Latency** Latency involves two related problems: tension maintenance (internal tensions and strains of actors) and pattern maintenance (displaying "appropriate" behavior). The social system must find a way to keep actors sufficiently motivated to play their roles (maintaining pattern patterns) and it must provide mechanisms and safety valves for actors so that they can release pent-up frustrations and other strains that they feel. This function is accomplished through such social institutions as the family, religion, education, and sports.

In their book *Economy and Society* (1957), Parsons and Smelser utilize their functional imperatives on a variety of figures. One of them is the figure of "The Differentiated Subsystems of Society" (p. 53). Starting with the macrosocial system of society, Parsons and Smelser (as described above) projected the adaptation problem on the economy; the goal attainment problem on the polity; the integration problem on an integrative subsystem that includes the legal system; and the latency issue on such subsystems as religion and education. However, in another figure, "Functional Differentiation of the Economy as a System" (p. 44), Parsons and Smelser projected the functional imperatives on a subsystem of the society, the economy. Here, the adaptation problem is delegated to the capitalization and investment sector; the goal attainment problem on to the production subsystem, including distribution and sales; the integration problem is the responsibility of the organization subsystem; and latency is the responsibility of the economic commitments. What can be learned from this is that the use of functional imperatives can be used on whole systems (society) and subsystems (organizations and groups).

The Structure of Social Systems

In *The Social System* (1951), Parsons wrote many chapters describing a variety of topologies in the structure of social systems. In chapter four of *The Social System*, Parsons described how subsystems are brought together to constitute more complex social systems. The social system is, with respect to its structurally significant components, a differentiated system. It is differentiated in terms of roles and the distribution process. Parsons (1951) classifies six headings of internal differentiation of social systems:

Relational Institutions

1. The categorization of actor-units as objects

2. The classification of role-orientation

Regulative Institutions

3. The "economy" of instrumentally oriented relationships

4. The "economy" of expressively oriented relationships

Cultural Institutions

5. The cultural orientation system (patterning)

Relational and Regulative Institutions

6. The integrative structure (social relational integration)

In chapter five, Parsons applied a variation of his pattern variables to a typology of structures that he labeled "Principal Types of Social Structure." The four categories:

1. **Universalistic-Achievement Pattern** Value-patterns, and a reward system for those who comply properly to roles.

2. **Universalistic-Ascription Pattern** Emphasis on classificatory and achievements valued instrumentally.

3. **Participation-Achievement Pattern** Combines achievement values with particularism.

4. **Particularistic-Ascriptive Pattern** There remains the combination of particularism with ascription as the definition of a dominant social value-orientation pattern. The absence of the achievement of instrumental orientations and the structures associated with them.

Also found in chapter five, Parsons devised "Empirical Clusterings of the Structural Components of Social Systems." These four systems are summarized below:

1. **Kinship Systems** Kinship, in terms of the possible combinations of the general structural elements of social systems, has a high degree of specificity. The fact that kinship looms large in every known society means that a great many other logi-

cally possible permutations of the structural elements exists. Kinship is constituted on the basis of biological relatedness.

2. **Instrumental Achievement Structures and Stratifications** This form of clustering has much more variability and therefore, a considerable narrower range of logically permutations and combinations.

3. **Territoriality, Force, and the Integration of the Power System.** The ability of society to exist implies some type of political recognition, a variation of law and order for control and existence, and very often a strong military. (In current times, Israel is an example of a country that exists primarily because of military power and political recognition on the part of most nations of the world. The territory was drawn up after World War II. Many other people do not recognize Israel as a legitimate state.)

4. **Religion and Value-Integration.** Religion is one of the very core starting points on which a society is formed. Religion gathers "like-minded" people together and reinforces core beliefs and values. The threat of sanctions for wrong-doing coupled with the guilt levied against norm violation serve as power motivators to integrate people.

The amount of work that Parsons put into developing his social action theory and structural systems analysis is truly remarkable. He also provided some fascinating sociological insights to the study of organizations.

A Sociological Approach to the Theory of Organizations

In his *Structure and Process in Modern Societies* (1960), Parsons provided a sociological view of organizations. There is clear evidence of Weberian thought, especially his use of the concepts of bureaucracy and authority. Parsons defined the term "organization" as a "broad type of collectivity which has assumed a particularly important place in modern industrial societies—the type to which the term 'bureaucracy' is most often applied" (Parsons, 1960:16). He mentioned common examples of organizations as a governmental bureau or department, a business enterprise, a college, and a hospital. The study of an organization represents a part of the greater study of social structures and social systems. Families and kinships may be viewed as quasi-organizations; whereas informal work groups, cliques of friends, and so on, are not technically examples of organizations.

The "primacy of orientation to the attainment of a specific goal" is the defining characteristic of an organization which distinguishes it from other types of social systems (Parsons, 1960:17). "This criterion has implications for both the external relations and the internal structure of the system referred to here as an organization" (Parsons, 1960:17). Since the organizational structure of the social system is responsible for goal-attainment, any moves made by this part of the system will affect the other elements of the system. "An organization is a system which, as the attainment of its goal, 'produces' an identifiable something which can be utilized in some way by another system; that is, the output of the organizations, for some other system, an input" (Parsons, 1960:17). For example, a business may produce a product to sell to another business, which may in turn sell it in the marketplace, or use the product in some other phase of the production process.

Organizations, just as larger social systems, have some sort of describable structure. Organizations may be evaluated in terms of their functional parts and their role within the system, or form the "cultural-institutional" point of view which examines the values of the system. The values, in turn, often directly feedback onto the functions of the organizational elements. As Parsons stated, "The main point of reference for analyzing the structure of any social system is its value pattern. This defines the basic orientation of the system to the situation in which it operates; hence it guides the activities of participant individuals" (1960:20). The values of the organization must always reflect the values of the greater social system since the organization is always defined as a subsystem of a social system.

As mentioned earlier, the organization, in its pursuit of goal-attainment, may be confronted by external and internal obstacles. The mobilization of resources demonstrates both concerns. "The problem of mobilizing fluid resources concerns one major aspect of the external relations of the organization to the situation in which it operates. Once possessing control of the necessary resources, then, it must have a set of mechanisms by which these resources can be brought to bear on the actual process of goal-implementation in a changing situation" (Parsons, 1960:28). An organization must secure necessary resources (external relations) in order to produce its own product, and in addition, it may have "marketing" problems attempting to sell its own product (external relations). Even after securing the necessary resources the organization must have the proper mechanisms of implementation to get these resources in the hands of the right people (internal structure). Other internal structural concerns include: policy decisions, allocative decisions, and coordination decisions.

The problem of power is another topic covered by Parsons in his sociological analysis of organizations. Social systems and organizations are often very complex, and therefore their efficiency are often dependent on people who can "get things done."

"Subject to the over-all control of an institutionalized value system in the society and its subsystems, the central phenomenon of organization is the mobilization of *power* for the attainment of the goals of the organization. The value system *legitimizes* the organization's goal, but it is only through power that its achievement can be made effective" (Parsons, 1960:41). In this sense then, power is the ability to mobilize resources in the interest of attaining the system's goal.

To conclude this subsection of Parsons' sociological work on organizations, it is fitting, and should not be surprising to the reader, that Parsons devised a classification system of the "Types of Organizations." A brief review is provided below:

1. **Organizations oriented to economic production.** This category is referring to business and production. Production is not limited to physical production (e.g., manufacturing), but applies to other areas of production as well (e.g., what contemporary society commonly refers to as the "service industry"—teaching, data entry, etc.).

2. **Organizations oriented to political goals.** This category of organization refers mostly to the government, and the allocation of power in the society. Parsons included the banking industry because of its purchasing power through the creation of "credit."

3. **Integrative organizations.** These organizations contribute primarily to ease conflicts between subsystems. The legal profession and courts of law are classed here. Political parties responsible for mobilizing support for candidates, and those who belong to political "interest groups," belong here as well.

4. **Pattern-maintenance organizations.** These are the organizations responsible for informing others of the basic moral beliefs and values of the social system.

The obvious examples here include religion and education. Parsons also added kinship groups along with an interesting choice of the arts.

As usual, Parsons justified his organizational classification scheme as something necessary in order to more easily understand the greater social system; and he added that these categories (as with all of his classification systems) can be further divided into other lower subsystems.

Social Change and Evolutionary Theory

Organizations and social systems seek to normalize behavior. Structural-functionalists warn that a disturbance in one element of the social system, will cause disruptions throughout the system. It has been argued that functionalists, such as Parsons, ignore social change, and in fact, they fail to address how change occurs. This is not true. Parsons did believe that societies seek to maintain equilibrium through the process of socialization and a certain level of force, and actors are expected to play their roles correctly. Inevitably, problems or new situations (e.g., technological advancements) arise that dramatically affect the social system. At the time Parsons wrote *The Social System* (1951), he did not think a theory of the processes of change of social systems was possible; but, he did imply that the analysis of social systems must be done in terms of the theory of social action. By the end of Parsons' career he began to spend a great deal of time on the issue of social change. In his book *Societies* (1966), Parsons outlined an evolutionary dimension to explain differences among societies. There is a strong biological component to his evolutionary explanation of social change.

First, how does *social change* occur? As previously mentioned, the social system seeks equilibrium. Equilibrium represents the ideal state of a system. The social system prefers to move at a deliberate pace, and can generally absorb small amounts of change that affect one part of the system by making adjustments to the other parts. There are many sources of change: excesses in either information or energy in the exchange among action systems; excesses of motivation; and, insufficient supply of either energy or information (Turner, 1978). These threats, or strain, on the social system can cause both external and internal adjustments. Strain is in contrast to equilibrium, it is a tendency to disequilibrium. But, strain does not automatically lead to radical change in the system. Change is just one possible outcome of strain. Another outcome could be the restoration of existing relationships. For Parsons, it depended on the success of the restoration process. Restoration processes could include such options as social control and assuring that safety valves are available to those feeling the strain.

Vested interests is another phenomenon that may cause social change. This derives from the nature of the processes of equilibrium in a boundary-maintenance function so far as it impinges on institutionalized patterns of action and relationships. Parsons (1951) believed that social change is never just an "alteration of pattern," but alteration by the overcoming of resistance. There is one apparent exception to this. Certain processes of empirical change are themselves institutionalized (e.g., scientific investigation and progress). Parsons (1951) concluded that it takes a plurality of events to cause social change. History has shown that human societies continually create new social institutions. Parsons believed that the processes and activities that lead to change can be identified and described in his *evolutionary* framework.

There are strong influences from Auguste Comte (law of three stages), Emile Durkheim (mechanical and organic societies), and Herbert Spencer (cultural evolution) on Parsons' *evolutionary theory*. Spencer had suggested that as the size of the system increases so too does its complexity, which in turn leads to the necessity of a division of labor, or differentiation. For Parsons, the idea of differentiation became critical in the evolutionary process. His evolutionary theory incorporated both processes and structures. Parsons' model of evolution had the following steps:

1. **Differentiation.** The system is made up of many subsystems, a change in one subsystem can potentially affect many other parts. Because of the ever-evolving differentiation, many new parts develop to take on roles once held by a different part (e.g., the creation of marketing and human resources departments with functions that once belonged to the executive board of the company). The system must keep up with external changes (e.g., in the market, or new legal restrictions), and internal structural changes (e.g., increased productivity, larger payroll, etc.); in short, it must show an *adaptive upgrading* quality. The system must change with the environment.

2. **Integration** This second step involves the process of inclusion. The system must find a way to operate with all the changes in the structure (differentiation). Mobilization and coordination become critical issues. As Ritzer (2000) explains, "A society undergoing evolution must move from a system of ascription to one of achievement. A wider array of skills and abilities is needed to handle the more diffuse subsystems. The generalized abilities of people must be freed from their ascriptive bonds so that they can be utilized by society" (p. 452). The growing complexity of the social system demands a larger supply of people that are motivated to contribute to the system.

3. **Value Generalization** In order for society itself to survive, it must adapt the general value system in order to involve all new members and structures of the system. A value system that attempts to meet the needs of all, becomes far more general and abstract. The move to generalized norms often offends specific smaller groups (those with a vested interest) and this in turn can lead to resistance of the new emerging norms, causing strain, and leading to further social change that the system must somehow differentiate and then integrate (Parsons, 1966).

Parsons (1966) traced the histories of many primitive societies (e.g., the Aboriginal Australians), and conducted cross-cultural studies (e.g., China, India, the Islamic empire, and Rome) in an attempt to document the organic components involved in *all* types of human sociocultural behavior. He developed stages in the evolution of societies: primitive, intermediate, and modern. He did all this (and more) in an attempt to further articulate his evolutionary theory.

Race, Class, and Gender

Throughout his works Parsons examined the effect of various demographic variables on social action. These issues are important to discuss because it shows that Parsons did not ignore the actor in the social system; and yet, he managed to always place the role of actors in terms of the social system.

1. **Race** Parsons revealed an academic and personal interest in race relations since his college-age interest in the Russian Revolution. In 1942, he published an article on fascism and Nazism, where he referred to racial antagonisms as sources of strain within a social system (Adams and Sydie, 2001). During the 1960s, race issues

were of primary concern for most Americans. This was especially true for sociologists. Parsons co-edited with Kenneth B. Clark *The Negro American* (1965), and in his Introduction, "Why 'Freedom Now,' Not Yesterday,?" Parsons explained why the racial issue was emerging so dramatically in the 1960s. "Its emergence now as a principal concern is in part at least the result of the nation's having cleared away its preoccupations with the Second World War and its aftermath, which included Korea and McCarthyism, and the end to the political quietism characteristic of the Eisenhower administration" (p. xxiii). Supreme Court decisions, boycotts, and mass demonstrations paved the way for heightened racial confrontations. Applying his evolutionary model, Parsons suggested that the survival of the system was dependent on a new level of institutionalization of values of equality. Mobilization and coordination of equality values remains unsolved today; as many people still suffer from racial inequality. In 1968, Parsons published an article in which he traced the origin of racial tensions in America to the relationship between Europeans and Africans and the instituting of slavery. The Europeans of the slave trade era possessed a superior social system spearheaded by advanced technologies (e.g., oceangoing ships and navigational instruments and skills) and marketing institutions, which made them far more powerful than the Africans (Kornblum, 1991). The imperialistic Europeans justified the social structure of slavery because slaves served a valuable function of building the new land.

2. **Class** Parsons saw class inequality as a result of the failure of a social system to properly integrate all members within the system. Stratification was seen as in-

evitable, especially given the reality of the scarcity of resources in any given society. Class inequality is a source of strain on society. From a functionalist perspective, inequality is not only inevitable, it is desirable (to a point) because it motivates people to work hard within the system if they hope to receive the rewards (generally) given to those who abide by the rules and play their roles correctly. Parsons was aware of the power elite theory, but questioned its validity. The basic premise of the power elite theory is that a limited number of very powerful people control the primary resources of society and work secretly behind the scenes to maintain the advantageous position. Parsons (1960) believed that since the power elite act in secrecy, they could not be observed or studied; therefore, the theory could neither be proved or disproved.

3. **Gender** Parsons traced differences in gender roles to the family. He argued that throughout time it was necessary for women to have babies in order for the species to survive. It was functional, then, for women to raise the children while the father became the provider. He correctly predicted that as greater numbers of women seek careers outside the family, the very structure of the family would be altered (Adams and Sydie, 2001). Any contemporary sociology course on the family will confirm the wide variety of family types today; in fact, the "traditional" family (which consists of the breadwinner father, the stay-at-home housewife, and the dependent children all living together in a single dwelling) constitutes a small percentage of family structures in American society. Parsons (1955) believed that the family serves as the primary agent of gender so-

cialization. In a highly differentiated society, the family must find a way to function (integrate itself) successfully within the greater social system. Its primary function today is to help develop the human personality, because personality is not "born," it is "made." Thus, anyone, male or female, with proper socialization and proper training of the social system, can learn to adapt and survive.

Relevancy

Talcott Parsons made tremendous contributions to the field of sociology. He revolutionized a way of thinking by formulating a grand theory, structural functionalism. His functionalist approach was centered around his social action theory and his analysis of social systems. His one-time dominant theoretical perspective has been criticized on many fronts. Criticisms of Parsons are generally critiques of functionalism itself. The primary criticism of Parsons' functionalism is that it fails to explain social change. As described in this chapter, Parsons did in fact attempt to explain social change (his theory of evolution), but his explanation was always in the context of strain on the system and the corresponding attempt to reach equilibrium. Emphasis of the social system is on the need for integration among the parts of society and the various actors. Consequently, a more legitimate criticism of Parsons' functionalistic theory is its conservative nature.

Because of the conservative nature of his theories, Parsons often ignored issues of conflict and power. Conflict is a cause of strain that must be stabilized so that the system can move along in a state of equilibrium. Parsons was aware of conflict, but failed to address it in any significant degree in his theories. The primary reason why he failed to explain conflict is because he did not elaborate on the role of power and how power

positions often dictate behavior. The reason many people perform their role, and act as they do, is not because it is functional to them, but because they find themselves on the short end of a power relationship. Parsons (1951) did acknowledge that one's participation in the social system is influenced by one's "location" in the relationship. In his article, "A Sociological Approach to the Theory of Organizations II" (1956), Parsons discussed what can be achieved with power, but he does not articulate what constitutes power, nor did he discuss power relationships. Parsons seemed to treat conflict and power as "givens" of normal life that do not need further examination. Even toward the end of his life, when he was surely aware of the criticisms of such theoretical shortcomings, Parsons failed to examine more closely these vital important variables of human action. In order to be a complete theory, functionalism needs to integrate the role of power and the effects and types of social conflict.

Parsons admired Weber and Durkheim for using empirical data to support their theories. Unfortunately, Parsons failed to produce a great empirical work of his own and, as a result, the validity of his theories come in question. "Parsons' strategy for theory building has revolved around the assumption that his system of concepts can generate testable systems of propositions that account for events in the empirical world. But if such a conceptual system inspires illegitimate teleologies and tautologous propositions, then its utility as a strategy for building sociological theory can be called into question" (Turner, 1978:62). Furthermore, his critics argue that structures and processes cannot be explained theoretically in terms of their functions to the system, they must have independent empirical validation. Parsons did not worry about such complaints as he indicated that there must be specialists in every field; some are specialists in research, he considered himself a specialist in theory. His preoccupation with developing sociological concepts in order to study human action reveals his commitment to social theory.

Parsons revealed a great deal of professionalism and "class" when he paid tribute to Pitirim Sorokin (a former department chair and harsh critic of Parsons) as a distinguished elder statesman of sociology. In "Christianity and Modern Industrial Society" (1963) Parsons stated, "In the sociological profession today Professor Sorokin and the present author are probably defined predominantly as antagonists who have taken widely different views on a variety of subjects" (p. 33). Parsons managed to disagree with Sorokin and at the same time compliment him—an often rare and refreshing trait in the competitive world of academia.

Despite the criticism of his grand theory, many elements of Parsons' theories remain relevant today, and most likely will remain relevant for some time to come. Although *functionalism* itself has come under attack from a variety of critics, it remains as one of the "Big Three" theories in sociology (along with Conflict Theory and Symbolic Interactionism). There are numerous reasons for its staying power, as many of the elements of functionalism are hard to ignore or dismiss. Society and social systems are comprised of interdependent parts, a major failure or breakdown in one part can cause harm to the entire system. Thus, for the sake of self-containment, the system will always seek equilibrium. The collapse of energy giant Enron (the one-time seventh-largest U.S. company, filed for Chapter 11 protection from creditors in December 2001) caused rippling effects throughout the financial industry. Many people lost their jobs, financial investors lost their life savings, and the charities that were dependent on Enron's contri-

butions were forced to close many of their social programs. All of the people hurt by this situation understand the value of maintaining a sense of equilibrium. An additional point that should be clear here is the fact that the financial system of the United States did not collapse, as other companies moved in on Enron's failure to help maintain the energy needs of Americans. Thus, the greater social system (society) reacted to Enron's collapse in an effort to maintain equilibrium.

The tragic events of September 11, 2001, illustrate clearly the systems model as articulated by Parsons. The terrorist attacks threatened the very core of the social system found in the United States. Upset with the American creeds of democracy, freedom of choice, and the right to pursue psychic and material happiness, terrorists attacked symbols of American wealth and political dominance (the World Trade Center twin towers and the Pentagon). The attacks on our social system affected far more than our collective psyches (let alone the loss of thousands of innocent lives); the ripple effect caused great changes in both the internal structure of America and external relationships with foreign nations. Among the internal social institutions affected by the terrorist attacks were the economic structure (the stock market nearly crashed, and trading had to be temporarily stopped until some sort of stability occurred); air travel had halted and new check-in policies were developed; the political system created new laws and created the Homeland Security Office; and the family structure was affected in that children needed an explanation for the attacks and had to be assured that they were safe. President George W. Bush took immediate action directed at the outside world (external needs). He declared that terrorist attacks will not go unpunished and declared "war" on terrorism. Furthermore, he made it very clear to every nation of the world, "You are either with us, or you are against us." Clearly, the whole social system of the United States was affected by the acts of terrorism displayed on "9–11"—as it is commonly called.

The second guiding principle of functionalism is the principle of a general consensus on values. It is this premise that upsets so many critics of functionalism, for they feel it reflects an intolerance to differing viewpoints, and is therefore conservative and supports the status quo. The truth remains, however, that in order for any social system (society, organization, family, or a love-relationship between two people) to remain intact and run smoothly, there *must* be some commitment toward general values, issues of morality, and goals of the relationship. Couples "drift" apart when they no longer share a commitment to the relationship; employees leave an organization when they realize that their attitudes and goals differ from those of the employer; and society risks dissolution when disturbances (internal conflicts, riots, protests, and civil war) cause such strain that the system itself is threatened. Incorporating necessary changes in the value system are often compromised by vested interest groups. For example, the legal system of the civil society of America giving women the right to control their own bodies by making abortion legal. Those who believe in democracy and freedom of choice support a value system that allows for personal choice in such "controversial" issues as abortion. Certain interest groups (usually religious-based) disagree with such freedoms and have attempted to force their value system onto the legal system of the United States. In short, there will *never* be a complete agreement on the values of any social system (micro or macro levels) and therefore critics of functionalism may believe they "won" this battle. On the other hand, functionalists will argue that a "general" agreement on most issues of right and wrong (e.g., unprovoked murder is wrong) does, and must, exist in order for the social system to survive.

Like most of the social thinkers that preceded him, Parsons had a generally positive view of the world and felt that societies evolve. The process of societal *evolution* and how fast society evolves is subject to many variables. One such variable is technology. Technological advancements change many aspects of everyday life, and yet the system attempts to adapt (in an attempt to reach equilibrium) and in many cases to incorporate such changes. In the past few years it has become commonplace for people to possess cell phones. Cell phone conversations in public places threaten the very core of common manners and proper behavior, as some people talk loudly without any consideration of those around them in very inappropriate places (e.g., restaurants, movie theaters, in the car, bathroom stalls, and even in the classroom). Cell phones were devised to help people in emergencies, but they are now being used by such people as joggers as they run and customers while they shop for groceries.

Among the most lasting relevant contributions of Parsons is his *sociological analysis of organizations*. Nearly all the activities we engage in are influenced by organizations. The books that we read are prepared by organizations; the products we consume are influenced by marketing organizations; social services are organizationally designed; newspapers and news programs discuss the organizational setting; most people work for organizations, and all universities are examples of organizations. Just think of the number of organizations any one person may come into contact with and utilize on a daily basis: radio and television stations, computers and computer game manufacturers, bus and taxicab services, phone service, health and fitness centers, freeways, movie theaters, and one's employer. All of these organizations have goals, means of integrating personnel, and mobilization efforts to reach their goals. When the organization runs smoothly, all people involved are happy. Think of how frustrating it is when someone gets up early in the morning to work out at a fitness center and then finds out that it is closed because the employee who was supposed to open the gym is late to work. This employee may be late because of some other organizational interference (e.g., the brand-new alarm clock that was purchased possessed a manufacturing defect and did not sound the alarm).

The role of organizations in society is ever expanding. Among the implications of this growth are: changes in society and the decreasing role of individual decision making. This results in an asymmetric relationship between corporate actors and individuals. This often leaves many individuals with feelings of alienation, anomie, and powerlessness. An organization can be viewed as a collection of jobs or social positions acting collectively as a unit (Ermann and Lundman, 1996). An organization is a social unit deliberately constructed to seek predetermined goals. Organizations generally move on even as individuals come and go. This fact underscores the idea that people are replaceable; that is, as one person leaves an organization, a replacement is trained to take over that position. Except for unusual circumstances, employees regularly come and go while the organization continues in an orderly fashion. Thus, when studying organizations, we must realize that, for the most part, people are replaceable and structures exist independently from persons.

Organizations play an important role within communities and they often have both negative and positive effects. On the positive side, organizations provide jobs, and when people are employed, the community is stronger; organizations provide social services (e.g., hospitals, police, churches, schools) that directly benefit the community; and organizations are active participants in the development and implementation of governmental or public policy; and when organizations cooperate and work with each other, many positive outcomes are possible. Unfortunately, organizations may have many negative effects in the community, that include the following: Some organizations (especially economic corporations) will abandon the community and relocate the business, this can be financially damaging to the community; the simple threat of relocation may lead the community to offering "sweetheart" deals to entice the organization to stay (e.g., tax breaks); and organizations are often the cause of many quality-of-life hazards—pollution, noise, traffic, depletion of natural resources, and a variety of disasters (e.g., toxic explosions). It should be clear that organizations play a huge role in society, and this fact underscores its importance to sociology.

Parsons is among the most recent of the "classical" social thinkers to be analyzed in this book. It is difficult to ascertain his true place in the history of sociological thought. He has been crowned as a "dominant figure" in sociology and then later treated as a "whipping boy" for all that is wrong with (functional) theory. It is too soon to determine his true place among the giants of sociology, but it is this author's contention that an interest in Parsons' work will be revitalized and that his place and role as a major figure in sociology will be realized.

13

George Homans
(1910–1989)

On August 11, 1910, George Caspar Homans was born in Boston to a wealthy Brahmin-style family. In his autobiography Homans (1984) describes the Brahmins as gentlemen and ladies who were conscious of their class standing. The Homanses resided at 164 Beacon Street—the better and "water" side of the street because it looked out over the Charles River basin—in the Back Bay district of Boston (Homans, 1984). The house belonged to his paternal grandmother, Helen Amory (Perkins) Homans.

George was the eldest of four children. He was followed by two sisters, Fanny and Helen, and a younger brother named Bobby. As with most families, the Homans children engaged in their fair share of verbal arguments at the dinner table and one time Fanny threw a lemon meringue pie in George's face. Their mother left the table disgusted (Homans, 1984).

George's grandparents were all a part of the upper class. Both of his grandfathers had died before George was born; his grandmother Adams died when he was one, and his grandmother Homans died when he was fourteen. Homans's mother, Abigail, was a niece of Henry Adams.

The Homans lineage consisted of three consecutive generations of successful med-

George Homans (1910–1989) American social thinker and founder of Social Exchange Theory.

ical surgeons, all residing in Boston, and all with the first name of John. It was a surprise to most when young George, as the eldest son, was not also named John. Interestingly, his mother had determined shortly after giving birth to her son that he was not the sort of person to make a good doctor. In a letter to his uncle Henry, Abigail wrote,

> His (George) nose has already assumed alarming proportions, while his head is a mass of lumps which will make him look very distinguished when as a bald old gentleman of eighty odd, he sits upon the bench dispensing justice!!! . . . He is to be named George Caspar for my brother, as the Homans family did not consider that I was the sort of person to produce a good doctor, and so reserved the name (John) for my brother-in-law Jack's benefit (Homans, 1984:1).

George was tormented by this name as a child because of a then-popular comic strip that had as its nonhero a spineless character called Caspar Milquetoast.

Abigail Homans served as president of the Good Government Association or "Goo-Goos" for a number of years. George's feelings toward his mother were mixed. He did not have the same level of emotional attachment to his mother as he had to his father. Homans states in his *Autobiography*, "She [his mother] had great qualities, but was not good all the way through as my father was" (1984:30). Abigail lived a long life and died at the age of ninety-five.

George greatly admired his father, Robert, and looked up to him with much pride. "My father was the best man I have ever known; he not only had an excellent mind but was morally good" (Homans, 1984:26). Robert Homans was the eldest of six children. Born in Boston, he went to Harvard as many of his relatives had done. Robert was eventually elected president of Harvard Law School and received considerable academic recognition. He later opened his own successful law firm—Hill, Barlow, and Homans.

Robert was a wonderful family man and a good athlete, something George would never be. Robert played baseball and tennis and was an excellent horseman, as was Abigail a wonderful horsewoman. Robert Homans despised the idea of a "horseless carriage" and never took the time to learn to drive a car; Abigail did all the driving in the family. George was a healthy young man, but small and weak. He knew that participation in certain sports, like football, would be out of the question, so in school he participated in cross-country running. With his compact size, George was adequate as a coxswain of the rowing crew. This worked out quite nicely, as rowing was a major sport at both of Homans' secondary schools. His father provided unconditional support and encouraged George to work hard in school and get good grades. Throughout George's accomplishments as a naval officer, a newspaper man, and finally, a scholar, Robert was always there as a source of support and inspiration (Homans, 1984). Robert died of cancer at the age of sixty-one.

George Homans would always value academics, and he took advantage of the outstanding library in his family home—something that can only happen in an financially privileged household. "Much of what I learned from books I learned not at school but at home, from our excellent library" (Homans, 1984:46). He also benefited from the top private schools in Boston until he eventually entered Harvard, following in the footsteps of previous generations of Homans (Homans, 1984). In September 1928, George entered the freshman class. As an English Literature major, he learned from Bernard DeVoto, who was his English instructor and tutor. Homans credited DeVoto as the biggest single influence on his intellectual life. Homans was particularly indebted to DeVoto for introducing him to Professor Lawrence Joseph Henderson.

DeVoto and Henderson were friends and it was Henderson who introduced DeVoto to sociology. In turn, it was DeVoto who introduced Homans to sociology. George then read Vilfredo Pareto and found him most agreeable (Homans, 1962).

George earned his bachelor's degree from Harvard in 1932, where he studied English literature. Homans did not study sociology as an undergraduate; "It never so much as occurred to me, although President Lowell had brought Professor Pitirim Sorokin to Harvard to found the Sociology Department in the very year I entered as a freshman" (Homans, 1984:63). Lacking a theoretical background in sociology, Homans (1984) acknowledged that he learned much practical sociology and became interested in the discipline by living in an environment in which people were highly conscious of social relations. He explained, this was especially true for microsociologists who were concerned with the face-to-face interactions of persons, compared to macrosociologists who were concerned with the characteristics of whole societies. "For us microsociologists the laws of sociology are the laws of snobbery, and an undergraduate of my background found Harvard to a high degree 'socially conscious'—in the bad sense of the phrase" (Homans, 1984:9).

Homans was fully aware of the snobbery associated with Harvard. The core of Homans' later theory on the structure of small groups was typified by his discussion of "final clubs"—fraternities and sororities (Wallace and Wolf, 1999). Membership to "final clubs" depended on a mixture of qualities—personal as well as those related to class, religion, and ethnic background (Wallace and Wolf, 1999).

Immediately following his graduation, Homans had hoped to pursue a career in journalism with William Allen White of the Emporia, Kansas–based *Gazette* (Martindale,

1981). However, as a result of the Great Depression, the newspaper failed and Homans was left unemployed but certainly not penniless (Ritzer, 2000). Residing in Cambridge and admittedly with nothing better to do, he decided to attend a seminar at Harvard in the fall of 1932 offered by Lawrence Joseph Henderson. A physiologist, Henderson was teaching a course on the theories of Vilfredo Pareto, whose sociology was then almost unknown in the United States.

His exposure to the works of Pareto would forever alter Homans' academic and professional pursuits. As a wealthy Bostonian who seemed to take the anticapitalist attack presented by Marxists personally, he welcomed the anti-Marxist ideas of Pareto. Homans (1962) explained:

> I took to Pareto because he made clear to me what I was already prepared to believe . . . Someone has said that much modern sociology is an effort to answer the arguments of the revolutionaries. As a Republican Bostonian who had not rejected his comparatively wealthy family, I felt during the thirties that I was under personal attack, above all from the Marxists. I was ready to believe Pareto because he provided me with a defense (p. 4).

A number of distinguished persons attended Henderson's seminar. Among them were Talcott Parsons, Bernard DeVoto, Crane Brinton, and Joseph Schumpeter (Martindale, 1981). Furthermore, his exposure to the ideas of Pareto left such an impression on Homans that he co-authored (with Charles Curtis) *An Introduction to Pareto*, published in 1934. "The publication of this book made Homans a sociologist even though Pareto's work was virtually the only sociology he had read up to that point" (Ritzer, 2000:55). The ideas of Pareto would continue to influence Homans even in his later works. This is especially true in his detailing the basic laws of psychology that guide human behavior, his application of general concepts associated with economics, and his desire to establish full deductive theories or explanations (Wallace and Wolf, 1999).

The publication of *An Introduction to Pareto* led directly to his appointment as junior fellow in sociology at Harvard in 1934. The Society of Fellows, formed by John Lowes in cooperation with President Lowell and Alfred North Whitehead, was created to explore the possibility of graduate training that was more adequate than that of the Ph.D. (Martindale, 1981 and Ritzer, 2000). Despite the fact that Homans himself never earned a Ph.D., he became one of the major sociological figures of his day (Ritzer, 2000). His experience with the Society of Fellows did, however, have a positive influence on Homans in that it brought him in direct contact with the new work in industrial sociology being developed by Elton Mayo, Wallace Donham, and Fritz Roethlisberger. Add to this, Homans was exposed to the work of functional anthropologists such as A. R. Radcliffe-Brown, Bronislaw Malinowski, and W. Lloyd Warner, all of whom found the works of Durkheim popular (Martindale, 1981). Homans now found himself in the center of an emerging school of sociological thought that came to be known as structural-functionalism. Homans's functionalist approach is demonstrated in his study of *English Villagers of the Thirteenth Century* (1941).

Homans was a junior fellow at Harvard from 1934 to 1939, and during this time he immersed himself in the field of sociology. In 1939, Homans became an instructor of sociology, remaining until 1941, when he left to serve in the United States Navy in support of America's war effort. He served his country for four and a half years, even though he was told that he would not have a job waiting for him at Harvard upon his return. But Homans was reemployed beginning with the spring term 1946, and given the position of associate professor of sociology in the Department of Social Relations founded and chaired by Parsons. Although Homans respected some of the ideas presented by Parsons, he would become highly critical of his style of theorizing (Ritzer, 2000). In fact, a long-running and public feud would develop between the two colleagues that often manifested itself in books and journals. Homans argued that Parsons's theory was not really a theory at all, but merely a vast system of intellectual categories of ideas that the social world somehow neatly fitted into. Homans believed that social theory should be centered around empirical observation and deductive reasoning. He felt that Parsons created theoretical constructs and then found examples to fit these preconceived categories.

During the 1950s, Homans was very productive as he amassed a large number of empirical observations (Ritzer, 2000). He became a full professor in sociology in 1953 and earned an M.A. in English in 1955 (Martindale, 1981). In 1950, Homans published *The Human Group*, which demonstrated a dramatic change in his theoretical position. Homans explained his theoretical shift as a result of his readings in experimental psychology, a belief in the logic of the scientific method, and his preference for the idea of individualism. He was especially impressed by the psychological behaviorism best expressed by his Harvard colleague, the psychologist B. F. Skinner. Skinner's ideas would play a major role in the thinking and development of Homans's exchange theory (Ritzer, 2000).

In *The Human Group* Homans analyzed the structures and processes of human groups in various settings ranging from a factory setting to the that of an aboriginal tribe found in the Pacific. It was an attempt to form a statement that could be applied to every circumstance and action a person might make. What single general proposition about human behavior have we established, Homans (1950) wondered. This was his first true attempt to set down general propositions that are applicable to small group research.

Homans would continue in his attempt to establish the basic principles that affect human activity. He detailed these principles, which later came to be known as exchange theory, in his 1961 publication of *Social Behavior: Its Elementary Forms*. Elementary forms of behaviors were those forms of behavior that appear and reappear whether or not people plan on these activities. He believed that all human behaviors could be explained by basic psychological explanations and principles. Furthermore, Homans stated that these principles could be utilized by all the social sciences, not just psychology and sociology. Homans (1961) indicated that "much of modern sociological theory seems to me to possess every virtue except that of explaining anything" (p. 10).

This shift in social thinking distanced Homans from the functionalism of Durkheim and further heightened his rift with Parsons; for he specifically footnoted to Parsons his theoretical fallacy to explain human behavior (Homans, 1961). In addition, Homans declared that he could explain social life by the reductionism of his psychological principles in an explicit rejection to Durkheim's antireductionist attitude. He described in length his indebtedness to the Skinnerian psychological approach and elementary economic theory as the means to explain human social life. These principles will be outlined later in this chapter.

With the 1961 edition of *The Human Group*, Homans' behavioristic sociology was essentially complete. Much of his work in the 1960s centered around his criticism of Parsons and other functionalists, along with

elaborating his own methodological principles (Martindale, 1981). These works are detailed in *Sentiments and Activities* (1962) and *The Nature of Social Science* as found in his introduction to "The Sociological Relevance of Behaviorism" (1969). Homans served as the president of the American Sociological Association (ASA) and in his 1964 address he followed the tradition of making controversial statements about the state of sociology. Homans verbally attacked functionalists, because of their rejection of the validity of using psychological propositions, by stating that functionalism was unable to generate any adequate explanations of human behavior. He stated, "Let us get men back in, and let us put some blood in them."

Homans spent his entire academic career at Harvard, and in 1988, while serving as professor emeritus, he was awarded the ASA's Distinguished Scholarship Award. The *Harvard Gazette* (March 6, 1992) obituary of Homans appeared as follows:

> Homans was a dedicated teacher who generously gave time to his students. In the way he related to students and colleagues, it was difficult to detect any difference based on their age, sex, rank, or social status. He had little patience in the late 1960s with the "wafflings of the foolish, hypocritical, and self-righteous 'liberals,'" but he believed in civility without regard to status and numbered among his friends, students and colleagues of all political persuasions.

Homans had acknowledged that sociologists make empirical discoveries, but the true task of sociology is not analytic—since the basic propositions of social science have already been established by behavioral psychology—but synthetic, displaying the relevance of behavioral psychology for human society. It is partially in the tradition of Homans and the demonstration of relevancy of social theory that this book is written.

Intellectual Influences

It is clear that the earliest significant academic influence on Homans came from Bernard DeVoto, who introduced George to Pareto. It was Pareto's works that led Homans in the direction of sociology. From the ideas of Pareto, Homans found justification for his own bourgeois background which had come under attack from Marxist theorists. Homans disagreed with Marx's analysis that the organization of the means of production determines all the other features of society. Homans (1967) stated, "This is more than a definition and resembles a proposition in that it relates two phenomena—the means of production and the other features of society—that are not single variables. At best they are whole clusters of undefined variables. And the relationship between the phenomenon is unspecified, except that the main direction of causation—determinism—is from the former to the latter" (p. 14). As a microsociologist, Homans criticized Marx's macro approach by stating, "the most amusing case is that of the Marxists, who theoretically believe in macroscopic laws inevitably converging on a certain result, but who will not let the laws alone to produce the result, and insist on helping them along" (Homans, 1967:104).

Because of his micro-orientation the most significant influences on Homans' works come from a variety of sources that attempt to explain small group analysis. These influences include such subject areas as biochemistry, behavioral psychology, functional anthropology, utilitarianism, and basic economics; and such social theorists as Lawrence Henderson, Elton Mayo, B. F. Skinner, and Georg Simmel.

Bernard DeVoto, Lawrence Henderson, and Elton Mayo

Shortly after entering Harvard, Homans came into close association with a junior member of the teaching staff, "and he, partly by chance, became the person who made the biggest single difference to my intellectual life. This was Bernard DeVoto, whom I soon was to call Benny" (Homans, 1984:85). Homans was very happy to have made such a close association with one of his teachers, as it was a standard complaint Harvard undergraduates made, that professors seldom made time for them outside of the classroom. Homans recognized then, as students do today, the value of associating with professors outside the confines of academia.

DeVoto was an instructor in English and a tutor. As an American Literature major, Homans was assigned to him as a tutee. Benny made it clear that he was a westerner from Utah, though not a Mormon. Benny had a certain "tough guy" stance and a stereotypical disdain for the elite "Eastern Establishment" that attracted Homans. In their very first meeting together Homans revealed that he was an Adams descendant, and that he neither drank nor smoked. DeVoto responded by asking, "What do you do, to smell like a man?" (Homans, 1984:86). Homans had no answer and reveals in his *Autobiography* that not long afterward he began to drink and some time later took up smoking. It was fairly common for Benny and George to meet off campus, including dining one time at the Ritz Hotel where DeVoto introduced Homans to his friend Alfred Knopf, the great publisher. Benny and George became long-time friends, and after each men had married the couples would continue to socialize. "Our main business was drinking, rationalized only by our singing . . . while Avis (Benny's wife) played the piano. The gallons of whiskey that got spilled over that piano!" (Homans, 1984:89).

Academically, DeVoto assigned numerous books for Homans to read. Among the most significant were Bernard Mandeville's *The Fable of the Bees*, and Pareto's *Sociologie generale* in the French translation; neither of which were English literature. Homans (1984) stated, "The greatest service Benny did me was to introduce me to Professor Lawrence Joseph Henderson" (p. 89).

When Homans first met Henderson, he asked him what he must do to become a sociologist. Henderson told him to learn about the work that he and his colleague Elton Mayo were conducting. This led Homans into direct contact with the new work found in industrial sociology by Henderson and Mayo at the Harvard Business School. Henderson, a biochemist, was studying the physiological characteristics of industrial work, and Mayo, a psychologist, was examining the human factors associated with industrial work. Mayo was the director of the famous studies conducted at the Hawthorne Plant of the Western Electric Company in Chicago. Mayo and his associates often noticed that workers used various forms of joking and sarcastic teasing to enforce the group's norms. The workers were fully aware of how much work they should turn out, both individually and as a group, in order to merit their pay. In the Bank Wiring Room workers hand-wired electrical circuits and it was common to see the members of a work group gang up and in a joking manner hit a fellow worker on the shoulder when he produced more than the other members of the group. This behavior was referred to as "binging." A worker was binged by his co-workers if he produced too much in a day or if he did not produce enough (Kornblum, 1991).

Mayo and his associates realized that binging was part of the work group's culture. Within this culture the group's norms of conduct and proper behavior were reinforced and maintained by the group's cultural standards.

Homans conducted his own follow-up studies of the Bank Wiring Room years later and concluded that workers shared a common body of sentiments.

A person should not turn out too much work. If he did, he was a "rate-buster." The theory was that if an excessive amount of work was turned out, the management would lower the piecework rate so that the employees would be in the position of doing more work for approximately the same pay. On the other hand, a person should not turn out too little work. If he did he was a "chiseler"; that is, he was getting paid for work he did not do. (Homans, 1951:235)

Consequently, the workers maintained a certain pace guaranteed to produce just enough work to keep management happy, but did not produce too much work in an attempt to keep fellow workers happy. Newcomers to the workforce were quickly indoctrinated into these shared sentiments in the workplace culture.

Much of Homans's *The Human Group* was a theoretical reanalysis of a series of previous studies of such diverse subjects as work groups in factories, street gangs, the kinship system in primitive societies, and the structure of a declining New England community (Coser, 1977). Homans was attempting to develop a theoretical scheme of interrelated propositions derived from observed regularities discovered in these studies. For example, he noted that increased interaction between persons would increase their liking for one another, but qualified this point by stating that this would only be true if they had roughly equal status positions. Consequently, if people with unequal status and power were placed in constant contact with one another, animosity would result.

Anthropology

Mayo instructed his students to read books by prominent social anthropologists, especially those that compared aboriginal and modern societies in terms of social rituals in productive work. At this time the cultural anthropologists were intellectually dominant, and friends of Homans in this group, such as Clyde Kluckhohn, insisted that every culture was unique. It was here that Homans perceived things quite differently. Homans believed that aboriginal societies were quite similar and repeated themselves (in basic behavioral modes) in places so far separated in time and place that they could not have borrowed cultural ideas from one another, and therefore, they certainly were not unique. Rather, Homans concluded that human nature was the same the world over.

Even though it is true that *The Human Group* was partially rooted in the functionalist tradition of Durkheim and of the British anthropologists Bronislaw Malinowski and A. R. Radcliffe-Brown, Homans's subsequent work abandoned this functional viewpoint in favor of an exchange perspective. Still, Homans was influenced by Malinowski's anthropological exchange considerations. Malinowski was concerned with the role that exchange plays in social life. He spent may years among the Trobriand Islanders of the Melanesian Islands, where he concluded that mutual exchange is the basis of social cohesion.

> Trobriand society is founded on the principle of legal status . . . [involving] well-balanced chains of reciprocal services. The whole division into totemic clans, clans of a local nature and into village communities, is characterized by . . . a game of give and take . . . [Moreover] reciprocity, the give-and-take principle, reigns supreme also . . . within the nearest groups of kinsmen . . . [The] most unselfish relation, that between a man and his sister, [is] founded on mutuality and the repayment of services (Malinowski, 1926:46).

The concept of reciprocity becomes a critical element in Homans' exchange theory. The concept of exchange itself was influenced by Malinowski's discussion of "The Gift." Anthropologists and exchange theorists argue that a crucial aspect of gift exchanges bind society together through mutual obligations and increases social cohesion (Wallace and Wolf, 1999).

After exposing Homans to the ideas of anthropology, Mayo then gave Homans a second group of books, mostly on Durkheim, which emphasized the research related to suicide. But, these readings only upset Homans, as he did not believe that the nature of society could determine the nature of the individual. Homans eventually broke away from the influence of Mayo, and his focus would turn to the brilliant works of B. F. Skinner.

B. F. Skinner and Psychological Behaviorism

With Burrhus Frederic Skinner's arrival at Harvard came psychological behaviorism, the famous pigeon studies, and the Skinner Box (an instrument to trace changes in animal behavior). B. F. Skinner was born in Susquehanna, Pennsylvania, in 1904. He earned his A.B. at Hamilton College in 1926, his M.A. in 1930, and his Ph.D. at Harvard in 1931. He became a research fellow and junior fellow at Harvard from 1931 to 1936, and from 1936 to 1945 he was on the teaching staff at the University of Minnesota. While at Minnesota, Skinner conducted war research sponsored by General Mills (1942–43). For the next three years Skinner chaired the psychology department at Indiana University. He became professor of psychology at Harvard in 1948 and remained there until his retirement as professor emeritus in 1974 (Martindale, 1981).

Skinner regarded theories such as structural functionalism, conflict, symbolic interactionism, ethnomethodology, and phenomenology as "mystical enterprises." He saw these theories as constructing mystical entities that distract sociologists from the only concrete entities of study, behavior, and the consequences that make such behavior more or less likely to occur. Culture is made by behaviors and concepts such as ideas and values are useless. What needs to be understood are things such as costs and rewards. Internal states are irrelevant because they are unobservable. (It should be noted that Homans did take into account a certain level of internal states.)

Skinner was a pioneer of operant behavior, and was fascinated by the prospects of the control of behavior of animals and human beings (Martindale, 1981). (Homans would use the word *activity* instead of operant.) At the heart of his psychology was the notion of the stimulus-response arc—when the subject is presented with a stimulus, a response is automatically triggered. In his studies of pigeons, Skinner proved that by reenforcing desired behavior he could train his birds to perform bizarre stunts. For example, he was able to get his pigeons to perform a parody of table tennis by rewarding them with corn (Martindale, 1981). Skinner learned that reinforcement control could be applied in schedules that are continuous or intermittent, which, in turn, may be converted into interval or ratio schedules. This same principle is applied to slot machines, where the "house" can determine the level of payouts.

Both imitation and willingness to follow instruction are the basis of reinforcement effectiveness. Skinner explained that language, the most significant human skill, arises on the basis of differential reenforcement, through the building of a basic repertoire of words and expressions. The biologically functional child is capable of learning language and does so by imitating the sounds of her parents. Through reinforcement, the child is encouraged and rewarded for furthering her vocabulary skills. Even creativity is explained through the principles of reinforcement, by the positive response that originality elicits among most humans.

Homans treated the social exchange between Skinner and his pigeons as the paradigm of all social exchange. Thus, in formulating his version of exchange theory, Homans turned to the behavioral school of experimental psychology founded by his friend Skinner (Wallace and Wolf, 1999). Homans's sociology is an attempt to build a theory about social life from the basic behavioristic propositions derived from B. F. Skinner's psychology of operant conditioning. Homans (1967) believed that all behavior can be reduced to psychological organismic behavior. Those people who dislike a theory based on pigeons simply suffer from "sentimental" problems.

Exchange theory is deterministic. There are two types of determinism: strong ontological (nature of being) and weak epistemological (nature of knowing). Homans falls into the category of the strong ontological, which denies conscious beings. Homans felt that consciousness was metaphysical—a leftover of religion. There is no soul, the mind replaces it. For Skinner, the mind is a "black box" and people simply react to stimuli. Therefore, the researcher merely needs to observe actual behavior. In regard to methodology, Homans' exchange theory advocates experiments. Experiments are used within the axiomatic theoretical format by using a few highly abstract statements, which leads to hypotheses, that can then be tested. This approach can be thought of in terms of the deductive-nomological approach which states that a general law can cover all similar situations and allows for outcomes to be deduced. For example, if all crows are black and one finds a bird that is not black, it is not a crow. This approach is a pure if–then relationship, it is deterministic.

Economics and Utilitarianism

Basic economic theory as developed by such great thinkers as Adam Smith, David Ricardo, and Carl Menger rests on certain premises about individual psychology and its implications for people's behavior in the marketplace (Wallace and Wolf, 1999). Rational choice theorists, such as those found in the exchange theory paradigm, have adopted four basic economic propositions. These propositions, as outlined by Wallace and Wolf (1999:299), are:

1. Individuals are rational profit maximizers, making decisions on the basis of their tastes and preferences.

2. The more of something an individual has, the less interested he or she will be in yet more of it.

3. The prices at which goods and services will be sold in a free market are determined directly by the tastes of prospective buyers and sellers. The greater the demand for a good, the more "valuable" it will be and the higher will be its price. The greater the supply, the less valuable it will be and the lower will be the price.

4. Goods will generally be more expensive if they are supplied by a monopolist than if they are supplied by a number of firms in competition with each other.

The first two propositions are clearly based on the psychological interests of persons. The last two propositions highlight the willingness of persons to pay market prices, especially if it means giving up other goods and/or services.

Homans adapted and applied these basic economic premises to human behavior. He argued that the parties involved in a social exchange approach it with a variety of interests or values such as material rewards (certain tangible goods and products) and nonmaterial rewards (enjoyment, power, self-esteem). Group equilibrium will occur when the rewards and costs to all parties involved in the exchange are in rough balance. Fair exchange is equated by Homans as "distributive justice."

Along with psychological behaviorism, Homans' exchange theory has its roots in utilitarianism. The utilitarian approach described people as self-interested in the sense of maximizing pleasure and avoiding pain (similar to hedonism). Utilitarians argued that behavior was more or less a moral activity according to the amount of utility it bestowed on individuals. Utilitarianism is a theory that the greatest good for the greatest number should be the main consideration in making a choice of actions.

Georg Simmel

Simmel was one of the first early major social theorists who attempted to identify universal characteristics of human behavior. He was especially interested in why people were moved to make contact with others. Like modern exchange theorists, he came to believe that their motive was to satisfy needs and pursue individual goals. Simmel suggested that even though people do not always receive equal returns, their interactions are always based on some expectation of reciprocity, and therefore should be viewed as kinds of exchanges (Wallace and Wolf, 1999). Simmel, then, sought to capture the fundamental nature of human life as an interactive process involving reciprocal relations, or exchange, within social associations (Farganis, 2000).

In 1958, Homans wrote an article for a special issue of the *American Journal of Sociology* in honor of Simmel. Homans suggested that Simmel was the ancestor of postwar small-group research, which he took to the growing edge of a scientific sociology. Homans urged small-group researchers to integrate laboratory experiments with quantified field work, and to reduce the propositions established to those of psychological explanations. He proudly stated in *Sentiments and Activities* (1962), "I hold myself to be an 'ultimate psychological reductionist'" (p. 279). Furthermore, Homans (1962) states that the special virtue of exchange theory is that it will bring sociology closer to economics, the oldest and most practical of the sciences of humanity.

Concepts and Contributions

As all of the primary influences on his work would seem to indicate, Homans's contributions to social theory center around exchange theory and its related concepts. His early works possessed a functionalist flair and a systems approach to the study of human behavior; but his later works mounted a full-scale attack on Parsons and all others who ignored his insistence on utilizing basic economic propositions and psychological principles in the explanation of human interaction.

Exchange Theory

Exchange theory illustrates an effort to take the principles of behaviorism, fuse them with other ideas, and apply them to the concerns of sociologists. Exchange theory originated during the 1950s, primarily through George Homans. Most of Homans' exchange theory can be viewed as a reaction against Parsons, Durkheim, and structural functionalism in general. Exchange theory is positivistic in that it assumes that human behavior can be explained by natural "laws."

Homans' basic view was that the study of sociology should concern itself with explaining individual behavior and interaction. He showed little interest in consciousness or in the various types of large-scale

structures and institutions that were of primary concern to most sociologists. His interest centered around the reinforcement patterns and the history of rewards and costs that lead individuals to do what they do (Ritzer, 2000). The most basic premise of exchange theory is that people will continue to engage in behaviors they find rewarding and cease to engage in behaviors where the costs have proven to be too high in the past.

Homans believed that self-interest was the universal motive that made the world go around and that individuals, just like Skinner's pigeons, modified their behavior in terms of positive or negative reinforcement provided by their environment (Coser, 1977). The human social world consisted of interacting persons exchanging rewards and punishments.

Because there is an *exchange* in behavior, Homans was concerned with the interactions between people. Exchange theory has a focus, then, on what people seem to be getting out of their interactions and what they in turn are contributing to the relationship. Homans clearly believed that in every interaction something is being exchanged. These exchanges were not limited to the economic realm (money or commodities), for incentives to socially behave (to take action) also come in the form of approval, esteem, love, affection, allegiance, and other nonmaterialistic or symbolic expressions. The larger the number of interacting members, the more complex these exchanges become.

When people become aware that they are being exploited or treated unfairly they will leave the relationship or quit the group (Homans, 1961). In Homans' industrial observations, he concluded that if workers feel that they are not being paid enough for their work they may form a union, bargain collectively with the employer, or even go on strike. But, in taking such action, workers must weigh the potential benefits against the costs that they may experience—losses in pay, in friendship, and perhaps even their job. Such choices are never easy, nor are the motivations always obvious. When multiple values are involved, the rational calculation of benefits and costs becomes very difficult.

For Homans, the human was seen as a rational calculator of pleasures and pains, always intending to maximize returns and minimize losses. Sociologists were to look for patterns of behavior to see how individuals conform and depart from normal expectations of behavior. The problem for the researcher is to weigh the value individuals place on certain rewards and costs.

In short, Homans' exchange theory "envisages social behavior as an exchange or activity, tangible, or intangible, and more or less rewarding or costly, between at least two persons" (1961:13). Homans outlined five clear-cut propositions that he felt explains all human behavior. These propositions are the cornerstone of his exchange theory.

Human Exchange Propositions

Homans (1967) made a strong point against the use of nonoperative definitions in the attempt to explain human behavior. Examples of nonoperating definitions include the definitions of some so-called central concepts in sociology and anthropology, concepts that theorists in these fields take to be the glories of their sciences. Concepts such as "role" and "culture" are nonoperating definitions because they do not define variables that appear in the testable propositions of social science. Concepts that allow for "operating definitions," however, can be distinguished as those concepts that are actually used. Homans uses as an example of an operative definition the concept of "frequency" to accompany his *value proposition*: The more valuable a man perceives the result of his action to be, the more frequently he will perform the action.

The explanation of a finding, whether it is a generalization or a proposition about a single event, is found in the process of showing that the finding follows as a logical conclusion, as a deduction, from one or more general propositions under specified given conditions. Homans stated that the content of the propositions and explanations are naturally different in the social sciences because the subject matter is different, but the requirements for a proposition and explanation are the same. An explanation is the deduction of empirical propositions from more general ones. Accordingly, in the matter of explanation, the problems of the social sciences are twofold: What are its general propositions and can empirical propositions be reliably deduced from them?

In his book *Social Behavior: Its Elementary Forms*, Homans defines the subject matter as the basic, common, everyday forms of behavior in which all humans engage. Homans does, however, begin with an analysis of animal behavior to establish the general and basic premises of his proposition. Animal studies allow for his testing of "operant conditioning." In Skinner's language, the pigeon's behavior in pecking the target is an operant; the grain is the reinforcer; and when the operant behavior is reinforced, the pigeon has undergone operant conditioning. Homans acknowledged that in human behavior it would be difficult to control for all factors necessary for operant conditioning. Consequently, behavior is referred to as an activity, not an operant.

The rate of reinforcement will vary with the "strength" of the reinforcer. Variable-ratio reinforcement exists as well. For example, gambling activity is reinforced both as variable ratio and in variable amounts. As for emotional behavior, humans are more apt to respond emotionally and have an infinitely greater capacity for expressing it. Emotional behavior can be strengthened by many reinforcers. Because of the emotional component of human behavior, sentiments can interfere in the determination of value and the choice of activities to engage in.

This leads to the discussion of the propositions themselves. Homans made it clear that these propositions are indeed psychological. They are psychological in two senses. First, they are usually stated and empirically tested by persons who consider themselves psychologists. Second, they are propositions about individual behavior, rather than propositions about groups or societies. Although a particular kind of reward may be valuable to members of one group, and a different kind of reward may be of value to another; and since the pursuit of different rewards may require different action, the same proposition is used. The proposition, "the more valuable the reward, the more frequent or probable the action that gets the reward," still holds true for both. Even if people differ genetically and biologically, they will still pursue action that is most likely to be rewarded (Homans, 1967).

Homans believed that all human behaviors can be explained by five general propositions. He stated:

The general propositions relate four main classes of variables to one another; frequency with which a person performs an action (in B. F. Skinner's language an operant); the frequency with which an action is followed by a reward, a punishment, or nothing at all (in Skinner's language, the frequency with which an action is reinforced, positively or negatively); the degree to reward or punishment experienced by the actor (in my language, not Skinner's, the value of the reinforcement); and finally the environmental conditions, stimuli, that attend a person's action. Note that a person need not get a reward because he performed a certain action. The reward may be the result of wholly different causes. To serve as a reinforcer, it is enough that it follows the ac-

tion, which leaves an opening for superstition behavior (Homans, 1984:334).

Of his five propositions, four of them were from Skinner, while the "frustration-aggression" proposition was stated in 1940 by Dollard in his book, *Frustration and Aggression*. The propositions are as follows:

1. *The Success Proposition:* **The Principle of Reward.** If in the past an activity was rewarded, then the individual is more likely to repeat the activity in the present. The shorter the interval of time between the behavior and the reward, the more likely the person is to repeat it. Furthermore, the more often a particular action of a person is rewarded, the more likely the person is to perform that same action. This is referred to as the success proposition because the individual is rewarded for certain courses of action and activity.

Homans explained that in the pursuit of *rewards* certain costs are incurred. A *cost* is described as a value foregone, and it is a negative *value*. A *profit* is measured in terms of successful rewards minus all costs. Thus, if a student receives a high grade (reward) after studying long hours (cost) for an exam, that student is likely to continue to study long hours for future exams (profit). If an athlete increases his performance level (reward) after taking a nap (cost) prior to the game, he is more likely to take naps before each of the remaining games (profit). This idea clearly reflects the influence of economics on Homans' exchange theory.

2. *The Stimulus Proposition:* **The Principle of Experience.** If a similar stimulus, or set of stimuli, present themselves and resemble an originally rewarded activity, the individual is likely to repeat that course of action. The more often, in a given period of time, an individual's activities reward the activity of another, the

more often the other will emit the activity. This proposition reflects the concepts of value and quantity. In quantity, frequency is measured by some sort of counting over a period of time. Such as the quantity of desired activities emitted during exchange. Value may be measured in terms of the "degree of reinforcement" an individual receives per exchange. Value is a matter of degree varying from one person to another, and it is equated with rewards. For example, parents who take away television-viewing privileges from their children will notice different results in the degree of reinforcement between the child who values watching television compared to the one who prefers to read. The punishment is further increased if the child will miss her favorite televised program. As another example, a fisherman who catches a large fish in a shady creek will be more likely to fish in shady areas in the future because his past experience was rewarding.

The connection between the stimuli and the action is subject to both *generalization* and *discrimination*. The individual works within bounds of how similar a stimulus must be to past rewarding stimuli in other to be considered as valuable as the original. For example, a grandchild tells her grandmother that she loves music and playing CDs (compact disks) on her new stereo. The grandmother, not thinking about what type of music her granddaughter listens to, assumes she will like a CD for a gift because she loves music (*generalization*), and purchases her a CD for a gift. But the grandchild does not like the Glenn Miller CD, preferring (*discrimination*) instead the new Pearl Jam release.

3. *The Value Proposition:* **Reward and Punishment, the Principle of Value of Outcome.** The more valuable to an individual a unit of the activity another gives him,

the more often he will emit activity rewarded by the activity of the other. Thus, if one person highly values the company of the other, she is far more likely to engage in behavior that the other finds desirable. However, Homans was quick to notice that this proposition needed to be altered, for if one person highly values the company of another, but the other is always accompanying the original, a feeling of satiation may occur.

Rewards, then, vary by degree of *value*. The value in question is always that of a given unit of the reward, no matter how that unit is defined. The variable, *value*, may take either a positive or negative form. The results of an individual's behavior that have positive values are called rewards; while the results that have negative ones are called punishments. Action that has the result of allowing an individual to avoid punishment is rewarded by that result, and that behavior is more likely to be performed in the future. Consequently, there are two classes of reward: intrinsic reward and the avoidance of punishment. Also, there are two classes of punishment: intrinsic punishment and the withholding of a reward. Punishment, or its threat, becomes a potentially powerful motivator of action.

Homans combines the first three propositions to form the "Rationality Proposition" or rational choice. These first three propositions assign value to our actions as individuals seek to collect favorable outcomes (rewards). As Homans explained, in choosing between alternative actions, a person will choose that one for which, as perceived by him at the time, the value, V, of the result, multiplied by the probability, p, of getting the result, is the greater. Thus, Action A equals p times V (A = pV). If a person faces a choice between two courses of actions, with the first, if successful, bringing him a result, let us say, three units of value to him, but he estimates the chance that his action will be successful as only one out of four, he may choose to pursue a different course of action. The second course of action will bring a result worth only two units, but he estimates its chance of success as one out of two. Thus, since 3 x 1/4 is less than 2 x 1/2, the rationality proposition predicts that the individual will take the second course of action (Homans, 1974). Although this may sound complicated, humans use this rational system daily. Decisions such as choosing what type of camcorder, automobile, or television to purchase is all determined by rationally calculating costs versus rewards.

4. *The Deprivation-Satiation Proposition:* **Principle of Diminishing Returns** Homans explained the effect of satiation as "The more often in the recent past a person has received a particular reward, the less valuable any further unit of that reward becomes for him [or her]" (1961:29). In other words, any behavior that is rewarding reaches a point where it begins to lose its value because it is too readily available (this is consistent with Simmel's thoughts). For example, making a snowman during a western New York winter in November is fun, but it loses its value by March when the snow has been readily available for five months. As for the deprivation aspect of this proposition, when an individual is forced to go a long period of time without the desired reward, she will begin to lose interest and move on, seeking other rewards from other sources. Homans referred to this as changes in kind of activity. Since human activities are not standardized exchanges incapable of change, people will change their activities to increase profits and rewards.

Homans further elaborated that the deprivation-satiation proposition is not very precise and is subject to the value of the reward in question in relation to the time it was last presented. Food can satiate people quickly, but it soon recovers its value; whereas most persons are not so easily satiated with money, power, sexual gratification, or status, if one can ever be wholly satiated by such rewards.

5. *The Aggression-Approval Proposition.* **Principle of Distributive Justice** Homans noted that when a behavior does not receive the expected reward, or is punished unexpectedly, the response is anger or aggression. Interestingly, the aggressor will find such aggression rewarding (1961:37). Additionally, when a person's action receives a greater reward than expected, or he does not receive a punishment when expected, he will be pleased; and is more likely to perform approving behavior.

The principle of *distributive justice* is applied here. Quite often individuals do not receive the same rewards as others; when this happens, frustration occurs. For example, students who have the same test score averages expect the same grade and workers who perform the same job functions expect equal pay. Homans (1961) explained that when someone feels cheated (the realization of unfair distributive justice) they are likely to display the emotional behavior called anger. At the very least, one who finds oneself at an unjust disadvantage learns to complain.

Antifunctionalist

In 1967, Homans wrote *The Nature of Social Science*, which was primarily in response to Parsons and structural-functionalism. Homans believed that theories must have propositions, and that Parsons's theories had none. Additionally, Homans felt that explanation (of behavior) was possible only through the use of propositions. Homans used

Skinner's psychological propositions and felt that all behaviors could be explained by using them. This leads to the discussion of the antagonists and the intended audience.

Homans argued that "explanation by concept" is not an explanation. Concepts such as "role" and "culture" are useless. Concepts and their definitions tell us that we are going to talk about behavior but, without propositions, lingering over nonoperating definitions may actually get in the way of the primary job of science—explanation. When nonoperating definitions are multiplied and elaborated into a nonoperating conceptual scheme (called a grand theory), such as that of Parsons, students are in a false sense of security that such a scheme can explain any phenomenon. Homans felt that the failure to state real propositions leads to a failure to create real theories. Parsons (and Shils) asserted that in interaction between any two persons, the actions of each other are sanctioned by the actions of the other. Homans felt that Parsons (and Shils) should have gone on to say that the more rewarding (valuable) to one man the action of the other, the more often will the first perform the action that provides him the desired reward; only then would they have stated a real proposition.

Homans confronted structural functionalists by directly attacking Durkheim on three main issues:

1. **The Issue of Emergence.** Homans believed all emergent social phenomena could be explained from psychological propositions.

2. **Durkheim's View of Psychology.** The psychology of Durkheim's day was very primitive and concentrated on instinctive forms of behavior.

3. **Durkheim's Method of Explanation.** Durkheim believed a social fact is ex-

plained when one can find the social facts that caused it. Homans was concerned with the relationship between cause and effect and argued that explanation was inevitably psychological.

Ekeh (1974) argues that Homans's orientation was directly against neo-Durkheimian anthropologist Claude Levi-Strauss. Levi-Strauss was of the French collectivist tradition, of which Durkheim was a major exponent. Homans was of the British individualistic tradition. Homans felt that he was doing battle with a newer version of Durkheimian theory and states that Levi-Strauss was the "last straw" that broke his patience with functionalism of the Durkheimian type. Durkheim and Levi-Strauss saw the actor as constrained by social facts, especially by the "collective unconscious." Homans disagreed with this perspective because the individual is accorded less of a place in the social process.

Homans also attacked the four types of explanation used in analyzing institutions by structural functionalists. The first type is structural. Homans argued that institutions which are correlated with others do not necessarily explain them. The second type of explanation is functional: the belief that an institution exists because society could not survive without it. Homans felt that there is inadequate evidence to prove such an assumption and that functional explanation in sociology is a failure. The third type, Homans labeled historical. The institution is seen as the end product of a historical process. Homans saw this historical explanation as basically a psychological one. The fourth type of explanation ties in with the historical explanation. All human institutions are products of processes of historical change. Homans argued that institutional change must be explained by sociologists and that definitions of change should be based upon psychological principles.

Homans summarized explanation as the process of showing how empirical findings follow from, can be deduced from, general propositions under particular given conditions. The general propositions are psychological and are propositions about the behavior of humans rather than about societies or other social groups.

The Group System

Homans was quite clear about the elements that comprise the *group system* (Martindale, 1981). These elements are: activity, interaction, sentiment, and norms. Activity refers to what the members of the group do as members. Interaction involves the relation of the activity of one member of the group to that of another. The sentiment of the group is seen as the sum of the feelings of group members with respect to the group. The norms of the group refers to a code of behavior adopted consciously or unconsciously by the group. Homans' group system is in the tradition of Pareto, who views a group as "external in contrast to internal system" (Martindale, 1981). The group is external in that it meets in response to the needs of outside environment. These environmental needs can be physical, technical and/or social. The group is an internal system because the elements of behavior are mutually depended.

In *The Human Group*, Homans defined a group as, "a number of persons who communicate with one another often over a span of time, and who are few enough so that each person is able to communicate with all the others not at secondhand, through other people, but face to face" (p. 1). Homans analyzed a series of previously conducted studies of groups found in a variety of environments, including: family, school cliques, co-workers, and so on.

Thus, Homans viewed a group as a plurality of people in interaction. When the members of the group maintain an active involvement with one another and share activity, interaction, sentiment and norms, they have formed a social system. The group (and community) responses to external needs and is internally maintained through interaction among the members. Changes to either the external or internal elements causes changes in the group system. The internal system is maintained through mutual dependence of interaction and sentiment by persons who interact on a regular basis.

Homans (1950) used the term *feedback*—borrowed from the property of electrical circuits (that he noted in his studies of the Bank Wiring Room)—to describe the relationship between the internal and external group systems. He stated that there is always a process of "buildup" in which the internal system is subject to change due to fluctuations in the external environment. The internal system is also subject to change as a result of fluctuations from the group members themselves. Changes in attitudes, sentiments, and norms among divisive members of the group will cause the need for an internal system's adjustment in activity.

Homans explained that the collapse of entire civilizations can be explained by the failure of a number of small groups to properly meet these group system's needs. "A civilization, if it is in turn to maintain itself, must preserve at least a few of the characteristics of the group . . . . Civilizations have failed in failing to solve this problem" (Homans, 1950:456).

Group Structure

Proper maintenance of the internal group system is at least partially depended on the *group structure* itself. Individual decision-making, on the part of group members, whether they behave selfishly or in the best interests of the group, will affect the effectiveness of group action. The action of group members is often dictated by one's status within the group structure; as each member has a varying degree of commitment to maintain the social system. Social behavior is an exchange of rewards (and costs) between persons. Unless all the members of a group are equal, social equality between any two of them implies that the members have previously become differentiated in esteem and then in recognized status (Homans, 1961).

The more valuable to other members of a group are the activities an individual emits to them, the higher is the esteem in which they hold that individual. The higher the esteem that one member holds, the lower the esteem that is available for the rest of the members of the group. The higher the rank of a person within a group, the more nearly his activities conform to the norms of the group (Homans, 1961).

However, regardless of individual esteem and status within the group structure, each member has certain role obligations. These role obligations are not always met, but generally they are. When these role obligations are met, the group has a better chance of survival (maintenance). Most members of the group will meet their group needs due to the acknowledgement of mutual obligations (Homans, 1961).

When the members of a group are trying to change the behavior of others, they will direct most interaction to the member whose behavior most needs changing, that is, the individual who has failed to meet group obligations. On the other hand, when the group influence has failed to produce the proper interaction adjustment requested of the deviant member, the group will greatly reduce their interaction with this person (Homans, 1961). Group members will offer social approval as a "generalized reinforcer" to those who provide activity they value, which increases the likelihood that approved action will continue. Group members generally conform to the expectations of the group because they find such activities and interactions rewarding. Thus, conformity is met with approval and acceptable behavior is more likely to continue.

Power and Authority

Homans (1961) felt that a person who influences other members has *authority*. An individual earns authority by acquiring esteem, and one acquires esteem by rewarding others. Similarly, *power* can be defined as the ability to provide valuable rewards. Those with power and authority are small in number, thus providing the seed of future conflict. The leader, when directing others, will inevitably cause members to incur costs. As long as the leader is also incurring costs this will help to avoid conflict. When the rewards that are distributed seem fair (distributive justice), the individual is satisfied. One is especially satisfied if the reward was received within a given period of time. Humans act as if they find it valuable to realize fair exchange, and they will expose emotional behavior toward this end (the pursuit of distributive justice).

Relevancy

It was George Homans' belief that all human behaviors could be explained by behavioral psychology. To that end he implemented a number of propositions, all psychological in origin, to comprise a theory of rational behavior centered around the assumption that individuals act to increase their rewards and decrease their costs. For all those theorists who disagree with his basic assumption, Homans argued that the burden of proof rests on their shoulders (Martindale, 1981).

Homans argued that self-interest was the universal motive for behavior and that people shape their behaviors in terms of positive or negative reinforcement provided by their environment (Coser, 1977). Thus, humans interact with one another by exchanging rewards and punishments. The individual is viewed as a rational being capable of calculating pleasures and pains and always motivated by maximizing profits. Homans paid little attention to consciousness or the various large-scale structures and institutions that were of primary concern to most sociologists. Instead, it is the history of reinforcement patterns that lead individuals to behave as they do. Consequently, to understand behavior, we need to understand an individual's history of rewards and costs (Ritzer, 2000). Behaviors that have been rewarded in the past are more likely to be continued in the present and the future. Conversely, behaviors that have been proven costly, or caused pain, in the past, are less likely to be repeated.

Initially, Homans was attracted to sociology through his exposure to the works of Pareto and his anti-Marxist sentiments. Soon after, Homans was introduced to the new work in industrial sociology being developed by such people as Elton Mayo and Fritz Roethlisberger. He was then exposed to the work of functional anthropologists and soon found himself in the tradition of structural functionalism. However, with the arrival of B. F. Skinner at Harvard, and his classic studies on operant conditioning, Homans' theoretical orientation would take a dramatic change in direction. Skinner and Homans would become trusted colleagues who respected each other works. Homans would come to agree with Skinner that any focus on internal states (consciousness) was pointless. Instead, behavior was a result of rewards and costs provided by the social environment and determined through the social exchange process between individuals.

Underlying all contemporary exchange theories are reformulations of certain basic utilitarian assumptions and concepts. For classical economists, humans are viewed as rationally seeking to maximize their material benefits, or utility (Turner, 1974).

Homans is, of course, best known for "creating" exchange theory. But nowhere in his descriptions of propositions does he use the term "exchange." In fact, he did not particularly care for the label "exchange theory," as it suggested that the theory was a special kind of theory, whereas he viewed it as a "general behavioral psychology" (Homans, 1984:338).

Exchange theory combines the principles of psychological behaviorism, basic economics and utilitarianism, with a focus on interactions between humans. These exchanges are not limited to the economic realm as individuals have incentives to socially behave in their pursuit of other forms of approval. Individuals will maintain the exchange relationship for as long as they find it rewarding, or if the abandonment of such an exchange will be too costly. For example, students may not want to attend an 8:30 A.M. class because they have to get up too early in the morning (costs), but they will continue to attend if the rewards are great enough (course credit toward graduation, it was the only class available to them, or the instructor finds a way to make the class relatively entertaining). Consequently, students will continue enrollment in the class because if they drop the course they will lose out on credit hours. The students have little to complain about attending a class at such an early hour because most people are already at work, or on their way to work. People work (cost of their time), of course, because they need the money (rewards) to pay their bills or to purchase items that they desire.

Homans proposed a number of propositions that he believed could explain any, or all, human behaviors. To demonstrate the relevancy of these propositions to today's world (and the future) is nearly pointless, as indeed, *any* behavior that one can think of can easily be answered by one or more of his propositions. The success proposition, for example, assumes that individuals will seek out, and maintain, interactions where the rewards outweigh the costs, thus providing a profit. Measurements of rewards are certainly not restricted to economics. The individual who wakes up early in the morning, despite being tired and feeling aches and pains, specifically to go jogging for 30–40 minutes, often in inclement weather, is not doing this for monetary reasons. The reward of the jogger presents itself in such forms as a cardiovascular workout, overall health benefits, to look fit and trim (which might attract different rewards in the form of physical attraction), sense of accomplishment, adrenaline rush, and so on.

The stimulus proposition proposes that if a stimulus similar to one that has been rewarded in the past presents itself, a course of action in pursuit of this new stimulus is likely to be pursued. For example, a person who enjoyed a vacation traveling in the past, is likely to pursue another travel vacation. This also explains why many people seem to date a certain "type" of person. An individual who finds one person attractive is likely to perceive similar persons attractive. If a movie viewer finds comedies entertaining, they are likely to watch other comedies. The list of examples is nearly endless.

The value proposition highlights the fact that certain behaviors are far more rewarding than others, and vary depending on the individual. The individual who greatly enjoys watching college football games is likely to forgo a number of other alternative courses of action on any given Saturday in the fall. The person with only a marginal interest in sports is likely to place little value on watching football, indoors, on television, when they could be outdoors enjoying the stimuli presented in the external environment.

However, as the deprivation-satiation proposition indicates, the value of the stimuli is affected by its availability. By mid-season, even the most die-hard football fan has reached a satiation point and a certain level of overexposure to football, all day, every Saturday, seems mildly redundant and is less rewarding. Consequently, other courses of action are likely to seem attractive. On the other hand, at the beginning of the football season the viewer is in a state of deprivation because he has gone months without viewing the games and, therefore, will highly value the upcoming contests. The end of the season is valued as well, for the viewer recognizes the season is almost over. Furthermore, the games at the end of the season have greater meaning because championships and bowl games may be at stake. This further indicates that some games are valued more than others because of their symbolic meaning. Championship games and games against one's rival are always more highly valued than the other regular season games.

The old adage, absence makes the heart grow fonder, comes into play here as well. Often, individuals take each other for granted, especially those whom one comes into contact with on a regular basis. When something that is cherished is removed for any period of time the desire for that object, or person, increases. Even the family pet is taken for granted on a daily basis, but when one returns home after a period of absence, both pet and owner are pleased to see one another. Again, examples to illustrate the validity of proposition are nearly endless.

Finally, the aggression-approval proposition dwells on subject areas not so obvious in everyday interaction. When one expects a certain reward and then does not receive it, they will most likely be upset and respond with anger or aggression. This aggressive behavior may be directed toward the guilty party or, in some cases, it is directed toward innocent persons. For example, if two people hope to receive an appointment of presidency for an association, it is clear that only one will be awarded the position. The loser of the appointment may take it out on the winner even though the winner was clearly a better candidate. The losing candidate has failed to acknowledge her own shortcomings at the expense of the other. This anger should have been directed toward the association (or self). The winner has every right to enjoy his success despite the loser's negativity. As Homans indicates, however, the loser may now take pleasure (reward) in directing her anger toward the winner.

There are times when a behavior that was expected to be punished is not. When this occurs the individual will predictably be happy. The same holds true when one receives more rewards (or a greater reward) than anticipated. Homans also indicated that individuals behave in such a way as to attain the approval of others. Many people find social approval a reward in itself. Thus, most people behave in socially acceptable means because they find such behavior rewarding. Acts of altruism are explained by this principle.

Contemporary research in the area of distributive justice has become more commonplace and fruitful. Younts and Mueller (2001) state, "justice perceptions—the degree of injustice that an individual perceives to exist in a situation—mediate the impact of rewards (both absolute and relative to those the individual believes are fair) on individual's emotional responses to injustice" (p. 140). They argue that justice perceptions act as a mediator in the justice evaluation process and that these findings have practical implications for understanding justice processes. Human Resource departments could find this information invaluable when dealing with co-worker problems and low morale.

Clearly, the validity of Homans' psychological propositions to explain human behavior in the small-group context remain relevant today and will continue to be so in the future.

Homans wrote extensively on the group system and the group structure. His ideas have maintained their relevancy, if for no other reason, because of the reality of the large number of small group interactions all humans engage in. As Homans indicated, all groups consist of the elements of activity, interaction, sentiment, and norms. One merely has to analyze any group that he participates in to find the validity of this. A study group, for example, involves such elements as all members showing up at the designated time and place with their books and notes (norms) prepared to discuss course materials (activity) with one another (interaction) in the pursuit of the goal to improve knowledge and to do well on the exam (sentiment).

Within the group structure itself the decision-making aspect will, to a great extent, dictate the effectiveness of group action. Evidence often reveals the fact that less work is accomplished in a group than when members pursue goals independently. Therefore, a strong leader is critical to group success. Inevitably, a leader always emerges from within the group structure. Taking the role of leader involves, among other things, designating role obligations of all the group members and emphasizing a course of action designed to meet the goals of the group.

The leader of the group has greater influence over the other members and enjoys a position of power and authority. Thus, the leader is in the position to distribute rewards and implement costs onto the other group members. This may lead to resentment directed toward the leader. The leader can respond in one of two primary ways. First, the leader may not care how others think as long as the job, or task, is completed. Second, the leader may be conscious of her position, and hoping to seek the approval of others, will demonstrate that she too has incurred some costs for the good of the group.

As with all theoretical orientations, exchange theory has its critics. One major criticism of Homans' theory is aimed at its failure to provide an adequate analysis of consciousness. Homans has been labeled as a reductionist by several of his critics, who attempted to show that his deductive schemes tended to be either tautological or *ad hoc* (Coser, 1977). His critics are displeased that he ignored the symbolic meanings of behavior, that he failed to deal with internal mental states, and that he ignored the norms and values that symbolically shape exchange relations. Turner (1974) doubts very much that all sociological behaviors are reducible to psychological principles. Yet, for Homans, the issue has always been one of how to explain with deductive—or axiomatic—systems the behavior studied by sociologists. He believed that if the social sciences possessed widely used general propositions about social aggregates that can actually explain behavior, they would be less concerned about the issue of reduction.

The criticism of reductionism does stimulate the question, should exchange theory incorporate the ideas of symbolic interactionism in order to address the issue of symbolic meanings of behavior? The answer, to a certain extent, is yes. As with exchange theory, symbolic interactionism is a microtheory, but it takes great effort to incorporate the concept of the "meanings" that impact the individual's behavior. Herbert Blumer (1969) believes that humans act toward things on the basis of meanings. These meanings are acquired through social interaction and are modified through an interpretive process. Consequently, meanings placed on items will have value. Value will differ for individuals based on individual social interaction and a varying degree of rewards received. For example, some people find viewing professional football games as rewarding, while others find shopping at garage sales rewarding.

Interactionist Harold Garfinkel pays special attention to the aspects of everyday life, commonplace activities, and the idea that individuals are accountable for their taken-for-granted realities that they themselves have created. Common understandings of realities imply a consistent shared agreement of interpretations of events (Garfinkel, 1967). It is important to realize that common meanings (if they really exist) do not equate to shared value interpretations among members of a society.

Mead's discussion on value has definite exchange implications. For Mead, value exists as an object for individuals within the exchange process. The act of exchange becomes complicated by the degree to which an object is valued. As the value of the object increases, so too does the attempt to control the object (Reck, 1964).

There are those who feel exchange theory should be integrated with symbolic interactionism, primarily with Mead's categories of mind, self, and society. Peter Singlemann has made such an attempt. Singlemann used these concepts of Mead's in an effort to establish convergence between exchange theory and symbolic interaction (Ritzer, 1983). Singlemann (1972) believes exchange theory is one of the most stimulating current sociological theories because it provides a general rationale for explaining human interaction while at the same time generating distinctive propositions for predicting concrete behaviors. He correctly points out that Homans's behaviorist approach ignores aspects of subjectively meaningful behavior. As Pareto had previously pointed out, and Homans failed to address, behavior has both "logical" as well as "nonlogical" aspects, but both provide the framework in which behavior is motivated (Singlemann, 1972).

For Singlemann, the mind "reflects the human capacity to conceive what the organism perceives, defines situations, evaluate phenomena, converts gestures into symbols, and exhibits pragmatic and goal-directed behavior" (1972:416). In other words, the actor perceives something as a reward, which must be defined as such, and therefore implies a symbolic position.

The self is concerned with the process where actors reflect on themselves as objects. Although this is somewhat interesting to exchange theorists, it is treated as trivial and almost irrelevant. It is not necessarily important to understand the process by which individuals decide what rewards to seek, but rather, it is the exchange relationship itself that is important. Therefore, exchange theorists merely treat the self as a "given" and proceed to more meaningful aspects—the exchange interaction. Skinner defined the self as simply "a repertoire of behavior" (1971:189).

As for the concept of "society," the constant construction and reconstruction of interaction patterns is what leads to its creation. Thus, the exchange process entails communication through the use of symbols.

The best way to deal with the reductionist critics of Homans' theory is to include the ideas that behavior can be both rational and irrational, and objectively and subjectively rewarding. Subjective rewards include the socially symbolic nature of human interaction. Furthermore, the ideas of Blumer and Garfinkel can be treated as mere "givens," and social theorists can proceed to the most important aspect of interaction—the exchange process.

Homans has also been criticized for being too micro in his orientation and for failure to address the macrostructural issues of society. Conflict theory has many exchange implications. Conflict theory is concerned with how stratification occurs, the kind and degree of inequality among groups and individuals, and their domination over one another (Ritzer, 1991). The bottom line is power, who has it, why do they have it, and how is it maintained? These are the very issues that exchange theory deals with through their concepts of distributive justice,

power, costs, rewards, punishments, and so on. Consequently, conflict theory is useless and unnecessary at the micro level when compared to exchange theory. Randall Collins (1975) believes that conflict theory is best equipped theory to bridge the gap between micro and macro concerns and issues. But this conclusion is flawed, as many recent exchange theorists have attempted to bridge the micro–macro levels of analysis.

Homans' greatest contribution to social theory is his development of social exchange theory. His relevancy to the third millennium rests with his influence on such theorists as Peter Blau, Richard Emerson, and Karen Cook; they have transformed exchange theory to address macro-level issues. In so doing, exchange theory is perhaps the most complete of all sociological theories in explaining human behavior.

Peter Blau was born in Vienna, Austria, in 1918, emigrated to the United States in 1939, and after serving in the military during World War II, he became an American citizen in 1943 (Farganis, 2000). In 1968, Blau won the Sorokin Award from the American Sociological Association for a book he co-authored with Otis Dudley, entitled *The American Occupational Structure.* However, it is his *Exchange and Power in Social Life,* published in 1964, that propelled Blau's status as a major theorist.

In *Exchange and Power in Social Life,* Blau acknowledged his devotion to Simmel's idea of exchange. Blau described social exchange as a central principle of social life, which is derived from primitive terms, and from which complex social forces are derived. Blau stated that social exchange theory can explain behavior in groups as well as in individuals. In short, he believed that social exchange may reflect any behavior oriented to socially mediated goals. In chapter one of *Exchange and Power,* Blau discussed the structure of social associations. He analyzed Durkheim's conception of suicide as a social fact by suggesting that a social fact emerges only when it has been transformed by association. Association itself is an active factor in producing social behavior, it creates social life.

Blau's conception of reciprocity in exchange implies the existence of balancing "forces" that create a strain toward equilibrium. The simultaneous operations of diverse balancing forces recurrently produce imbalances in social life, and the resulting dialectic between reciprocity and imbalance gives social structures their distinctive nature and dynamics (Blau, 1964). Human beings choose between alternative potential associates or courses of action by evaluating the experiences, or expected experiences, of each in terms of preference ranking and then select the best alternative. Blau believed that the main force that draws people together is social attraction (Farganis, 2000). Attraction is defined in terms of potential rewards to be awarded for participating in the social exchange. When there are inadequate rewards, the deterioration of the social ties between individuals, and groups, is (more) likely to occur. Irrational as well as rational behaviors are governed by these considerations. Of particular importance is the realization that not all individuals (or groups) prefer or value the same alternatives equally. Blau also makes distinctions between intrinsically rewarding exchanges (love relationships) and associations primarily concerned with extrinsic benefits (getting paid to tutor a student).

The formation of a group involves the development of integrative bonds that unite individuals in a cohesive unit. Some of the integrative bonds discussed by Blau (1964) include:

1. **Impressing Others.** Expectations of rewards make association attractive. Strategies to appear impressive include taking risks, performing role distance, and the ability to exhibit both strain and ease depending on the social occasion.

2. **Social Approval.** Humans are anxious to receive social approval for their decisions and actions, for their opinions, and suggestions. The approving agreement of others helps to confirm their judgments, to justify their conduct, and to validate their beliefs. Preoccupation with impressing others impedes both expressive involvement and instrumental endeavors. Restraints imposed by social approval are confined to circles of significant others.

3. **Attractiveness.** Opinions that are met with approval, and one's approval of another's opinion, increase one's level of attractiveness; whereas serious and persistent conflicts of opinions lead to personal rejections (unattractiveness). The role of first impressions is involved in perceived attractiveness, for they may be self-fulfilling as well as self-defeating. One must be cautious of first impressions for their reflections may be distorted. Bluffing is a mechanism utilized by some people in hopes of creating a positive early impression, however, the cost of having a bluff called may be too high. For example, at a social gathering where an individual knows few people and claims to be a medical doctor, when in reality he is not, this bluff will backfire when a medical emergency arises and that person cannot properly execute the claimed role (bluff is called).

4. **Love.** Love is the extreme case of intrinsic attraction. Love appears to make human beings unselfish, since they themselves enjoy giving pleasures to those they love, but this selfless devotion generally rests on an interest in maintaining the other's love. The exchange process is most evident in love attachments, but the dynamics are different because the specified rewards are not as

clear as in social exchanges. In love relationships, there quite often is one person who is "more in love" than the other. This has been referred to as "the principle of least interest." The person "in less love" has the power advantage (an edge), and may manipulate this advantage to gain more rewards. Although expressions of affections stimulate another's love, freely granting them depreciates their value, which is the dilemma of love!

Group cohesion promotes the development of consensus on normative standards and the effective enforcement of these shared norms because integrative ties of fellowship enhance the significance of the informal sanctions of the group (such as disapproval and ostracism) for its individuals members. Whereas social control strengthens the group as a whole, social support strengthens its members individually, particularly in relation to outsiders (Blau, 1964).

Simmel's discussion of the dyad and the triad influenced Blau's conception of power. The simple addition of a third person to a two-person group radically changes the structure of the group. The power of an individual over another depends entirely on the social alternatives, or the lack of alternatives, of the subjected individual. Unilateral exchange generates differentiation of power. The exercise of power, as judged by norms of fairness, evokes social approval or disapproval, which may lead to legitimate organization and to social opposition, respectively. Collective approval of power legitimates that power, collective disapproval of power engenders opposition. Furthermore, equilibrium forces on one level are disequilibrating forces on another (Blau, 1964).

Processes of social association can be conceptualized, following Homans' lead, as an exchange of social activity, tangible or intangible, and more or less regarding or costly,

between at least two persons (Blau, 1964). Exchanges of gifts in simpler societies served latent functions of establishing bonds of friendship and to establish superordination over others. The basic foundation of any social exchange involves the availability of a reward by one person being offered to another person at a certain cost. The relationship continues as long as both persons find the exchange mutually beneficial, or necessary. A variety of conditions affect processes of social exchange: the stage in the development and the character of the relationship between exchange partners; the nature of the benefits that enter into the transactions; the costs incurred in providing them; and the social context in which the exchanges take place.

Blau was clearly influenced by Homans' work, but he attempted to remedy some of the perceived deficiencies of Homans' conceptualizations and to reconcile them within the structural perspective (Coser, 1977). For Blau, studying face-to-face interaction was just the beginning attempt to explain larger concerns, such as social structures. Blau felt that there were three basic reasons why one should look beyond micro-level interaction patterns. First, humans rarely pursue one goal and forget about all others. Second, humans are inconsistent with their performances. Third, humans never have complete information regarding alternative behaviors that might be available.

Where Blau left off, contemporary theorists Richard Emerson and Karen Cook (among others) have continued to transform the microsociological perspective of exchange theory to the macro-level (Ritzer, 2000). Emerson emphasized the concepts of power and dependence and the alternatives available to people. The dependence variable is measured by how much the resources to be obtained are valued (Wallace and Wolf, 1999). In other words, what costs are willing to be incurred in other to obtain valuable resources. For example, how willing is the United States to turn its back on the dictatorship government of Kuwait and its repressive government on the rights of its citizens, in order to obtain its oil? Or consider the Nike corporation and its willingness to forgo the public relations nightmare of alleged child-labor law violations (among other complaints) in its Vietnam factories (costs) so that they could reduce manufacturing costs and consequently increase profits (rewards).

Cook and Emerson have conducted a number of laboratory studies of exchange relationships in order to determine what costs people are willing to endure in their pursuits of rewards (Wallace and Wolf, 1999). Studies of exchange situations also demonstrate that the experience of frequent exchange itself creates a positive feeling toward other members of the exchange network (Lawler and Yoon, 1996). Lawler and his colleagues have explained exchange relationships by the term "relational cohesion." Thus reflecting an emotional element, but also a macro element, as integral aspects of exchange theory. "Empirical studies such as those of Emerson, Cook, Lawler, and others have extended

Homans's formulations and underlined the distinctive characteristics of social exchange" (Wallace and Wolf, 1999:321).

Exchange theory has experienced and enjoys an evolutionary growth in credibility. From the basic level of exchange described by George Homans and expanded upon by Peter Blau (especially at the group level), to a "network analysis" approach by such contemporary thinkers as Emerson and Cook. Perhaps the best illustration, or evidence, of the bright future of exchange theory is Gary Becker's winning of the prestigious Nobel Prize for economics in 1992. Becker believes people make rational choices about various behaviors based on economic theories such as cost-benefit and incentives. Becker believes behavior can be analyzed and predicted in terms of time and pleasure "costs" as well as with the economic concept of money. He equates long term marriage with capital, and refers to children as consumer durables (Smith, 1992).

Homans' brilliant works and contributions to social theory are only at the early stages of recognition. His insights of human behavior will continue to inspire social thought well into the third millennium.

14

Contributions from Women to Classical Social Theory

The absence of a chapter on a female classical social thinker does not reflect the fact that women did not contribute significantly to social theory; rather, it reflects the patriarchal reality of the social structure found in nearly all societies throughout most of human history. There have been a number of women who have contributed to social theory and social activism, leading to a revised way of thinking about the role of women in society. This chapter provides a brief review of a number of women who deserve recognition for their participation in the formulating of social thought.

The story of sociology is generally a history of men (e.g., Comte, Spencer, Marx, Durkheim, and so forth) and their contributions to the formation of the field. Missing from many social theory books was any significant mention of women. It was as if women were "invisible" from early sociology. "'Invisibility' suggests not being seen, that is, never having one's presence acknowledged as significant" (Lengermann and Niebrugge-Brantley, 1998). Interestingly, some of the women to be discussed in this chapter originally received their credit in sociology because they were linked to men in sociology.

The women to be discussed in this chapter are: Harriet Martineau (1802–1876),

Beatrice Potter Webb (1858–1943), Anna Julia Cooper (1859–1964), Ida Wells-Barnett (1862–1931), Charlotte Perkins Gilman (1860–1935), Jane Addams (1860–1935), Marianne Weber (1870–1954) and Elizabeth Cady Stanton (1815—1902). Stanton is included here partly because of the "uniqueness" she brings to any volume on the discussion of women contributors to social theory; but mostly because it allows for the sociological examination of her wonderful insights into human behavior. Also, discussion of Stanton allows for an introduction to the "Ladies of Seneca Falls." Seneca Falls, New York, is considered the birthplace of the Women's Rights Movement. It is the work of these women that led to the development of the feminist movement.

The women whose recognition in the past were linked primarily to men include: Martineau, as Comte's translator; Weber, as the wife of a genius (Max); Webb as Sidney's partner; Addams, as "secular saint;" and Gilman, as the eccentric genius of such publications as *The Yellow Wallpaper* (Lengermann and Niebrugge-Brantley, 1998). All of these women, however, made significant contributions to sociological thought in their own right.

Harriet Martineau (1802–1876)

Harriet Martineau was born in Norwich, England, on June 12, 1802. She lived during the period that witnessed the beginnings of sociology; and although she is best known as Auguste Comte's translator, she herself was a prolific writer. Harriet was the sixth of eight children born to Thomas and Elizabeth (Rankin) Martineau. Martineau was raised in a loving and nurturing family environment. She was often ill as a child and suffered from many physical limitations: she could not taste or smell, and she lost most of her hearing when she was twelve. Her family was slow to recognize her hearing disability and she did not receive her "ear trumpet" (a hearing-assistance aid) until she was eighteen. Harriet enjoyed reading and writing and was always self-disciplined to study. Martineau was encouraged to speak her mind and stand by her social and ethical beliefs. This was congruent with the English Dissenting tradition (Herbert Spencer was a Dissenter) that characterized Norwich. The city of Norwich was prosperous in industry and possessed an intellectual culture that embraced the dissention tradition. "Dissenters belonged to a range of Protestant sects— Baptist, Methodist, Quaker, Presbyterian, and Unitarian—that refused to accept Anglicanism, the state religion of Britain, and were thus barred from various civil rights such as voting and attending university" (Lengermann and Niebrugge-Brantley, 1998). The Martineau family were Unitarians who emphasized the value of education and did not believe in worshiping a God; instead, they encouraged a commitment to meeting social needs. Harriet and her sisters, who were all home-schooled, enjoyed a higher level of education than compared to most British women, but she regretted for her whole life that she was barred from attending a university.

Thomas Martineau was a successful textile manufacturer. He was a hard worker and understood that the success of his business was dependent on happy employees who were sharing in the profits of industry. The phenomenon of the "Industrial Revolution" transformed the entire socio-economic makeup of England, and this was especially true in Norwich. By the 1820s the Martineau family business and most of the prosperity of Norwich disappeared because of industrialization (Webb, 1960). Harriet took note of these events and came to believe that society was greatly influenced by two variables: politics and economics. "Political economy," the emerging science of economics, as it was known then, became a common topic of conversation in the Martineau family. These experiences would greatly influence Harriet's future writings in social science.

The 1820s were a turbulent period for Martineau: The family fortune was quickly disappearing; an engagement she had ended; all of England was suffering from an economic crisis; her father passed away in 1826; and in 1829 the family business completely collapsed (Lengermann and Niebrugge-Brantley, 1998). Oddly, Martineau became engaged to a second man, a Unitarian minister with "weak nerves." When he collapsed into insanity, Martineau was relieved, and she even refused to visit him in the hospital. He finally died a month later (Hoecker-Drysdale, 1992). The family's new economic reality dictated that Harriet would have to begin working to support herself and assist the family. She lived at home with her mother and began to write fictional tales on economic issues for the *Monthly Repository*. Interestingly, she had published an article anonymously in 1822, "Female Writers on Practical Divinity," in the *Monthly Repository* (a Unitarian journal).

In 1830, Martineau produced 52 pieces for the *Repository*, "plus a novel, a book-length religious history, and essays for contests sponsored by the Unitarian Association" (Lengermann and Niebrugge-Brantley, 1998). She was clearly taking advantage of her Unitarian background in order to get published; but it is hard to fault her for this, as she was establishing her name for future publications.

Present-day critics of Martineau do fault her, and point to this high output of mostly general journalistic articles, essays, and commentaries, as evidence of her lightweight intellectual status (Adams and Sydie, 2001). Martineau's writings can be defended on at least two fronts (Adams and Sydie, 2001). First, she was writing for a wage; this was her livelihood and she was economically dependent on this income (she did not set out purposely to be an academic writer). Second, she possessed the ability to describe rather difficult subject matters in a more popular style of writing—she was attempting to appeal to an audience that did not necessarily include academia. She wanted to reach the masses. Returning from an inspirational visit to Ireland, financed by the Unitarian prize money she had won, Martineau decided to write a series of short tales illustrating the principles of political economy. After a lengthy and difficult search for a publisher, Martineau's patience and writing would be vindicated. The first volumes of her *Illustrations of Political Economy* (1832) became a runaway bestseller. In these volumes she wrote about the ideas of such people as Adam Smith, David Ricardo, Thomas Malthus, and James Mill. She produced 25 volumes in the following 24 months, each volume of about 33,000 words. By 1834, the series was selling at the unbelievable rate of 10,000 per month. She was easily outselling such notable writers of her time as Charles Dickens (Hoecker-Drysdale, 1992).

Martineau's name was now recognizable and she turned her attention toward the creation of a science of society. She visited the United States for two years (1834–36) and wrote three books about her experience: *Society in America* (1836), *How to Observe Morals and Manners* (1838), and *Retrospect of Western Travel* (1838). Martineau (1836) describes her visit to America as a wonderful experience: She traveled to twenty of the then 24 states; she visited Congress; had dinner with President Jackson; she liked Americans and they seemed to like her; and she met abolitionist proponents William Lloyd Garrison and Maria Westin Chapman (with whom she maintained lasting friendships). Having written against slavery as early as 1830, Martineau was easily able to identify with the abolitionist cause. *How to Observe Morals and Manners* was her first text on sociological research techniques. She had started the methodological portion of the book before she left for the United States, and then applied and expanded the research strategies in her extensive American field trip. By the end of the 1830s Martineau was acknowledged as a leading social analyst, which led to a request from her publishers that she become editor of a newly proposed sociology periodical (Hoecker-Drysdale, 1992). She turned them down, and instead concentrated of her own writings in sociology and other interest areas.

During the 1840s Martineau published many books and articles. Among them were: *The Hour and the Man* (1841), a fictional account of Toussaint L'Ouverture, the black liberator of Haiti; *The Playfellow* (1841), very popular children's adventure stories; *Life in the Sick-Room* (1844), written after she had recovered from an illness due to gynecological problems; *Letters on Mesmerism* (1845), a controversial book because she promoted mesmerism (hypnotism) and proclaimed how it had helped her recovery; *Eastern Life: Past and Present* (1848) a sociological and religious account of her trip through the Middle East; and *Household Education* (1849), a sociological, pro-family examination of the early socialization process of children (Lengermann and Niebrugge-Brantley, 1998). On a personal note, in 1845, Martineau had purchased land at Ambleside, England, and designed and had built The Knoll, a family farm type dwelling. She would live there until her death on June 27, 1876.

Martineau's quality production continued through the 1850s. In 1851, she co-authored with friend and philosopher, Henry George Atkinson, *Letters on the Laws of Man's Nature*, where the authors state that, "the mind can be studied scientifically as material reality that forms ideas out of experience. She rejected the idealist thesis that the mind has immanent categories issuing directly from God" (Lengermann and Niebrugge-Brantley, 1998). She was promoting her atheism. In 1852 she published *Letters from Ireland*, a book written about her travels throughout Ireland and her analysis of the Irish people. In 1853, she made the contribution to sociology that most students are made aware of, her translation of Comte's six-volume *Positive Philosophy*. Martineau had come to believe that many educated middle-class English people had begun to lose their sense of moral direction during the 1840s and 1850s. Martineau (1853) wrote in the preface of her translation of *Positive Philosophy*, that a large number of English people were adrift because ideals of morality were in a state of fluctuation (Vol.I:viii). As Coser (1977) explains, "Harriet Martineau here alludes to the crisis of belief that came to be widespread in the forties. Educated men were increasingly deprived of the kind of certainties that used to be provided by traditional religion. Whereas earlier in the century those who had lost faith were sustained by the utilitarian morality of Bentham and the elder Mill, this alternative was no longer viable for the later generation" (p. 121).

In 1855, Martineau became ill again, and this time, fearing her death was imminent, she began writing her autobiography. She recovered, but limited her writing to mostly journalistic pieces. On her death bed at her beloved The Knoll, Martineau (1877) wrote that she had no regrets about her life, and she saw all of humanity advancing under the law of progress.

Significant Contributions to Sociology

Martineau's name usually surfaces as a mere footnote in sociology, and even then, it is usually mentioned because she translated Comte's works into English, but she did more than simply translate Comte's ideas (she actually managed to condense and clarify much of his work), she also wrote about social issues of her time. She traveled to different countries and was able to provide cross-cultural analysis on a diverse sets of beliefs (e.g., religion). Martineau was responsible for educating the public on guiding principles of sociology. If Comte is labeled the "Father of Sociology," it might be proper to label Martineau as the "Mother of Sociology." Lengermann and Niebrugge-Brantley (2000) refer to her as a "founding mother" of sociology. Martineau shared with her contemporaries a general belief in progress, that human society was constantly moving forward and becoming better. She noted, however, that progress is sometimes interrupted by various crises.

Among Martineau's contributions to sociology was her insistence on defining subject matter methodologically. The subject matter, according to Martineau, should be social life in society. This was especially true in terms of answering the question, "What constitutes a better life for people?" Examination of current living standards would allow the social scientist an opportunity to describe details that would make life better (progress). In an attempt to create a "science of society," sociology should be grounded in systematic, empirical observation. Furthermore, in order for the masses to make personal and political decisions that would help enrich their lives, this "science of society" should be made accessible to a general readership. Martineau involved herself in extensive travel, where she began to apply her systematic scientific inquiry to an understanding of society. From the time she first started traveling until she died, Martineau would conduct sociological analysis (Lengermann and Niebrugge-Brantley, 1998).

Martineau believed that any analysis of society must include its morals (cultural values and beliefs) and manners (social interaction). She recommended that nothing should be overlooked in the methodological pursuit of an accurate portrayal of the subject matter. She suggested that data should be sought in such places as cemeteries and prisons. Tombstone inscriptions found at cemeteries reveal the morals of the community in which the dead had resided; and because there is a prevailing moral code of *De mortuis nil nisi bonum* (do not speak negatively of the dead) epitaphs everywhere indicate what were considered good qualities (Martineau, 1838). Studies of prisons are important as they reflect the morals and manners of society that are most important; because those who violate certain norms (morals) will be punished by society and find themselves in prison. In her analysis of America's democratic ideal of social equality, Martineau (1836) noticed an inconsistency in the form of the unequal status of women. She noted that the Constitution guarantees equality and

democracy, but not for women. This observation would help create her feminist thinking, especially her analysis of the role of women in relation to the institution of marriage. Martineau would maintain a lifetime commitment to the betterment of women's role in society. Of sociological significance was her article "Female Industry" (1859), which analyzed women's work in Great Britain and concluded with the overall importance of female labor to the national wealth (Lengermann and Niebrugge-Brantley, 1998). Her concern over the enslavement of Blacks is another feature of her work in *Society in America*.

Martineau (1838) speaks of the importance of researchers remaining detached (impartiality) from their subjects and of remaining careful not to impose their own values (an ethnocentric view) onto their study. Martineau seemed to violate this very principle in her study of tombstone inscriptions and the corresponding idea that only good things are said about a person in epitaphs. The point is, if the sociologist wants to truly understand the morals and manners of people, one must investigate the "bad" things that people do as well. She did not advocate complete value-neutrality but believed that a researcher's own biases (if any) should be acknowledged in the study. Martineau (1838) felt that the sociologist should try and develop a systematic understanding of the subject in order to better understand the meanings of an activity for the actor (Lengermann and Niebrugge-Brantley, 2000). Sympathy toward the subject is a skill that separates sociology from geology or general statistics. A researcher who fails to understand the meaning of an event that the actor participates in does not gain the full methodological picture (Martineau, 1838). Her approach is similar to Weber's *verstehen* or the Chicago School's use of sympathetic introspection.

Martineau believed that sociology should be a critical and ethical field, that is, it should work toward improving society and pointing out its ills. This is completely in tune with the prevailing theme of the early sociologists as moral reformers (see chapter one). Martineau was not a brilliant writer, nor was she an imaginative genius. But, as Thomas (1985) concludes, "Her gift was, in many respects, a more taxing and demanding one, for she set herself the task of recording the sights, the events, and the people of her own time with a steady, careful, and patient eye" (p. 132). The ability to accurately capture social reality and put it to writing is praiseworthy for anyone. Martineau is truly a sociologist deserving of proper recognition for her contributions to the development of the field.

Beatrice Potter Webb (1858–1943)

Martha Beatrice Potter was born on January 22, 1858, at Standish House, on the edge of the Cotswolds, near Gloucester, England (Webb, 1982). She was the eighth daughter born to Richard Potter, a businessman and Laurencina Heyworth. Beatrice was four years old when her brother, and male heir, was born; she was seven when he died. Beatrice learned early on in her life the gendered nature of her society. Webb (1926) explains that she lived, "in the shadow of my baby brother's birth and death" (p. 58). Gender issues were a major preoccupation for Webb since early on in her life. "She seems to have experienced some basic discomfiture in gender identity, which while not the determining factor in her life, certainly left her with mixed feelings about being female. The particularity of her response is perhaps demonstrated by the fact that all of her sisters made conventionally good marriages and went on to live lives of

conventional female service" (Lengermann and Niebrugge-Brantley, 1998).

Richard Potter made his living as a railroad speculator and became a very wealthy industrialist. Laurencina was a close personal friend of Herbert Spencer, a frequent visitor to the Webb household. Richard first met Spencer when he was displaying a flying-machine (a type of airplane) that he had invented. Potter was fascinated by this and offered to finance its production; unfortunately, Spencer's flying machine never got off the ground (Muggeridge and Adam, 1968). Spencer (1904) described Webb's parents as having an ideal marriage, "the most admirable pair I have ever met" (p. 19). Both Richard and Laurencina's fathers had risen to industrial power early in the nineteenth century. This economically advantageous lifestyle afforded Beatrice's parents (both of liberal provincial backgrounds) an opportunity to take a passionate interest in every detail of their children's upbringing (Muggeridge and Adam, 1968). The Potter house was filled with books and intelligent friends. The girls were encouraged to read widely and to discuss candidly their impressions of what they read (Webb, 1932). The nine girls were free to roam about a very large country house farm filled with ponies, dogs, and cats. They would enjoy elaborate picnics and lavish birthdays. There were servants to take care of all their needs. The Potter home was one with many luxuries.

Beatrice, like her sisters, was homeschooled. In *My Apprenticeship* (1926), the only volume she completed of her planned autobiographical trilogy, Beatrice described her education as very broad, which included: speculation of religion and philosophy, along with the study of literature and the classics, modern languages, history, mathematics, and science.

Laurencina Potter, Beatrice's mother, was described as being nearly as perfect as a human being could be. She was raised by her father to see herself as a "paragon of virtue," and her family treated her as such (Muggeridge and Adam, 1968). From the time she first met Richard Potter in Rome, where they fell immediately in love, he treated her as an "angel" as well. Richard was from a "broken" home and made every effort to assure a happy and successful marriage and family with Laurencina. In 1882, Laurencina died, and Beatrice became her father's best friend and close companion, running his households in London and in the country (Webb, 1982). She enjoyed the stimulating conversation of houseguests such as Spencer. "Herbert Spencer never married, but—like other eminent Victorian bachelors—he loved little girls. In those days mothers were merely touched and amused if an elderly unmarried friend fell in love with their pre-pubescent daughters . . . . He said they served as 'vicarious objects of the philoprogenitive instinct'" (Muggeridge and Adam, 1968:40). Spencer enjoyed the bevy of little girls at Standish, and they looked forward to Spencer's visits.

As a teenager, Beatrice Potter traveled to America with her father as he attended to an extended business trip. In her diary she wrote about such subjects as having a right to question conventional religion, but then stated that one has a duty to create a belief system of one's own. She would spend most of her life in search of her own belief system (Lengermann and Niebrugge-Brantley, 1998). As a young woman, Beatrice felt the social pressures of society's expectation that she should be looking for a husband. She was of a privileged background and taught to believe that she could accomplish whatever she put her mind to. Unfortunately, employment opportunities for women of this era were very limited. Potter faced quite a dilemma throughout the 1880s. She was "well-to-do, intelligent and attractive, Beatrice was apparently set for a conventionally successful marriage. But, her upbringing . . . . left her with a profound inner conflict between emotion and intellect, between her feminine instincts and her desire to be independent and successful in a man's world . . . ." (Webb, 1982). Beatrice was torn between her perceived duty to get married and her fond desire to make "something of herself." She pursued odd jobs in an attempt to find herself and she pursued with obsessive passion the Radical politician Joseph Chamberlain (Webb, 1982). Nothing came of the obsession but, "she sought relief from that self-tormenting attachment in the anodyne of work in the East End of London" (Webb, 1982:xii). Potter became a "rent collector" in the Katherine Buildings, a poverty-ravaged housing slum. She was horrified and demoralized by the poor conditions that these people were living in. This was her first real witness of the differences between the wealthy class and the working class of England.

Through a family connection, Beatrice found a job working with her cousin-in-law, Charles Booth, an author and social researcher. Through Booth, Potter learned all the techniques of social research; quantitative and qualitative; personal interviewing; observation studies; content analysis; and statistical analysis. Her work with Booth convinced Potter to pursue a career as "a brain worker," a phrase she used often in an attempt to identify with other workers (Lengermann and Niebrugge-Brantley, 1998). She was also convinced that she needed to do something to help the less-fortunate; and she decided that she would give her life to charity work, along with the dutiful quest of figuring out how to make the lives of the working-class better. Potter finally had her own sense of direction in life.

In 1891, living off a pension received following the death of her father, Potter pub-

Fabian ideologist

lished her most influential single-authored book, *The Co-operative Movement in Great Britain*. Her personal life was taking a turn for the better as well. She had met Sidney Webb, a fast-rising civil servant and Fabian ideologist, a year earlier. Her immediate interest in Webb was strictly as a friend and intellectual partner. On July 23, 1892, Webb won over the reluctant Beatrice Potter. She insisted that the wedding be based on equality, and that it should be a working partnership (Webb, 1982). Although she had begun to come to terms with the idea that she might end up a working "spinster," she had not really turned against marriage. She was quoted to say in 1889 (the year just prior to meeting Webb), "God knows celibacy is painful to a woman" (Webb, 1982:232). Their marriage had become quite the topic of conversation, as they were both socialites, and both well on their way to reshaping English society. For the rest of her life, Beatrice Potter Webb worked with her husband on a variety of social issues. Among their many collaborative publications: *The History of Trade Unionism* (1894); the companion volume, *Industrial Democracy* (1897); *The History of Liquor Licensing in England* (1903); *The Parish and the County* (1906); *The Manor and the Borough* (1908); *The Story of the King's Highway* (1913); *English Prisons under Local Government* (1922); *English Poor Law History: The Old Poor Law* (1927); *English Poor Law History: The Last Hundred Years* (1929); *Methods of Social Study* (1932); and their last work of social science, *Soviet Communism: A New Civilization* (1937). Clearly, the Webbs were proficient in their level of production. Besides their publications, the Webbs created the London School of Economics and Political Science (1895) and Beatrice founded the *New Statesman*, a periodical concerning itself with sociological issues. Potter Webb lived in Chicago for a while and conducted social research on urban poverty in an at-

tempt to develop reform legislation. In 1928, Beatrice and Sidney Webb retired to Hampshire, where they lived until their deaths—1943 for Beatrice, and 1947 for Sidney.

Significant Contributions to Sociology

Beatrice Potter Webb helped to break the gender barrier found in professional fields, including in sociology. Webb maintained a strong commitment to the proposition that in order to claim to be a science, sociological work must be arrived at inductively, and grounded in the practice of rigorous empirical investigation. Empirical research aids sociology because it allows the social scientist to show that society is a system of emergent social structures, rather than a by-product of individual action. She felt that the goal of sociology should be to discover how economic equity can be arrived at through a democratic decision-making process. The empirical research conducted by the Webbs, "became an intellectual and political partnership which left a policy-oriented body of empirical research that laid the foundation for the twentieth-century British welfare state" (Lengermann and Niebrugge-Brantley, 2000).

It was Potter Webb's work with Booth that first introduced her to the importance of utilizing empirical data; but it is also where she came to the view that the capitalist system was slowly destroying the British working class, and that it was the working-class people who would suffer the most. She studied the working-class, empirically, in order to find ways to make their lives better. This was quite a transformation for Webb, because, as a child, she not only enjoyed the benefits of wealth, she was raised by the Spencerian application of social evolution. Spencer, more or less, blamed poverty on individuals who were selected against, because they were not "fit" for the environment (e.g., society's economic structure). She learned of Malthus' idea that charity leads to overpopulation by allowing the unfit to survive and produce more unfit children. The very idea of governmental interference in the natural order of things went directly against the tenets of social evolution. It is quite amazing that Potter Webb became the caring, generous, crusader of the working-poor.

While conducting empirical research on the working poor, Potter Webb became convinced that poverty was caused by social conditions. The problem of poverty was structural, not individual unfitness as proposed by Spencer. She felt that capitalism should be replaced by socialism. British socialism is essentially pragmatic, and not similar to Marx's radical conception of a reconstruction of society. When Potter married Webb, she became associated with the "Young Fabians" and Fabian socialism. The Fabians believed that society should be modified through slow and bloodless reform. "They christened themselves after the Roman general Fabius: 'For the right moment you must wait, as Fabius did most patiently when warring against Hannibal, though many censured his delays; but when the time comes you must strike hard as Fabius did or your waiting will be vain and fruitless'" (Muggeridge and Adam, 1967:131). The Fabians positioned themselves in government and attempted to shape policy in the socialist perspective. They believed in social progress (evolution), but they believed that it must be given directional assistance. According to Webb (1983) the workers need to be led because, "judging from our knowledge of the Labour movement we can expect *no* leader from the working class. Our only hope is in permeating the young middle-class men,

catching them for collectivism before they have enlisted on the other side" (p. 77).

Webb never described herself as a feminist; in fact, many contemporary feminists shun her works because of her antisuffrage stance of the 1880s and 1890s. Her simple reasoning for not identifying with the feminist movement was because she personally never experienced anything negative resulting from her gender. She had visited the Hull House on her trip to the United States, and Jane Addams read her *The Co-operative Movement in Great Britain* (Lengermann and Niebrugge-Brantley, 1998). It so happens that Webb's primary concern was the plight of the poor, not of women.

Beatrice Potter Webb was among the early female sociologists. She attempted to develop legislation that would help the working-class poor. In keeping with the true sociological tradition, Webb insisted on the use of empirical data to support theory and social policy. She is a worthy contributor to the field of sociology.

Anna Julia Cooper (1858–1964)

"Cooper was born Anna Julia Hayward in Raleigh, North Carolina, in 1858, the daughter of Hannah Stanley Haywood, an African American woman who was a slave and 'presumably,' in Cooper's words, of George Washington Hayward, her mother's white master" (Alexander, 1995:338). Her mother was a slave but Anna described her as the finest woman she had ever known. Her mother could read the Bible and write a little bit. Anna Hayward was born during the Civil War and freed by the Emancipation Proclamation Act of 1863. She was quite a smart young girl, but had to battle racism, sexism, and limited finances in her pursuit of an education. She attended St. Augustine's Normal and Collegiate Institute, an Episcopal school for African Americans. She was such a bright student that she was a tutor since the age of nine. Hayward was admitted to Oberlin College, one of the few colleges that allowed Blacks, and earned her bachelor's degree in 1884 and an honorary master's degree in 1887. Hayward would support herself as a teacher in the Washington D. C., school system for the rest of her life (Lengermann and Niebrugge-Brantley, 2000). In 1887, Anna Cooper would marry George A. C. Cooper, a native of the British West Indies. After his death two years later, she would never remarry.

Cooper valued education and the subsequent status it afforded her. She believed that she was bestowed with a Heavenly "intelligent consciousness" that pushed her in the direction of education (Alexander, 1995). Cooper felt that it was her destiny to enlighten the masses and to help reshape society. She campaigned against racism throughout her life. In 1892, she published *A Voice from the South*, her collection of essays on the issues of race, gender, education, and other topics. Throughout her teaching career, Cooper continued to work toward her Ph.D., by studying during summer recess and various academic leaves. She attended Columbia University and the Sorbonne, in Paris. Her dedication and commitment finally paid off when she successfully defended her dissertation, *Slavery and the French Revolutionists (1788–1805)*, at the age of sixty-five. Her dissertation was written in French and made available in English in 1988. It is with these two books that Cooper demonstrated her ability as, "a significant sociological theorist of race and society both in the United States and globally . . . " (Lengermann and Niebrugge-Brantley, 2000).

Significant Contributions to Sociology

The post–Civil War era was not kind to African Americans. The climate of Cooper's time includes: lynchings at an all time high; overt and covert racism evident throughout the nation; an economic depression that increased tensions in 1893; a confederation of Black women being formed in Boston (1895); and many other Blacks who were speaking out against racism. In *A Voice from the South*, Cooper spoke out against: the white women's movement for its racist exclusions; the emerging Black male leaders' refusal to fight for the rights of Black women; the negative portrayal of Blacks in literature; and U.S. expansionism (Alexander, 1995). Her core belief was that racism was the result of an unequal power structure found in society.

Cooper was a theorist who sought, "self-consciously, to describe the patterns of social life and to stimulate herself in that work of theoretical creation" (Lengermann and Niebrugge-Brantley, 2000:314). Cooper attempted to support her theories, as would any good sociologist, with statistical data and historical documentation. She applied her theories primarily to issues of race and gender. Cooper served as an inspiration to many, and in her writings, "she forges a space for the African-American woman intellectual, working and thinking at the turn of the century" (Alexander, 1995:355).

Ida Wells-Barnett (1862–1931)

Ida Wells-Barnett was a fearless civil rights crusader, suffragist, women's rights advocate, journalist, and speaker. She was born in Holly Springs, Mississippi in 1862, and died in Chicago, Illinois in 1931, at the age of sixty-nine. Her parents were slaves who gained freedom after the Civil War. After they gained freedom, Ida's father, Jim Wells, was able to find employment as a carpenter with the man with whom he had apprenticed. Ida's mother, Elizabeth Warrenton

Wells, worked as a cook for her husband's boss, and the whole family lived on his land. Elizabeth Wells enrolled at Rust College, an institution started by white Northerners for the education of freedmen, so that she could learn to read her Bible (Lengermann and Niebrugge-Brantley, 1998).

In her autobiography, *Crusade for Justice* (1970), Wells-Barnett credited her parents with instilling in her an interest for politics and a guiding principle of fighting for justice. She recalled that when her father's boss asked for her father's vote (it was a common practice in those days for a white boss to demand his black employees vote as he dictated) he refused; Jim Wells resisted, moved off his boss's land, and started his own carpentry business. Ida Wells followed in her mother's footsteps and attended school at Rust College. When Ida was just fourteen, her parents and youngest sibling fell victim to yellow fever. Symbolic of the responsibility and perseverance that characterized her life, Ida kept the family together by working as a teacher until 1883. She continued her studies at Rust during this period. In 1883 she moved to Memphis to live with her aunt. As an educated black woman, Ida quickly found that her teaching, writing, and public speaking skills were in high demand. Teaching salaries were also much higher in Memphis than compared to rural Mississippi. Ida expanded her own education by attending both Fiske and LeMoyne Institute.

It was in Memphis where Ida first began to fight for racial and gender equality. She worked as a journalist and started a one-woman campaign against lynching in 1883, by writing a series of articles detailing, with empirical data, the horrors and racial terrorism that lynching represented (Lengermann and Niebrugge-Brantley, 2000). In 1884, Ida Wells was ordered to move from her seat on a railroad car. A white man wanted to sit

Ida Wells-Barnett (1862–1931) African American civil rights crusader, suffragist, women's rights advocate, journalist, and speaker.
Source: CORBIS

down, and Blacks were supposed to sit in the "smoker" cars, which were generally very dirty. Despite the 1875 Civil Rights Act banning discrimination on the basis of race in theaters, hotels, and other public accommodations, several railroad companies ignored this law. It is interesting to note that her defiant act was before *Plessy v. Ferguson* (1896), the U.S. Supreme Court decision that established the doctrine of "separate but equal," which legalized racial segregation. Wells was forcefully removed from the train and the white passengers cheered. When she returned to Memphis, she immediately hired an attorney to sue the Chesapeake, Ohio and Southwestern Rail Road Company. She won the decision in the lower court but lost in the Court of Appeals. She was ordered to pay court costs of $200. From this point on Wells-Barnett was identified as a dissident. She decided to dedicate the rest of her life to fight for the rights of Blacks and women.

Her suit against the railroad company (and against Jim Crow tactics) sparked her career as a journalist. Many newspapers wanted to hear about the experience of the twenty-five-year-old school teacher who stood up against white supremacy. Her writing career progressed in papers geared toward African American and Christian audiences. In 1889, Wells became a writer and part owner of the *Free Speech and Headlight*, a paper primarily owned by Rev. R. Nightingale. He forced his large congregation to subscribe to the paper. The success of her writing career led Wells-Barnett to leave her job as a teacher. She often wrote about the horrors of lynching, and in her first antilynching pamphlet, *Southern Horrors*, she described a case involving one of her close friends, Thomas Moss. Moss and two of his friends, Calvin McDowell and Henry Stewart, owned a successful grocery store called the People's Grocery. Their success was cutting into the profits of white-owned grocers. A group of angry white men decided to do something about this matter and attacked the owners of People's Market. Moss and his friends fought back and one of them shot one of the attacking white men. The black men were arrested, but a lynch-mob broke into the jail, dragged them away from town, and brutally murdered all three.

Upset by the way the white media covered the event, Wells-Barnett began a campaign against lynching and wrote about it in *The Free Speech*. "Her articles in *The Free Speech* provided ideological clarity and served as an organizing tool locally, nationally and internationally" (Boyd, 1994:9). She led a campaign of a mass exodus of Blacks from Memphis and her open campaign against white patriarchal chivalry (even suggesting that white women might desire black male companionship) so offended Whites that they destroyed the press offices of *Free Speech*. A white-owned newspaper in Memphis called for the lynching of Wells-Barnett, but she was attending an African Methodist Episcopal Church convention in Philadelphia (Boyd, 1994). It became clear, however, that she could no longer live in Memphis, so she moved to Chicago and continued her journalistic attacks on southern injustices. She would live in Chicago for most of her adult life. Wells-Barnett was a friend of Jane Addams the activist, and her work at Hull House.

Chicago was host to the 1893 World's Columbian Exposition, which black Americans were not allowed to attend. In a response to this overt act of racism, Ida Wells wrote and published a pamphlet, *The Reason Why the Colored American Is Not in The World's Columbian Exposition*. The introduction was translated into German and French, and the pamphlet, which included a copy of "Lynch Law"—an essay that explains the racist psychology of American society—was distributed to patrons of the exposition (Boyd, 1994). That same year, a black women's organization founded the World's Congress of Representative Women, in order to secure representation of Blacks in the exposition. Wells-Barnett would remain a prominent figure in the women's movement. She was instrumental in the founding of the National Association of Colored Women, the National Afro-American Council, and the National Association for the Advancement of Colored People. She was now a leader of campaigns for women's suffrage. Wells-Barnett, along with Jane Addams successfully blocked the establishment of segregated schools in Chicago.

In 1895, Ida Wells married F. L. Barnett, a Chicago lawyer and editor of a Black newspaper. In the same year she published her second major work on lynching, *A Red Record*. She used data from White newspapers as a part of her statistical analysis of lynching. Wells-Barnett would remain as social activist and writer for the rest of her life. She died on March 25, 1931, in Chicago.

Significant Contributions to Sociology

Ida Wells-Barnett, like Anna Julia Cooper, was directly influenced by her immediate environment. Born slaves, freed early on in childhood, but realizing the racist nature of society, they both possessed an intellectual and activist desire to make a positive contribution to society. They both fought for the rights of women and Blacks. Their theories were based on the premise that Blacks and women are oppressed because of the unequal distribution of power in society. Cooper and Wells-Barnett believed that oppression creates a dominate-dominated class structure. Domination by the power group is patterned by five factors: history (sets of events that lead to power discrimination); ideology (distortions and exaggerations of select events); material resources (possession of resources equals power); manners (routinization of everyday interactions between dominants and subordinates); and passion (the key to domination rests on emotion, a desire to control) (Lengermann and Niebrugge-Brantley, 1998). Cooper and Wells-Barnett both wished for a society without domination, a society that allowed for peaceful coexistence, or equilibrium.

Unfortunately, American society was not in a state of racial equilibrium, and class struggles coexisted with racial and sexual discrimination. Wells-Barnett wrote articles that demanded justice. She called upon Blacks and women to become politically active, to fight inequality. She used lynching as her exemplar of racial injustice. She spoke internationally on the topic and linked it to racial and class inequality. For Wells-Barnett, lynching involved the combination of racial and gender issues. "She dissolves the rationale for the lynching of black men offered by white society, the myth that the victim has raped a white woman. She provides case studies of the emotional/sexual attraction between white women and black men as a normal part of social relations in the South and of the attraction of white men to black women" (Lengermann and Niebrugge-Brantley, 2000). Publishing ideas such as this during this particular era reflects very radical behavior. But, it was this very behavior and spirited commitment to activism that provided Wells-Barnett with her huge following and support among those in the Black community.

Ida Wells-Barnett launched an international campaign against lynching and significantly influenced the ideological direction of black women's organizations. But as the years went on, Wells-Barnett often endured political and gender discrimination from within and outside the Afro American community. "Wells' political integrity and strong sense of social urgency was compatible with her earliest associates, but during the more conservative era of the early twentieth century, this radicalism distanced her from the new leadership of the left" (Boyd, 1994:12). She has been vindicated in the advent of black women's studies.

Wells-Barnett contributed to sociology by means of her analysis of racial and gender issues; especially as they pertain to class inequality and injustice. "In the study of Wells' life and words, we find insight into the complex and peculiar predicament of the black female experience" (Boyd, 1994:13).

Charlotte Perkins Gilman (1860–1935)

Charlotte Anna Perkins was born on July 3, 1860, in Hartford, Connecticut. She was the great-niece of abolitionist advocate Harriet Beecher Stowe, author of *Uncle Tom's Cabin*. "Her childhood was characterized by loneliness, isolation, and poverty, particularly after her father, a gifted but temperamental librarian and fiction writer, abandoned the family when Charlotte was nine. Contributing to her emotional insecurity was her mother's tendency to withhold affection, which left Charlotte exceedingly wary of personal relationships" (Gilman, 1998:xi). Economic hardship caused the Perkins family to move nineteen times in just eighteen years. Transferring from school to school led Charlotte to become largely self-educated. She would visit the library on her own, and read about ancient history and civilization. Charlotte's childhood developed a strong, hardworking, and independent woman.

As a teenager, Charlotte Perkins became involved in a loving relationship with her friend, Martha Luther. They were together for four years until Martha left Charlotte in 1881, to marry a man, and then moved away. Perkins was devastated, and described in *The Living of Charlotte Perkins Gilman* (1935) that the break-up was the most lasting pain she had ever known. In January 1882, Charlotte was still dealing with loss of Luther, when she was introduced to Charles Walter Stetson, a handsome young man. Stetson pursued Perkins for two years until she finally agreed to marry him. Predictably, the marriage was a failure. Charlotte suffered a nervous breakdown and was institutionalized. The critical trigger of Perkins Gilman's chronic depression was her relationship with Stetson, although the origins of her depression had clearly been established early on in her life.

Charlotte Perkins had refused Stetson's marriage proposals for two reasons. The most obvious of these reasons was her uncertainty regarding her sexual orientation; she had warned him of the difficulties of pursuing an intimate relationship with her (Gilman, 1935). Second, Perkins was concerned that if she married, she would not have time to pursue a career, and she very much wanted to make her mark on society through social activism. She was totally alarmed when she found out she was pregnant. Since she had feared marriage would interfere with a career, motherhood was viewed as a curse. Katherine Beecher Stetson was born on March 23, 1885, just a little more than ten months after Charlotte and Walter were married (Gilman, 1998). Charlotte fell into a deeper depression and was sent to a Philadelphia sanitarium. Upon release, and subsequent attempts to reconcile her marriage, the depression that Charlotte Stetson felt led her to abandon her husband and move to California. She took her daughter with her, but due to economic deprivation she decided in 1894, the year her divorce became final, to turn Katherine over to Stetson and his new wife. "Determined to have an independent lifestyle, Gilman helped effect the marriage of her best friend to her former husband and turned her daughter over to them while she pursued her public and professional career" (Lengermann and Niebrugge-Brantley, 2000:298).

During the 1890s Perkins published numerous articles and edited a weekly magazine, the *Impress*. She joined the lecture circuit speaking on socialist issues and on women's rights throughout the United States and in England (Gilman, 1998). In 1898, Gilman gained international acclaim with the publication of *Women and Economics*, her ground-breaking work that would go through nine editions in her lifetime, and was translated into seven languages. Her two other major sociological publications are, *The Home* (1903), and *Man-Made World* (1911). Her literary reputation was established with her quasi-autobiographical short story depicting the mental and emotional disintegration of a young wife and mother, "The Yellow Wall-Paper" (1892). She wrote a number of popular short essays that were serialized as *Herland, With Her in Ourland*, and *The Dress of Women*. "Gilman wrote and published *The Forerunner* as an educational, sociological enterprise. The influence of works like *The Dress of Women*, presented over the course of a year in twelve monthly installments, was limited primarily to the regular readers of her magazine" (Gilman, 2002:xii). Perkins Gilman expected a large readership that would include "Gilman Circles" of small face-to-face groups who would discuss the contents of her writings. Sales were poor, and her, perhaps delusional, hope to amass a wider audience to her work never materialized. Perkins Gilman was, however, a well-known sociologist during her era. She presented papers at annual meetings of the American Sociological Association and published articles in the *American Journal of Sociology*.

As for Charlotte Perkins' personal life, she decided to give marriage one more try. "In 1900, after several passionate attachments with other women, she married a cousin, Houghton Gilman, who was considerably younger than she and who supported her need for independence and public visibility in what was to be a very satisfactory marriage for them both" (Lengermann and Niebrugge-Brantley, 2000:298). The marriage lasted for thirty-four happy years, until George Houghton Gilman died of a massive cerebral hemorrhage. "During the early years of their marriage, Katherine lived with Charlotte and Houghton much of the time and alternately with her father and stepmother, Grace" (Gilman, 1998:xiv). Charlotte

Gilman, struck with inoperable breast cancer, would take her own life on August 17, 1935.

Significant Contributions to Sociology

"Gilman participated in several important intellectual movements, including: cultural feminism, reform Darwinism, feminist pragmatism, Fabian socialism, and Nationalism that shared interests in changing the economy and women's social status through social reform movements" (Gilman, 2002:xiii). Some of these movements were national or international, while others were of local concerns. Lengermann and Niebrugge-Brantley (1998) state that, "Gilman was influenced by three configurations of thought popularly expressed in her era: (1) reform social darwinism; (2) Progressivism, particularly those strands of its reform ideology that drew on non-Marxian or utopian socialism; and (3) feminism, the growing mobilization by women for rights, including the right to vote and the right to economic independence" (p. 112). Gilman admired Thorstein Veblen, a man who had an integral role in Gilman's *The Dress of Women*. She particularly enjoyed his concept of *conspicuous consumption* and his application of the term to gender issues. Gilman believed much of Veblen's works were a defense of women. In his *The Theory of the Leisure Class*, Veblen discussed the problematic nature of displaying the wealth of men and families through women's adornment and leisure. Veblen devoted an entire chapter, "Dress as an Expression of the Pecuniary Culture," that parallels Gilman's work in *The Dress of Women* (Gilman, 2002). Gilman also applied the words "savage" and "barbarian" in similar ways to Veblen's usage; as a means to refer to stages in social evolution. Furthermore, both Veblen and Gilman were described as immoral because of their sexual lives, Gilman because of her lesbianism, divorce, joint custody of a child with an ex-husband and his wife, a marriage arranged by Charlotte; and Veblen (as detailed in chapter ten) because of his public affairs and adulterous behavior.

In *The Dress of Women*, Gilman (2002) stated that, "Once recognizing that human clothing in material and structure is part of our social life; that cloth is a living tissue evolved by us for social use as much as fur or feathers are evolved for individual use; then we are prepared to recognize also the action of evolutionary forces on this tissue, in all its forms and uses" (p. 15). Clothing, then, becomes a social element beyond its most obvious function to cover the body and keep it warm in cold weather. Through conspicuous consumption, clothing becomes a weapon of wealth and a public display of power. Gilman did not solely blame individuals for their display of leisure consumption; in addition, she discussed the influence of the clothing industry as a powerful economic force capable of intimidating and initiating social action. The relevance of this analysis should not be lost on any sociologist who examines the role popular culture on decision-making. Parents understand that the clothing industry has successfully penetrated the minds of young consumers to "look" a certain way. Social class differences become quite evident with the issues of clothing, fashion, and style. Gilman (2002) clearly expressed her views of the producers and consumers of fashion as, "the people contentedly, eagerly, delightedly, practicing this unspeakable foolish slavery to the whims and notions, and the economic demands, of a group less worthy to rule than any Church or Court of past—the darling leaders of the demi-monde, the poor puppets of a so-called 'Society' whose major occupation is to exhibit clothes, and a group of greedy and presuming tradesmen and their

employees" (p. 117). Gilman even attempted to understand the psychology behind people who consume clothing at the conspicuous level. Gilman clearly demonstrated a critical sociological theoretical approach to this, and other studies.

Prior to her first real sociological writing, Gilman published the "The Yellow Wall-Paper," in *New England Magazine* (1892). This short story was written in two days, during the summer of 1890, during Gilman's "first year of freedom" that followed her permanent separation from Walter Stetson (Gilman, 1935). Loosely based on her experiences while undergoing therapy, critics claim that her writings are a reflection of progressive insanity. She insisted that the real purpose of "The Yellow Wall-Paper" was to convince Dr. S. Weir Mitchell (the doctor who treated her) of the error of his ways of treating nervous breakdowns (Knight, 1997). Today, "The Yellow Wall-Paper" remains a definitive feminist statement that continues to spark controversy (Knight, 1997). Charlotte Perkins Gilman is generally ignored in contemporary sociology; but her works make for wonderful additions to women's studies, American literature, and short fiction.

Jane Addams (1860–1935)

Jane Addams was born in Cedarville, Illinois on September 6, 1860, to Sarah and John Addams. Jane's parents had lost three babies (1850, 1855, and 1859) prior to Jane's birth and prayed that the other five children would remain healthy. Both John and Sarah Addams were descended from immigrants who arrived in the United States in the early eighteenth century (Diliberto, 1999). Jane attended Rockford Female Seminary, although she did not look forward to it upon her arrival in 1877. "Jane admitted she was distraught to be starting at 'humdrum

Rockford."' With its weak academic program, its emphasis on religion, and its rigid code of conduct, Rockford seemed stuck in the pre–Civil War past" (Diliberto, 1999:60). This was an era when women where first being allowed to attend college, and Rockford was one of dozens of female seminaries that had transformed itself into a real college. Upon Jane's arrival at Rockford, the college did not even offer degrees. John Addams was among the more enlightened men of the time and he encouraged his daughters to pursue higher education. Jane had hoped to convince her father to let her transfer to Smith after one year at Rockford, but he would not allow it. Luckily for Addams, just months before she was to receive her "testimonial"—a certificate used in place of a degree—the Rockford board of trustees voted to allow degrees to those students who had completed the four-year academic program. Addams excelled in this academically weaker environment and graduated as valedictorian in 1881.

Like many college students, Jane was hoping to "find herself" at college, and she was open to new experiences. "Jane's avidity for new experience led her, as it has college students in other eras, to experiment with drugs. One morning she and four friends swallowed crushed opium pills, hoping to induce hallucinations that would help them better understand *Confessions*, by the English essayist and opium addict De Quincey, which they planned to read once the drug took effect" (Diliberto, 1999:72). Addams discovered that she enjoyed public debate and took part in Rockford's public examination, an annual event where a panel of ministers and politicians would test the young women's knowledge of a variety of topics. In the fall of 1880, a group of men from Knox College in Galesburg, Illinois, tried to block Jane and other female debaters from participating in the state debate contest. They did

Jane Addams (1860–1935) American social worker and founder of Hull House.
Source: Courtesy of the Library of Congress

not think it was proper for women and men to share a stage in public debate—etiquette books of the late 1800s agreed (Diliberto, 1999). This was a period of time, after all, where women were first entering college, and were expected to be raising large families. Many of Jane's friends dropped out of college to get married. Jane was not about to marry a man. She was an ardent feminist, and feminists of this era often viewed heterosexual love as disgusting. Furthermore, "many feminists of the nineteenth-century believed that women were degraded by having sex with men" (Diliberto, 1999:75).

On August 17, 1881, John Addams died. He had a huge estate and left half to his wife Ann Haldeman (Sarah had passed away when Jane was just two years old) and the other half was divided between Jane and her two sisters and brother. Jane's share included a 247-acre farm, sixty acres of timberland in Stephenson County, eighty acres in Dakota, Illinois, stocks and bonds, and $50,000—the equivalent of nearly one million dollars in 1998 (Diliberto, 1999). Ann, Jane's stepmother, wanted her to get married and attempted to unite her son George with Jane. It seems that Ann was worried that her son might be gay, and she felt the marriage between Jane and George would benefit both of them. Jane was horrified by the idea. The year 1883 was especially memorable to Addams; she visited Ireland and England, but also suffered her first nervous breakdown. Throughout the 1880s Addams seemed unsure of herself, and wondered what she should do with the rest of her life. She would travel to Europe again and find inspiration in London. She was, at first, alarmed at the urban decay of London, characterized by: prostitutes, drunken men, crippled children begging on the streets, streets covered with garbage and animal blood from the open slaughterhouses, and news of an unknown assailant the reporters called "Jack the Ripper" (Diliberto, 1999). But Addams also discovered in London Toynbee Hall, a "settlement" house designed to provide "relief" to the less-fortunate (e.g., money, food, clothes, and other services). The idea and image of creating some sort of equivalent settlement house in America would lead to Jane Addams' greatest contribution to society and ultimately, sociology.

In 1889, Jane Addams and Ellen Gates Starr arranged to rent the second floor of a subdivided former mansion on Halsted Street, an area of working-class immigrants. They planned on creating a settlement house modeled on Toynbee Hall, and named it "Hull House" after Chicago millionaire Charles Hull, the original owner

(Lengermann and Niebrugge-Brantley, 1998). Addams and Starr had some definite ideas on what they hoped to accomplish at Hull House, but they also realized that new programs would have to be created as new needs arouse. "Their plan, which Addams recounts in *Twenty Years at Hull-House* (1919/1990), was to try to learn and help by living simply as neighbors among the poor . . . they embarked upon a range of social experiments including social clubs, garbage collection, apartments for working women, consumer cooperation, evening classes, trade unions, industrial reform legislation, investigations of working conditions, debating societies, and intervening in strikes, unemployment, and hysteria about anarchists (many of whom took part in Hull House debates)" (Lengermann and Niebrugge-Brantley, 2000:303). From the start, the settlement was a refuge for many of the children in the neighborhood, "whose harsh lives were often cut short by industrial accidents and the many epidemics that raged through their squalid homes" (Diliberto, 1999:158). For the older children, Hull House provided an educational program.

Hull House was a success story in every way. It offered literary clubs, academic clubs, sewing lessons, kindergarten and daycare facilities for children of working mothers, and so much more. In fact, Hull House was so successful it "expanded from a single floor to a city-block complex of building including an art gallery, coffee shop, gymnasium, library, theater, museum of labor, dining rooms, music rooms, and housing facilities" (Lengermann and Niebrugge-Brantley, 1998:68). Hull House was now a collaborative enterprise assisting thousands of people, including recent immigrants such as the Italians, Russian and Polish Jews, Irish, Germans and Greeks, and even the Bohemians found refuge there. Many other educated women who shared Addams' activism and reform attitude joined her at Hull House, among them, Florence Kelley, Dr. Alice Hamilton, Julia Lathrop, Sophonisba Breckinridge, and Grace and Edith Abbott.

Significant Contributions to Sociology

Jane Addams made a significant difference in Chicago with her Hull House settlement. Her most important contributions to sociology are directly linked to her experiences at Hull House. The communal atmosphere of Hull House led Addams to develop a sociological theory based on the idea that people must begin to work collectively and cooperatively. Sociological themes of cooperation and progressive growth are the foundation of her major publications: *Democracy and Social Ethics* (1902), *Newer Ideals of Peace* (1907), *Twenty Years at Hull House,* (1910), *The Long Road of Women's Memory* (1916), *Peace and Bread in Times of War* (1922), and *The Second Twenty Years at Hull House* (1930). Her sociological outlook on society implied that diverse people must learn to accept and tolerate one another.

Addams involved modified versions of progressivism, reform social Darwinism, philosophic pragmatism and social gospel Christianity into her general social theory (Lengermann and Niebrugge-Brantley, 1998). In an attempt to prove that the social Darwinistic, laissez-faire philosophy of government coexist with social reform, Addams proposed *reform social Darwinism.* She believed that humans had already progressed to the point where they could control evolution and therefore owed a duty to help the less fortunate. The reform social Darwinism principle stated that, "evolutionary law demanded that people find ways to work in combination with each other to secure a social environment in which all people could develop fully" (Lengermann and Niebrugge-Brantley,

1998:73). Her progressive Darwinistic approach also possessed a "social gospel" in order to provide proper moral guidance in decision-making and social action. In the tradition of the Chicago School and the sociology that dominated that geographic area, Addams' theoretical ideology involved a "hands-on approach" to the study of human behavior. She believed that sociologists must go "native," and live with those that they study. Her micro-orientation leads to the individual as the basic unit of study, and it is the individual and her interactions with the community that most dominated Addams' social theory.

Addams' theories and research reflect a feminist framework. She wrote from a gendered standpoint; employed a focus on women's lives in her research (e.g., housewives, domestics, sweatshop laborers, prostitutes); and demonstrated a commitment to changing the role of women in society. Hull House itself, despite all the other programs it offered diverse people, was as much a sanctuary for female friendship and a source for professional, practical, and material support for women. "When Addams wrote sociology, she did not have the men of the academy as her primary audience, but the thousands of women she knew through social reform work, lecture tours, personal correspondence, and as the intended readership for her articles in popular magazines. She understood the work that she and other women activists were doing to be sociology—a sociology created primarily by women out of their life experiences" (Lengermann and Niebrugge-Brantley, 1998:70).

Addams was an activist and a person who believed in social, moral change. Hull House residents, neighbors, and supporters forged a powerful reform movement. Among the projects that they launched were the Immigrants' Protective League, the

Juvenile Protective Association, the first juvenile court in the nation, and a Juvenile Psychopathic Clinic. Through their efforts, the Illinois legislature enacted protective legislation for women and children (1903), the Federal Children's Bureau (1912), and passage of a federal child labor law (1916). The efforts and successes of the Hull House reformers would be expanded to the national level. Addams began to realize that the passing of laws would not be enough to guarantee the end of poverty, and as a result she attempted to find the root causes of poverty. She joined a number of labor groups and discussed with the working poor the reasons for poverty. Armed with specifics, Addams attempted to get lawmakers to legislate for the protection of immigrants from exploitation; limiting the working hours of women; mandating schooling for children; recognizing labor unions; and providing industrial safety. She worked in the efforts to secure women's rights to vote, she was a member of the Chicago municipal suffrage, and became first vice-president of the National American Women Suffrage Association in 1911. Addams even became the first woman to second the nomination of a presidential candidate, Theodore Roosevelt, at the Progressive Party convention of 1912.

Addams was not without controversy. When horrible working conditions led to workers' protests and the subsequent Haymarket riot, Addams was personally attacked for her support of the workers. It resulted in a great loss of donor support for Hull House. Addams would supplement the settlement from her own resources. She was also criticized for her effort to stop the United States involvement in World War I. There was a great deal of patriotism at the time of the war, and her diplomatic attempts to thwart war were not popular among the masses. Many people labeled her a socialist, an anarchist, and a communist. Addams was even expelled from the Daughters of the American

Revolution (1917). She made the FBI's list of "most dangerous radicals" during the "Red Scare" decade of the 1920s. However, despite these controversies, Addams had, by now, achieved international acclaim. Her participation in numerous charities and associations were highlighted by: her election as the first president of the Women's International League for Peace and Freedom (a position she held until her death); her involvement with the creation of the American Civil Liberties Union; and her activism with the NAACP.

Jane Addams was many things to many people. Her Hull House settlement seemed to vindicate her beliefs that society should work more cooperatively. Much of the governmental "interference" designed toward reform social Darwinism advocated by Addams became policy under President Franklin Roosevelt. Perhaps her crowning achievement came in the form of her receiving a Nobel Peace Prize in 1931. Despite her failing health, Addams worked at Hull House to the end of her life. She died on May 21, 1935. Thousands of people came to her funeral at Hull House before she was taken to Cedarville to be buried.

Marianne Weber (1870–1954)

Marianne Schnitger Weber was born on August 2, 1870, in Oerlinghausen, Germany. Marianne is mostly remembered today as Max Weber's wife and proponent of his work after his death. She also played an important role in helping organize Max's works while he lived. "[Max] Weber's work was fragmentary and disconnected, 'found in journals or left unedited.' Marianne Weber's persistence and devotion played no little part in its collection and publication. *Economy and Society* was in large part written 'without benefit of footnotes and other customary scholarly paraphernalia'" (Mommsen and Osterhammel, 1987:383). Marianne was the grandniece of Max Weber

Sr., father of her future husband. Her mother Anna, who came from a wealthy family, married Eduard Schnitger, a man who the Weber family felt was beneath her. Schnitger was a country doctor in an era when such a position was not considered prestigious. Marianne was born within the first year of this marriage, but became motherless when Anna died two years later after giving birth to a second child (Lengermann and Niebrugge-Brantley, 1998). Shortly after the death of his wife, Eduard began to show signs of a mental illness. Marianne was sent to live with her paternal grandmother and an aunt in a small country town. At age sixteen, her wealthy grandfather Weber sent her to be educated at a fashionable finishing school in Hanover (Weber, 1975). After completing her studies in Hanover, Marianne returned to the country to live with her mother's married sister, Alwine. Marianne was bored there because she relished an intellectual environment. In 1891, she was invited to spend a few weeks with the Weber family in Berlin. "In that affluent and sophisticated family, Marianne at last caught a glimpse of the life she wanted" (Lengermann and Niebrugge-Brantley, 1998:195). She could hardly get her fill of such a cultural and intellectual atmosphere (Weber, 1975). A year later, she went back to Berlin to live with the Weber family. Two very important elements took place during this second visit. First, she formed a solid "mother–daughter"-type relationship with Helene Weber. Helene was like the mother that Marianne never really had, and Marianne became Helene's confidant. Second, Marianne became "interested" in her cousin Max. She was extremely happy to discover he felt the same way about her, and became engaged to marry. Determined to be an active part of her future husband's academic career, Marianne helped Max with an investigation of farmworkers he had undertaken for the Evangelical Social Congress. She wanted to familiarize herself with scholarship as soon as possible (Adams and Sydie, 2001).

The early years of their marriage found Max consumed with academic activity, intellectual production, and leftist politics. Marianne was becoming a sociologist in her own right, as she was producing sociological research on marriage and the legal position of women in that institution. Weber (1975/1926) argued for a reform of marriage, not a substitute for marriage. Marianne Weber was also among the leading women of Germany in the liberal feminist movement. "In 1918 German women obtained the vote, and in 1919 Marianne Weber became the first member of the Baden parliament" (Adams and Sydie, 2001:172). In 1897, Max Weber (see chapter seven) had a "falling out" with his father, and, shortly thereafter, and before reconciliation, his father passed away. Max was devastated and went into a state of depression, and was in and out of mental institutions for years. During this period, Marianne took over the role of public speaker in the marriage, and became actively involved in sociopolitical issues.

By 1904, Max had recovered from his nervous collapse, and would manage to find a proper blend between scholarship and leisure. In this same year, the Webers visited the United States to attend a scholarly conference held during the Universal Exposition in St. Louis. Max looked forward to visiting American so that he could further examine the role of Protestantism and capitalism. He had accepted the editorship of a new journal in social science, *Archiv fur Sozialwissenschaft und Sozcialpolitik*. His article, *The Protestant Ethic and the Spirit of Capitalism*, published in that journal, is now famous. Max Weber concluded that Americans were passionate only about mundane pursuits (e.g., economic wealth, consumer goods) and that their pursuits were minus any religious and ethical meaning. Marianne was far more condemning of Americans' behavior. Her religiously inspired criticism of the United States included doubts of the very core of America's ideology—freedom. She felt that freedom had brought immorality to millions "living under the scourge of gold" (Mommsen and Osterhammel, 1987:217). The Webers gathered with other German intellectuals in Tonawanda, New York and in between visits to nearby Niagara Falls, they would compare empirical evidence of American's economic, materialistic system. During this American tour, Marianne was expanding her own sociological self. She met both Jane Addams and Florence Kelley, and "between 1904 and 1907 she published several papers on women's experience, engaging critically with the theories of Charlotte Perkins Gilman" (Lengermann and Niebrugge-Brantley, 1998:197). In 1907, Marianne published her famous *Ehefrau und Mutter in der Rechtsentwicklung* (Marriage, Motherhood, and the Law). In that same year, Marianne's grandfather Karl died, leaving her and Max free from financial worry. Max and Marianne were living a life of economic comfort which allowed both of them to actively pursue intellectual interests. Marianne created her own "intellectual salon" where gifted speakers, including some of Max's colleagues (e.g., Robert Michels and Georg Simmel) joined with prominent feminist speakers. Unfortunately for Marianne, one of Max's interests involved a sexual relationship with their mutual friend Else Jaffe (Green, 1974). "In 1910, the Webers were in Venice with the Jaffes, friends from Heidelberg. Edgar Jaffe was Max Weber's publisher and coeditor on the *Archiv*; Else Jaffe, one of Marianne's friends, had briefly been one of Max's students" (Adams and Sydie, 2001:189). The first time Max and Else became lovers was when Marianne attended a feminist conference. Their relationship continued until Max's death, and Else was even at his bedside, along with Marianne, during his dying days (Adams and Sydie, 2001). Max claimed to have maintained his

affection for Marianne during this whole period, and Marianne did stay with Max; but her writings would reveal her own emerging sense of power and critical confidence. Among her publications are: "The Question of Divorce" (1909), "Authority and Autonomy in Marriage" (1912), "On the Value of Housework" (1912), "Women and Objective Culture" (1913), all of which can be found in *Frauenfragen und Frauengedanken* (Reflections on Women and Women's Issues) (1919).

Max and Marianne remained married and to all appearances (to the outside world) displayed allegiance to one another. Max would defend her from antifeminist attacks, and Marianne remained committed to the idea of marriage and would work hard after Max's death to make sure his intellectual legacy remained in tact. It often seems odd that a couple could remain together after one of the two is known to have cheated on the other; but this is not a new development and a contemporary parallel might be drawn to Bill and Hillary Clinton. Former United States' president Bill Clinton has been involved in extramarital affairs, and yet, his feminist wife Hillary has (at least externally) remained committed to the relationship while still maintaining creditability in the feminist world with her work on female empowerment. After her husband's death, Marianne would remain busy in the intellectual world. She published eight books in all, and worked on feminist issues until the Nazis came into power in Germany, in 1933. She managed to publish *Erfülltes Leben* ("The Fulfilled Life") in an underground press. Weber survived the war, but she was devastated to learn of the true horrors created by the Nazis during World War II. Her last years of life paid witness to the construction of a prosperous and democratic West Germany. Many of the participants of her Heidelberg intellectual salon were actively involved in this reconstruction. On March 12, 1954, Marianne Weber died in Heidelberg.

Significant Contributions to Sociology

Many students of social theory first hear of Marianne Weber as the wife of Max Weber, and then they hear of her influence on the next generation of social thinkers (e.g., Talcott Parsons) through her interpretations and teachings of Max Weber's sociology. But Marianne Weber made her own significant theoretical contributions to sociology, mostly in the areas of feminism and in marriage and family. Germany had been unified in 1871 under the authoritarian and militaristic regime of the monarchy of Prussia led by Bismarck. Bismarck instilled an unquestioned male-dominated society (Lengermann and Niebrugge-Brantley, 1998). Industrialization allowed for the creation of an emerging middle class, and political activists who attempted to make many changes in government and civil society. The feminist movement began in Germany during the late 1800s and was spearheaded by an active attempt to reach economic and political equality. Around 1905, a new power group of the German feminists emerged, and their primary concern of sexual autonomy led to what is known as "the erotic movement."

Helene Stocker became the leader of the erotic movement in 1906, and under her leadership problems of sexual politics and matrimonial law became the most important issues. "Within the bourgeois women's movement, this shift of interest triggered off violent disagreements about the relation between sexual and economic emancipation. The Association [Association for the Protection of Mothers] attacked the conventional ossification of bourgeois marriage and

propagated as an alternative a 'new ethic,' whereby women could claim the right to engage in sexual relations regardless of material and legal considerations" (Mommsen and Osterhammel, 1987:486). What these women were proposing, according to Max Weber, was the right to "free love" and to the illegitimate child. He viewed the erotic movement as crass hedonism and ethically immoral. (Note the relevance of this material to contemporary society, where within just the past few years it has become, more or less, acceptable for women to have a child on her own and without a paternal-figure role model.) Marianne Weber agreed with her husband's stance and wrote in her book, *Ehefrau und Mutter in der Rechtsentwicklung,* that the standpoint of the women's movement should be with the equality of women, and less concerned with moral emancipation. In 1907, Marianne Weber gave a lecture at the Evangelical-Social Congress in Strasbourg. In this talk, "she defends the ethical and legal norms of modern marriage by drawing on the theory of rationalization, introducing evolutionary motifs" (Mommsen and Osterhammel, 1987:487). Weber made it clear that she believed marriage should be a lasting, exclusive life-companionship relationship between man and woman, with mutual obligations. Thus, she made two critical points. First, women should be treated equally in the social system, especially the social institution of marriage. Second, she viewed marriage strictly as a union between a man and a woman; thus alienating many other feminists.

Weber was certainly a feminist, "she defended a women's right to, capability of, and need for sexual pleasure in the face of late Victorian sentiments that idealized the asexual woman" (Adams and Sydie, 2001:191). She believed that women should have the right to freedom from a patriarchal marital relationship. Her feminist sociology was centered on the realization that Germany, as with most societies, was based on a patriarchal social structure and social organization model. She stressed that women should have the right to financial independence, including perhaps the idea that a housewife should be paid for her domestic chores. (Note: The idea of a housewife being paid for her work has been discussed so often in feminists' circles that it is now a part of popular culture; especially in the form of story lines on television shows.) Weber believed that under a patriarchical society, the system is designed so that males can reach fulfillment of essential needs; whereas women are expected to be subordinate to the male and help him reach his full potential. Weber concluded that this system needs to be changed, so that women may also reach their full potential.

The Ladies of Seneca Falls

Feminism was begun in the United States by those who advocated equal rights for women. The origins of feminism are also found in the abolitionist movement of the 1830s (Anderson, 1997). The exact birthplace of feminism is Seneca Falls, New York. As Miriam Gurko (1974) asks and answers, "Who were the ladies of Seneca Falls? Originally there were five: five ladies sitting around a tea table in 1848 in the small town of Waterloo in upstate New York" (p. 2). The leader of this group was Elizabeth Cady Stanton, the others were: Quaker preacher Lucretia Mott of Philadelphia, her sister Martha Wright, Jane Hunt, and Mary Ann McClintock. They proposed to do the nearly unthinkable, to call a woman's rights convention. The five ladies committed to take action despite the fact they had no idea how to organize such a meeting. There would be many obstacles to organizing a woman's rights gathering. Many of the prevailing so-

cial institutions were designed to keep women subordinate to men. The existing sociopolitical structure worked against them. For example, "Once a woman married, she forfeited her legal existence. She couldn't sign a contract, make a will, or sue in a court of law. If she received property from her father or other source, her husband could sell it and keep the money for himself" (Gurko, 1974:8). If she didn't marry, she would be mocked as an "old maid." The church was another social institution determined to keep a woman in her place. Women where instructed to know their place—the home. The social institution of education worked against women, as college doors were not opened to them. And, the press often led the public in denouncing any woman's effort to improve her social standing. Gurko (1974) provides what she describes as a typical comment on a woman's rights convention from the now-defunct *Syracuse Daily Star*, "which labeled the proceedings as a mass of corruption, heresies, ridiculous nonsense, and reeking vulgarities which these bad women have vomited forth for the past three days" (p. 10). As Stanton and Mott would point out, the most devastating barrier to women's rights was the acceptance of these ideological beliefs by so many women.

Despite all these obstacles, the Women's Rights Convention would be held in the Wesleyan Methodist Chapel, Seneca Falls, New York, on July 19–20, 1848. More than 300 people attended this first convention of women's rights. In a replica copy of the minutes, it states that the convention was gathered to discuss the social, civil, and religious condition of woman, and called on by the Women of Seneca County, New York. The "Declaration of Sentiments" was offered for the acceptance of the convention; after a few changes were suggested, the declaration was accepted as the guiding theme of the convention. The "Declaration of Sentiments" was modeled after the "Declaration of

Independence." For example, paragraph two begins, "We hold these truths to be self-evident; that all men and women are created equal" (Source: Women's Rights National Historical Park Service). The "Declaration" states that women have been victims of tyranny by men, "The history of mankind is a history of repeated injuries and usurpations on the part of man toward woman, having in direct object the establishment of an absolute tyranny over her" (Source: "Declaration of Sentiments"). The document set demands for equality in such areas as custody laws, property rights, educational opportunities, and the participation in the church, professions, and politics. This convention was the beginning of a seventy-two year battle to gain women the right to vote in the United States. In 1920, the United States became the seventeenth country in the world to given women the right to vote. The first country to do so was New Zealand in 1893. Interestingly, the U.S.S.R. was the seventh nation to give women the right to vote (1917).

Elizabeth Cady Stanton (1815–1902)

Elizabeth Cady Stanton led the call for the Convention and wrote the first draft of the "Declaration of Sentiments" out of a strong sense of injustice and righteous indignation at the plight of women. "Elizabeth Cady Stanton was the best known and most conspicuous advocate of women's rights in the nineteenth century. For almost fifty years she led the first women's movements in America. She set its agenda, drafted its documents, and articulated its ideology" (Griffith, 1984:xiii). For most girls in the early nineteenth century, the normal course of things included modest education, marriage, raising a family, and keeping a house. But it was quite clear from early on, that young Elizabeth Cady was not about to follow the normal course of action.

Born in Johnstown, New York, in 1815, Elizabeth was the seventh of the eleven children of Daniel and Margaret Livingston Cady. Named for Sir William Johnson, an Englishman who bought the site from the Indians before the Revolution, Johnstown was an intellectual and industrial center in the early nineteenth century. The Cayadadutta River at the north end of the village supplied power for factories (Griffith, 1984). The Cady family thrived in this environment and were very wealthy, socially prominent, and politically active. Her parents encouraged Elizabeth to pursue her childhood interests in traditionally held activities such as debating, learning Greek, and horseback riding; she excelled at all of them. She did very well in school but did not attend college because no colleges were open to women. She did attend the Troy Female Seminary, and received the most advanced education available to a woman in her era (Source: Women's Rights National Historical Park).

Stanton was influenced by family members (the Livingston name tied her to the old Dutch aristocracy in New York), outstanding teachers and the preaching of Charles Grandison Finney during the Great Troy Revival of 1831. Finney had claimed to have seen Christ on a main street in Rochester, New York, and felt he had a mission similar to St. Paul (Griffith, 1984). Stanton was raised as a Presbyterian with the gloomy Calvinistic outlook of a punitive God. Finney's strenuous style and revival enthusiasm had quite an effect on impressionable adolescents, and Elizabeth was awe-struck as well. He taught that man and woman had free will to choose between salvation and damnation. When someone confessed their sins to him, Finney granted "conversion" to a reaffirmation of faith and an acceptance of an obligation to perfect oneself and one's community (this is similar to the conversion process of being "born again"). Elizabeth

Elizabeth Cady Stanton (1815–1897) American social reformer, suffragist, author of "Declaration of Sentiments."
Source: National Archives and Records Administration

Cady's conversion left her feeling bad instead of good, and her family forbade any further discussion of religion or mention of Finney. This experience would lead her to religious indecision and eventually religious superstitions would give way to ideas based on rational, scientific facts. But some good came out of this experience as well. She had always loved to debate and she did admire Finney's ability to command the attention of his audience.

Elizabeth Cady spent many summers at the home of her cousin Gerrit Smith, a wealthy radical reformer. She learned about and became committed to antislavery, temperance, and other reforms. In 1839,

Elizabeth Cady met Henry Brewster Stanton, who was an eloquent speaker of the abolitionist movement, and one of its most capable and courageous leaders. The abolitionist movement was not very popular among the masses, and he was repeatedly attacked by violent mobs. Henry Stanton was also the financial secretary of the American Anti-Slavery Society (Gurko, 1974). Elizabeth and Henry quickly fell in love with each other and announced their engagement less than one month after first meeting. Her family and friends objected to the marriage. Her father Judge Cady, disapproved of abolitionists, especially a nonaffluent one who presumed to marry his daughter. She initially broke off the engagement but continued to see him. A year later, when Henry informed Elizabeth that he was going to London as a delegate to the World Anti-Slavery Convention, he asked her one more time to marry him; she accepted. In the wedding vows, the word "obey" was omitted, and she objected to being called "Mrs. Henry Stanton" on the basis of equality. The couple would travel to London together, further inflaming Elizabeth Cady Stanton's desire for future activism. "The antagonism to women evident in the debate aroused Elizabeth Cady Stanton more than the antislavery questions on the agenda. She was angry at the injustice of the situation and impatient with the hypocrisy of the abolitionists. The opposition of the most liberal leaders of the most radical movement of the era to a question of women's rights stunned her" (Griffith, 1984:37). Her outrage at the London meeting ignited her interest in women's rights. But it was also at this meeting that Cady Stanton met Lucretia Mott, and formed an enduring friendship.

After an extended European trip, the newlywed couple returned to Johnstown. Henry, in an attempt to mend family feeling, decided to study law with his father-in-law

Judge Cady. He clerked for fifteen months. On March 2, 1842, the first of the three boys was born to Elizabeth while she and Henry were still living at the Cady family home. After Henry Stanton finished his law studies, the family settled in Boston, where they became active in reform work and in the city's intellectual and cultural life. In 1846, the Stantons moved to Seneca Falls, New York. She was experiencing the life of an average middle-class white housewife. Henry was often away working, while Cady Stanton was raising three sons and taking care of a house. She missed the intellectual stimulation she enjoyed in Boston. The true nature of her discontent surfaced at a tea party in Waterloo, New York, at the home of Jane Hunt in early July 1848. "Cady Stanton vividly described her unhappiness to four women friends: Lucretia Mott, Martha Wright, Mary Ann McClintock, and Jane Hunt. The group decided then and there to call a convention to discuss the status of women" (Source: Women's Rights National Historical Park). A week later they met again, drafted the "Declaration of Sentiments," and the convention was on. This meeting was the formal beginning of the women's rights movement, and Cady Stanton was the leader. After the convention she continued to work for women's rights, she wrote extensively, but family responsibilities prevented her from traveling and speaking outside the local area. In 1862, the Stanton family moved to New York City. Here, she articulated that the women's rights movement should be a broad platform of change for women, including: woman suffrage, dress reform, girls' sports, equal employment, property rights, equal wages, divorce and custody law reform, collective households, coeducation, birth control, and religious reform (Source: Women's Rights National Historical Park). When her children were grown, she began to travel the country to discuss women's issues. She helped write the three-volume *History of Woman Suffrage* (1887), before publishing her controversial autobiography, *Woman's Bible* (1895). The *Woman's Bible* was a series of commentaries on biblical passages that were antiwoman. Cady Stanton took exception, for example, to the passage that states God made man, man was lonely, so God made woman. She believed this to be insulting to women. The clergy said of her interpretations, that it was the work of the devil. Even many women suffragettes disagreed with the tenets of her book. It was a "controversial" end to a women's-rights crusader.

Lucretia Coffin Mott (1793–1880)

Lucretia Coffin Mott was one of the most active and successful reformers of the nineteenth century. A devout Quaker, she attributed her strength and courage to divine inspiration. She believed that all people possess "divine" elements, and consequently, all people are equal.

Lucretia Coffin grew up on Nantucket Island, off the coast of Cape Cod. Her father, Thomas Coffin, Jr., was a sea captain, who was away from home for long stretches of time as he chased sperm whales over the deep. Her mother, Anna Folger Coffin, a successful storekeeper, was herself a model of strength and self-reliance for her daughter. The Coffin family were Quakers, and as such, women were allowed to speak freely, they had a right to an education, and they could be ministers, something quite unthinkable in nearly any other religion. Lucretia Coffin Mott would become a minister herself while still in her twenties. The very fact that she was raised in Nantucket benefited her as a woman. "The island was a great whaling and fishing center, with the men away at sea for months at a time. In the absence of their husbands, the Nantucket housewives not only managed all the family affairs, but often set up small businesses of their own" (Gurko, 1974:52). Thus, as a child, Lucretia saw women in a position of authority.

Lucretia loved the island and was heartbroken when the family moved away when she was eleven and a half. They first moved from Nantucket to Boston, and then to Philadelphia, the center of Quaker life. Lucretia started school at age four and later attended the Nine Partners boarding school in Duchess County, New York. An outstanding student, she joined the faculty after graduation and met another young teacher, James Mott. They were married in Philadelphia in 1811. In keeping with their Quaker beliefs, the marriage was quite egalitarian. Religious faith was very important to both of the both of them. With the advent of the War of 1812, Thomas Coffin took a gamble and invested all of his money in a factory for the manufacture of cut nails, a new product of the Industrial Revolution. The gamble paid off as he earned huge sums of money from his factory. On August 3, 1812, Lucretia gave birth to her first child, Anna.

As a minister in the Quaker church, Lucretia's life was consumed with social issues. Her work was becoming increasingly affected by the growing controversy within the church over the issue of slavery. Some Quakers, including Mott, spoke out against slavery and the injustice of human bondage. However, many of the conservative elders felt such discussion were inappropriate. In 1827, the more liberal "Hicksites" broke away from the authoritarian Orthodox Friends church. The Hicksites believed it was their religious duty to protest slavery, but the Orthodox church dismissed them as heretics. Mott believed that religion must be based on "inward spiritual grace," not upon rigid creeds or fixed ceremonial rituals. Mott felt that religion, "must be based on justice

as well as upon reason and 'inner light,' it must be express itself in 'practical godliness' " (Gurko, 1974:54).

Lucretia Mott became aware that throughout Delaware, New Jersey, and Pennsylvania, Quaker men and women were becoming increasingly troubled by the growing power and authority of the Philadelphia elders. Protest against the elders reached its peak with their treatment of the prophetlike minister Elias Hicks, a man who preached against slavery, and whom Lucretia and James Mott had entertained in their home (Bacon, 1999). The elders denounced his antislavery speeches. This was the last straw for Mott. She joined the Hicksites in 1828, and became more actively involved in the antislavery struggle. Their home became an active station in the Underground Railway. James Mott joined the Free Produce Society, refusing to sell slavemade products, including cotton and sugar, in the Mott store. In 1833, delegates came to Philadelphia to form the American Anti-Slavery Society. Lucretia Mott was one of four women invited to attend the conventions, but only as observers. They would not be permitted to join the new society. Instead, Mott met with local abolitionist women, black and white, to organize the Philadelphia Female Antislavery Society. The local white community was horrified by the idea of interracial organizations, and publicly protested the women's group. Let by Mott, the organization insisted that Blacks and Whites working together was an important step in combatting racism, and educated others, by their example, of interracial friendship and cooperation (source: Women's Rights National Historical Park).

Her battle against slavery was constantly interrupted by the "woman question." Mott was forced to fight two battles at once; one against slavery/racism, and one against sexism. Women were routinely denied access to leadership positions in the male-dominated antislavery societies and were discouraged from participating in public activities (e.g., public debates, and serving as delegates to national conventions). These issues finally came to a boil at the 1840 World Antislavery Convention in London. Mott and seven other women attended as representatives of female antislavery societies, but the male delegates were divided over whether to recognize the women as "legitimate" delegates. Seated with the Motts was Elizabeth Cady Stanton, who struck up a friendship with Lucretia. They decided to discuss women's rights issues when they returned to the United States.

It would be eight years before Stanton and Mott were able to act on this decision. Mott was traveling throughout upstate New York and was invited to a tea party at the home of Jane Hunt, a Waterloo Hicksite Quaker. As described previously in this chapter, it was this famous tea party that set into motion the women's rights convention to be held in Seneca Falls. Mott championed a wide-variety of causes beyond antislavery and women's rights; she was a lifelong peace activist who opposed the Civil War (even though many follow activists tried to convince her that this was the only way to end slavery); she was in favor of Indian rights and opposed to white aggression against native tribes and the taking of their lands; and she challenged intolerance and prejudice of any form. She continued her work until her death in 1880.

Growth of the Women's Rights Movements

As concluding remarks for this section on the "Ladies of Seneca Falls," it should be clear that the "birthplace" of feminism is arguably Seneca Falls, New York; but the movement had surfaced in various forms

throughout the United States, and other parts of the world. Women like Harriet Tubman, born a slave, uneducated, apprenticed as a weaver, always deeply spiritual (who claimed to have visions from God), escaped from slavery when her master died in 1849. She obviously basked in the glory of her newfound freedom; but this did not last for long, as she worried her sister and her two children and others who were still slaves. She decided to try and rescue them. Her determination to help free other slaves led to the forming of the Underground Railroad. It is believed that she led over 300 slaves to freedom. She is often referred to as the "Moses of her people" (source: Women's Rights National Historical Park). She would go on to create a Home for Indigent and Aged Negroes on her own property in Auburn, New York.

Susan B. Anthony was a friend of Cady Stanton, and as a single woman she had the time to travel and make speeches promoting women's rights. She would visit Stanton in Seneca Falls and then take her speeches and writings with her to travel throughout the country campaigning for women's rights. Susan Anthony was active in the women's movement by her own right. She also joined the Rochester (New York) Daughters of Temperance and became its president. Anthony was a highly competent organizer and fundraiser. She served as a delegate to the many temperance conventions in upstate New York. Susan Anthony was not among the original ladies of Seneca Falls, but she became close to many of them.

Final Thoughts

The various reforms sought by the Ladies of Seneca Falls took some time. More and more female conventions were held, legislation would eventually be passed that granted freedom to slaves and the right to vote for women. The plight of women was not completely rectified during the classical period of social thought but much progress has been made. The feminist movement gained new momentum in the late 1960s (e.g., the formation of the National Organization for Women in 1966 by Betty Friedan and associates) and continued in the 1970s (e.g., the Equal Rights Amendment passes both houses in 1972, the Roe v. Wade U.S. Supreme Court decision that granted women the right to an abortion in 1973). The role of women has increased dramatically in the United States over the past couple of centuries. But as usual with most types of major social change, it comes too quickly for some, and not quickly enough for others.

Women will have a bigger role in modern society and in contemporary social theory; and they will come to agree with most of the core tenets of beliefs articulated by the classical theorists that came before them (e.g., the progressive nature of society, the role of power in social relationships and social organization, the impact of limited and scarce resources on an aggregate of people or entire social system).

Bibliography

ABC News Special. 1997. "Love, Lust & Marriage: Why We Stay and Why We Stray." Televised presentation October 21.

Aboulafia, Mitchell. 1986. *The Mediating Self: Mead, Sartre, and Self-Determination.* New Haven: Yale University Press.

Abraham, Gary. 1992. *Max Weber and the Jewish Question: A Study of the Social Outlook of His Sociology.* Urbana: University of Illinois Press.

Acton, H. B. 1967. *What Marx Really Said.* New York: Schocken.

Adams, Bert, and R. Sydie. 2001. *Sociological Theory.* Thousand Oaks, CA: Pine Forge Press.

Addams, Jane. 1906. *The Modern City and the Municipal Franchise for Women.* New York: National American Woman Suffrage Associates.

———. 1910. *Twenty Years at Hull-House.* New York: Macmillian.

———. 1916. *The Long Road of Women's Memory.* New York: Macmillian.

———. 1922. *Peace and Bread in the Time of War.* New York: Macmillian.

———. 1930. *The Second Twenty Years at Hull-House.* New York: Macmillian.

Adler, Patricia, and Peter Adler. 2000. "The Gloried Self," pp. 185–197 in *Social Theory,* edited by Roberta Garner. Orchard Park, NY: Broadview.

Alexander, Elizabeth. 1995. "We Must Be About Our Father's Business: Anna Julia Cooper and the In-Corporation of the Nineteenth-Century African-American Woman Intellectual." *Signs.* Winter: 336–356.

Althusser, Louis. 1971. "Ideology and Ideological State Apparatuses," pp. 121–173 in *Lenin and Philosophy* edited by Louis Althusser. New York.

Anderson, E. 1994. "The Code of the Streets." *The Atlantic Monthly.* May: 81–94.

Anderson, Margaret. 1997. *Thinking About Women: Sociological Perspectives on Sex and Gender.* Boston: Allyn & Bacon.

Andreski, Stanislav. 1971. *Herbert Spencer: Structure, Function and Evolution.* London: Michael Joseph.

Aron, Raymond. 1970. *Main Currents in Sociological Thought.* Garden City, NY: Doubleday.

Aschcraft, Richard. 1987. *Locke's Two Treatises of Government.* London: Allen & Unwin.

Ashley, David, and David Orenstein. 1985. *Sociological Theory.* Boston: Allyn & Bacon.

Ayers, Michael. 1999. *Locke.* New York: Routledge.

Babbitt, Irving. 1919. *Rousseau and Romanticism.* Boston: Houghton Mifflin.

Bacon, Margaret. 1999. *Valiant Friend: The Life of Lucretia Mott.* Philadelphia: Friends General Conference.

Bailey, Leon. 1994. *Critical Theory and the Sociology of Knowledge*. New York: Peter Lang.

Bailey, Thomas, David Kennedy and Elizabeth Cohen. 1998. *The American Pageant: Volume II, Since 1865*. Boston: Houghton Mifflin.

Baldwin, John. 1986. *George Herbert Mead: A Unifying Theory for Sociology*. Beverly Hills: Sage Publishing.

Barnet, R. 1980. *The Lean Years*. New York: Simon & Schuster.

Baron, Robert, and Donn Byrne. 1997. *Social Psychology*, 8th edition. Boston: Allyn & Bacon.

Battistelli, Fabrizio. 1993. "War and Militarism in the Thought of Herbert Spencer." *International Journal of Comparative Sociology*. Vol. XXXIV, 3–4:192–209.

Bauer, Bruno. 1843. "The Jewish Question." *Deutsch-Französiche Jahrbücher*. Cologne.

Baum, Gregory. 1977. *Truth Beyond Relativism: Karl Mannheim's Sociology of Knowledge*. Milwaukee, WI: Marquette University Press.

Beer, Ann. 1978. *Herbert Spencer*. London: MacMillan.

Bender, Thomas. 1991. *Community and Social Change in America*. Baltimore: John Hopkins University Press.

Bergin, A. E., R. D. Stinchfield, T. A. Gasko, K. S. Masters, and C. E. Sullivan. 1998. "Religiousness and Mental Health Reconsidered: A Study of an Intrinsically Religious Sample." *Journal of Counseling Psychology*. 34:91–98.

Berlin, Isiah. 1971. *Karl Marx: His Life and Environment*, 3rd ed. New York: Oxford University Press.

Birnbaum, Pierre, and Jane Marie Todd. 1995. "French Jewish Sociologists Between Reason and Faith: The Impact of the Dreyfus Affair." *Jewish Social Studies*. 2:1–35.

Blau, Peter. 1964. *Exchange and Power in Social Life*. New York: Wiley.

Bloom, David, and Adi Bender. 1993. "Labor and the Emerging World Economy." *Population Bulletin*. 48(October):1–39.

Blum, Ronald. 2002. "Salaries Up Average 5.2%, Hit Record $2.023 Billion." *USA Today*. April 4:4C.

Blumer, Herbert. 1969. *Symbolic Interaction*. Englewood Cliffs, NJ: Prentice-Hall.

Bohlim, Ray. 1997. "The Little Lamb that Made a Monkey of Us—Can Humans Be Cloned Like Sheep?" Available: www.probe.org/lambsclon.

Borstein, Seth. 2001. "Global Warming Will Raise Temperature 5 Degrees by 2100, New Study Predicts." *Buffalo News*. July 29:H6.

Boyd, Melba Joyce. 1994. "Canon Configuration for Ida B. Wells-Barnett." *The Black Scholar*, Vol 24, No.1:8–13.

Brazill, William. 1970. *The Young Hegelians*. Yale University Press.

Breckman, Warren. 1999. *Marx, the Young Hegelians and the Origins of Radical Social Theory*. Cambridge: University Press.

Brickner, M., S. Harkins, and T. Ostrom. 1986. "Personal Involvement: Thought Provoking Implications for Social Loafing." *Journal of Personality and Social Psychology*. 51:763–769.

Broome, J. H. 1963. *Rousseau: A Study of His Thought*. Alva, Scotland: Edward Arnold Publishers.

Buffalo News. 2000. "May Day Protestors Clash with Police in U.S. Cities." May 2:A2.

———. 2000. "Tensions Force Scrapping of Genocide Resolution." October 20:A3.

Burger, Thomas. 1976. *Max Weber's Theory of Concept Formation: History, Laws and Ideal Types*. Durham, NC: Duke University Press.

Burgess, John. 2000. "Richest Nations Get Wake-up Call on Poverty Issues." *Washington Post*. April 18.

Camic, Charles. 1991. *Talcott Parsons: The Early Essays*. Chicago: University of Chicago Press.

Carlebach, Julius. 1978. *Karl Marx and the Radical Critique of Judaism*. Boston: Routledge & Kegan Paul.

Carlsnaes, Walter. 1981. *The Concept of Ideology and Political Analysis*. Westport, CT: Greenwood.

Carnegie, Andrew. 1920. *Autobiography of Andrew Carnegie*. Boston: Houghton Mifflin.

Carneiro, Robert, editor. 1967. *The Evolution of Society: Selections From Herbert Spencer's Principles of Sociology*. Chicago: University of Chicago Press.

Carr, E. H. 1934. *Karl Marx, A Study in Fanaticism*. London: Dent.

Catton, W. R. 1980. *Overshoot: The Ecological Basis of Revolutionary Change*. Urbana: University of Illinois Press.

Chamberlin, K., and S. Zika. 1992. "Religiosity Meaning in Life, and Psychological Well-Being," pp. 138–148 in *Religion and Mental Health*, edited by John Schumaker. New York: Oxford Press.

Chriss, James J. 1993. "Durkheim's Cult of the Individual as Civil Religion: Its Appropriation by Erving Goffman." *Sociological Spectrum*. 13:251–275.

Coakley, Jay. 2001. *Sport in Society*. Boston: McGraw-Hill.

Cockerham, William. 1995. *The Global Society*. New York: McGraw-Hill.

Collins, Randall. 1974. *Conflict Sociology: Toward an Explanatory Science*. New York: Academic Press.

———. 1975. *Conflict Sociology*. New York: Academic Press.

Collins, Randall, and Sal Restivo. 1983. "Development, Diversity and Conflict in the Sociology of Science." *The Sociological Quarterly*. Vol. 24 (spring): 185–200.

Comte, Auguste. 1851. *System of Positive Polity*, Vol. 1. New York: Burt Franklin.

———. 1852. *System of Positive Polity*, Vol.2. New York: Burt Franklin.

———. 1854. *System of Positive Polity*, Vol.4. New York: Burt Franklin.

———. 1891. *The Catechism of Positive Religion*. Clifton, NJ: Kelley.

———. 1896. *Positive Philosophy*, translated by Harriet Martineau. London: Bell.

———. 1912. *Systeme de Politique Positive*, 4th ed. Paris: Cres.

———. 1975. "Auguste Comte and Positivism: The Essential Writings," edited with an intro-duction by Gertrud Lenzen. New York: Harper.

Cook, Karen, and J. M. Whitmeyer. 1992. "Two Approaches to Social Structure: Exchange theory and Network Analysis." *Annual Review of Sociology*. 18:109–127.

Cook, Karen, and Karen Hegtvedt. 1983. "Distributive Justice, Equity and Equality." *Annual Review of Sociology*. 9:217–241.

Cooley, Charles. 1899. *Personal Competition*. New York: Macmillan.

———. 1902. *Human Nature and the Social Order*. New York: Scribners.

———. 1909. *Social Organization*. New York: Scribners.

———. 1918. *Social Process*. New York: Scribners.

———. 1927. *Life and the Student*. New York: Alfred A. Knopf.

———. 1930. *Sociological Theory and Social Research*, introduction and notes by Robert Cooley Angell. New York: Henry Holt.

———. 1964. *Human Nature and the Social Order*. New York: Schocken Books.

Cooper, Derick. 1991. "On the Concept of Alienation." *International Journal of Contemporary Sociology*. 28:7–26.

Cooper, Richard, and Richard Layard, editors. 2002. *What the Future Holds*. Cambridge, MA: MIT Press.

Coser, Lewis, and Irving Howe, editors. 1954. "Images of Socialism," pp. 29–47 in *Legacy of Dissent*, edited by Nicolaus Mills. New York: Simon & Schuster.

———. 1973. *The New Conservatives: A Critique from the Left*. New York: Quadrangle/New York Times Books.

———. 1977. *Masters of Sociological Thought*, 2nd ed. New York: Harcourt, Brace & Jovanovich.

Cranston, Maurice. 1983. *Jean-Jacques: The Early Life and Work of Jean-Jacques Rousseau, 1712–1754*. Suffolk, Great Britain: Chaucer Press.

———. 1986. *Philosophers and Pamphleteers: Political Theorists of the Enlightenment*. Oxford, Great Britain: Chaucer Press.

Crocker, Lester G. 1968. *Jean-Jacques Rousseau: The Quest, 1712–1758*, Vol.1. New York: Macmillan.

Cullen, Daniel E. 1983. *Freedom in Rousseau's Political Philosophy*. DeKalb, IL: Northern Illinois University Press.

Curtis, Bruce. 1981. *William Graham Sumner*. Boston: Twayne.

Curtis, James E., and John W. Petras. 1970. *The Sociology of Knowledge, A Reader*. New York: Praeger.

Cuzzort, R. P. 1969. *Humanity and Modern Sociological Thought*. New York: Holt, Rinehart and Winston.

Dahrendorf, Ralf. 1959. *Class and Class Theory in Industrial Society*. Stanford, CA: University Press.

Dant, Tim. 1996. "Fetishism and the Social Value of Objects." *Sociological Review*. 44:495–516.

Darwin, Charles. 2000. *The Voyage of the Beagle*, with a introduction by H. James Birx. Amherst, NY: Prometheus.

de Bonard, Louis. 1862. *Essai analytique sur les lois naturelles*. Paris: Migne.

———. 1864. *Œuvres*. Paris: Migne.

Delaney, Tim. 1993. "Fragmentation and the 1992 Los Angeles Riots." Paper presented at the annual meeting of the Pacific Sociological Louis Association.

———. 2000a. "The Building Blocks of Religion." *New Zealand Rationalist & Humanist Journal*. (Winter):2–8.

———. 2000b. "Humanistic Issues in Genetic Engineering, Fertility, and Cloning," pp. 214–219 in *Science and Society*, edited by H. James Birx. St. Petersburg, Russia: Russian Academy of Sciences.

———. 2001. *Community, Sport and Leisure*. Auburn, NY: Legend Books.

———. 2002a. "Karl Marx and Social Change: From Early Capitalism to Emerging Capitalism," pp. 41–70 in *Values, Society & Evolution*, edited by James Birx and Tim Delaney. Auburn, NY: Legend Books.

———. 2002b. "The Value of Multiculturalism," pp. 169–180 in *Values, Society & Evolution*, ed-ited by James Birx and Tim Delaney. Auburn, NY: Legend Books.

Delaney, Tim, and Allene Wilcox. 2002. "Sports and the Role of the Media," pp. 199–215 in *Values, Society & Evolution*. Auburn, NY: Legend Books.

DeLey, Herbert. 1966. *Marcel Proust et le duc de Saint-Simon*. Urbana: University of Illinois Press.

Devine, Elizabeth, Michael Held, James Vinson & George Walsh, eds. 1983. *Thinkers of the Twentieth Century*. Detroit: Gale Research.

Diliberto, Gioia. 1999. *A Useful Woman*. New York: Scribner.

Dorfman, Joseph. 1934. *Thorstein Veblen and His America*. New York: Viking.

Douglas, Jack. 1980. *Introduction to the Sociologies of Everyday Life*. Boston: Allyn & Bacon.

Dronberger, Ilse. 1971. *The Political Thought of Max Weber: In Quest of Statesmanship*. New York: Meredith Corporation.

Duncan, D. 1908. *The Life and Letters of Herbert Spencer*. London: Methuen.

Durkheim, Emile. 1928. *Socialism*. New York: Collier Books.

———. 1938 [1895]. *The Rules of Sociological Method*. New York: Free Press.

———. 1951 [1895]. *Suicide*. New York: Free Press.

———. 1957. *Professional Ethics and Civil Morals*. London: Routledge & Kegan Paul.

———. 1962 [1928]. *Socialism*. New York; Collier.

———. 1965 [1912]. *The Elementary Forms of Religious Life*. New York: Free Press.

———. 1965. *Montesquieu and Rousseau; Forerunners of Sociology*. Ann Arbor: University of Michigan Press.

———. 1973a [1914]. "The Dualism of Human Nature and Its Social Condition," pp. 149–163 in *Emile Durkheim: On Morality and Society*, edited by K. Bellah. Chicago: University of Chicago Press.

———. 1973b [1925]. *Moral Education: A Study in the Theory and Application of the Sociology of Education*. New York: Free Press.

———. 1984. *The Division of Labor in Society*, translated by W. D. Halls. New York; Free Press.

———. 1993 [1887]. *Ethics and the Sociology of Morals*. Buffalo: Prometheus.

Edwards, Paul. 1997. *The Encyclopedia of Philosophy*. New York: Macmillan.

Ekeh, Peter. 1974. *Social Exchange Theory: The Two Traditions*. Cambridge: Harvard University Press.

Ellensburg, Stephen. 1976. *Rousseau's Political Philosophy*. Ithaca, NY: Collier Books.

Ellul, Jacques. 1964. *The Technological Society*. New York: Vintage.

Emerson, Richard. 1972a. "Exchange Theory, Part I: A Psychological Basis for Social Basis for Social Exchange," pp. 38–57 in *Sociological Theories in Progress*, Vol. 2, edited by J. Berger, M. Zelditch, and B. Anderson. Boston: Houghton Mifflin.

———. 1972b. "Exchange Theory, Part II: Exchange Relations and Networks," pp. 58–87 in *Sociological Theories in Progress*, edited by J. Berger, Zelditch, and B. Anderson. Boston: Houghton Mifflin.

Engels, Frederick. 1869. "Karl Marx," translated by Joan and Trevor Walmsley in *Die Zukunft* (185): August 11.

———. 1883. "On the Death of Karl Marx." *Der Sozialdemokrat*. No. 13.

Ermann, M. David, and Richard Lundman. 1996. *Corporate and Governmental Deviance*, 5th edition. Oxford: Oxford University Press.

Etzkorn, Peter. 1968. *Georg Simmel*. New York: Teachers College Press.

Farganis, James. 2000. *Readings in Social Theory*, 3rd edition. Boston: McGraw Hill.

Faris, Robert. 1967. *Chicago Sociology 1920–1932*. San Francisco: Chandler.

Farley, John. 1998. *Sociology*, 4th edition. Upper Saddle River, NJ: Prentice-Hall.

Farrington, Karen. 2000. *The History of Torture & Execution*. New York: Lyons Press.

Flaherty, Julie. 1999. "Bricks, Mortar and Sociology." *The New York Times*. June 20:BU7.

Fontana, Andrea, and James Frey. 1983. "The Place Kicker in Professional Football: Simmel's Stranger Revisited." *Qualitative Sociology*. 6(1) Winter: 308–321.

Foster, Janet. 1990. *Crime and Community in the City*. New York: Routledge.

Fracoise, Michel. 2001. "McDonald's the Testing Ground for Russia's New Unionists." *AFP Moscow, Russia*. March 8.

Freund, Julien. 1968. *The Sociology of Max Weber*. New York; Random House.

Frisby, David. 1981. *Sociological Impressionism: A Reassessment of George Simmel's Social Theory*. London: Heinemann.

———. 1984. *Georg Simmel*. Chichester, England: Ellis Horwood.

Fry, Dieter, and Robert Wickland. 1980. "Self-Awareness Theory: When the Self Makes a Difference, pp. 7–48 in *The Self in Social Psychology*, edited by Daniel Wegner and Robin Vallacher. New York: Oxford University Press.

Garfinkel, Harold. 1967. *Studies in Ethnomethodology*. Englewood Cliffs, NJ: Prentice-Hall.

Garner, Roberta (editor). 2000. *Social Theory*. Orchard Park, NY: Broadview.

Gay, Peter. 1969. *The Enlightenment: An Interpretation*. New York: Norton & Company.

Geertz, C. 1973. "The Growth of Culture and the Evolution of Mind." *The Interpretation of Culture*. New York: Basic.

Gerth, Hans, and C. Wright Mills. 1946. *From Max Weber: Essays in Sociology*. New York: Oxford University Press.

Giddens, Anthony. 1971. *Capitalism and Modern Social Theory*. Cambridge: University Press.

———. 1972. *Emile Durkheim: Selected Writings*. New York: Cambridge University Press.

———. 1978. *Durkheim*. New York: Penguin Books.

———. 1987. *Sociology: A Brief But Critical Introduction*, 2nd edition. New York: Harcourt, Brace & Jovanovich.

Gildin, Hilail. 1983. *Rousseau's Social Contract: The Design of the Argument*. Chicago: University of Chicago Press.

Gilman, Charlotte Perkins. 1887. "The Right to Earn Money." *Woman's Journal*. 18 (January 8):12.

———. 1892/1973. *The Yellow Wall-Paper*. New York: Feminist Press.

———. 1898. *Women and Economics*. Boston: Small and Maynard.

———. 1935. *The Living of Charlotte Perkins Gilman*. New York: D. Appleton-Century Company.

———. 1998. *The Abridged Diaries of Charlotte Perkins Gilman*, edited by Denise D. Knight. Charlottesville, VA: University of Virginia Press.

———. 2002. *The Dress of Women*, edited with an introduction by Michael R. Hill and Mary Jo. Deegan. Westport, CT: Greenwood Press.

Glock, Charles, and Rodney Stark. 1965. *Religion and Society in Tension*. Chicago: Rand McNally.

Goffman, Erving. 1959. *Presentation of Self in Everyday Life*. Garden City, NY: Anchor.

Goode, Erich. 1988. *Sociology*, 2nd edition. Englewood Cliffs, NJ: Prentice-Hall.

Gough, J. W. 1968. *John Locke's Political Philosophy: Eight Studies*. London: Oxford Press.

Green, Martin. 1974. *The Von Richtofen Sisters*. New York: Basic.

Griffith, Elisabeth. 1984. *In Her Own Right*. New York: Oxford University Press.

Gurko, Miriam. 1974. *The Ladies of Seneca Falls*. New York: Schocken Books.

Habermas, Jürgen. 1987. *The Theory of Communicating Action*. Boston: Beacon Press.

Hadden, Richard W. 1997. *Sociological Theory*. Orchard Park, NY: Broadview.

Hall, Richard. 1987. *Organizations: Structures, Processes, and Outcomes*, 4th edition. Englewood Cliffs, NJ: Prentice-Hall.

Hamid, Nicholas P. 1993. "Self-Monitoring and Ethnic Group Membership." *Psychological Reports*, 72:1347–1350.

Hartle, Ann. 1983. *The Modern Self in Rousseau's Confessions: A Reply to St. Augustine*. Notre Dame: University of Notre Dame Press.

Hegtvedt, Karen, Elanie Thompson, and Karen Cook. 1993. "Power and Equity: What Counts in Attributions for Exchange Outcomes?" *Social Psychology Quarterly*. Vol.56(2):100–119.

Heilbroner, Robert L. 1970. *Between Capitalism and Socialism*. New York: Random House.

Heller, Agnes. 1976. *The Theory of Need in Marx*. New York: St. Martins.

Henslin, James. 1993. *Sociology*. Boston: Allyn & Bacon

———. 1994. *Social Problems*. Englewood Cliffs, NJ: Prentice-Hall.

Hewitt, John. 1998. *The Myth of Self-Esteem*. New York: St. Martin's Press.

Hinkle, Roscoe. 1967. "Charles Horton Cooley's General Sociological Orientation." *The Sociological Quarterly*. Vol.8(11):5–20.

Hobbes, Thomas. 1971. *Leviathan*, edited by Michael Oakeshoti. New York: Collier-Macmillian.

———. 1990. *Thomas Hobbes and Political Theory*, edited by Mary G. Dietz. Lawrence, KS: University Press of Kansas.

Hoecker-Drysdale, Susan. 1992. *Harriet Martineau: The First Woman Sociologist*. Oxford, England: Berg Publishers.

Hofstader, Richard. 1955. *Social Darwinism in American Thought*. Boston: Beacon Press, Harcourt, Bernard.

———. 2001. *Illusion of Order*. Cambridge, MA: Harvard University Press.

Homans, George and Charles Curtis. 1934. *An Introduction to Pareto*. New York: Knopf.

Homans, George. 1941. *English Villagers of the Thirteenth Century*. Cambridge, MA: Harvard University Press.

———. 1950. *The Human Group*. New York: Harcourt & Brace.

———. 1951. "The Western Electric Researches," in *Human Factors in Management*, edited by S. D. Hoslett. New York: Harper.

———. 1958. "Social Behavior as Exchange." *American Journal of Sociology*. 63:597–606.

———. 1961. *Social Behavior: Its Elementary Forms*. New York: Harcourt, Brace and World.

———. 1962. *Sentiments and Activities*. New York: The Free Press.

———. 1964. "Bringing Men Back In." *American Sociological Review*. 29:Dec.

———. 1967. *The Nature of Social Science*. New York: Harcourt, Brace and World.

———. 1969. "The Sociological Relevance of Behaviorism," pp. 1–24 in *Behavioral Sociology*, edited by R. Burgess and D. Bushell. New York: Columbia University Press.

———. 1984. *Coming to My Senses: The Autobiography of a Sociologist*. New Brunswick, NJ: Transaction Books.

Hook, Sydney. 1962. *From Hegel to Marx*. Ann Arbor, MI: University Press.

Hudson, William. 1974. *An Introduction to the Philosophy of Herbert Spencer*. New York: Haskell.

Iggers, Georg G. 1958. *The Cult of Authority; The Political Philosophy of the Saint-Simonians, A Chapter in the Intellectual History of Totalitarianism*. The Hague: Nijhoff.

James, William. 1948 [1890]. *Principles of Psychology*. Cleveland: World Publishing.

Joas, Hans. 1985. *George Herbert Mead: A Contemporary Re-Examination of his Thought*. Cambridge: MIT Press.

Kalberg, Stephen. 1980. "Max Weber's Types of Rationality: Cornerstones for the Analysis of Rationalization Processes in History." *American Journal of Sociology*. 85:1145–1179.

Kallen, Horace. 1956. *The Social Dynamics of George H. Mead*. Washington, DC: Public Affairs Press.

Karau, S., and K. Williams. 1993. "Social Loafing: A Meta-Analytic Review and Theoretical Integration." *Journal of Personality and Social Psychology*. 65: 681–706.

Kasler, Dirk. 1988. *Max Weber: An Introduction to His Life and Work*. Chicago: University of Chicago Press.

Kennedy, James. 1978. *Herbert Spencer*. Boston: Twayne.

Knight, Denise. 1997. *Charlotte Perkins Gilman*. New York: Twayne.

Kornblum, William. 1991. *Sociology*, 2nd edition. Austin, TX: Holt, Rinehart & Winston.

———. 1994. *Sociology*, 3rd edition. Fort Worth, TX: Harcourt Brace.

La Capra, Dominick. 1972. *Emile Durkheim: Sociologist and Philosopher*. Ithaca, NY: Cornell University Press.

Laslet, Peter, editor. 1960. *John Locke, Two Treatises of Government*. New York: American Library.

Latane, Bibb, and John Darley. 1970. *The Unresponsive Bystander: Why Doesn't He Help?* New York: Appleton-Century-Crofts.

Lawler, Edward, and Jeongkoo Yoon. 1996. "Commitment in Exchange Relations: Test of a Theory of Relational Cohesion." *American Sociological Review*. 61 February):89–108.

Lawrence, P. A. 1976. *George Simmel: Sociologist and European*. New York: Barnes & Noble.

Lea, G. 1982. "Religion, Mental Health, and Clinical Issues." *Journal of Religion and Health*. 21:336–351.

Lee, Yueh Ting. 1993. "In-Group Preference and Homogeneity Among African American and Chinese American Students." *Journal of Social Psychology*, 133:225–235.

Lengermann, Patricia Madoo, and Jill Niebrugge-Brantley. 1998. *The Women Founders*. Boston: McGraw Hill.

———. 2000. "Early Women Sociologists and Classical Sociological Theory: 1830–1930," pp. 289–321, in *Classical Sociological Theory*, written by George Ritzer. Boston: McGraw Hill.

Lenin, Vladimir. 1896. "Biographical Article on Friedrich Engels," in *Collected Works*. Moscow: Progress.

Levine, Donald. 1971. *Georg Simmel*. Chicago: University of Chicago Press.

Lewes, G. H. 1853. *Philosophy of the Sciences*. London: Bohn.

Lichtheim, George. 1970. *A Short History of Socialism*. New York: Prager.

Locke, John. 1967. *Two Treatises of Government: A Critical Edition*, introduction by Peter Laslett. London: Cambridge.

———. 1991. *Letter Concerning Toleration*, translated by William Popple. London: Routledge.

Los Angeles Times. 1993. "Garbage: Landfills Yield Recycling Clues." July 17:A2.

———. 1996. " 'Luther Year' in Germany." February 18:C3.

Low-Beer, Ann. 1969. *Herbert Spencer*. London: Macmillian.

Lukes, Steven. 1972. *Emile Durkheim: His Life and Work*. New York: Harper & Row.

Maclean, Kenneth. 1962. *John Locke and English Literature of the Eighteenth Century*. New York; Russell & Russell.

MacPherson, C. B. 1962. *The Political Theory of Possessive Individualism: Hobbes to Locke*. Oxford: Clarerdon.

Macrae, Donald. 1974. *Max Weber*. New York: Viking.

Malinowski, Bronislaw. 1926. *Crime and Custom in Savage Society*. London: Routledge and Kegan Paul.

Maney, Kevin. 1999. "Web Weaves Shift in Balance of Power." *USA Today*. September 22:3B.

Mannheim, Karl. 1936. *Ideology and Utopia*. New York: Harvest Books.

———. 1936. "The Sociology of Knowledge," pp. 264–311 in *Ideology and Utopia* by Karl Mannheim. New York: Harcourt, Brace & World.

———. 1940. *Man and Society: In An Age of Reconstruction*. London: Routledge & Kegan Paul.

———. 1943. *Diagnosis of Our Time*. London: Routledge & Kegan Paul.

———. 1952. *Essays on the Sociology of Knowledge*. New York: Oxford University Press.

———. 1953. "The Structural Analysis of Epistemology," pp. 15–73 in *Mannheim, Essays on Sociology and Social Psychology*. New York: Oxford University Press.

———. 1962. *An Introduction to the Sociology of Education*. London: Routledge & Kegan Paul.

———. 1971. "The Problem of a Sociology of Knowledge," pp. 5–115 in *From Karl Mannheim*, edited by K. H. Wolff. New York: Oxford University Press.

———. 1982. *Karl Mannheim: Structures of Thinking*, edited by Kettler, Meja, and Stehr. London: Routledge & Kegan Paul.

———. 1993. "The Sociology of Intellectures." *Theory, Culture, and Society*. 10:69–80.

Manuel, Frank. 1956. *The New World of Henri Saint-Simon*. Cambridge: Harvard University Press.

Martindale, Don. 1988. *The Nature and Types of Sociological Theory*. Prospect Heights, IL: Waveland Press.

Martineau, Harriet. 1822 "Female Writers on Practical Divinity." *Monthly Repository*, 17:593–96.

———. 1832–34. *Illustrations of Political Economy*. 9 vols. London: Charles Fox.

———. 1836–37. *Society in America*, 2 vols. New York: Saunders and Otley.

———. 1838. *How to Observe Morals and Manners*. London: Charles Knight and Company.

———. 1841. *The Hour and the Man: An Historical Romance*, 3 vols. London: Cassell.

———. 1841. *The Playfellow*, 4 vols. London: Charles Knight and Company.

———. 1844. *Life in the Sick-Room: Essays by an Invalid*. London: Edward Moxon.

———. 1845. *Letters on Mesmerism*. London: Edward Moxon.

———. 1848. *Eastern Life: Past and Present*, 3 vols. London: Edward Moxon.

———. 1852. *Letters From Ireland*. London: John Chapman.

———. 1853. *The Positive Philosophy of Auguste Comte, Freely Translated and Condensed by Harriet Martineau*. London: John Chapman.

———. 1859. "Female Industry." *Edinburgh Review*. 109:293–336.

———. 1877. *Harriet Martineau's Autobiography, with Memorials by Maria Westin Chapman*, 3 vols. London: Elder.

Martineau, Harriet, and Henry George Atkinson. 1851. *Letters on the Laws of Man's Nature and Development*. London: John Chapman.

Martinich, Aloysius. 1999. *Hobbes—A Biography*. Oakleigh, Australia: Cambridge University Press.

Marx, Elanor. 1897. "Biographical Comments on Karl Marx." *Neue Zeit*. Vol.1.

Marx, Karl. 1964. *The Economic & Philosophic Manuscripts of 1844*, edited by Dirk Strunk. New York: International Publishers.

Marx, Karl, and Friedrich Engels. 1970 [1845–46]. *The German Ideology, Part I*, edited by C. J. Arthuer. New York: International Publishers.

———. 1978. "Manifesto of the Communist Party," pp. 469–500 in *The Marx and Engels Reader*, edited by Robert Tucker. New York: Norton.

———. 1980. *Collected Works*. New York: International Publishers.

Mazlish, Bruce. 1993. *A New Science: The Breakdown of Connections and the Birth of Sociology*. University Park, PA: Pennsylvania State University Press.

McLellan, David. 1969. *The Young Hegelians and Karl Marx*. New York: Macmillian.

———. 1987. *Marxism and Religion*. New York: Harper and Row.

———. 1990. *Karl Marx: Selected Writings*. Oxford: Oxford Press.

Mead, George H. 1964. *On Social Psychology*, edited by Anselm Strauss. Chicago: University Press.

Mead, George Herbert. 1934. *Mind, Self & Society*, edited and with introduction by Charles W. Morris. Chicago: University of Chicago Press.

———. 1936. *Movements of Thought in the Nineteenth Century*. Chicago: University of Chicago Press.

———. 1938. *The Philosophy of the Act*. Chicago: University of Chicago Press.

———. 1964. *Selected Writings*, edited by Andrew Reck. Indianapolis, IN: Bobbs-Merrill.

———. 1982. *The Individual and the Social Self: Unpublished Work of George Herbert Mead*. Chicago: University of Chicago Press.

Medical Ethics. 1999. "Understanding Cloning." Available: www.learner.org/cgi-bin/de-livery/e...medicalethics/cloning/index

Meltzer, Bernard, John Petras, & Larry Reynolds. 1975. *Symbolic Interactionism—Genesis, Varieties & Criticisms*. Boston: Routledge & Kegan Paul.

Merton, Robert. 1949. *Social Theory and Social Structure*. New York; Free Press.

Mestrovic, Stjepan G. 1988. *Emile Durkheim and the Reformation of Sociology*. Totowa, NJ: Rowman and Littlefield.

Michelmore, Bill. 2000. "Cataracts Big Suicide Lure." *Buffalo News*. May 1:A1.

Mill, John Stuart. 1873. *Auguste Comte and Positivism*. London: Trubner & Row

Miller, David. 1973. *George Herbert Mead; Self, Language, and the World*. Austin: University of Texas Press.

Miller, S.M. 1963. *Max Weber*. New York: Crowell.

Mills, C. Wright. 1959. *The Sociological Imagination*. New York: Oxford University Press.

Mitchell, J. Clyde. 1974. "Social Networks." *Annual Review of Anthropology*. 3:279–99.

Mommsen, Wolfgang. 1989. *The Political and Social Theory of Max Weber*. Chicago: University of Chicago Press.

Mommsen, Wolfgang, and Jurgen Osterhammel, editors. 1987. *Max Weber and His Contemporaries*. Boston: Allen & Unwin.

Moscow Times. 2001. "Putin Says More Cars Are Needed." June 7:5.

Muggeridge, Kitty, and Ruth Adam. 1968. *Beatrice Webb*. New York: Knopf.

Murdock, George Peter. 1935. "Comparative Data on Division of Labor by Sex." *Social Forces*, 15:551–553.

Naylor, R. T. 2002. *Wages of Crime*. Ithaca, NY: Cornell University Press.

Neisser, Hans. 1965. *On the Sociology of Knowledge*. New York: James H. Heineman.

Nisbet, Robert. 1965. *Emile Durkheim*. Englewood Cliffs, NJ: Prentice-Hall.

———. 1969. *The Quest for Community*. New York: Oxford University Press.

———. 1974. *The Sociology of Emile Durkheim*. New York: Oxford University Press.

Nixon, Howard II and James H. Frey. 1996. *A Sociology of Sport*. Belmont, CA: Wadsworth.

Noone, John B. 1980. *Rousseau's Social Contract: A Conceptual Analysis*. Athens: University of Georgia Press.

Ogburn, William Fielding. 1922/1964. *Social Change*. New York: Viking.

———. 1942. "Inventions, Population and History" in American Council of Learned Socities, *Studies in the History of Culture*. Freeport, NY: Books for Libraries Press.

Ollman, Bertell. 1976. *Alienation*, 2nd edition. Cambridge MA: University Press.

Pampel, Fred. 2000. *Sociological Lines and Ideas*. New York: Worth Publishers.

Parsons, Talcott. 1942. "Some Sociological Aspects of the Fascist Movements." *Social Forces*, 21:138–147.

———. 1949 [1937]. *The Structure of Social Action*. Glencoe, IL: Dorsey Press.

———. 1951. *The Social System*. Glencoe, IL: Free Press.

———. 1954. *Essays in Sociological Theory*. Glencoe, IL: Free Press.

———. 1956. "A Sociological Approach to the Theory of Organizations I" *Administrative Science Quarterly*. June:63–85.

———. 1956. "A Sociological Approach to the Theory of Organizations II." *Administrative Science Quarterly*. Sept:225–239.

———. 1960. *Structure and Process in Modern Societies*. New York: Free Press.

———. 1963. "Christianity and Modern Industrial Society," pp. 33–70 in *Sociological Theory, Values, and Socio-Cultural Change*, edited by Edward A. Tiryakian. Glencoe, IL: Free Press.

———. 1965. *The Negro American*, editor. Boston: Houghton Mifflin.

———. 1966. *Societies*. Englewood Cliffs, NJ: Prentice Hall.

———. 1968. "The Problem of Polarization Along the Axis of Color," in *Color and Race*, edited by J. H. Franklin. Boston: Beacon Press.

———. 1968. "Cooley and the Problem of Internalization" in *Cooley and Social Analysis*, edited by Albert Reiss. Ann Arbor; University of Michigan Press.

———. 1971. *The System of Modern Sociology*. Englewood Cliffs, NJ: Prentice Hall.

Parsons, Talcott, and Neil Smelser. 1957. *Economy and Society*. New York: Free Press.

Parsons, Talcott, and Robert Bales. 1955. *Family, Socialization and Interaction*. Glencoe, IL: Free Press.

Parvin, M. 1973. "Economic Determinants of Political Unrest: An Economic Approach." *Journal of Conflict Resolution*. 17:271–96.

Peel, J. 1971. *Herbert Spencer: The Evolution of a Sociologist*. New York: Basic.

Perrin, Robert. 1963. *Herbert Spencer*. New York: Garland.

Perrow, Charles. 1986. *Complex Organizations*, 3rd edition. New York: Random House.

Peterson, L. R., and A. Roy. 1985. "Religiosity, Anxiety, and Meaning and Purpose: Religious Consequences for Psychological Well-Being." *Review of Religious Research*. 27:49–62.

Pfuetz, Paul. 1954. *Self, Society and Existence; Human Nature and Dialogue in the Thoughts of George Herbert Mead and Martin Buber*. New York: Harper Torch Books.

Phillips, John. 1993. *Sociology of Sport*. Boston: Allyn & Bacon.

Pickering, Mary. 1993. *Auguste Comte: An Intellectual Biography*, Vol.1. Cambridge: Cambridge University Press.

———. 1996. "Angels and Demons in the Moral Vision of Auguste Comte." *Journal of Women's History*. Summer Vol. 8(2):10–17.

Pressler, Charles, and Fabio Dasilua. 1996. *Sociology and Interpretation: From Weber to Habermas*. Albany: State University of New York Press.

Raison, Timothy. 1969. *The Founding Fathers of Social Science*. Baltimore, MD: Penguin.

Rammstedt, Otthein. 1991. "On Simmel's Aesthetics: Argumentation in the Journal *Jugend*, 1897–1906." *Theory, Culture, and Society*. 8:125–144.

Reck, Andrew. 1964. *Selective Writings; George Herbert Mead*. Chicago: University of Chicago Press.

Rempel, Warren F. 1965. *The Role of Value in Karl Mannheim's Sociology of Knowledge*. The Hague, The Netherlands: Mouton & Company.

Reynolds, Larry. 1993. *Interactionism: Exposition and Critique*, 3rd edition. Dix Hills, NY: General Hall.

Ritzer, George. 1981. "The Failure to Integrate Theory and Practice: The Case of the Sociological Work." *Journal of Applied Behavioral Science*. Jul/Aug/Sep:376–380.

———. 1983. *Sociological Theory*, 2nd edition. New York: Knopf.

———. 1988. *Contemporary Sociological Theory*, 2nd edition. New York: Knopf.

———. 1990. *Frontiers of Social Theory*. New York: Columbus Press.

———. 1993. *The McDonaldization of Society*. Newbury Park, CA: Pine Forge Press.

———. 1996. *The McDonaldization of Society*, 2nd edition. Thousand Oaks, CA: Pine Forge Press.

———. 2000a. *The McDonaldization of Society*. Thousand Oaks, CA: Pine Forge Press.

———. 2000b. *Sociological Theory*, 5th edition. Boston: McGraw Hill.

———. 2000c. *Classical Social Theory*, 3rd edition. Boston: McGraw Hill.

Roche de Coppens, Peter. 1976. *Ideal Man in Classical Theory: The Views of Comte, Durkheim, Pareto, and Weber*. London: Pennsylvania State University Press.

Rose, Peter. 1981. *They and We*, 3rd ed. New York: Random House.

Rousseau, Jean-Jacques. 1973. *The Social Contract and Discourses*, edited by G. D. H. Cole. New York: Dutton.

Ryan, John, and William Wentworth. 1999. *Media and Society*. Boston: Allyn and Bacon.

Sabine, George. 1965. *A History of Political Theory*. New York: Holt, Rinehart & Winston.

Saint-Simon, Claude Henri. 1976. *The Political Thought of Saint-Simon*, edited by Ghita Ionesco. London: Oxford Press.

Scharff, Robert. 1995. *Comte After Positivism*. New York: Cambridge.

Scheffler, Israel. 1974. *Four Pragmatists: A Critical Introduction to Pierce, James, Mead, and Dewey*. New York: Humanities Press.

Schellenberg, James. 1978. *Masters of Social Psychology*. New York: Oxford University Press.

Schiller, Friedrich. 1967. *On the Aesthetic Education of Man in a Series of Letters*, edited by Wilkinson and Willoughby. New York: Oxford Press.

Schluchter, Wolfgang. 1981. *The Rise of Western Rationalism: Max Weber's Developmental History*. Berkley: University of California Press.

Schumaker, John. 1992. "Mental Health Consequences of Irreligion," pp. 54–69 in *Religion and Mental Health*, edited by John Schumaker. New York: Oxford University Press.

Seidman, Steven. 1983. *Liberalism and the Origins of European Social Theory*. Los Angeles: University Press.

Shalin, Dmitri 1986. "Pragmatism and Social Interactionism." *American Sociological Review*. 51:9–29.

———. 1992. "Critical Theory and the Pragmatist Challenge." *American Journal of Sociology*. Vol. 98, No. 2(Sept):237–79.

———. 2000. "George Herbert Mead," pp. 302–344 in *The Blackwell Companion to Major Social Theorists*, edited by George Ritzer. Malden, MA: Blackwell Publishers.

Shibutani, T. and K. Kwan. 1965. *Ethnic Stratification: A Comparative Approach*. New York: Macmillan.

Shister, Gail. 2001. " 'Nation' Pushes Past 'This Week' in Sunday Ratings." *Buffalo News*. May 22:C4.

Sills, David, editor. 1968. *International Encyclopedia of the Social Science*, Vol. 3. New York: Macmillan

Simmel, Georg. 1890. "Über soziale differenzierung." *Staats—und Sozialwissenschaftliche Sprachwissenschaft.* XX:6–46.

———. 1893. "Moral Deficiencies as Determining Intellectual Functions." *International Journal of Ethics.* 111:490–507.

———. 1895. "The Problem of Sociology." *Annals of the American Academy of Political and Social Science.* VI:412–23.

———. 1896. "Friedrich Nietzsche: Eine Moral Philsophische Silhovette." *Seitschrift fur Philosphie und Philosophische Kritk.* CVII:202–05.

———. 1896–97. "Superiority and Subordination as Subject-matter for Sociology." *American Journal of Sociology,* 167–89.

———. 1897–99. "The Persistence of the Social Group." *American Journal of Sociology,* 662–98.

———. 1900. *Philosophie des Geldes.* Leipzig: Duncker und Humblot.

———. 1950 [1906]. "The Secret and the Secret Society," pp. 307–376 in *The Sociology of Georg Simmel,* edited and translated by K. Wolff. New York: Free Press.

———. 1955 [1908]. *Conflict and the Web of Group Affiliates.* New York: Free Press.

———. 1959 [1908]. "The Problem of Sociology," pp. 310–336 in *Essays in Sociology, Philosophy and Aesthetics,* edited by K. Wolff. New York: Harper Torch Books.

———. 1964. "The Web of Group Affiliations," translated by Reinhard Bendix, edited by Kurt H. Wolff, Reinhard Bendix, *Simmel: Translation of Chapters from "Soziologie."* New York: The Free Press.

———. 1965. *Makers of Modern Social Science,* edited by Lewis Coser. Englewood Cliffs, NJ: Prentice Hall.

———. 1971 [1903]. "The Metropolis and Mental Life," pp. 324–339 in *George Simmel,* edited by D. Levine. Chicago: University of Chicago Press.

———. 1971 [1904]. "Fashion," pp. 294–323 in *George Simmel,* edited by Levine. Chicago: University of Chicago Press.

———. 1971 [1908]. "The Poor," pp. 150–178 in *Georg Simmel,* edited by D. Levine. Chicago: Chicago Press.

———. 1971 [1908]. "The Stranger," pp. 143–199 in *Georg Simmel,* edited by Levine. Chicago: Chicago Press.

Simpson, George. 1963. *Emile Durkheim.* New York: Crowell.

———. 1969. *Auguste Comte: Sire of Sociology.* New York: Crowell.

Singer, Sam. 1995. *Human Genetic.* Freeman Publishing.

Singlemann, Peter. 1992. "Exchange as Symbolic Interaction: Convergence Between Two Theoretical Perspectives." *American Sociological Review.* Vol. 37 (Aug):414–424.

Skinner, B. F. 1971. *Beyond Freedom and Dignity.* New York: Knopf.

Slater, Don. 1997. *Consumer Culture and Modernity.* Cambridge: Polity Press.

Smith, Lynn. 1992. "Women, Work, and the Nobel." *Los Angeles Times.* October 21.

Smith, P. 1962. *A History of Modern Culture.* New York: Collier.

Snyder, E. 1991. "Sociology of Nostalgia: Sport Halls of Fame and Museums in America." *Sociology of Sport Journal.* 8:228–238.

So, Alvin, 1990. "Class Theory or Class Analysis? A Re-examination of Marx's Unfinished Chapter of Class." *Critical Sociology.* 17:35–55.

Spencer, Herbert. 1851. *Social Statics.* London: Chapman.

———. 1855. *The Principles of Psychology.* London: Chapman.

———. 1860. *The Social Organism.* London: Greenwood.

———. 1862. *First Principles.* New York: Appleton.

———. 1864. *Reasons for Dissenting from the Philosophy of Comte.* Available: www.marxists.org/reference/subject/philosophy/works/spencer

———. 1864. *The Principles of Biology.* New York: Appleton.

———. 1896. *Synthetic Philosophy of Herbert Spencer*. New York: Appleton.

———. 1896. *The Study of Sociology*. New York: Appleton.

———. 1898. *Principles of Sociology*. New York: Appleton.

———. 1904. *An Autobiography*. New York: Appleton.

———. 1908. *Social Statics and the Man Versus the State*. New York: Appleton.

Spykman, Nicholas. 1965. *The Social Theory of Georg Simmel*. New York: Atherton.

Squadrito, Kathleen M. 1979. *John Locke*. Boston: Twayne Publishers.

Stammer, Otto, editor. 1971. *Max Weber and Sociology Today*. New York: Harper & Row.

Standley, Arline Reilein. 1981. *Auguste Comte*. Boston: Twayne.

Stanton, Elizabeth, and Matilda Joslyn Gage, editors. 1887. *History of Woman Suffrage*, 3 Vols. Rochester, NY: Susan B. Anthony.

———. 1895. *The Woman's Bible*. New York: European Publishing Company.

Stashenko, Joel. 2000. "Quick Draw Said to Target Minorities." *Buffalo News*. April 1:D2.

Stenski, Ivan. 1997. *Durkheim and the Jews of France*. Chicago: University of Chicago Press.

Stone, Gregory. 1955. "American Sports: Play and Display." *Chicago Review*, 9(3):83–100.

Strauss, Anselm. 1956. *The Social Psychology of George Herbert Mead*. Chicago: University Press.

———. 1964. *George Herbert Mead on Social Psychology: Selected Papers*. Chicago: University of Chicago Press.

Stumpf, Samuel. 1994. *Philosophy, History & Problems*, 5th edition. New York: McGraw-Hill.

Swedberg, Richard. 1998. *Max Weber and the Idea of Economic Sociology*. Princeton, NJ: Princeton University Press.

Syracuse Post Standard. 1997. "Ancient City Uncovered; Residents met Columbus." March 25:A5.

———. 1999. "Our Near the End Awards: The Best of the Rest." November 11.

Tabb, William, and Larry Sawers, editors. 1984. *Marxism and the Metropolis*, 2nd edition. New York: Oxford University Press.

Thayer, H. S. 1968. *Meaning and Action: A Critical History of Pragmatism*. New York: Bobbs-Merrill.

Thibaut, John and Harold Kelley. 1959. *The Social Psychology of Groups*. New York: Wiley.

Thompson, Kenneth. 1975. *Auguste Comte: The Foundation of Sociology*. New York: Wiley & Sons.

———. 1982. *Emile Durkheim*. London: Tavistock.

Thomson, Garret. 1993. *Descartes to Kant*. Prospect Heights, IL: Waveland Press.

Tole, Lise Ann. 1993. "Durkheim on Religion and Moral Community in Modernity." *Sociological Inquiry*. 63:1–29.

Tucker, Robert. 1978. *The Marx-Engels Reader*. New York: Norton.

Turnbull, Linda, Elaine Hendrix, and Borden Dent. 2001. *Atlas of Crime*. Phoenix: Oryx Press.

Turner, Bryan. 1990. *Theories of Modernity and Post-Modernity*. London: Sage.

Turner, Jonathan and Adalberto Aguiree. 1998. *American Ethnicity: The Dynamics and Consequences of Discrimination*, 2nd edition. Boston: McGraw-Hill.

Turner, Jonathan H. 1972. *American Society: Problems of Structure*, 2nd edition. New York: Harper–Row.

———. 1972. *Patterns of Social Organization: A Survey of Social Institutions*. New York: McGraw-Hill.

———. 1974. *The Structure of Sociological Theory*. Homewood, IL: Dorsey Press.

———. 1977. *Social Problems in America*. New York: Harper & Row.

———. 1978. *The Structure of Sociological Theory*. Homewood, IL: Dorsey Press.

———. 1981. "The Forgotten Theoretical Giant; Herbert Spencer's Models and Principles."

Revue Européenne des Sciences Sociales. 19(59): 79–95.

———. 1982. *The Structure of Sociological Theory,* 2nd edition. Homewood, IL: Dorsey Press.

———. 1984 *Societal Stratification; A Theoretical Analysis.* New York: Columbia University Press.

———. 1985. *Herbert Spencer: A Renewed Appreciation.* Beverly Hills, CA: Sage.

———. 1987. *Social Theory Today.* Stanford, CA: Stanford University Press.

———. 1988. *A Theory of Social Interaction.* Stanford, CA: Stanford University Press.

———. 1990. "The Past, Present, and Future of Theory in American Sociology," pp. 371–391 in *Frontiers of Social Theory: The New Syntheses,* edited by George Ritzer. New York: Columbia University Press.

———. 1993. *Classical Sociological Theory: A Positivists' Perspective.* Chicago, IL: Nelson-Hall.

———. 2001. "Historical Forces Behind Bureaucratization." *Sociology,* 2nd edition. New York: Harper & Row.

Van Hoorn, Willem, and Thom Verhave. 1984. "The Temporization of the Self." *Historical Social Psychology,* edited by Kenneth J. Gergen and Mary Gergen. New Jersey: Lawrence Erlbaum Associates.

Veblen, Thorstein. 1894. "The Economic Theory of Woman's Dress" in *Political Science Monthly,* Vol. XLVI (Nov.).

———. 1898. "Why Is Economics Not an Evolutionary Science?" *The Quarterly Journal of Economics,* Vol. XII:56–81.

———. 1899. *The Theory of Leisure Class.* New York: Macmillian.

———. 1904. *The Theory of Business Enterprise.* New York: Scribner's Sons.

———. 1914. *The Instinct of Workmanship and the State of Industrial Arts.* New York: Macmillian.

———. 1915. "The Opportunity of Japan." *The Journal of Race Development,* Vol. VI (July).

———. 1915/1942. *Imperial Germany and the Industrial Revolution.* New York:Viking.

———. 1918/1957. *The Higher Learning in America,* edited by M. Hacker. New York: Hill and Wang.

———. 1919/1961. *The Place of Science in Modern Civilisation.* New York: Russell & Russell.

———. 1921. *The Engineers and the Price System.* New York: Viking.

———. 1923. *Absentee Ownership and Business Enterprise in Recent Times: The Case for America.* New York: Viking.

———. 1947. *What Veblen Taught,* edited by Wesley C. Mitchell. New York: Viking.

———. 1963. *Thorstein Veblen,* edited by Bernard Rosenberg. New York: Viking.

———. 1964. *The Writings of Thorstein Veblen,* edited by Leon Ardzrooni. New York: Viking.

Wallace, David. 1967. "Reflection on the Education of George Herbert Mead." *American Journal of Sociology.* Vol. 72(4):396–408.

Wallace, Ruth and Alison Wolf, (3rd edition, 1991) 5th edition. 1999. *Contemporary Sociological Theory.* Upper Saddle River, NJ: Prentice Hall.

Ward, Russell. 1998. "Rituals, First Impressions and the Opening Day Home Advantage." *Sociology of Sport Journal.* 15:279–293.

Waters, Malcohm. 1995. *Globalization.* London: Routledge.

Webb, Beatrice Potter. 1891/1904. *The Co-operative Movement in Great Britain.* London: Swan, Sonnenschein and Company.

———. 1926. *My Apprenticeship.* London: Longmans Green.

———. 1982. *The Diary of Beatrice Webb,* Vol. 1, edited by Norman and Jeanne MacKenzie. Cambridge, MA: Harvard University Press.

———. 1983. *The Diary of Beatrice Webb,* Vol. 2 Edited by Norman and Jeanne Mackenzie. Cambridge, MA: Harvard University Press.

Webb, Robert K. 1960. *Harriet Martineau: A Radical Victorian.* New York: Columbia University Press.

Weber, Marianne. 1975/1988. *Max Weber; A Biography.* New Brunswick, NJ: Transaction Books.

———. 1926/1975. *Max Weber: A Biography*, translated and edited by Harry Zohn. New York: Wiley & Sons.

Weber, Max 1946. *From Max Weber: Essays in Sociology*, translated and edited by H. Gerth and C. Wright Mills. New York: Oxford University Press.

———. 1947. *The Theory of Social and Economic Organization*, translated by A. M. Parsons and T. Parsons. New York: Free Press.

———. 1949 [1903–1917]. *The Methodology of the Social Sciences*, Edward Shils and Henry Rinch, editors. New York: Free Press.

———. 1958 [1904–1905]. *The Protestant Ethic and the Spirit of Capitalism*. New York: Scribners.

———. 1958 [1915]. "Religious Rejections of the World and Their Directions," pp. 323–359 in *From Max Weber: Essays in Sociology*, edited by H. Gerth and C. W. Mills. New York: Oxford University Press.

———. 1958 [1916–1917]. *The Religion of India: The Sociology of Hinduism and Buddhism*. Glencoe, IL: Free Press.

———. 1958 [1921]. *The Rational and Social Foundations of Music*. Carbondale: Southern Illinois University Press.

———. 1963 [1921]. *The Sociology of Religion*. Boston: Beacon Press.

———. 1964 [1916]. *The Religion of China: Confucianism and Taoism*. New York: Macmillan.

———. 1964. *Basic Concepts in Sociology*. New York: Citadel Press.

———. 1968 [1921]. *Economy and Society*, 3 vols. Totowa, NJ: Bedminstor Press.

———. 1976 [1896–1906]. *The Agrarian Sociology of Ancient Civilizations*. London: NLB.

———. 1976 [1903–1906]. *Roscher and Knies; The Logical Problems of Historical Economics*. New York: Free Press.

———. 1978. *Economy and Society*, edited by Guenter Roth and Claus Wittich. Berkley: University of California Press.

———. 1978. *Selections in Translation*, edited by W. Runciman, translated by Matthews. New York: Oxford University Press.

———. 1985 [1906]. " 'Churches' and 'Sects' in North America: An Ecclesiastical Social-Political Sketch." Sociological Theory. 3:7–13.

Weingartner, Rudolph. 1962. *Experience and Culture: The Philosophy of Georg Simmel*. Middetown, CT: Wesleyan University Press.

Weinstein, David. 1998. *Herbert Spencer's Liberal Utilitarianism*. Cambridge: University Press.

Weldon, E., and L. Mustari. 1988. "Felt Dispensability in Groups of Co-Actors: The Effects of Shared Responsibility and Explicit Anonymity on Cognitive Effort. *Organizational Behavior and Human Decision Processes*. 41:330–351.

Wells-Barnett, Ida. 1895. *A Red Record*. Chicago: Donohue and Henneberry.

———. 1900/1969. "Mob Rule in New Orleans," reprinted in *On Lynchings*. New York: Arno.

———. 1970. *Crusade for Justice: The Autobiography of Ida B. Wells*, edited by Alfreda M. Duston. Chicago: University of Chicago Press.

Westley, Frances. 1983. *The Complex Forms of Religious Life: A Durkheimian View of New Religious Movements*. Chico, CA: Scholars Press.

Whitehouse, Tom. 1998. "From the Wild: Feral Boy Prefers Living with Dogs." *Daily Breeze*. July 17:A7.

Will, George, F. 2000. "Meet the Latest Trend Group, Bobos." *Washington Post*. April 9.

Williams, Dara. 1999. "Neighbors Torn About When to Act on Their Suspicions." *Buffalo News*. September 10.

Williams K., S. Harkins, and B. Latane. 1981. "Identifiability as a Deterrent to Social Loafing: Two Cheering Experiments." *Journal of Personality and Social Psychology*. 40:303–311.

Wilshire, David. 1978. *The Social and Political Thought of Herbert Spencer*. Oxford; University Press.

Wilson, Edward. 1975. *Sociobiology*. Cambridge, MA: Harvard Press.

Wilson, James and George Kelling. 1982. "Broken Windows." *Atlantic Monthly*. March:29–38.

Witter, R. A., W. A. Stock, M. A. Okum, and M. J. Harring. 1995. "Religion and Subjective Well-Being in Adulthood: A Quantitative Analysis." *Review of Religious Research*. 23:332–342.

Wolff, Kurt. 1950. *The Sociology of Georg Simmel*. New York: Free Press.

Younts, Wesley, and Charles Mueller. 2001. "Justice Processes; Specifying the Mediating Role of Perceptions of Distributive Justice.' *American Sociological Review*. Vol. 66 (February):125–145.

Yuille, Judith. 1991. *Karl Marx: From Trier to Highgate*. London: Highgate Cemetery.

Yulton, John. 1956. *John Locke and the Way of Ideas*. London: Oxford University Press.

Zeitlin, Irving. 1968. *Ideology and the Development of Sociological Thought*. Englewood Cliffs, NJ: Prentice Hall.

———. 1981. *Ideology and the Development of Sociological Theory*, 2nd edition. Englewood, Cliffs, NJ: Prentice Hall.

Index